HENRY R. LUCE
AND THE RISE OF THE
AMERICAN NEWS MEDIA

HENRY R. LUCE
AND THE RISE OF THE
AMERICAN NEWS MEDIA

James L. Baughman

with a new afterword by the author

The Johns Hopkins University Press
Baltimore and London

To Milt, Julia, Tom, and Kate

Copyright © 1987 G. K. Hall & Co.
New material copyright © 2001 The Johns Hopkins University Press
All rights reserved
Printed in the United States of America on acid-free paper

Originally published in hardcover by Twayne Publishers,
a division of G. K. Hall & Co., 1987
Johns Hopkins Paperbacks edition, 2001
2 4 6 8 9 7 5 3 1

To quote and cite from the oral histories of Eric Hodgins, Clare Boothe Luce,
T. S. Matthews, and Henry A. Wallace, permission is granted by the Trustees of
Columbia University in the City of New York.

The Johns Hopkins University Press
2715 North Charles Street
Baltimore, Maryland 21218-4363
www.press.jhu.edu

Library of Congress Cataloging-in-Publication Data

Baughman, James L., 1952–
Henry R. Luce and the rise of the American news media / James L. Baughman.—
Johns Hopkins paperbacks ed.
p.   cm.
Originally published: Boston : Twayne Publishers, 1987, in Twayne's twentieth-
century American biography series ; no. 5.
Includes bibliographical references and index.
ISBN 0-8018-6716-9 (alk. paper)
1. Luce, Henry Robinson, 1898–1967. 2. Journalists—United States—Biography.
3. Publishers and publishing—United States—Biography. I. Title.

PN4874.L76B38   2001
070.5′092—dc21
[B]   00-053469

A catalog record of this book is available from the British Library.

CONTENTS

FOREWORD

In 1948, a rival magazine called the editor of *Time, Life,* and *Fortune* the closest equivalent to "a Lord of the Press as America can now produce." The appellation suited Henry Robinson Luce. Not only did his publishing empire outstrip all competitors in size, circulation, profits, and influence, but the man also enjoyed a status in the United States that resembled the standing of Fleet Street's press lords in Britain. Moreover, those press lords and Luce flourished under the same conditions of modern industrial society. They seized upon technology to turn out vast runs of low-priced, illustrated journals; furnished the means for huge commercial and manufacturing concerns to advertise their wares to multitudinous, widely scattered customers; and capitalized on near universal literacy to feed the hunger of hordes of readers for information about swiftly changing news and fashion. Moreover, in common with his British counterparts, Luce belonged to an age of empire, and he similarly gloried in his nation's global reach to spread its power, culture, and ideals.

Yet, for all such likenesses, Henry Luce remained distinctly American. As James L. Baughman so sensitively portrays him in this biography, Luce was both more and less than a press lord transplanted across the Atlantic ocean. His own fantastic success in business and his devotion to the capitalist system notwithstanding, Luce thought of himself solely as a journalist. He always carried the title of "editor," never "publisher," "president," or "chairman." Unlike his British counterparts and the earlier American press magnates, Luce built his empire on magazines, not newspapers. His magazines rarely gathered news through reporters; rather, as with *Time*, they interpreted news through writers, or, as with *Life*, illustrated news through photographers. Conversely, despite *Life's* promotion of photojournalism and Luce's successful newsreel venture, "The March of Time," the editor differed from later "media" tycoons in his stubborn, sometimes financially costly, commitment to both the printed word and literary and cultural standards.

Luce's public standing likewise contained glaring contradictions. As Baughman makes clear, this head of a press empire never became a pillar of any establishment, social, financial, political, or cultural. Although Luce was a graduate of Yale and member of Skull and Bones, he always viewed himself as a rough-edged outsider in uppercrust circles, and he prided himself on having made, not inherited, his fortune. At no time did he regard wealth as an end in itself, and he favored much social welfare legislation and governmental economic regulation. His magazines' thinly veiled Republican partisanship after 1940 did not make Luce an uncritical or opportunistic partisan, and he stirred up mistrust and opposition in liberal and conservative Republican camps. Nor did Luce's efforts through *Time* and *Life* to elevate public taste and popularize advanced writers, thinkers, and artists earn him much appreciation among intellectuals, who sneered at him and his publications. In short, this builder of the greatest publishing empire of twentieth-century America was a many-sided, complex man, and Baughman portrays Luce's character and accomplishments in their full fascination.

John Milton Cooper, Jr.

ACKNOWLEDGMENTS

Although indebted to numerous librarians and archivists, I am especially grateful to Allen Stokes of the South Caroliniana Library, University of South Carolina, Elaine Felsher of the Time Inc. Archives, Jeri Nunn of the Oral History Research Office, Columbia University, and the indefatigable staffs of the Sterling Memorial Library, Yale University, and the Interlibrary Loan Department, University of Wisconsin-Madison Library.

I thank Henry Luce III for allowing me to interview him in June 1984, granting me access to his father's boyhood correspondence in the Time Inc. Archives, and permitting me to quote from his father's unpublished letters and memoranda. His cooperation should not, however, be construed as an endorsement of this enterprise.

Several of those who have written on Luce and Time Inc. assisted me as well, including Noel Busch, Robert T. Elson, Laura Z. Hobson, and W. A. Swanberg. Roy Hoopes generously permitted me to read chapters from his biography of Ralph Ingersoll prior to its publication.

Others to be thanked include William Appleyard, who guided me to materials on Luce at the Hotchkiss School; William B. Blankenburg, who read one chapter and talked me through several more; Hedley Donovan, former editor-in-chief of Time Inc., who granted me access to his oral history at Columbia University; Mrs. C. D. Jackson, for permission to review her husband's papers at the Eisenhower Library; Wilmott Ragsdale, a great colleague and inspiration, who had worked for Luce; and the Cleveland Indians, for their chronic inability to distract me during much of the time I conducted research and wrote the manuscript. For counsel or Luce-related favors, I am also indebted to Barbara Bellows, Jane Brown, Gordon and Ruth Cote, Merle Curti, Caroline Dow, Lawrence W. Lichty, Louis W. Liebovich, Jeffrey Marcus, Jim Murray, Dianne Paley, Gary Pettey, Hoyt Purvis, Valentin H. Rabe, Christine I. Schelshorn, David Schuyler, George Talbot, Charles F. Van Fossan, Stephen L. Vaughn, Lu Winters, Randall Woods, and Xinshu Zhao.

My students at the University of Wisconsin-Madison are to be thanked as well, notably the stalwart few who enrolled in a special seminar I offered on Luce in the fall of 1984. For another class, Sara Zimmerman wrote a paper on *Fortune* and the Vietnam war that proved especially useful, as did independent research projects by Jay Rath and Max Silverman.

Special thanks must go to Virginia Trapino for putting the manuscript and many revisions on the word processor; to James L. Hoyt, director of the School of Journalism and Mass Communication, for his encouragement; several research assistants, Andrew Feldman, Richard Digby-Junger, Deborah Barber, and Jeffrey Merron, for their diligence; and to Gerald Marwell, John Nitti, and the University of Wisconsin Graduate School Faculty for grants in support of the research and writing of this work.

I am grateful to Sharon Dunwoody, James and Polly Fosdick, Sally F. Griffith, Carl F. Kaestle, Vance Kepley, Jr., Jan Lewis, Jack M. McLeod, Albro Martin, David Paul Nord, Shiela Reaves, and Donald Ritchie, for commenting on individual chapters. Philip Ranlet reviewed and patiently attempted to salvage the entire work. Despite innumerable good suggestions and corrections, however, they must all be deemed innocent of any and all errors and interpretations.

For their helpfulness and understanding, I thank Anne Jones, John Amburg, and Lewis DeSimone of G.K. Hall/Twayne. For keeping my spirits up and most of the hyphens out, I am grateful to John Milton Cooper, Jr., the editor of this series, a great historian and friend.

Like many middle-class Americans, I grew up reading Henry Luce's publications. My family took *Time* and *Life* and intermittently *Sports Illustrated*. On occasion, my father brought from work *Fortune*, which too was consumed. For these preliminary research materials and much more, I thank my parents, Ann and Lewis Baughman. To another Time Inc. family—my brother, Milton Day Baughman, his wife, Julia, their children, Tom and Kate—this work is dedicated.

Finally, my cat, Andre Thornton Baughman, frequently disrupted my work and but for his interruptions, I would have corrected every error and annoying or dissatisfying argument in this book.

1

INTRODUCTION

The New Press Lord, 1940

He stood just over six feet tall, had pale blue eyes and, in his early fort-
ies, receding sandy-colored hair, just starting to gray. Although he
chain-smoked cigarettes, he rarely drank or ate to excess. Such moderation combined with an overabundance of nervous energy kept him
trim. Aside from a habitual seriousness of expression, his most distinctive features were bushy eyebrows. If not so overwhelming as those of
such famous contemporaries as labor leader John L. Lewis and Attorney
General Frank Murphy, the beetle brows were the physical characteristics that those meeting him for the first time invariably noticed immediately. Newcomers might note, too, odd speech patterns, such as
speaking too quickly, his mind racing ahead of his words, or sometimes,
a stammer, due to a boyhood speech defect.

In the late 1930s, he was America's single most powerful and innovative mass communicator. During the preceding decade and a half,
with several other young men fresh from the nation's Ivy League colleges, Henry Robinson Luce had started distinctive and popular magazines. Taken together these publications provided a more gripping and
coherent view of the world than was to be found in similar periodicals
and daily newspapers. They had also transformed Luce's company,
Time Inc., into a substantial concern. Luce and his partner had raised

eighty-six thousand dollars to start their first magazine, *Time*, in 1923. In 1941, the revenues from *Time* and other Luce enterprises reached forty-five million.[1]

Although up to one out of every five Americans might look at a Luce periodical during a given week, his magazines in 1940 commanded greatest favor among journalists and the middle class. More correspondents in Washington read *Time* than any other magazine; there and elsewhere many admired and modeled their own work after *Time*'s peculiar and omniscient mode of news writing. It commanded an audience well outside the federal city. Younger, better-educated members of the middle class had begun to consider *Time* required reading. Their wealthier neighbors not only took *Time*, but *Fortune*, Luce's lavishly illustrated business monthly.

The most read of any Luce publications in 1940 was his latest creation, *Life*. Published weekly, *Life* introduced its readers to photojournalism. *Life* used pictures to accomplish what *Time* labored to achieve with words: offer a compelling summary of the week. In barber shops and beauty parlors, on trains and in two million homes, Americans thumbed through the glossy-paged picture magazine. Pollster George Gallup discovered, according to one *Time* correspondent, "that the biggest publicity break a movie can get is a two-page layout of stills in *Life*,"—better, indeed, "than a page-one news break in all U.S. newspapers."[2]

More and more Luce found acknowledgments of his rank as a minister of information. At his Hyde Park home President Roosevelt was sufficiently annoyed by *Time*'s coverage of election night 1940 to demand a correction. The writer's details were all wrong, the president complained, and yet the story had been written in the "know-how" style characteristic of *Time* that persuaded the reader of its veracity.[3] A year later, Luce loomed in a screen biography based on one of Luce's failing rivals, newspaper mogul William Randolph Hearst. Only two decades earlier, as Luce and Briton Hadden began planning *Time*, Hearst published newspapers in virtually every major American city. He was widely regarded as the nation's most powerful and dangerous publisher. *Citizen Kane*, however, showed Hearst's empire in decline and a new one emerging: Time Inc. "With the breaking up of the old personal newspaper empires," *Business Week* reported later, "Henry Robinson Luce comes as close to being a Lord of the Press as America can now produce."[4]

The Missionary, 1940–1967

Had Luce died in 1940 he would have been remembered for his inventions. Instead, he lived another thirty-seven years and came to be hated, even after his death, for his prejudices. Until the late 1930s, Luce's publications could convey contradictory points of view. Liberals and radicals at *Fortune* and *Time* swiped at capitalism and imperialism; one foreign affairs editor at *Time* could not disguise an infatuation with fascism. More frequently, Luce's magazines seemed merely smug. All of this started to change as Luce himself turned his attentions more toward public affairs. It was perhaps inevitable. Born in China, the son of an American missionary educator, Luce regarded journalism as a "calling," a positive, educative force. Then, too, his father's career had symbolized to his son America's potential for good works. The son's material success reaffirmed a boyhood appreciation of capitalism. Starting in 1940, Time Inc. publications at times deliberately presented the news in ways that revealed Luce's preoccupations. The magazines continued to summarize events in typical *Time* fashion, but after 1939 they regularly ridiculed opponents of certain policies Luce advocated. The intellectually dishonest or simply mediocre champions of Luce's causes more likely obtained good coverage. Years of editorial cleverness were now being used to promote the foreign policies of Henry Luce. "No restraint bound him," recalled one of his correspondents, "in using his magazines to spread the message of his conscience."[5]

Luce's concern for the world began with the Second World War. Like many members of the Eastern Establishment—an informal collection of publishers and political and financial leaders—Luce viewed the early victories of Nazi Germany with alarm. No longer, Luce argued, could America afford her traditional isolation from the world. Even if Britain stopped Hitler, Luce correctly surmised, the war would leave her too exhausted to play the great world power. Americans had to be made to accept the "inevitable": armed intervention to save Europe and a new postwar order dominated by the United States—Luce called it the American Century.

Luce's vision of American hegemony still faced obstacles. Some powerful conservative elements within the Republican party and some newspapers, most notably the *Chicago Tribune*, fiercely opposed Luce's new imperialism. Abroad, the Soviet Union began late in the war to assert its own will over Eastern Europe. Even before the disintegration of the U.S.-Soviet alliance, Luce's magazines, in 1944 and 1945, started to question Russia's intentions for the postwar world. Stalin, like Hitler, seemed bent on upsetting a balance of power favorable to the United States.

Once again Luce's magazines framed news stories to leave little doubt that America must face up to this new aggressor. In the 1950s, Time Inc. publications fostered a consensus enveloping and deadening discussions of American foreign policy. Critics of America's containment of the Soviet Union—on the left and right—were brutally handled, and every confrontation with the Communist world and even the neutral block celebrated. Luce himself told a Senate committee in June 1960, "I do not think there can be a peaceful co-existence between the Communist empire and the free world."[6]

The Costs of Commitment

Luce's magazines had been attacked since the 1930s. *Time*'s initially unusual style pained some critics; *Life* appeared to make too many compromises to achieve greater circulations. In the 1950s and 1960s, such criticisms increased; both periodicals were accused of cultivating "middlebrow" cultural tastes and *Time* of highly prejudiced political reporting, presented as objective synthesis. *Time*, remarked one former editor, "is the most successful liar of our times."[7]

Nevertheless, it was Luce's close association with a vigorously anticommunist foreign policy that cost his reputation dearly. Luce became, wrote Joseph Epstein, "a great grey eminence whom everyone, with tar brush in hand, painted black."[8] No other publisher of his rank had offered, in his own words, such resolute calls for American hegemony. And to those in the late 1960s outraged over the cost of that globalism in Vietnam, Luce and his magazines bore much of the responsibility. "The Lucepress had led, not followed, the nation into war," biographer W. A. Swanberg wrote. Luce stood guilty of "manipulating 50 million people weekly."[9]

Such appraisals can be misleading. Most Americans did not regularly read a Luce magazine; in a given week, far more were likely to scan a daily newspaper and listen to a radio newscast than to examine an issue of *Life*. Nor did every subscriber absorb whole the arguments in all the articles in each issue. Luce's publications alone did not frame or structure readers' view of the world; for many, they served as supplements to friends and neighbors, newspapers, and broadcast news services. These other voices, in turn, often echoed Luce. By the late 1940s, virtually all the popular press shared his hostility toward the Soviet Union. But not all advocated what came to be Luce's moralistic approach to foreign policy. Nor were Harry's ardent views on China found in every national and local news service. Nevertheless, rival mass communicators had come to accept the fundamental premises of the American Century.

Then, too, Luce's role was most often limited to that of a publicist, not an initiator, of policies. When the Roosevelt administration refused to place him on a special commission reviewing postwar economic policy, he could only publish, as opposed to participate in, its determinations. Later in the decade, his lobbying for China, under siege from Communist insurgents, went largely unheeded until it served the political needs of Republicans in Congress; they and Luce then watched helplessly as the United States abandoned any attempt to save China from the Communists. In the 1950s and 1960s, Luce received more attention from both Republican and Democratic presidents. Yet they approached him after making decisions, not before. Luce served as an information minister, not foreign secretary.

The Press Revolutionary

To note the limits of Luce's power and the representative nature of his opinions is not to diminish the importance of his journalism. His most severe critics would blame him for what he argued. Too conveniently or self-servingly they ignore how many not on Luce's payroll shared his basic assumptions about the Cold War. It is not, then, so much *what* information he conveyed as *how* he did it. *Time* and *Life,* and to a lesser extent *Fortune* and "The March of Time," helped to change the practices of American journalism. Luce and his collaborators deliberately sought to create new ways of relaying the news. And by succeeding, Luce helped to alter the profession forever.

Luce's formula involved little more than cleverly summarizing the week's news in print *(Time)* or pictures *(Life)* in ways that left readers with a concise, entertaining, and frequently inadequate version of an event or trend. Complex "running" stories were simplified. Normally, the *Time* entry emphasized "personality." *Time,* in fact, invented the newsmagazine "cover story," usually on an individual as metaphor for what was or should be happening. "Knowing," if irrelevant, details flavored an entry. Above all, *Time, Life* and *Fortune* stories possessed "omniscience," an all-knowing point-of-view. Often Luce's journalism offered little but the illusion of information. Readers, knowingly or not, surrendered to *Time* writers the right to sift through facts. Some subscribers wanted *Time* and other Luce publications to "mediate" information for them. Working in businesses increasingly dependent on national and international events, they sought a succinct or "efficient" view of the world. Other readers experienced a crisis over information in the 1920s and 1930s. From the outset, *Time* sought those casual or ineffective newspaper subscribers, ones whose inability to absorb the news left them with a fear of inadequacy. The whole realm of knowledge, of government, technology and business, had expanded and complicated life. Although more Americans had gone to college than ever before, most institutions of higher education at the turn of the century had begun to abandon the idea that the whole of human endeavor could be understood. An increasing number of college students, like Luce and his classmates at Yale, had begun to "concentrate" in certain fields. Work itself became more focused, with people accordingly less aware of more things. To this ignorance, Luce and his partner, Briton Hadden, consciously played. *Time* would summarize and explain trends not only in politics and diplomacy, but in the arts and sciences, clearly, cleverly, knowingly. Analyzing a 1934 radio program that assessed literature and the theatre, historian Joan Shelley Rubin saw *Swift's Premium Hour* fulfilling a similar function. The programs "did not pretend to provide literary analysis or to teach the audience to arrive at its own critical judgments. Their function was instead to create in the listener the sense that she or he was 'in the know' about the arts."[10] The Olympian *Time* writer would similarly determine what a weekly news item "meant." "The dream," a former *Time* writer observed, "was that an external truth exists this week and can be expressed in 500 words by a talented writer after he has read the week's New York newspaper clippings."[11]

In time, Luce's formula of the directed synthesis could be seen in competing news services: in radio and television news reports, in an increasing number of newspaper columns and analyses. His legacy thus concerns a transformation of American journalism from information to synthesis, and another episode of what Raymond Williams has called "the long revolution," the centuries-long struggle, first through literacy, to gain access to the printed word, and then, through new mass media, to achieve a mastery of a more complicated order. The most successful mass media managers devised forms that rendered a more complex and crowded world comprehensible. By succeeding, this mass communicator created a harmony, whereas individual experience or physical isolation might only have fostered faction or worse—to the purposeful Luce—disengagement.[12]

Because Luce's publications sought to create and control a national consensus, he chose his causes more carefully than some detractors have admitted. Most of the time he looked to others within the establishment or government, or to commentators like Walter Lippmann, before committing his publications. Deeply ambitious, he hated to lose. "He could, and often did, mount sustained campaigns," wrote William F. Buckley, Jr., "but the goals were carefully chosen, and above all they were realizable. Luce had an aversion to lost causes."[13]

Luce's career, then, took two stages. The first and more vital involved the evolution of new types of information media, the news magazine, the thoughtful business periodical, the photoweekly. By the very late 1930s, these inventions had become innovations, popular and profitable. At this point, the publisher began to assume an interest in public affairs. Although still a publisher, never a politician, Luce became a "public man," more concerned about presidential politics, world affairs, and the quality of life of the American middle class. For him, this second act was more frustrating. Not until his last years did he overcome a restlessness about his works, his country, even his personal life. Yet he never lost the confidence he had as a young man that his journalism could inform the millions and hold the modern state together.

2

THE MISSIONARY'S SON
1898–1920

The man whose magazines claimed to influence large numbers of Americans and their communities did not experience a typical American childhood. The son of Presbyterian missionaries, Henry Robinson Luce was born and spent all but one of his first fourteen years in China. His America consisted of missionary compounds, then private schools. Through a family benefactor, he did return to the United States in 1914 to attended Hotchkiss, an exclusive school for boys in Connecticut; like his father, Luce went to Yale, then as later, a higher education reserved for few.

Boyhood influences and experiences were similarly uncharacteristic. They left him extraordinarily self-confident. He had overcome adversities. And he had accepted from his father a will to succeed.

The Missionary Father

Luce's father, Henry Winters Luce, had grown up in Scranton, Pennsylvania, then a booming mining and manufacturing center. Despite an invitation to join a good hometown law firm, Henry chose upon graduation from Yale to attend divinity school. Like many young men and women of the middle classes in the 1890s, Luce had been swept up in the religious Student Volunteer Movement. Inspired by the preaching of Dwight Moody, the movement had been founded in 1888 to draw young people into missionary work, both at home and abroad, and was closely associated with the new Young Men's Christian Association and Young Women's Christian Association. Luce and two Yale classmates, Horace Pitkin and Sherwood Eddy, took up the movement's charge and went to the Union Theological Seminary. There and at Princeton's theological school, Henry Winters Luce prepared for the Presbyterian ministry.

Although Luce, Pitkin, and Eddy possessed an evangelical fervor, all were exposed to the emerging liberal or modernist theology of the decade. All three, Eddy recalled, eschewed the "old hell-fire appeal" in favor of a more reasoned emphasis on Christian nurture associated with the Congregationalist theologian Horace Bushnell (1802–76).[1] Bushnell stressed that through child-rearing one could develop in the child a religious "moral agency." Earlier Protestant writers—and most missionaries—had constructed their views around the concept of original sin. Bushnell differed by concentrating on the child's moral possibilities. To him, child-rearing and education were all important.

As Luce prepared for ordination in 1897, he married Elizabeth Root of Utica, New York. Her ancestors, like Henry's, first settled in America in the 1640s. She, too, had been involved in the movement as a YWCA worker among Scranton's working classes in the south side. And she had come to share Henry's purpose.

Luce had already elected to become a missionary in China. The world's most populous nation, China presented Henry with an unparalleled opportunity for conversion. Japan's humiliating defeat of China in the 1894–95 war, missionary organizers argued, had deeply shaken the Middle Kingdom, making its millions ripe for Protestantism. Moreover, as one of the few non-Western and non-Christian nations ostensibly free of foreign rule, China seemed America's duty, the greatest application of what came to be dubbed America's "sentimental imperialism" of charity and missionary work.[2]

That task to Luce and others called for a new attitude toward preaching in the Orient. Ordaining Luce in May 1897, his Scranton pastor, Charles E. Robinson, admonished him to "have a good common-sense Christianity about you. . . . Strive to learn the Chinese ways of looking at things and adapt yourself according to the true interpretations of the words of Christ." The new missionary should "not try to Americanize the Chinese."[3] The elder Luce heeded Robinson.

Studying the language and culture and preaching in Chinese attire, Luce separated himself from the older generation of missionaries who preached in English a harsh and incomprehensible religion, offering little, Eddy recalled, but eternal punishment, constant images of "millions of 'heathen' going every hour into 'Christian graves.'"[4] This is not to understate Luce's religiosity; his was a religious certainty foreign to a later, less believing generation. Yet compared to older converters, the elder Luce was better educated and less provincial in his view of the world. Moreover, the ministries of Luce and others touched by the Social Gospel paid less attention to theology in favor of attending to the social needs of the Chinese. Education, the creation of Christian schools and colleges, could be especially effective tools of conversion.

The Missionary Son

On 3 April 1898, Elizabeth Luce gave birth to their first child, Henry Robinson Luce, in Tengchow (Penglai). The Luces shifted from one harsh outpost of God to another; for no more than five years did the family stay in one place, and a China missionary's home was always primitive when compared to what a Scranton attorney's house would have been. Indeed, the Luces did not have a "home" until Harry was nine, when Mrs. Cyrus H. McCormick, heir to the McCormick reaper fortune and patron of many overseas missions, endowed a small cottage for them. The ever-changing locations of the family left young Henry sad at not having an American "hometown" and also made him forever restless; throughout his life he moved himself and briefly *Time*'s headquarters around the country.

Wherever the family went, Luce displayed a penchant for leading. Other missionary children came to the Luce residence. Harry organized and directed their activities. Younger siblings deferred to the firstborn. When he set up a war game using blocks in the nursery, they were careful not to interfere. "We never touched the blocks," one of his sisters remembered, "it was his war." Meeting Harry during the family's 1906 visit to the United States, Mrs. McCormick wrote his mother, "it seems natural for him to be a ruler."[5]

Playmates were most often other American children. Like most missionary children, Harry had little contact with Chinese his own age. He spent his idle time with a younger brother and two sisters and the children of other missionaries. Although his father shared some of his knowledge of Chinese language and culture, Harry came to regret his relative insularity and some who knew him later thought he allotted too much of his adult life compensating for this childhood isolation.[6]

Along with other missionary children, Luce developed a special loyalty to America. His father possessed a deep and unquiet patriotism, which the son accepted whole. Then, too, young Harry transferred a reverence for his father to the missionary experience itself and America abroad. He came to see America as the selfless Western power. The Germans and British in north China, Luce recalled, could be brutal or condescending; Americans, in contrast, behaved unselfishly toward the Chinese. These boyhood impressions never left him. Nor did his image of America, which from his distance had assumed marvelous qualities. "I probably gained a too romantic, too idealistic view of America," Luce recalled later. Like Pearl Buck as a child, Harry proved a constant patriot. It was an earnestness he never lost, confessing "I never went through any special period of disillusionment with America."[7]

Harry's patriotism was one of many signs of his father's influence, the most decisive of his childhood. A forceful presence, Henry Winters Luce took his paternal responsibilities seriously. The elder Luce applied Bushnell's theories to the rearing of his own children. The Luce children were not, in strict Victorian fashion, to be good as much as they were to understand being good. The elder Luce used family discourse as a means of Christian nurture. He wanted Harry to question and discuss right and wrong. A patient teacher, the father allowed argument, all the while sure of his own views. Again, it was a quality Luce himself came to display. At Hotchkiss and Yale, he regularly participated in school debates. Later, at Time Inc., he welcomed contentiousness from those to his left and right. From those like senior editor John Shaw Billings who carried no ideological baggage, Luce rarely solicited opinions.

Then, too, Luce's parents nurtured in Harry an active and wide-ranging curiosity. As a small boy, Harry consumed books in the substantial family library. The elder Luce, though devout, did not limit discussions to matters of God and mammon or to the travails of translating certain biblical passages into North Chinese. And again the son followed the father, all too faithfully; as an editor and dinner guest, Harry Luce could be exhaustingly curious about things. Relatedly, Henry Winters Luce's stress on education impressed his son. Even journalism could be an instrument of mission work by making one, Luce late in his life quoted his father, "at home with the world."[8]

As a small boy, young Harry found himself absorbing his father's interest in journalism. The family took many American periodicals, all of which Luce began reading at an early age. In the family compound he started a hand-written newspaper. He also studied copies of the 1891–92 *Yale Courant*, which the elder Luce had edited while in college. Luce had revived the *Courant* by insisting that it be a showcase for the "easier, lighter literary powers" of Yale men. The best stories were his own, descriptions of Yale and New Haven and his own frailties. Of his inability to arise from bed some mornings: "A noisy alarm clock, effective at first, became in time only too soothing to his morning drowsiness." Although already acquiring a deep religiosity, Luce had no difficulty confessing in one column to being easily distracted by young female worshippers while listening to a sermon.[9]

More than any single trait, however, Henry Winters Luce inculcated his ambition into his firstborn. A man of no modest designs for a Christian China, the missionary father found himself more and more back in America, raising funds not for small and isolated mission schools but for one of several American-operated universities in China. Without insisting that Harry follow him into the ministry, he did expect nothing less than success of his namesake. "Character is destiny," he extolled Harry. "Use your native Lucepower."[10] Thornton Wilder, who knew Luce in China, spoke of the effect of such exhortation: "In Harry it took the shape of a shy—joyless power drive."[11]

The young Luce, indeed, lacked Henry Winters Luce's humorous or lighthearted manner, to say nothing of what one contemporary called a "winning smile." Photos of him as a boy and young man rarely show the beginnings of a grin. At Yale, the story went, his best friend saw him frowning and hunched, deep in thought, and cried, "Watch out Harry, you'll drop the college!"

Luce's sobriety may also have related to a stutter that afflicted him as a child. The speech defect probably resulted from a traumatic tonsillectomy. It left him embarrassed, all but forcing him to excel at his studies, although his father's demands for excellence provided an even greater incentive. When he was first away at school, the stutter proved so chronic that classmates had to read aloud for him his answers in Latin and Greek. Still, he refused to let the defect frustrate his course. In prep school and college, he proved a skilled orator. Off-the-cuff, casual conversation, though, remained a struggle. When Luce tried nervously in the early twenties to sell *Time* shares to potential backers or later to win a heated cocktail party debate, the stutter might return.

Nevertheless, he kept at it and as an older man could speak freely and forcefully. Informal chitchat, however, never came easily.

In childhood, his speech defect, even his nationality, were sorely tested. At ten, Luce was sent to a British boarding school at Chefoo (Yantai). The British presence in the Middle Kingdom was substantial. The assumptions about China being "America's burden" notwithstanding, there were more British than American missionaries in China as late as 1910. Britain also had considerable business interests as well as a military presence in China. And as Britain ranked as the great power of 1908, the English children and teachers at Chefoo could not veil a conceit about their nationality or contempt for all things and children American. (Or Chinese: the school offered no instruction on Chinese culture.) Instead, English custom and manner predominated. On Sundays, Luce along with the other Yankee children dressed in imperial white pith helmets and white suits with knee-length pants and marched to Church of England services. Seven days a week the Americans were bullied. The British insisted on a unique pronunciation of Ohio; the student not conforming was beaten by the instructor in class and mocked by peers afterwards. To his parents in 1909, Luce wrote, "I have arrived at this smelly old prison once again, hang it."[12]

Chefoo teachers, when not ridiculing the Yankees, offered a strict, traditional instruction that helped Luce later. The student erring on a translation or formula was flogged. To avoid that fate Luce worked hard. Never again, he remembered, would school be such a challenge. In 1913, his parents sent him to America to attend the Hotchkiss School. There, Chefoo's rigors served him well; he had scant trouble excelling. Luce ranked first in Lester Brown's Greek class, and Brown had a reputation as a hard taskmaster. But Luce had expected no less. "The easiest part of my life," he wrote his parents on arriving, "will be my studies."[13]

Hotchkiss was not, however, free of indignities. Despite Mrs. McCormick's help, Luce had to help meet his expenses by working in the school chapel and library. Waiting tables, he had to suffer the snobbery of those who did not. Their class consciousness brought about his one momentary disenchantment with America, he confided to Mrs. McCormick. "When I came to America," he wrote in 1916, "I found more snobbery in two weeks than I had hoped to find in two decades."[14]

He withstood such taunting. Already Luce possessed a remarkable self-confidence. As a child modeling his father by composing sermons, Luce referred several times to 2 Timothy, Chapters, 1–2, 6–9. "For

God hath not given us the spirit of fear; but of power, and of love, and of a sound mind" (2 Tim. 1:7).[15] Mrs. McCormick wrote of Henry at eight, "already mature beyond his years—his perception acts with lightning rapidity, and things have to move quick to keep pace with him."[16] Harry's letters to his parents over the next eight years conveyed an increasing self-reliance, which in turn fashioned a quiet but unmistakable self-assurance. Perhaps overcoming his stutter and surviving Chefoo shaped this facet of his personality. His odyssey from China to Connecticut, by way of Europe to see a speech therapist, had been made alone. By then he had no difficulty getting on without his parents. Intellectually precocious, Luce at fourteen was criticizing James Bryce's *American Commonwealth* for its dated quality and recommending serious magazines to his father. "Judging from his weekly letters," Harry Winters Luce wrote in 1916, Harry's "soul is surging like a sea with thoughts and reflections which sometimes almost startle us when we think that he is only eighteen."[17]

At Hotchkiss, Luce stood up to the tyrannical headmaster, H. G. Buehler, who had complained that young Harry was shirking his library cleaning duties. Luce politely disagreed. After the headmaster wrote to inform the elder Luce of his dissatisfaction, the son quietly stood his ground, with no fear of his father. After the horrors of Chefoo, no school authority could frighten him. And he was confident his father would see his side. Luce even belittled Buehler, promising to have him "figure in my first novel."[18]

Soon after arriving at Hotchkiss, Luce decided that he would not follow his father into the ministry. In one of his first Hotchkiss papers, Luce sought to justify a secular course while revealing just how inner-directed he had become. He hailed Franklin's classic *Autobiography*. Franklin's "industry," a single-minded purposefulness, deeply impressed Luce. If this trait was "sometimes very obnoxious," Franklin's works nevertheless benefited both himself and his society. "The ardent way in which he strove" constituted "the secret of his own personal and moral uplift." To Luce, "the lesson is—what you would do, you can do. Do it!"[19]

Three years later, Luce wrote in praise of another secular historical figure, Charles Sumner, the abolitionist senator from Massachusetts. Like Franklin, Sumner suffered from an excess of self-absorption that he, in contrast to the colonial printer, could not disguise. Scholars increasingly found Sumner's righteousness unpalatable. But Luce, the missionary's son in search of lay role models, admired Gamaliel Bradford's *Yale Review* profile of Sumner. Bradford praised the senator "as the high proclaimer of moral law."[20]

Luce's secular course and ambition could be seen in the children of other clergymen spreading the gospel at home or abroad. Most sons and daughters of China missionaries appear to have been like Luce overachievers. A 1936 study of Yale alumni in *Who's Who in America* found missionary children far more likely to succeed than the children of graduates in any other profession. And few—one out of ten—took up the Lord's work. Instead, ministers' children, whether raised at home or abroad, walked a secular path.[21] When early in his adolescence Luce determined not to become a minister, he had arrived at a conclusion that other offspring of preachers and bishops, including Pearl Buck, Dean Acheson, Bruce Barton, William Benton, and Robert Hutchins, were making.

Journalism continued to command Luce's attentions. In his last year at Chefoo, he had been designated "editor-in-chief" of a planned student publication. "Does that not sound an elephantine title!" he reported proudly.[22] At Hotchkiss, he pursued his interest in journalism, with his father's editorship of the *Courant* a frequent reference. Assuming control of the *Hotchkiss Literary Monthly* he completely revamped the periodical. Luce added a joke column and like his father insisted on liveliness overall. He also included more illustrations, even putting out a special pictorial supplement.[23] The man who oversaw the creation of *Life* twenty years later was displaying a sense of the visual at eighteen.

The Collaborator

While laboring on the *"Lit,"* Luce made a friend in Briton Hadden, the editor of a rival school publication. It proved the most important association in Luce's life, and the least expected. In most ways Hadden was Luce's opposite. Hadden did not have to reckon with a strong father figure; his had died in 1906. Hadden had grown up not abroad but in a comfortable middle-class Brooklyn neighborhood. Then, too, he had personality traits absent in Luce: cynicism, flamboyance, irreverence. Only in his self-assurance and love of journalism did Hadden resemble Luce.

As editor of the *Hotchkiss Record,* Hadden had also displayed editorial skills unusual in an adolescent. He prized lively writing and solicited argument. The *Record*'s editorial columns frequently raised a host of issues, usually in a mocking way. Hadden delighted in commenting on the *Lit*'s progress under friend Harry, and in not always a cordial manner. Hadden's flippancy extended to reporting the Great War. In an otherwise serious set of war dispatches on the *Record*'s page-one left column, 28 January 1916, Hadden added the fictitious entry: "MONTENEGRO STILL FIRM . . . Contrary to last week's reports, Montenegro has not surrendered. Her army is retreating to Albania to join the Swedish forces." During his tenure, the *Record* introduced stories with a heavy statistical bias. How much did Yale men earn? (Most Hotchkiss men then went to Yale.) How much did the average senior weigh? What were the career plans of the class of '16? (Most planned to go into business.)[24] This fascination with numbers, often meaningless, like the average weight of a senior, was to be evident in *Time* under Hadden and his successors.

Possessed of an adolescent arrogance he never outgrew, Hadden had begun to rethink the ways newspapers reported news. He found two major failings in American journalism. One involved style: news copy, he concluded, should be more lively and concise. Homer provided the ready model. Required reading at Hotchkiss, the *Iliad* possessed a vivid, efficient, and distinctive sentence order. Telescoped phrases like "far-darting Apollo," "rolling-eyed Greeks"—constructions then avoided in American English—intrigued him. Hadden's other criticism involved the ever-increasing volume of information. Put simply, Hadden had determined that there was too much news in newspapers. As editor of the *Record* in the fall of 1915, Hadden had introduced a new feature: a special column digesting the news of the week, necessary, he said, "for those of us who do not find time to read the detailed accounts in the daily papers."[25]

Less the innovator, Luce nevertheless appeared nearly as fascinated as Hadden by journalism itself. The summer before entering Yale, Luce worked for a Massachusetts daily, the *Springfield Republican*, clerking in the business office and doing a little reporting. He also found a role model, an ace political correspondent named Haas. "He's four-square," Luce informed his parents, who no doubt appreciated knowing that Haas violated his profession's stereotype by not drinking. He also defended journalism as a proper, middle-class profession. "There's not a game on the face of the earth that requires more manhood of every kind than the reporting game," he told Luce. "There's hardly a firm in this city, respectable or otherwise, that I don't know a great deal about. And not one of them takes the physical, intellectual or nervous energy that a man simply must put into the reporting business."[26]

The free and easy associations of journalism appealed to Luce as well. In a missionary compound, he had led easily. At Chefoo and Hotchkiss, however, he had to compete with others, many his social betters, none afflicted with his speech defect. Making friends proved a struggle, one he determined, ever his father's son, to wage. It would be less of an ordeal in the fourth estate. "It is the personal element in all newspaper work which attracts me to it," he wrote after his summer in Springfield. "Real human sympathy, and the power of wide friendship is not inherent in me. Therefore would I have it."[27]

Entering Yale in September 1916, Luce still found college journalism an enormous temptation. He and Hadden survived the keen competition to win slots on the *Yale Daily News*, the school's premier student publication. Although Luce's father had all but ordered him to make Phi Beta Kappa, Harry in planning his freshman year had confessed "if it came down to an issue between Phi Beta Kappa and the *News*, I would take the former. But if, practically a key and a *News* charm were laid before me now I am afraid my hands would almost unconsciously grasp the latter." When Hadden defeated him in January 1918 for the chief editorial post at the *Daily News*, Luce wrote his parents, "My fondest college ambition is unachieved."[28]

With Luce his chief assistant, Hadden set out to reshape the *Daily News* along the lines of the *Hotchkiss Record*. Newswriting conventions should be avoided. More world and national news should be included, in summary form, in each edition. One of Hadden's professors shared his passion for synthesis. "Everybody in America reads—from the messengerboy to the corporation president," Henry Seidel Canby wrote in 1915. Yet Canby sensed that consumers suffered from an excess of information. Americans "read too much to read intelligently." College students, his at least, could not even keep pace. "It is an old reproach against the college student that he is idle and lazy. Our present race of undergraduates are energetic beyond belief," too busy with classwork, clubs, athletics, to keep up with one or more newspapers, seven days a week, or all the magazines of opinion available to him.[29]

Curriculum changes at Yale and other colleges further justified a new journalistic summary. Yale had become a place of specialization. Following the lead of Harvard, Cornell, and Johns Hopkins, Yale's faculty had submitted to "the elective revolution" and eliminated most course requirements. Mostly at the expense of the classics, more courses were offered in the new social sciences. The elective revolution conveyed the expanding universe of formal learning. Students decades earlier had far less to learn, particularly in the physical sciences. Indeed, in the eighteenth century, Yale students could conceivably have been taught and read about all that then made for human knowledge. Wrote one college president, "We have found the specialist efficient in producing knowledge but need the journalist to put it to work."[30]

Hadden's journalism offered a solution. With Canby he assumed that people everywhere were similar to Yalies, too busy to follow the day-to-day occurrences with care. And the explosion of knowledge made this capacity to summarize effectively all the more important. Hadden the adolescent had foreseen the great opportunity for the innovative mass communicator: generalizing reams of information for an increasingly specialized audience.

This function proved difficult to perform. Although Hadden saw the need, the prep school and college newspapers under his direction were not dramatically different from numbers edited before or after his regimes. Indeed, Hadden and Luce were to find, even as they entered the real world, that the goal of synthesis was easier to see than to reach.

More evident was Hadden's contempt for another journalistic convention, objectivity. In his first editorial as *Daily News* chairman, Hadden declared that the paper would "of course, endeavor first, last, and always to mirror Public Opinion." But Hadden then declared the occasional impossibility of his goal. At times, "there is no Public Opinion. The point in question may appear neither black nor white—because everybody persists in calling it gray." The board on such occasions "will presume to express its own opinion." The *Daily News* "will call a spade a spade and will take sides whenever sides are to be taken. True journalism admits of no No-Man's-Land."[31]

The Hero

Hadden and Luce's politics were readily apparent at both Hotchkiss and Yale. Both young men were ardent Bull Moose Republicans, and their hero was former president Theodore Roosevelt, leader of the Progressive insurgency of 1912. Henry Winters Luce had been a great admirer of the colonel and while still in competition with Hadden at Hotchkiss, Harry had scored the coup of persuading Roosevelt to do a column for the *Literary Monthly*. Roosevelt's ostentatious cries for manliness appealed to Hadden, who dreamed of being a baseball player. Luce, taught by his father to lead, admired Roosevelt for his strong leadership. The colonel's high nationalism attracted the once persecuted patriot. Then, too, Roosevelt's near religious approach to political discourse—his 1912 "battle for the Lord"—struck a responsive chord in the missionary's son. Years later Luce wrote, "My own political hero has been Theodore Roosevelt who, fallible though he was, did not hesitate to assert that 'righteousness' is relevant to politics and all public affairs of men and women."[32]

Roosevelt's nationalism and advocacy of war with Germany left the greatest impression on Luce and Hadden. Sentiment for intervention came first and proved the strongest in the Northeast. On 7 May 1915, a German U-boat sank the liner *Lusitania,* with many well-to-do New Yorkers and "four well-known Yale men" aboard, as one historian of the college wrote.[33] The incident provided Roosevelt and others with a call to arms. In the summer of 1916, eastern college men participated in preparedness camps supervised by a Roosevelt follower, General Leonard Wood. Some actually enlisted in British, French, and Italian units. The prospect of fighting seemed grand, while the gruesome reality of trench warfare was hardly understood. Both Luce and Hadden supported Roosevelt's cries for preparedness. Hadden's *Record* in April 1916 recommended attending one of the special summer training camps for would-be warriors. The experience offered "the prospect of spending a real vacation at moderate cost." Then with uncharacteristic seriousness, Hadden added, "There is a grander motive than these, however, the cause of the country itself."[34] Although Luce doubted the value of the camps, he did see a spiritual purpose served: the camps would foster national unity. When America entered the war in April 1917, Luce unsuccessfully sought to join former secretary of state Elihu Root's special mission to Russia, and then signed on with Hadden to be an army officer.[35]

The Great War and Confirmation

At Camp Jackson, South Carolina, in the hot summer of 1918, Luce and Hadden encountered for the first time the rest of America: working class and farm boys. The contrast could not have been greater. Luce had lived in China and traveled through Europe. Hadden's Brooklyn in 1910 ranked as the nation's third largest city. Yet the recruits they led were from very small hamlets or parts of Brooklyn foreign to Hadden. Most of their men had little education. One survey indicated that just under 18 percent of white draftees had even attended high school. A majority of the enlistees had quit school between the fifth and seventh grades.[36] Up to half of the farm boys now in khaki had never left their home counties and seemed like the semiliterate ball player Jack Keefe in Ring Lardner's *You Know Me, Al.*

The soldiers' ignorance of current events most affected Luce. At Camp Jackson he was ordered to explain the war to his platoon. Draft boards in rural areas had contended with resisters objecting not out of conscience but out of ignorance. To his horror, Luce realized that many of his men were unaware of the *Lusitania*'s sinking, to say nothing of the less newsworthy incidents leading to war. So Luce overcame his stutter to lecture his platoon two or three times a week on America's cause and Germany's barbarism. His talk on the *Lusitania,* based on his memory of the *New York Times* account, proved his most successful. "They had never heard the story and were on the edge of their chairs," he recalled. They "couldn't wait to get 'over there' and fix the Huns."[37]

The rank's gross unawareness of current events helped to upset an older view of the rationality of the reader. A more sober element of American journalism, led by Adolph Ochs, whose *New York Times* had enjoyed new life as the good, gray, antisensationalist "newspaper of record," had believed, like John Stuart Mill, in the capacity of women and men to follow events in detail and draw conclusions from them. Yet the ignorance of the troops in a supposedly literate society had reinforced the thinking of those like Walter Lippmann, who had already begun to question this assumption. Lippmann afterwards ridiculed the paradigm of the "omnicompetent citizen" and spoke of the "failure of self-governing people to transcend their casual experience and their prejudice."[38]

The war had another meaning for those covering it. The complexity of the campaign along the western front baffled the older journalist. No longer could a war correspondent sit atop one ridge and know what had happened. Battles were now fought along miles of trenches. Reporters had to rely on colleagues and army information officers to know all the facts and outcomes. For some, this reliance on rivals and officers was profoundly disillusioning.[39]

Luce endured none of this uneasiness. He never saw action; the war ended with unexpected swiftness in November 1918. Thus he never confronted the maze of modern combat that reporters and platoon leaders faced. He had not lost his confidence in a journalist's capacity for understanding. Nor was war itself challenged as an instrument of national policy.

The Assumptions of Senior Year

Returning to Yale, Luce held to other orthodoxies, notably an enthusiasm for a "New Era" of business and finance. Mrs. McCormick's personal attentions and generosity had long conditioned Harry's thinking about the economic order.[40] The McCormick Harvester "trust"—once a Progressive target—had subsidized his education and helped his father to build a Christian university near Peking. Surely such giant enterprises should be deemed socially positive institutions. Classmates similarly not only accepted the new, large-scale industrialized American economy but eagerly awaited careers managing it. Henry Winters Luce's path into the ministry or such related noncommercial callings as education no longer appealed to most Yale undergraduates. They adhered to what George Santayana called a "muscular Christianity" that held, Joseph Epstein later observed, "business to be the duty of the best young men."[41]

Luce no longer resented the wealth of peers for whom he had waited tables at Hotchkiss. Wanting to "belong," he celebrated his admission to Yale's exclusive Skull and Bones club. He made associations that served him and Hadden well, especially when in a few years they sought investors for a new magazine. "Membership in the Skull and Bones," wrote Hadden's cousin, "is thus often considered by undergraduates to be not only a campus accolade but also a down payment or insurance policy for progress in the future."[42]

The Yale faculty honored Harry as well. He realized his father's expectation by being admitted to the Phi Beta Kappa his junior year. Classmates his senior year approached him for help in courses he himself had not taken, Luce's mother learned from one of Harry's friends.[43] Majoring in Greek, he won the Hugh Chamberlain Prize for earning the highest mark in Yale's history on his comprehensive examination. Class poet, he was graduated summa cum laude.

Luce's boyhood nationalism had helped him to win another distinction. Several months before commencement in 1920, Luce overcame his stutter and won the De Forest oration contest with a plea for an expansive American foreign policy. The first year of peace troubled him. With the Senate rejection of the Treaty of Versailles and League of Nations membership, advocated by President Wilson, America seemed to be retreating from world affairs in favor of an isolation of egoistic materialism. The nation's unprecedented industrial, agricultural, and financial triumphs "testify to a natural strength whose bulk the world has never seen, and which even now is beyond the capacity of anyone's understanding." Still, America's inclination to withdraw from the world arena suggested a lack of purpose. "Is our greatness after all great merely for the sake of greatness? Does America, in short, believe in anything?" Luce offered a missionary's vision. Predicting an American Century to occur within twenty years, he offered the articles of faith—in capitalism and democracy—that he came to put in his magazines and that never left him. In two decades, Luce declared,

> American interests shall be respected, American citizens entitled to trade and to live in every corner of the globe, American business ideals recognized wherever the trader goes; second, that America may be counted upon to do her share in the solution of every international difficulty, that she will be the great friend of the lame, the halt and the blind among nations, the comrade of all nations that struggle to rise to higher planes of social and political organization, and withal the implacable and the immediate foe of whatever nation shall offer to disturb the peace of the world.

For America, he cried, there could be no higher calling. "If this shall be," he asserted, "then the America of this century shall have glory and honor which the kings do bring, and a [one] more magnificent yet than the honor of our fathers. For if America will be a defender of good faith throughout the world, hers will be adventure more brilliant than Eldorado, hers a moral and ethical attitude unapproached by the Puritans, a democracy broader than we have ever dreamed, an aristocracy of incomparable nobility."[44]

Luce's own aspirations remained journalistic. Forsaking the ministry might disappoint his father, but journalism, too, could be a calling. "The rewards in newspaper work are not great," he wrote Mrs. McCormick his senior year, "but on the other hand, the writing, the mixing in public affairs of [the] moment, the possibilities of exerting influence for good—all these appeal very strongly to me."[45]

3

TIME BEGINS
1921–1923

Since prep school, Luce had considered journalism to be his first choice of a career. A measured self-awareness contained higher literary ambitions. Although Luce had been considered, Thornton Wilder recalled, along with himself and Stephen Vincent Benet, to be one of the three outstanding poets of Yale's class of 1920, Luce was less certain. He did fancy himself capable of writing a novel but he concluded that his literary skills were best suited to journalism. With many weighing the field, Luce considered the fourth estate to be—at the very least—a waiting room, something he could do until he finally settled on a calling, perhaps public office.[1]

As earlier, Luce left his immediate future in the hands of the family benefactor, Mrs. Cyrus McCormick. She agreed to pay for a year's graduate study in history at Oxford in 1920–21. Returning, Luce again went to Chicago, this time to take up her offer of a job with her family's mammoth farm machinery firm. Then fate and the 1921 recession intervened. The company could not after all hire him. Given his background in journalism, the McCormick family secured him a beginning reporter's position at the *Chicago Daily News*.

In the early twenties, proper Chicagoans considered the *Daily News* one of the nation's great newspapers. Its sobriety did make it Chicago's one serious sheet. Under the editorship of Victor Lawson, the

Daily News distinguished itself from the *Chicago Tribune* and Hearst's *Herald-American* by emphasizing national and foreign news. Like the *New York Times,* to which Chicagoans compared it, the *Daily News* was "serious," little tinged by the sensationalism of the 1890s that still afflicted Hearst's sheets. Like the *Times,* the *Daily News* determined to be dull; its writing stiff and wordy, its layout drab. It appealed to an older middle-class Chicago, so much so that for years in-house jokesters held that the paper "lost a reader every time it printed an obituary."[2]

Skills or insights Luce had displayed as a younger man were not apparent during his tour with the *Daily News.* Like staff neophytes on every paper, Luce had to follow the rigid style of his employer or suffer the rewrite man, if not dismissal. His copy was indistinguishable from other dry and wordy entries in the paper.[3]

His friend Hadden was having the same experience. Like Luce, he chanced to get a job with a prestigious daily, the *New York World.* And he too found working for a large paper, with its rigid, formulaic writing strictures, dissatisfying. Innovations and irreverence tried at Yale or Hotchkiss were not welcome.

The New Venture

Together the two plotted a journalistic escape. Reunited at the *Baltimore News* late in 1921, they began to plan a new type of publication, "a weekly paper of our own, totally different from anything now being given to the American public," Luce wrote Mrs. McCormick.[4] Briefly in Baltimore, then in New York, where they set up operations in a dreary Lower East Side warehouse, Luce and Hadden worked on prototypes. Drawing on their Yale ties and self-assurance, they talked their way into the offices of various prominent business leaders and publishers. Nationally known editors like Walter Lippmann of the *New York World,* Glenn Frank of *Century Magazine,* and Edward Bok of the *Ladies' Home Journal* met with the young men. Many offered encouragement and ideas. Some, like public relations counsel Edward L. Bernays, frankly predicted failure.[5]

Luce and Hadden proposed a weekly summary of the most important news. Since Hotchkiss, Hadden had been thinking about newspapers and their shortcomings. The better newspapers, he had determined, contained too much information, even for the typical upper- and upper middle-class man to absorb. Waving a copy of the newspaper "of record," the *New York Times,* Hadden asked who, even stuck on a commuter train, could read such a thick, eight-column, small-type chronicle of the day before, complete with transcripts of two-hour speeches? No one, Hadden contended. As a result, consumers even of the *Times* were only dimly informed. What was needed was a weekly newspaper or magazine that synthesized the reams of information in the *Times* and other dailies.

Nor was Hadden alone in this view. Editors, with few exceptions lacking systematic readership surveys, presented indiscriminately vast amounts of news. "Readers get a voluminous daily newspaper, comparable to the average novel in length," a Florida journalism professor wrote. "Consequently, the public reads the newspapers with an inevitable aimlessness and gets out of them only a superficial smattering of the day's news."[6] In a January 1925 article, "What Difference Does It Make?" advertising agent Bruce Barton complained of the newspapers' overabundance of information. Dropping his evening paper—Barton had been taking two dailies—he declared himself "freed of that nightly bondage forever."[7]

Newswriting itself placed another strain on readers. Most prestigious newspapers in America after World War I did not prize concise, sprightly copy. In Chicago, the liveliest paper was Hearst's *Herald-American.* But Hadden did not seek Hearst's readers, whom Hadden dismissed as "gum-chewers"; he wanted a middle- and upper-class audience served by such papers as the *Chicago Daily News,* the *Baltimore Sun,* or the *New York Times.* These papers, however, dared only to be dull. Editors frowned upon short and readable opening paragraphs or "leads." Indeed, "lively" copy was suspect. The ideal start encompassed the formula, "Who, What, Why, When, Where, and How," and no matter if it ran over twenty-five words and lost readers in the process. In the *Chicago Tribune* of 24 September 1921, a page-one story on the German-American peace treaty began, "There will be no official participation by the United States except by the express authorization of congress in the administration of German reparations, if the senate ratifies the German, Austrian, and Hungarian peace treaties with the reservations recommended by the foreign relations committee today." After meeting with Hadden's composition professor at Yale, Henry Seidel Canby, Luce concluded, "We have got to have a style which is condensed but not telegraphic. As it is now, people have to think too hard as they read."[8]

Style also involved structure. Writers for most dailies and all the wire services in the early twenties normally wrote backwards, that is, with the most important set of facts first. A religiosity toward accuracy, in turn, crowded copy with qualifiers and commas. H. L. Mencken recalled that at the *Sun*, "the Bible of Baltimore," editors "fostered a sober, matter-of-fact style [on] its men. The best of them burst through these trammels but the rank and file tended to write like bookkeepers."[9]

Sometimes an innovative stylist triumphed. As America in 1921 prepared to dedicate the Tomb of the Unknown Soldier, Kenneth Simpson of the Associated Press wrote a feature violating every AP rule. The lead lacked the formula. Minor detail gave the piece a striking and sad flavor ("Sodden skies and a gray, creeping, chilling rain all through the day seemed to mark the mourning"). Some sentences were short, some inverted. No bookkeeper composed it. And, as if to rattle a thousand tradition-bound copy editors, Simpson's story deeply touched readers as no standard wire service account would have.[10]

Hadden sensed this appetite for the unorthodox. Long infatuated with style for its own sake, he experimented with inverted sentences in the manner of the *Iliad*. ("To many-fountained Ida they came.") Hadden delighted in Homer's multiple adjectives before a subject ("the goddess white-armed Hera," "horse-taming Diomedes").[11] In a February 1922 letter to his mother, Hadden referred not to his editor-in-chief, Harwood, and the city editor, Steuart, with the grammarian's appositive, commas and articles, but to "Editor-in-Chief Harwood" and "City Editor Steuart."[12] Positions became titles, every man a (no article) President (no comma) Harding. This style, however novel, had its advantages. It combined efficiency with detail. Although at times excruciatingly different from the then accepted prose, Hadden's approach ate less space or linage all the while giving the impression that the writer was thoroughly familiar with the subject.

Luce, too, had studied Homer and others in search of stylistic models. Describing an Easter 1917 trip to Detroit, he wrote his parents, "Puppets of Time and Fortune are we all." After touring a Ford Motor Company plant: "greatly to be admired and respected was the great extent of the system of it all."[13] Luce admired the English critic and satirist Max Beerbohm, who avoided the stuffy and dry hand of many peers in favor of a style capable of vivid, knowing description. ("The clatter of dominoes shuffled on marble tables," he wrote in one essay Luce noted enjoying; and mockful speech tags, " 'No', he droned.")[14] In his fiction, too, Beerbohm inverted sentences ("Very still the air was"). His theatre criticism conveyed a self-confidence seen early and often in young Luce. George Bernard Shaw, Beerbohm observed, "was not born to write serious plays. He has too irresponsible a sense of humor."[15] That Beerbohm could at best be premature or at worst wrong in his assessments did not seem important to Luce, only that he was certain.

With Hadden, Luce reconsidered the very structure of a news story. Rather than organize facts by their significance in the manner of the AP, Luce and Hadden would arrange them as true "stories," with a beginning, middle, and end. Their classical education helped to inspire them to propose an Aristotelian order for the typical magazine entry. Moreover, Luce's father had perfected such a sequence in his introduction of a "Campus Note Book" in the *Yale Courant* in 1891–92, copies of which young Henry had pored over as a child.

Nothing tarnished these boyhood models. Luce and Hadden never worked long enough at one paper to have the accepted practices inculcated into them. Both plotted their magazine with high opinions of their stylistic capacities, which no editor or peer had worn down. Perhaps understandably: Hadden and Luce were Yale men, far better educated than the cast of characters pecking out stories in the typical big city newsroom. Journalism in the early 1920s was still, in Lippmann's words, "a refuge for the vaguely talented." There were able reporters and editors, many with college educations, a few graduates of the new schools of journalism. But Lippmann observed in 1920, "They are eminences on a rather flat plateau." Journalism still lacked the prestige of such middle-class callings as the law and medicine; pay and working conditions could be dreadful. "Reporting is not a dignified profession for which men will invest the time and cost of an education," Lippmann wrote, "but an underpaid, insecure, anonymous form of drudgery, conducted on catch-as-catch can principles."[16]

Luce and Hadden, then, envisioned a "news-magazine" that freed themselves and its readers from the shortcomings of American journalism. The news would be written and organized differently. A week's events would be compartmentalized into regular departments and summarized in entries of no more than four hundred words (seven inches of type). The new journal, Luce and Hadden wrote in their prospectus, would deal "*briefly* with EVERY HAPPENING OF IMPORTANCE."

Luce and Hadden found such an approach warranted if only because of an overabundance of information. They assumed that their typical subscriber took the *New York Times,* a newspaper never afraid to bury the unsuspecting in detail. The *Times*'s completeness was their magazine's raison d'être. The week Hadden and Luce resigned from the

Baltimore News to start their magazine, 5–12 February 1922, the *Times* carried twenty-four articles, averaging eighty-three lines, on the Irish civil war. The few Irish-Americans taking the *Times* might read each story. Hadden, however, considered the typical *Times* reader too busy, too restless, to take in each day's entry. Yet the *Times* had no Sunday review of the news, no columnist to summarize and explain the Irish Question. Their magazine would.

It would be called, appropriately enough, *Time*. "No publication," Luce and Hadden argued, "had adapted itself to the time which busy men are able to spend on simply keeping informed." *Time* would relieve readers of the dread of missing "the necessary news" because they had not read carefully a day's newspaper. Reading *Time* would absorb less than an hour yet live up to the magazine's motto, "to keep men well-informed."

The idea of a weekly summary of the news dated to *Niles' Weekly Register*, a Baltimore newspaper (1811–49). In 1892, philosopher John Dewey planned a new version of Hezekiah Niles's work, to be called "thought news." Dewey's paper was "not to go beyond the fact," while interpreting the information presented raw in the daily papers.[17] The new century saw several magazines, *Current History*, *Current Opinion*, *Review of Reviews*, *World's Work*, the *Independent*, attempt in part or whole to synthesize the latest events.

Demand was not hard to locate. In the mid-1910s, Walter Dill Scott, professor of psychology at Northwestern University, conducted a survey of twenty-three hundred of Chicago's leading business and professional men. Most spent about fifteen minutes an evening reading a paper. Despite the new emphasis on features and sports in Chicago's dailies, most replying to Scott's questionnaire said they took papers for local, national, and financial *news*. Those who complained about their dailies spoke of their prejudices or wordiness. "All that is desired," Scott concluded from his respondents' letters, "is a *brief* but comprehensive publication of the news."[18]

The New Certainty

Time would be no mere summary. Its style and structure would distinguish it from standard copy, but so would its tone. Hadden and Luce insisted that *Time* have a point-of-view. That is, *Time* would not be objective in the deadening fashion of the AP. Rather, like the *Yale Daily News* under Hadden, *Time* would not deny the correctness or banality of one side or another.

So doing, Luce and Hadden prepared to challenge not only the first canon of the Associated Press but the watchword of their primary news source, the *New York Times.* Publisher Adolph Ochs of the *Times* abhorred opinion, to the point of regretting having an editorial page only less than one for sports. This is not to say that Ochs lacked a bias. The *Times*'s coverage of the Russian civil war, Lippmann and Charles Merz found, had been thoroughly anti-Bolshevik. The *Times*, press critic Silas Bent complained, "slew Lenin and captured Petrograd."[19] More often, however, the newspaper of record was just that, dry and detailed, and a burden to read. At the Columbia University School of Journalism, press critic A. J. Liebling recalled, "the pattern held up to us was Adolph Ochs' colorless, odorless, and especially tasteless *Times* of 1923, a political hermaphrodite capable of intercourse with conservatives of both parties at the same time."[20]

The problem was not that the *Times* and other papers so lacked opinion as analysis. The safest course for any daily—or magazine—wishing to avoid partisanship was to provide nothing more than information. Editorials might advocate, they rarely analyzed. Readers were still expected to decide what was significant about a story. Daily journalism, Silas Bent complained, "deals with crises and ignores developmental trends."[21] The *New Yorker* magazine's 1925 prospectus declared, "as compared to the newspaper, *The New Yorker* will be interpretive rather than stenographic."

Twenty years earlier, the nation's best journalists were less stenographic than encyclopedic in conveying information. Great "muckraking" magazine writers like Ida Tarbell, Lincoln Steffens, and Ray Stannard Baker composed extended exposés of "evil" trusts and political corruption. Sharing a nineteenth-century ideal of citizenship, the muckrakers assumed that like-minded readers would devote hours to such stories, and that reform would follow. These journalists, wrote one historian, believed they "would rouse the public to contemporary evils by overwhelming them with facts."[22] Later looking at his articles, Baker concluded that some had been too long: "They ought to have been 'reader digested'—but [I] don't see quite how that could have been done, since facts, facts piled up to the point of dry certitude, was what the American people then needed and wanted."[23]

The New Reader

The middle class, which made up the bulk of the muckrakers' readership, came to lose interest in their journalism. Legislation enacted in the wake of their exposés seemingly quieted the demand for still more inquiries. Perhaps the muckrakers' relentlessly gloomy portraits of the political culture encouraged a mass disaffection toward politics. Then, too, new distractions emerged. An expanding number of Americans found ways of escaping home and reading. More went to the picture shows or ball games; many bought their first automobiles and took frequent trips. Men's clubs like the Rotary became fashionable. Younger men of the bourgeoisie joined country clubs and took up golf. Such new leisure activities, recorded "faithfully" by sociologists Robert and Helen Lynd in *Middletown,* made reading more of a luxury. "Our lives, even in our so-called leisure hours," wrote a mechanical engineer in 1930, "are hectically speeded up." Returning home, he asked,

> Do we settle down with a quiet smile to a thought-provoking or soul-enlarging book? No, we go to the movies, or to that gattling-gun variety of entertainment called a revue. We skim the headlines on the way to the office and vote accordingly. On Sundays we rush about in cars at forty miles an hour (or more) cursing those ahead for blocking traffic. Or we play golf and yell "fore!" at every man we catch sight of. . . . We have roving minds. The novel is being replaced by the short story. . . . The two-and-three hour orations . . . have to be compressed into twenty minutes or nobody will listen. Leisurely thinking, which means, or at least may mean, deep, continuous, sustained thinking, is rare.[24]

Magazines tried to respond to this new sense of perpetual motion. Those like *Century* or *Judge* unable to adjust ceased publication. Others—the *North American Review* and the *Independent*—saw their circulations drop. *Forum* tried a livelier layout. *Liberty* actually posted the time needed to read an article. *Collier's* experimented with a one-page short story. Indeed, perhaps the most successful magazine of the 1920s, *Reader's Digest,* reprinted abbreviated versions of pieces originating elsewhere. "To be brisk, curt, concise, telegraphic, and bright became the verbal mode of the hour," Charles and Mary Beard wrote. "To print nothing that would take more than ten or fifteen minutes to read became almost a ruling fashion. Even so complicated a matter as the collapse of American railways could be summarized and disposed of presumably in a few 'crystal clear' paragraphs for readers who had but ten minutes to spare from their looking."[25]

Still, the most popular magazines refrained from guiding their readers. Like the prestige dailies, widely read periodicals not only eschewed advocacy but very often ideological consistency and analysis as well. Popular journals like the *Saturday Evening Post* and *Collier's* ran articles by free-lance writers of various persuasions. If few radicals made their way onto the pages of the *Ladies' Home Journal*, the perspectives of the accepted were by no means harmonious. The *New York Times* subscriber too busy to reach his or her own conclusion found few guideposts in the more widely read magazines. There were plenty of lamps—the *Nation* and the *New Republic*, for example—but few bothered to take either publication. Although the age's most popular journal, the *Saturday Evening Post*, had a reactionary editor, the *Post*'s run of fiction and nonfiction stories by different nonstaff writers betrayed no stalwart bent. The *Post* and other mass-circulating magazines, observed one historian in 1930, "tended toward colorlessness in opinion."[26]

None better exemplified the drabness of the early 1920s magazines than the weekly *Literary Digest*. Founded in 1890, the *Digest* commanded an estimated nine hundred thousand circulation in 1922. Yet it lacked a personality. Staff members summarized but rarely judged events, relying instead on extensive quotations from American and overseas newspapers. The subscriber was treated then not to what the *Digest* writers thought but to the conclusions of a Philadelphia, Saint Louis or Mexico City editor. The *Digest*, a New Haven newspaper complained, suffered from a "slavish devotion to the utterances of many newspapers" and "has made a success of disavowing omni-science."[27] A Luce contemporary remembered the *Digest* as "a dull and stodgy publication with an immense circulation."[28]

Time, Luce and Hadden argued, would differ from the *Digest*. In forty departments, *Time* would cover more news, giving less space to each item than the *Digest*, which consisted of fewer but larger stories. Furthermore, *Time*, unlike the *Digest*, would have opinions. Articles would not quote various voices but speak from one. This persuasion would not be narrowly partisan or ideological. It would be omnipresent. Just as Hadden as *Yale Daily News* editor in 1919 had belied the absoluteness of objectivity, he and Luce declared in their prospectus that some issues and events all but demanded a position. "The *Digest*, in giving both sides of a question, gives little or no hint as to which side it considers to be right," they wrote. "*Time* gives both sides, but clearly indicates which side it believes to have the stronger position."

The Ideology of the New Era

Luce and Hadden gave some hint of their biases. With great confidence in America's future, they promoted *Time* early in 1923 as a "magazine devoted to Summarizing Progress."[29] The Great War's horrors may have shattered a generation of European intellectuals, contributors to the *New Republic,* and those writing chapters in Harold Stearns's depressing collection of essays, *Civilization in the United States* (1922); one scholar of the twenties later dismissed Stearns's work as "a curious document . . . a grim and melancholy index of failure in almost every field of human activity and expression."[30] But other young Americans on the make shared George Babbitt's cheery outlook. In exile, F. Scott Fitzgerald, like *Time*'s founders, anxious to join the class of the well-to-do he had known at college, shared their vision of America in the world. Echoing Luce's 1920 De Forest oration, Fitzgerald wrote Edmund Wilson a year later, "God damn the continent of Europe. It is merely of antiquarian interest," adding that "we will be the Romans in the next generations as the English are now."[31]

Politically, Luce and Hadden identified themselves and their project with the more foward-looking Republicanism of Secretary of Commerce Herbert Hoover. The great engineer, a national hero for his humanitarian work in the Great War, led a party elite of leaders in government, journalism, and business attempting to recast the GOP into the mold of a "new individualism" wary of government bureaucracies. (In *Time*'s prospectus, Luce and Hadden admitted to "a general distrust of the present tendency toward increasing interference by government.") But the new individualism they embraced was not reactionary. Relying on enlightened management and trade associations, Hoover and others looked for a middle ground between what Glenn Frank called "a rampant unsocial individualism on the one hand and an inefficient amateur bureaucracy on the other."[32]

The new individualism of men like Hoover, Frank, and industrialist Owen Young shaped the ideology of *Time*'s founders. They had no use for the decade's liberals, some of them Yale classmates. Yet they also decried the Republican Party's old guard. *Time*'s first number, 3 March 1923, featured a cover story on conservative representative and former House Speaker Joseph G. Cannon; it all but celebrated his departure from public life. The same issue could not veil the editors' disapproval of isolationist opposition to American entry into the World Court. Unlike the *Literary Digest, Time* concluded. The story ended with the confident if erroneous assertion of "a growing sense of American discontent with isolation."[33]

There were less political influences. Hadden admired the decade's great iconoclasts, novelist Sinclair Lewis and journalist H. L. Mencken. The sarcasm of both men appealed to Hadden, who took only baseball seriously. Lewis and Mencken both parodied the American burgher, the middle-class, middle western provincial. Luce remarked later, "The world's greatest reporter is Sinclair Lewis."[34] From his popularity Luce and Hadden realized that *Time,* unlike the *Literary Digest* or the *Saturday Evening Post,* did not have to play exclusively to a small-town Indiana sophistication.

Nevertheless, Luce and Hadden refrained from shaping *Time* only to please the readers of Lewis's *Main Street* or Mencken's *Smart Set. Time* needed a younger George Babbitt's subscription. The magazine was intended for college men their own age in Gopher Prairie and Zenith. Early issues of *Time* even criticized Mencken for his unrelenting abuse of middle-class convention. "For the most part," *Time* observed in October 1927, Mencken "is engaged upon no more important a task than flattening pennies." Nor did Lewis always survive the *Time* of the twenties. *Arrowsmith*'s reviewer all but dismissed Lewis as "the Nation's semi-official castigator."[35]

Walter Lippmann ranked as the greatest influence. Ten years older than *Time*'s founders, graduate of Harvard, former assistant of muckraker Lincoln Steffens and once an editor of the *New Republic*, Lippmann wrote often and searchingly about the shortcomings of American journalism. Although his sway over the profession as a whole has been overstated, his writings did affect Luce and Hadden. To Lippmann, the complexity of modern life demanded more of the fourth estate. Traditional notions about citizenship were failing in part because of newspapers. They reported events inadequately, relying on popular stereotypes or the editor's prejudices. Journalism needed to be less episodic and more analytical. The people, Lippmann wrote in 1922, "cannot govern by episodes, incidents, and eruptions." Newspapers "have become a bundle of 'problems,' which the population as a whole reading the press as a whole, is supposed to solve."[36] When Mrs. McCormick questioned

Luce's "purpose," he replied, "The hope of Democracy is Intelligence and the food of Intelligence is Information."[37]

Luce and Hadden showed their prototype of *Time* to Lippmann, who agreed to be a charter subscriber, a distinction Luce and Hadden in turn publicized. They repaid Lippmann by often quoting him extensively—not like the *Literary Digest,* which would reproduce a dozen different editorial pages—when filing national stories. "He is no Menckenesque boobshouter," *Time* said of the *World*'s editor in September 1927. "He seizes upon the phenomena of democracy which come to his editorial desk, clarifies them in a style bursting with logic, empty of ballyhoo."[38]

Luce and Hadden's reliance on Lippmann was reciprocated in kind. In Lippmann's world the future of journalism belonged to young men like Hadden and Luce. The profession would improve, Lippmann argued, as the better-educated swelled the rank-and-file. A new breed of more intelligent reporters would not be the easy prey of the new, notorious company and government "publicity men," a frequently evoked phantom in contemplations of twenties journalism.

Hadden and Luce tried to realize Lippmann's prophecy in two ways. Not only would graduates of the "better schools" swell *Time*'s editorial ranks, but they would justify the magazine's very creation. More and more people from the middle class went to college. Between 1910 and 1920, the number attending colleges and universities rose from 266,654 to 462,445. In 1926, three years after *Time* began, enrollments reached 767,263. This new, younger and better-educated middle class, Hadden and Luce argued, would be *Time* readers. Most were not Mencken's provincials. College had given them a more outward or "cosmopolitan" worldview. "It is estimated that there are over 1,000,000 people in the United States with a college education," Luce and Hadden noted in their prospectus. "*Time* is aiming at every one of those 1,000,000."

Although approximately three of every eight college students were women, Luce and Hadden's 1922 prospectus and *Time*'s promotional materials through the decade referred only to men. Even the advertising had a male-only hue. The founders did consider and then drop the idea of a "fashion" department. The new staff was similarly male. Indeed, not one woman held one of the twenty initial editorial and business positions. Women served only as "researchers," checkers of obscure or important details.

Time's staff also tilted toward New Haven. Of the magazine's first twenty editors, writers, and business managers, fourteen—including Stephen Vincent Benet and Archibald MacLeish—held Yale degrees, with only two from Yale's arch rival. Two had been *Daily News* chairmen. Almost all were in their twenties, too young to know just how many conventions Hadden and Luce expected to upset. Yale historian George Pierson later wrote, "The roster of [*Time's*] first editors and contributors reads like a Yale College catalog."[39]

The Yale connection aided them in other ways. Hadden was no better off financially than Luce; neither had the capital needed to start a national weekly. Yet the young men estimated that a hundred thousand dollars would be required to finance the venture. How could this much be raised? The brother-in-law of one college acquaintance drew up a frequently used stock scheme whereby Hadden and Luce, though virtually penniless, retained control of the company. They held preferred stock and then sold the common to rich classmates and their associates and families in the New York area. Promoting their plan, the young men did not impress everyone. Hadden could be abrasive; Luce could fall into a stutter when nervous, which was often during this period. But they had enough initial encouragement—one classmate put up four thousand dollars—to expand their market of potential college-friend stockholders. In the summer of 1922, Hadden and his cousin John S. Martin sought still more underwriters by visiting country clubs from New York to Chicago in Martin's new roadster. Yale associates in these new upper-class enclaves welcomed them with open arms and thousand-dollar investments. Having belonged to Yale's exclusive Skull and Bones aided them all the more, as that connection led Luce and Hadden to the home of Mrs. William L. Harkness of New York and their largest single catch, twenty thousand dollars. Although short of their hundred-thousand-dollar goal, the young men now had enough— eighty-six thousand dollars—for *Time* to begin.

Vol. 1., No. 1

Late in 1922 and early in 1923, Hadden and Luce labored furiously in a grim print shop on East 17th Street to prepare the first number. They and their staff shredded the *Times* into departmental piles for rewriting. Lippmann had disliked a typewritten prototype done in December, which had consisted of little more than a collection of two-to-three-sentence entries on individual newsmakers. A 30 December specimen issue came closer to the creators' objectives. The week's news was organized under seventeen departments. Almost all the entries were brief, no longer than a paragraph. "Knowing" description crept in: "Senator Norris is a good citizen from the Middle West who wears his watch chain on his belt."

Late in February came the first issue. *Time*, volume one, number one, was thirty pages long. Luce contributed throughout, with the minister's son handling the Religion Department on his own. As in the specimen issue, most stories were short. Otherwise there was little indication of Hadden's reconceptualization of newswriting. Despite Hadden's fetish for style, almost all the writing was flat, some of it wordy.

Time, volume 1, number 1, did provide clues to both men's political, class, and ethnic insularity. The Education Department discussed only Yale's classical languages program. Under National Affairs came the news that "So-called 'Big Business' wants immigration increased." A means had to be found "to increase the influx of hardy, industrious northern Europeans and [that] would diminish the number of southern Europeans."[40]

Even those in accord with such a narrow view of public issues hardly paused at the advent of *Time*. Of their million collegemen, nine thousand took number one, most of them in the New York area. Vendors returned half of the five thousand newsstand copies. "When *Time* actually appeared," Hadden's cousin recalled, "the results of this publishing revolution was a burst of total apathy on the part of the U.S. press and public."[41] It would take time for America's "busy man" to discover *Time* and for its founders to realize their magazine's goals. The boys would in due course find their audience, though its size and membership would be unexpected.

Elizabeth Luce holding
fourth child, Sheldon.
Harry, Elisabeth, and
Emmavail, 1909.
*Courtesy of Nettie Fowler
McCormick Collection,
State Historical Society of
Wisconsin.*

Emmavail, Elisabeth, and Henry, May 1911.
*Courtesy of Nettie Fowler McCormick Collection,
State Historical Society of Wisconsin.*

The Luces in Switzerland, August 1913.
Courtesy of Nettie Fowler McCormick Collection,
State Historical Society of Wisconsin.

Harry about to enter the Hotchkiss School, 1913.
Courtesy of Nettie Fowler McCormick Collection,
State Historical Society of Wisconsin.

Harry roughing it, 1916.
Courtesy of Nettie Fowler McCormick Collection.
State Historical Society of Wisconsin.

Harry in the American Expeditionary Force, 1918.
Courtesy of Nettie Fowler McCormick Collection,
State Historical Society of Wisconsin.

Harry in the early 1930s; *Time* and *Fortune* underway, *Life* ahead.
Courtesy of Cleveland Press Collection, Cleveland State University Library.

4

"TIME WILL TELL"
1923–1938

When Luce and Hadden first approached New York's well-to-do Yale alumni in 1922 to seek investors for a new magazine, most argued that the venture would too much resemble the *Literary Digest* to succeed. That year, 900,000 Americans took the *Digest*. And the advent of *Time* in March 1923 had no appreciable effect on the *Digest*, which in 1925 had an estimated 1.4 million subscribers, as against Hadden and Luce's magazine's just over 100,000. A relatively small number responded to the young men's slogan "*Time* Will Tell."

By 1938, however, Luce and Hadden had proven the Yale money on Wall Street wrong. *Time*, not the *Literary Digest*, was being imitated. A group of former *Time* writers had begun a rival newsmagazine, *News-week*. Luce could ignore it for the time being. His magazine was becoming a fixture in the middle-class home, and the *Digest* about to fold. Already Luce was a millionaire, and his fame was such that the *New Yorker* in October 1936 ran a profile on him written entirely in Timese. Although Luce and his staff hated the parody, it did signal how far they had come. A spiteful rival, the first of many, felt bound to mock them.

The Struggle, 1923–1928

Time's first years hardly portended great days. Fewer than twenty thousand took the magazine at the end of 1923; the company lost $39,454.

In 1924, it made a profit as circulation neared seventy thousand. Yet a cash shortfall late in 1925 almost killed the young enterprise. A Cleveland bank's loan and an unexpected gush of renewed subscriptions successfully set back creditors.

There were editorial struggles as well. Individual entries did achieve the summary quality Luce and Hadden wanted; many, even cover stories or pieces on major national news, ran to only two or three paragraphs. But that capacity for abbreviation only made the magazine seem a more concise version of the *Digest*. Like the *Digest*, *Time* quoted extensively from a speech, editorial, or court decision. Then, too, early stories suffered from a certain flatness in cadence. Only by the late twenties did *Time* begin to acquire a distinctive tone. Luce and Hadden's conception, a *Time* executive later acknowledged, "would require many months and years of hard work to bring to fruition."[1]

Although both were listed as editors, Hadden handled most editorial tasks while Luce served as business manager until 1928, when they switched posts for a year. Hadden clearly deserves the most credit for *Time*'s formulation, though Luce closely followed and participated in many of his college friend's decisions. Luce long afterwards had to live with the charge that he had been *Time*'s chief accountant and Hadden the magazine's inventor.

Unlike Hadden, Luce was determined to see *Time*'s circulation rise above the "better" middle-class periodicals. Without expecting *Time* to reach the same number as the *Saturday Evening Post*, the nation's largest circulating magazine, Luce drew no satisfaction from a select audience of young and affluent commuters with whom Hadden seemed preoccupied. "My ambition," he told one applicant for a *Time* position in 1927, "is to top the top magazine in the quality group."[2]

In December 1923, Harry found the time to marry. Visiting Rome during his year abroad after finishing Yale, he met Lila Hotz, of a well-to-do Chicago family. The two shared an enthusiasm for poetry. When Lila returned to Chicago in the fall of 1921, Harry courted her with a single-mindedness otherwise seen only in his worldly pursuits. Still, marriage had to be delayed because of Lila's stepfather's objections. He considered Harry "a person of no position," Luce told Mrs. McCormick in February 1922. "He was apparently convinced that I am thoroughly worthless."[3]

After several years of marriage, Harry demonstrated his worthiness, but at a price. While Lila bore him two sons, Henry III and Peter Paul, Harry found less and less time for domestic life. Making *Time* a success absorbed him. And he found it more and more difficult to separate himself from his work in other ways. He preferred the company of people who could inform him, sharing a new fact or philosophy. Small talk, whether from Lila or one of her dinner guests, had no utility to Harry. Lila, in turn, made little effort to enter Harry's world; she was content to study the arts and poetry and have friends over to tea, with Harry slipping in the back door to avoid having to chat with them. At infrequently attended social gatherings, Lila was outgoing and warm; Luce was preoccupied with work, always checking his watch. They were usually among the first guests to leave. As a father, too, he was distant. His sixty-to-seventy-hour work weeks left to Lila the major tasks of raising a family.

Luce's labors began to bear fruit. By 1925, *Time* had more subscribers than Mencken's *American Mercury*. The magazine enjoyed a high renewal rate. Enough did so to sustain the periodical. (Advertising revenues did not subsidize *Time*'s production costs.) Hadden seemed content with a growing if still modest circulation. To Hadden, it gave *Time* a clubbish quality. Two men on a commuter train and each carrying *Time* had a basis for comradeship. One reader in 1929 wrote to thank the publishers: having a copy of *Time* helped him to get a date.

Still another confirmation came after August 1925, when at Luce's urging *Time* moved its offices to Cleveland. Putting out the magazine there, Harry reasoned, would be less costly, and he enjoyed playing the young success story more noticeable in a smaller metropolis. Hadden hated the shift. The relocation did teach them an unexpected lesson about their audience and daily journalism. Both men had assumed their typical reader read the *New York Times* or a similarly dull and detailed chronicle. *Time* itself relied on the *New York Times*. In Cleveland, however, they took one of the city's dailies, the *Plain Dealer*, only to realize how exceptional the *Times* was in its comprehensiveness. The *Plain Dealer*, "though one of the great newspaper properties of America, made no pretense of printing all the news that was fit to print," Noel Busch, Hadden's cousin, wrote. Its editors, like their counterparts in most communities, ran what they thought their readers wanted. Local and state news, of scant use to *Time*, displaced national and international stories that the *Times* carried. It had not occurred to Luce and Hadden, having lived too long along the New Haven-New York axis, that most of their potential audience read not "the newspaper of record" but ones that did not even begin to cover national and world news in depth. "The discovery of the *Plain Dealer*'s inadequacies as a journalistic free-lunch counter was a bonanza for *Time*," Busch wrote. "It showed Hadden and Luce that the main reason so many people were ill-informed was not merely that they were too busy or too lazy to keep up with what was happening" by reading the *Times*.[4] With Cleveland too far from Times Square, Luce and Hadden returned to New York in August 1927.

The dispute over where to base *Time*'s operations had been only one sign that Luce and Hadden, if still friends, were drifting apart. Each was responding to the prospect of middle age and success differently. Luce became ever more serious, Hadden ever more adolescent. He continued to chew gum, play catch, and drink with his writers. At times, Harry sensed that Brit was becoming bored with it all.

Early in 1929, Hadden fell ill. He had been unexpectedly listless in the office and Luce and others insisted that he rest. Late in February, Hadden died of a streptococcus infection of the blood stream. Devastated, Luce told a co-worker, "I do not know what I shall do without him."[5] He had, indeed, lost not only a friend, but his only equal at Time Inc. And Harry took no chances. Borrowing the money, Luce bought enough of Hadden's stock to secure effective control of the magazine.

Planning new publications beginning in 1929, Luce turned over much of the day-to-day responsibility for editing *Time* to others. Hadden's successors proved faithful to his intentions for the magazine. In Hadden's place as editor, Luce named John S. Martin, another of Hadden's cousins, who had helped to solicit investors for *Time* in 1922 and had worked closely with both on the magazine itself. Martin was fiercely devoted to his cousin's ideas and under him *Time* achieved the tone Hadden had sought. Four years later, John Shaw Billings replaced Martin as *Time*'s managing editor. Billings had no loyalty to Hadden, who had died soon after he joined *Time* fulltime. Yet like Hadden, Billings, as a college student and young reporter for the *Brooklyn Eagle*, had studied and admired unconventional writing forms. His free-lance and private writings showed an enthusiasm for unusual sentence order, for rethinking newswriting generally. As managing editor he did nothing to reverse the course Hadden and his cousin had set for *Time*.

Time was an editor's magazine. Even as senior newspaper reporters gradually began to enjoy some autonomy and command by-lines, *Time* stories remained unsigned and most often reflected the values of the editors. "Martin was pretty dogmatic," Billings wrote after one story conference in 1931. "It was evident he wanted to express the ultimate editorial view and suppress the views of associates. He is so cocksure."[6]

In other ways, *Time* was a collective enterprise. Compared to a newspaper, which might have one reporter compose and one or more editors review copy, *Time* had three or more individuals engaged in writing most entries. Initially, none actually witnessed events. Only in the early 1930s did *Time* begin to do some reporting. Even as late as 1937 Martin told an editors' group, "We don't pretend to be reporters at *Time*. We are rewrite men."[7] Staff writers assembled stories from files of clips taken from the *New York Times* and other papers. Female "checkers" dutifully visited the public library to corroborate facts not clear in each pile. One scanned out-of-town papers for bizarre occurrences (similar to those listed in the Americana section of the *American Mercury*). One observer later recalled the anomaly of researchers who knew the facts but not the story and writers who knew the story but not the facts.[8]

Group journalism constituted a bureaucratization of newswriting. Although not wholly new to magazine publishing, *Time's* organizational "system," like that of the emerging corporation, was held together through rigid, hierarchical lines of authority. It transformed the once relatively autonomous magazine "contributor" into an anonymous employee, whose role, wrote one, became "isolated, dependent, and fragmented."[9]

Luce detested the phrase, but he was deeply committed to "group journalism." His own career seemed to prove the validity of the practice. Burdened with a stammer and peculiar personality, Luce could never play Jack Armstrong at Hotchkiss or Yale. He had always required alter egos, first Hadden, then Martin, and later others. Often his opposites, they were instrumental to his success.

Luce himself could be an exasperating supervisor. Although his writers found him unpretentious despite *Time's* success, Luce nevertheless had set views about the magazine's organization and style. He could also be insensitive to those adhering to them. Luce, Billings complained in his diary, rarely praised good work. Other writers thought Luce, when he annually edited *Time* for two weeks, encouraging, an easier wielder of the blue pencil. He could even be challenged. The writer simply had to have the will to do so. On occasion, the editor-in-chief could be generous. When Billings's wife was going through a difficult pregnancy, Luce offered them the weekend use of his New Jer-

sey estate. More often, Luce could be coldly inattentive to his employees' feelings; a certain shyness, from boyhood, prevented frequent and
easy displays of collegiality.[10]

"Facts" as Knowledge

As journalists, everyone at *Time* shared an infatuation with "facts."
The founders had, indeed, planned to call their enterprise *Facts*. To
promote *Time*, Hadden in 1924 and 1928 experimented with producing
quiz programs on the radio, among the first on the new medium.
Twenty questions were asked; *Time* subscribers, the program's an-
nouncer noted at the beginning and end of the show, could answer
each. Sometimes "news" could be defined as unimportant detail. Luce
delighted in copy that included a little item of which he had been unaware. Billings boasted in 1933, "We can ask what dress Queen Mary
wore last Thursday and have an answer in twenty minutes."[11] Literary
critic Alfred Kazin recalled the frustration of wooing a *Time* checker.
"My admiration for her was not reciprocated," he wrote. "She liked intellectuals with a great sense of fact—psychiatrists, biologists, lawyers—
and she had sized me up as someone not clearly useful."[12]

The minutiae disguised the amateur quality of the staff. *Time*'s editors, writers, and checkers were not experts in their fields. To Luce and
Martin, however, that lack of expertise made *Time* more effective at
conveying information, whether on science or modern art. A *Time*
staffer need only have, as Martin put it, a "nodding acquaintance" with
complex knowledge. Moreover, like Luce and Hadden, most *Time*
workers lacked great experience in journalism. Martin confessed to an
editors' group in 1937, "Not more than four or five of us ever worked
on a daily paper."[13]

To T. S. Matthews, who joined *Time* in 1929, the magazine's
writers confused facts for knowledge. *Time* men and women may have,
like Matthews and his former colleagues at the *New Republic*, attended
the "better" schools. Yet "that didn't mean they were well educated or,
in fact, educated at all." Rather, Matthews likened his new coworkers
not to the smartest classmates at his alma mater, Princeton, but to
those who had done well only by cramming for exams at the last moment, by rote memorization of particulars. "The result was much the
same," he wrote, "slickness, smartness, bluff."[14]

The Style

Attention to the small and inconsequential nevertheless began in the late twenties to give *Time* the identity it needed among competing news services. To *Time* writers this approach called for a vivid imagery absent in the daily newspapers and the staid *Literary Digest*. "Newspapers are one-dimensional pictures of news," Billings remarked in 1933, and "news in one dimension is hard to remember." *Time* offered "body and color." Echoing Lippmann's *Public Opinion*, Billings noted, "It is easier to remember what can be seen in a mind's picture—five men filing into President Roosevelt's executive office, Secretary Woodin sitting on a table, swinging his legs."[15]

Time writers thus often noted the physical features of a news setting or newsmaker. They gave a *Time* entry a visual flavor at a time when more and more Americans, mainly because of the diffusion of photography and the motion picture, possessed a greater iconographic sensibility. An eye for detail also conveniently left readers with the false impression that *Time* writers had attended the event covered rather than relied on a pile of newspaper clips and the weather report. The "knowing" and sometimes unkind item, moreover, gave a story authority. In August 1927, for example, President Coolidge addressed a "swarthy audience" of Sioux Indians. H. L. Mencken was a "stocky Dutchman whose appearance suggests the beer drinking of which he is notoriously fond."[16] As in *The Iliad*, figures were described as well as listed: *bald-domed, black-bereted, blubber-lipped, dirt-poor, multichinned, Yankee-shrewd, Maine-born,* and *cloudily-understood*. Such phrasing saved space and struck readers. "Homer wrote about 'high-helmed Hector,' " John Martin remarked, "and a reader of today is, we believe, more likely to be interested in the doings of 'white-crested Senator Johnson' than in those of 'Senator Johnson, Rep., Calif.' "[17]

By the late twenties *Time* writers followed not only Homer but sportswriters in giving an individual a news title. This type of expression allowed the writer, in the interest of economy, to eliminate the appositive. Instead of Clark Griffith, manager of the Washington Senators, the *Brooklyn Eagle* in Hadden's youth had referred to "Manager Griffith of the Washingtons."[18] After several years, *Time* writers, too, alluded to "Novelist Adams," "Editor Bowles," "Motormaker Chrysler," "Publisher Pershing," "Moderator Davis," even "Kidnappee Chiang." The form proved especially useful in photo caption lines, for a "Farmer Campbell" or "Banker Pierson."

Hadden and Martin similarly sought to make *Time* distinctive through the invention or borrowing of words. "Obviously," an Arkansas speech professor observed in a formal study of *Time* writers' vocabulary, "their Roget is always at their elbow."[19] So were compilations from a little notebook in which Luce's partner had recorded words or phrases for adoption in *Time*. The Japanese expression, *tycoon*, came to be applied to "Motormaker" Chrysler and others. From Hindu, *Time* writers began using *pundit*. Hadden's imperative to condense the news also fostered new words like *cinemactor*, *cinemusical*, *cinemoppet*, *radioactor*, and *socialite*.

Finally, *Time* conveyed the news as "stories." Hadden and Luce unknowingly revived a literary style that larger newspapers and wire services had abandoned in the late nineteenth century in favor of one that ritualistically organized individual news items in order of the importance of the information in each. Unlike newspaper reporters, *Time* contributors did not have to justify to an editor or reader their entries by their first paragraph "leads." *Time* staff members instead adopted a linear form. "Our writers," Martin noted, "are required to present in each piece of any length a story with a definite literary form, a beginning, a middle and an end."[20] With color and "significant" facts added to give them a lively tone, *Time* entries came to have an eyewitness or documentary quality lacking in most newspaper accounts. A *Time* editor remarked in 1940 that "the basis of good *Time* writing is narrative, and the basis of good narrative is to tell events 1). in the order in which they occur; 2). in the form in which an observer might have seen them—so that readers can imagine themselves on the scene."[21]

In "The Death of Coolidge," Billings chose not to start his story with the most important set of facts, as he would have at the *Brooklyn Eagle*, but to tell two tales: one of the news spreading around the country to Coolidge's contemporaries, and another, of the funeral. Billings took a thick pile of clippings to tell the story of the former president's last day and funeral. Through small details, the writer captured the mood of Coolidge's home and the reactions of his political allies and rivals when the news came. Billings applied a colorful visual imagery most reporters eschewed in his description of cars going to the gravesite: "Twenty motorcars made the trip through a wet, cheerless afternoon. Their tires droned a dirge on the rutty mud." Near the end came the one-sentence paragraph, "That night snow fell blotting out all trace of the new grave." "It reads like something out of a novel," one of Billings's former colleagues on a daily declared of an earlier Billings's *Time* story.[22] Neither he nor the *Time* subscriber would have guessed that the writer had not been to the funeral; he had composed the story without leaving his office in New York.

Individuals as News

Structural and stylistic peculiarities alone did not differentiate *Time* from the rest of the news media. Whereas the *Literary Digest* or the less widely read and liberal *New Republic* treated news as a web of issues, *Time* from the beginning stressed personalities. *Time*'s cover from the start featured a newsmaker. Between 1923 and 1931, the cover focused on one individual just under 95 percent of the time.[23] Inside, too, individuals frequently defined news. The magazine's first section, National Affairs, invariably began with the subsection The President's Week regardless of whether the president had done anything during those seven days. Before the Great Depression, which all but forced the chief executive into an active role, the presidency section often consisted of little more than miscellaneous and irrelevant items. Although no doubt humanizing the first family for many readers, this organization annoyed some. A Detroit man canceling his subscription late in 1926 complained that "although I am nominally at least a Republican, your waste of two or three pages in each issue discussing the favorite colors of Mrs. Coolidge, President Coolidge's colds and indisposition and such drivel is sickening."[24] Still, *Time* pursued personality. Beginning in 1928, *Time* designated a Man of the Year. Under the People section in 1937, the magazine ran the slogan *Names make news*.

Time's stress on the "newsmaker" led to certain distortions. Overseas coverage often played up royalty, despite their irrelevance to the modern political order. The classic instance came in 1936, when foreign affairs editor Laird Goldsborough devoted columns to the love affair of Edward VIII of Great Britain. In the 9 November 1936 issue, Goldsborough's story on Edward ran to just over four columns, the Spanish civil war entry to half a column.[25]

Still, organizing information around individuals offered a palatable if sometimes woefully incomplete way of conveying current events. Nor was it unique to *Time*. In *News and Human Interest Story* (1940), sociologist Helen McGill Hughes found that newspapers had a new preoccupation with persons, the enthusiasm for which she regarded as a sign of a recently urbanized and less rooted culture.[26] It was one of the ironies of a more complex world that those who wrote and read the news came to reduce events and tendencies to one or two individuals. Even in the twenties, when politics supposedly stood still, the size and role of the federal government grew. Yet *Time* then and later often framed discussions of government around one man, the president.

Time's emphasis on individuals was not new to the periodical press or unique to the culture of the new era. Vast increases in magazine readership in the 1890s could be attributed in part to editors' greater reliance on biographical profiles. A decade later, the muckrakers on occasion viewed social and political problems as the products of bad men, like Rockefeller in Ida Tarbell's *History of the Standard Oil Company*; often, a heroic and incorruptible alternative, like Tom Johnson in Lincoln Steffens's *Shame of the Cities*, waited in the wings. In the twenties, this focus on persons accelerated. Motion picture companies had already begun to emphasize "stars" like Douglas Fairbanks over the stories filmed. Developments in aviation were explained in terms of the single feats of Charles Lindbergh, Robert Byrd, and Amelia Earhart. Henry Ford and Walter Chrysler became metaphors for the booming automobile industry. Baseball copy came to involve the exploits of one figure, Babe Ruth of Hadden's beloved Yankees. Even in popular literature and the histories of Strachey and others, personality became the new focus.[27]

Omniscience

The journalism of persons might have been transparent enough to many readers had Luce and Hadden not similarly adopted a tone of omniscience. With "facts" and "surroundings of facts" *Time* stories were not only summaries of weekly events, shaped around personalities, but shared an all-knowing air. The inclusion of the irrelevant, the physical features of a player or setting, partly achieved this effect. So did the vigorous editorial consistency, which made the magazine appear to be the product of a single intelligence. *Time*, a Chicago-based writer observed, "often reads as though it were all written by the same person."[28] Luce himself acknowledged in 1934, "*Time* is conceived of as written by one man, not any one man you can see, but a sort of superman—the sum total of the very men (perhaps sometimes only three or four) who really 'make it.' " To Martin, *Time* must have the "lunar detachment" of "the man in the moon at the end of the current century."[29] And he ruthlessly sought to see that tone in each *Time* entry, usually

with success. Of a writer having difficulty learning *Time* style, one editor complained, "His writing just lacks significance."[30]

The pose of omniscience allowed *Time* to draw conclusions in ways
no newspaper or the *Literary Digest* dared. Early and often the magazine
ran stories on Negroes accused by hysterical white southerners of various crimes and hanged without trial. But while a newspaper like the
New York World might damn the practice only on the editorial page
and the *Digest* then reprint that criticism, *Time*'s 9 January 1928 story
on lynching began: "Lynching is an institution preserved in the U.S.
for Negroes by primitive white people." Similarly, the lead for a story
late that month started, "The Sixth Pan-American Conference accomplished absolutely nothing last week." Six years later, newspapers covered a week of the London Naval Conference extensively. *Time*
summarized the meeting's importance in one paragraph, focusing on, of
all things, the U.S. envoy playing golf with the Japanese negotiator.[31]

Time's omniscience could take the form of a bias usually only
hinted at until the final paragraph. A flattering May 1932 cover story
on former secretary of war Newton D. Baker, one of *Time*'s initial investors, and his possible nomination for president ended, "If he is nom-
inated by the Democrats at Chicago, the next campaign will not lack
literate eloquence from at least one side of the field." Five years later,
an entry on President Roosevelt's just announced and controversial
court reorganization proposal observed, "As obviously as the President's
message was an argument for a change in the judiciary on the simple
grounds of good government, his major proposal had an ulterior motive. It was patently contrived to let him override the Supreme Court
as now constituted by adding or replacing Justices to support the legal
contentions of the New Deal."[32]

Such opinionated analyses had more impact because of the magazine's peculiar format. Even a bitterly partisan newspaper carried such
assessments only after the reporter located a source echoing his or,
more likely, his editor's, prejudices. Correspondents for the *Chicago Tribune* and other newspapers (most were hostile to the court plan) relied
on political or legal authorities they could quote. By the early 1930s,
however, *Time* quoted others less and spoke its own mind more.
Its writers did not remove themselves through attribution from their
opinions. Moreover, because only some foreign news and reviews had
by-lines, the reader had no clue as to who drew what conclusion.
Although this practice denied writers the identity and status some
wanted, for readers it had the necessary effect. Individual newspaper

columns ("One Man's Opinion," "In This Corner") and magazine opinion pieces bearing a person's name could be dismissed as the products of mere individuals. *Time*'s entry, written with a distinctive and assured hand, gave the impression that a larger body or Luce's "superman" had weighed a problem and decided its importance.

The writer for *Time* thus found himself under the greatest pressure to reflect the assurance of the founders and be able to conclude. Since adolescence, Luce and Hadden believed in themselves and their capacity to synthesize information. They expected no less of their staff. *Time* was a magazine of supremely confident young men. The founders had no doubt, wrote David Cort, an early *Time* staffer, that "an external truth exists this week and can be expressed in 500 words by a talented writer after he has read the week's New York newspaper clippings." To those hesitating, they cried, "Make up your mind!"[33]

Time's willingness to "know" distinguished it from newspapers and the *Literary Digest*. Compared to *Time*, the *Digest* ran longer stories, but ones without conclusions; instead, it quoted from the week's newspaper editorials. Prestigious newspapers tended to overwhelm readers with information or offer them objective wire service copy. Opinion came only on the editorial page. Other dailies deliberately confused reporting and advocacy. *Time* took stands unlike the objective papers and wire services, yet did so with more subtlety than the partisan sheets. Competing with newspapers, *Time* also enjoyed the advantages of a weekly deadline. Newspapers presented information in terms of single episodes, what one sociologist later dubbed "eventism." Week to week *Time* could synthesize many individual occurrences, tell one story and often derive conclusions from it. The pattern often owed more to hindsight than to wisdom.

Yet even with a week's pause for reflection that those working for dailies lacked, *Time* occasionally misjudged developments. After Franklin Roosevelt's poor showing in some 1932 presidential primaries, a *Time* entry observed, "Mr. Roosevelt's protestations of interest in the forgotten man have brought him just nowhere." Why? *Time* knew. "The people of the East know about Mr. Roosevelt and gradually have taken his measure. They just do not believe in him. They have detected something hollow in him, something synthetic, something pretended and calculated." That Roosevelt could go on to win his party's nomination and decisively defeat President Hoover in November was not broached. Like Lippmann, whose anti-Roosevelt column *Time* had quoted approvingly, the magazine did not masquerade its underestimation of the New Yorker. Two months later, the magazine assured readers Adolf Hitler would not come to power in Germany. *Time* incorrectly forecast a naval arms limitation agreement in 1934; a friendly golf game reported between the American and Japanese diplomats was not, after all, a metaphor for the negotiations.[34] Again, other analysts erred as well. But few passed off opinion as information so skillfully.

In this regard *Time* proved true to Luce and Hadden's original specifications. *Time* possessed opinions: it avoided the odorlessness of the *New York Times* or the *Literary Digest* yet without becoming a party organ. Although both men remained Republicans, their magazine occasionally criticized Coolidge and Hoover. Luce himself lost enthusiasm for the Great Engineer and voted for his Democratic opponent in 1928. "I did a Presidency which was really an editorial on Hoover's political troubles, blaming him for them," Billings wrote in late February 1930. "I have a growing antipathy toward the President."[35] Compared to many dailies, *Time* offered objective summaries of the 1936 Roosevelt-Landon campaign. *Time* did claim on the eve of the balloting that in New England Roosevelt's "most enthusiastic crowd appeared in Socialist Bridgeport." But it also reported Landon's hostile audiences in New York and Los Angeles, clues to his impending humiliation at the polls.[36]

In the arts, *Time* strove to be cautious. Matthews had to fight to get a cover story on James Joyce. On learning that another was planned for John Dos Passos, Luce suggested Carl Sandburg would be more fitting. Compared to "little" magazines, *Time* took few risks. Matthews recalled, editors "always wanted the Book of the Month Club choice well-reviewed, the popular stuff." A frustrated literary critic later judged Luce to be one of "the two great enemies of literary talent in our time."[37]

Overall, *Time*'s first decade and a half was less prejudiced than sneering. The magazine described an older, less refined generation of politicians—Republican and Democratic—in the most unflattering ways. President Hoover's campaign manager in June 1932 was "large, chunky, slow-minded Everett Sanders." A candidate for the U.S. Senate in Georgia that year was the "son of the State's prolific, tobacco-chewing chief justice."[38] Nor did the sophisticated but leftward-leaning escape the magazine's judgmental manner: The *New Republic* was dismissed as "pinko," the *Nation* belittled for its affinity for lost causes. Such a tone, though, added to *Time*'s pose as arbiter of the great center.

Occasionally *Time* writers went too far, seeing only a white and Protestant middle. Although highly critical of lynching, *Time* called transgressing blacks "blackamoors" or "blackamorons." So doing, Noel Busch shamelessly recalled, maintained "the Olympian impartiality which was essential to *Time*'s basic attitude toward all controversy."[39] Jews were upset by a veiled anti-Semitism in the magazine, especially after the biases of Foreign Affairs Editor Goldsborough combined with the editors' love of news titles to create the reference to the French politician, "Jew Blum." Allegations of anti-Semitism disturbed Luce, who in turn demanded that his (overwhelmingly Protestant) staff show more sensitivity to the feelings of *Time*'s Jewish readers. For some it was too late. The editor of the *New Yorker* wrote Luce in 1936, "two Jewish gentlemen were at dinner with me last night and, upon mention of *Time*, one of them charged that you were anti-Semitic, and asked the other if he didn't think so too. The other fellow said he's read *Time* a lot and he didn't think you were anti-Semitic, especially—you were just anti-everything, he said: 'anti-Semitic, anti-Italian, anti-Scandinavian, anti-black widow spider. It's just their pose.' "[40]

Finding an Audience

Time's "pose" nevertheless did appeal to many Americans. Between 1925 and 1930, *Time*'s circulation increased threefold to three hundred thousand. In the next six years it doubled and neared one million by the decade's end. Of *Time*, *Harper's* editor Bernard de Voto wrote in 1937, "Everyone reads it, everyone relies on it for part of his information about the modern scene."[41]

But *Time* was not the magazine of everyone. Subscribers were more likely to have "cosmopolitan" tastes in information; that is, they were more interested in national and world affairs and in the arts and sciences than the average newspaper reader. *Time*, the magazine proclaimed in 1935, "does not appeal to Oscar Stillwater, resident of Hicksville, whose interests range no further than the county line. Nor to Manhattan's Josephine Puddle, who thinks everything west of the Palisades is wilderness." In fact, *Time* was relatively little read in the largest cities, where the prestige papers served the cosmopolitan taste. Rather, *Time* was to be found most often in those medium-sized cities of one hundred fifty to three hundred thousand persons where newspapers stressed local news. Luce himself concluded that the typical *Time* reader was "the gentleman from Indiana."[42]

Time readers were usually among the wealthier members of their communities. Most Americans regarded magazines as luxury items, for which few had the time or money. Time proved no exception. A 1931 Time survey of readers in Appleton, Wisconsin, found that 60 percent of all Time subscribers had annual incomes of over $5,000. Just over a third earned more than $10,000. Nationwide, two years earlier, 1 percent of all families earned $10,000 or more; the average income was $2,335. Of thirty thousand subscribers sampled in 1931, 71 percent owned the homes in which they lived, compared to a 1930 national average of 46 percent.[43] By 1941, as Time reached the one million mark, more of the middle class joined in subscribing. Advertisers learned that 64 percent of all subscribers earned more than $3,000 annually; 18.8 percent of all families had incomes that high.[44]

Business executives and proprietors formed the bulk of Time's readership. In the early 1930s, a New York advertising agency survey found more bankers reading Time than any other magazine, including the Saturday Evening Post and Literary Digest. Time's own study of subscribers listed the presidents of Coca Cola and General Motors as well as the chairmen of Eastman Kodak and General Electric. More often, Time's business readers consisted of executives closer to Luce's age and on the make as vice-presidents.[45] A Boston-based survey declared that Time was the business classes' favorite magazine, the one most likely to be read upon delivery—and cover to cover. While the circulations of business periodicals like Forbes and Nation's Business between 1932 and 1937 remained fairly level, Time's continued to grow.[46] A 1939 Time Inc. study indicated that 60 percent of all subscribers were businessmen and women; 18.5 percent were professionals: doctors, engineers, lawyers, and educators.[47] Advertising promoted products only the country club and wood-paneled station wagon set could afford: expensive hotels and private schools and camps, air travel, overseas telephone services, office equipment and supplies.

Luce and Hadden had, after all, designed their magazine for the small and large capitalist too busy to give his newspaper a close day-to-day reading. David Cort put it more sourly, "Time was directed at the literate Philistine reader who was assumed to be in such a hurry that only great charm and provocativeness could stop him long enough to read anything."[48] Time's emphasis on conciseness and "facts" appealed to the "practical" men of enterprise of modern America. Describing the first generation of capitalists, the new burghers of western Europe, historian Carl Becker in 1935 captured the typical Time readers. "They are occupied with immediately practical affairs, with defined and determinable rights, with concrete things and their disposal and their calculable cash value," Becker wrote. "The burgher mind is subdued to what it works in: chiefly occupied with practical affairs and material values, it seeks to impose on the outer world and relations an ordered and measurable and predictable behavior."[49]

Time similarly served the needs of those "new burghers" participating in the emerging organizational society. The long-term integration of once locally oriented business and financial activities into ones serving or affected by new regional and national markets caused many small city financiers and manufacturers as well as middle- and upper-level executives of new corporate bureaucracies to seek a systematic presentation of world and national events. For this reader, economic well-being made *Time* a necessary supplement to hometown dailies that likely emphasized local politics, bank holdups, and warehouse fires.[50]

Time's business readership may explain why the magazine displeased certain critics. As Cort observed, *Time* was not written for the more literate and liberal takers of the *New Republic*. Many admiring *Time*'s approach took it anyway. But *Time* had always been meant for the comfortable burghers, most of whom shared Luce's support for Republican capitalism. "Our journalism," Luce wrote in May 1939, "is concerned with the middle and upper middle class."[51]

Time helped to meet this middle-class audience's cultural needs as well. The magazine's "back of the book" departments on the arts, literature, and theater together served as one of several components of a national cultural machinery arising in the 1920s and 1930s to direct middle-class taste. Some four hundred thousand bought the five-foot shelf of books endorsed by former Harvard University president Charles W. Eliot. Fifteen minutes of reading a day, Eliot averred, made one "educated." The Book-of-the-Month Club decided for members which of the many new books published each year were worth having. Radio programs in the 1930s hosted by Alexander Woollcott and William Lyon Phelps similarly selected literature for the busy American bourgeois. Phelps argued, wrote one historian, "that the attainment of culture was not a matter of actively acquiring aesthetic sensitivity or critical understanding but of passively receiving inside information."[52] *Time* promised much the same. "From every important news-source," one ad declared, "*Time*'s editors condense, vivify, present the facts in brief, lucid paragraphs. . . . Each page brings to the reader a *final report* on a whole world of news."[53]

The success of *Time*'s formula suggested a middle-class unease about information. The new distractions of leisure time joined with the ever greater specialization of education and work to deny people the hours and sensibilities needed to master a more complex culture. In self-promotion, *Time* seized upon this anxiety by running ads asking, "Do you recognize the kind of man who never quite knows what he is talking about?"[54] and under the Miscellany department carrying the comment, "*Time* brings all things."

The Alternatives

Indeed, the middle-class acceptance of *Time*, as Luce and Hadden had surmised, owed the most to the shortcomings of the newspaper of the 1920s and 1930s. The respectable or "prestige" press of the largest cities inundated readers with serious news while caring little for readability. Elsewhere—as the founders discovered operating *Time* out of Cleveland—newspapers stressed local and state news, to the disadvantage of the cosmopolitan consumer concerned with national and international events.

America, unlike England, lacked national newspapers. Those with a specialized focus, like the *Wall Street Journal*, had not yet found a way of achieving national distribution and had modest circulations. Most dailies tried to serve the conflicting tastes of hometown audiences, to appeal to all elements of a community in search of the largest possible circulation. As a result, papers usually played up crime, natural disasters, train or aircraft accidents, all of general consumer interest if of little national importance. Affairs of state were not ignored, though they could be obscured by the emphasis on so much else. Although this model of "gatekeeping," of carrying certain stories at the expense of others, did not upset most readers, it did leave a cosmopolitan minority hungry for less sensational and less localized news. Soon after returning to California in 1933, former president Hoover arranged for the airmail delivery of thirty dailies. The local papers, he complained, could not satisfy his appetite for national and world news.[55]

A changing news agenda added to the confusion. In the middle and late 1920s, many newspapers and the major wire service boosted their coverage of human interest stories, murders, sports, and various "stunts" identified with the new era. Spurred by the success of the new big-city tabloids, dailies as staid as the *New York Times* and William

Allen White's *Emporia Gazette*, as well as the Associated Press, took up what came to be known as "jazz journalism." The AP "has simply enlarged the field of its interests. It is striving to report every phase of the human spectacle," the *Kansas City Star* observed. The AP by-line "now is appearing over dispatches that are gay as well as grave."[56] Although readers in small and large markets had demanded this broader report of society, the growing list of what made for "news" put new demands on them, making what was important as opposed to interesting more difficult to discern.

The greater attention to spectacular murders and other crimes in the 1920s and 1930s could be seen in many dailies. All New York papers, not just the tabloids, greatly augmented their coverage of crime. "It was nothing unusual," Silas Bent wrote in 1927, "to see in New York newspapers as much as twenty columns devoted to a single day's proceedings in two second rate murder trials."[57] The wire services as well offered subscribers across the country copy on the more lurid proceedings. In Boston, as playwrights like Eugene O'Neill reckoned with prudish censors, most dailies freely offended church and civic groups with flamboyant tales of mayhem.

This journalism of "ballyhoo" also involved grossly overcovering some events. The death of film actor Rudolph Valentino and the visit of Queen Marie of Rumania received far more play in many papers than their significance warranted. Perhaps no event obtained more excessive coverage than the solo transatlantic flight of Charles Lindbergh in May 1927. New York's six largest dailies devoted an average of thirteen pages to news of Lindbergh's arrival in Paris.[58] Newspapers across the country joined in this extraordinary treatment of the Lone Eagle's exploits. The kidnapping of Lindbergh's infant son in 1932 commanded even more sustained coverage as did accounts of the investigation and trial of the man accused of the deed.

Time stood out against the newspapers' new ordering of events. The magazine's strict departmentalization of the news did not collapse with the flight of *The Spirit of St. Louis* or the murder of a New Jersey minister and his choir director. Although eventually naming Lindbergh Man of the Year, *Time* covered his flight on page twenty-six of a forty-page issue. Similarly, the magazine waited eight weeks after the kidnapping before putting the Lindbergh baby on the cover. *Time* thus kept its journalistic bearings, keeping the "serious" reader informed of national and international affairs while local editors tried to decide how much to run of a wire service account of gangster clashes or flagpole sittings.

Time's steadfastness became all the more important after 1929. The depression compelled a demand for what many editors had chosen to obscure. The frivolous gave way to the pressing. Mass misery and government's response to it reminded readers of the complexities and treacherousness of modern life, of how much economic and political events could, after all, affect their lives. Dailies had no choice but to take on a new seriousness. By 1934, the United Press trunk lines carried three times as much Washington news as in 1930.[59] Compared to a daily newspaper, however, Time was prepared to cover America in depression. For readers, the magazine's blend of information and interpretation made what was occurring more manageable. Time's emphasis on the presidency, which earlier only partly related to the newsworthiness of the chief executive's week, suddenly seemed inspired. As Hoover and then Roosevelt endeavored to reverse the economic downturn, their office assumed a new significance for Americans.

Newspapers and later in the decade radio news belatedly attempted what Luce and Hadden had prescribed in their Time prospectus eight years earlier: news had to be analyzed as well as conveyed. Radio networks employed commentators like H. V. Kaltenborn to interpret events. Even the Associated Press sought more searching and less descriptive copy. Larger papers began to allow their most prominent correspondents to interpret as well as to present information.

Perhaps the most telling change was the advent of the analytical news column. In 1931, the Herald Tribune hired Lippmann to write a thrice-weekly news analysis, "Today and Tomorrow." Although many papers had political columns, most did not so much explain events as share gossip. Lippmann was the first to provide sustained analysis. Others, like Dorothy Thompson and Raymond Clapper, soon followed. Syndicated, the new analyst reached audiences heretofore at the mercy of the provincialism of a local editor; some 160 newspapers carried Lippmann in 1939. Now readers had editorials offering the kind of national view found in Time. The new syndicated columnist, wrote one British journalist, "is a liberated leader-writer."[60]

By the mid-1930s some major dailies imitated Time by adding to their Sunday editions a weekly review of the news. Although the New York World had long published such a section, it had included relatively few entries; by the mid-1930s, the Kansas City Star, Richmond News

Leader, Cincinnati Enquirer, and *New York Times* published supplements synthesizing the major news developments of the week; in 1936, the Associated Press began offering members materials for a weekly news review. No longer did some editors assume that readers had absorbed all the information covered day to day. Most grudgingly acknowledged *Time's* leadership in the new journalism of synthesis. The *Chicago Tribune* actually criticized Luce's news magazine; unlike *Time*, the *Tribune's* weekly review "will avoid the smart aleck style of drawing conclusions from unrelated facts set together in suspicious nearness. It is simple to say in one sentence that Miss Vera Loos lives at 2 Easy Street and in the next sentence that Senator Trombone was seen to pause to mop his brow in front of 2 Easy Street."[61]

In most regards, however, newspapers were slow to change. Stylistic rituals nurtured over several decades proved hard to abandon, even as George Gallup's surveys of news readers found consumers dissatisfied with newswriting and layout. Since Pulitzer's time, newspapers had organized information around departments or "pages" for such topics as sports and society. But none could match *Time's* neat and succinct ordering of the world. "Lay critics of the press have long complained," wrote Herbert Brucker in 1937, "that they get a confused picture of the news from our newspapers, and if newspapermen can put themselves in the position of the objective man from Mars they may agree." Before his Columbia journalism school students, Brucker held up *Time* as a model when they experimented with layouts. To Brucker and others, objective accounts could be written with such attention to accuracy and attribution as to confuse the lay reader. Most wire-service copy still lacked analysis. Member newspapers contributed much material, not all of it distinguished or—in the case of southern dailies on the racial issues—disinterested.[62]

Except for the introduction of news reviews and columns, big city papers languished. The *Detroit Free Press* in the 1930s, one house historian observed, "still came across as a tired institution in its coverage and presentation of news."[63] Boston's dailies constituted what Oswald Garrison Villard called a "journalistic poorfarm." The publisher of the city's largest circulating paper, the *Globe*, "had led the profession downward." A historian of the *Globe* later dubbed the thirties his paper's "dimmest period. But this was a dim period for the press generally."[64] In Washington, the local papers' inadequacies drove some to take a New York daily. Almost all appeared resistant to the new. Even the nation's two best papers, the *New York Times* and *Herald Tribune*, Villard found, were content merely to inform. Both, he wrote, "are positively committed to the established order. Neither can claim to be an originator of causes." Of the *Los Angeles Times*'s owner, a harsh George Seldes observed, "No one ever heard [Harry] Chandler say anything which could be interpreted even vaguely as humanitarian, altruistic, liberal or progressively intelligent."[65]

The new political order of the 1930s partly explained the newspapers' malaise. After a pause, most publishers declared war on the Roosevelt presidency. For many dailies, this antagonism filtered down to ostensibly "objective" accounts of the administration. For others, it rested exclusively on the editorial page. Of those newspapers endorsing a candidate in 1936, 63 percent backed Roosevelt's Republican opponent. In Massachusetts, only two papers favored a second term.[66]

For the first time since the advent of the mass-circulation press in the late nineteenth century, newspapers found themselves out of step with public opinion. Until the 1930s, the publishers outside the South could endorse Republican candidates without fear of offending the vast majority of their readers; the GOP was the majority party. But Roosevelt fashioned a new partisan alignment that left publishers politically isolated. Particularly in the major cities, the *New Republic* found, newspapers opposing the New Deal were far removed from their readers. In Los Angeles pro-Roosevelt newspapers had a 74,252 combined circulation, yet Roosevelt polled ten times as many votes there. No Detroit daily backed Roosevelt, who nevertheless outpolled Landon in the Motor City two to one. In Chicago, where the *Tribune* had vigorously slanted all copy against the New Deal, and only one rival favored the incumbent, Roosevelt carried forty-eight of the city's fifty wards.[67]

How had this prejudice worked? For smaller dailies, relatively neutral wire copy filled the national news hole, though some editors altered portions favorable to the New Deal. Anti-Roosevelt publishers made a point of carrying those syndicated columnists who regarded Roosevelt with distaste. And most analysts by the 1936 campaign had problems with the New Deal; even Lippmann, once a protégé of the Socialists, voted for Landon. One of his more popular rivals, Mark Sullivan, suggested in a November 1935 column that the forthcoming presidential election might be America's last, and went on to liken the New Deal to German fascism. Sullivan's writing, observed one contemporary, "stands like a ruined monument to an age that has gone."[68]

Some of the bigger papers, able to report the campaign, went to extremes. The reactionary *New York Evening Sun* announced that the

Social Security Act would compel workers to wear metal tags. After police broke up gangster activities in northern Wisconsin, the *Tribune* ran the story under the headline: ROOSEVELT AREA IN WISCONSIN IS HOTBED OF VICE. The *Tribune*'s Soviet Union correspondent indicated that Moscow had ordered American Communists to back Roosevelt. Later, a news item in Hearst's *New York American* declared that the Communist party's "real candidate" was not nominee Earl Browder but Franklin Roosevelt.[69]

The excesses of such papers caused some aligned with the administration to overestimate the anti-Deal prejudices of the press. Many anti-Roosevelt dailies carried relatively objective accounts of presidential speeches and news conferences. The administration's elaborate public information machinery effectively shaped the agenda and tone of Washington reportage. The editorial page offered many anti-Roosevelt publishers their only enclave.[70]

Nevertheless, the war that some publishers fought with the New Deal invited severe repercussions. For the first time since the late 1790s, members of one political party, led by Secretary of the Interior Harold Ickes, not only openly criticized newspapers but hinted at the need for federal regulation. An exasperated director of the University of Wisconsin's journalism school privately considered advocating newspaper licensing. He and others were not alone. Surveys revealed that most Americans no longer trusted their newspapers. More and more followed the administration's advice and turned to radio with its live transmission of events that newspapers might distort. The publisher of the *New York Times* warned of "a growing disposition on the part of the public to view with skepticism that which they read in their newspapers and to distrust newspaper motives."[71]

If only by default, then, *Time* had replaced many dailies in their informational function and reliability. The politics of the thirties had caused some newspapers to revert to a nineteenth-century partisanship. Although Luce shared his rivals' disillusionment with Roosevelt—and his magazine could not be regarded as neutral toward the New Deal, *Time*'s coverage hardly displayed the tilt evident in a Hearst or McCormick sheet. The magazine frequently criticized the reactionary chains for their excesses, as in the 12 October 1936 number dismissive of the Hearst charge of Communist ties to Roosevelt. Already Hearst's editors were under instructions to "see that any mention of [Time Inc.'s] doings scrupulously avoids anything in the nature of a boost."[72]

Luce and his publication came much closer to an objective standard that most of his readers, whatever their anti–New Deal politics, welcomed. *Time* readers wanted to be told the "facts," however unpleasant, that Landon's campaign was faltering, that Roosevelt was likely to win. Indeed, many who supported Roosevelt took *Time*. De Voto praised the magazine. "*Time* has made itself indispensable," he wrote in 1937. "Its coverage is amazing, its accuracy good, its editorializing stimulating and frequently fair."[73] "Mr. Luce's publications have maintained for seven years a critical attitude toward the Roosevelt administration," Dorothy Thompson wrote three years later. "It has not, however, been a blindly partisan attitude. It has not been critical for the sake of criticizing, but critical according to the views of objective reality of the editors and writers."[74]

Time as Model and Target

Among journalists, *Time* enjoyed a wide following. From the beginning, *Time* subscribers included Lippmann and other knights of the fourth estate. In April 1924, *Time* listed just under five hundred editors and publishers as readers. *Time*'s extensive treatment of the press explained some of this popularity. Many, too, were attracted to *Time*'s novel style and organization. Journalism students at the University of Minnesota, a professor reported late in 1927, found *Time* an inspiration. "They all wished assiduously to mimick *Time*'s style."[75] "*Time* is not only a threatening competitor but a worthwhile stylebook," a Springfield, Missouri, editor confessed two years later. "For thoroughness of detail, vividness of description and the graphic simplicity of its literary style, *Time* is far ahead of most newspapers." "Today the pattern seems to be the short, crisp, comma-studded phraseology typical of *Time*," *Variety* noted. "But editors avow it is the biggest nuisance in journalism today." Nonetheless, chain newspaper operators at home and abroad like Frank Gannett and Lord Beaverbrook began to encourage their staff members to read *Time*. Some needed no hints. Washington correspondents in the mid-1930s, sociologist Leo Rosten found, were more likely to take *Time* than any other magazine.[76]

Not everyone celebrated *Time*'s new place in American journalism. In 1936 and 1937, the *New Yorker* and the *Nation* ran highly critical assessments of Luce and his creation. A *New Yorker* profile of Luce by Wolcott Gibbs satirized the magazine's peculiar style: inverted sentences, "knowing" descriptions, invented news titles, neologisms.

"Backward ran sentences until reeled the mind," Gibbs wrote, who spoke of an "ambitious, gimlet-eyed, Baby Tycoon Henry Robinson Luce."[77] Several months later, the *Nation* carried a more disturbing barrage by a former Time Inc. writer, Dwight Macdonald. In what proved to be the first of several generations of such criticisms, Macdonald assailed *Time* not for its style but for its prejudices. *Time*, Macdonald contended, was as guilty as any daily of political distortions. Macdonald went on to liken Luce to Hearst; whereas Hearst relied on ignorance and passion to twist information, Macdonald wrote, "Luce and his editors at least *think* their conclusions are determined by the weight of evidence."[78]

Both attacks, however, tended to ignore *Time*'s implications for American journalism. *Time*'s peculiar prose, so offensive to Gibbs and his editor, could eventually be abandoned. Relaying prejudice as news, which Macdonald found rampant, could be better understood by recognizing the magazine's disproportionately upper and uppermiddle class audience. Then, too, much of the bias Macdonald located was, as he himself admitted, more apparent in some newspapers. The real hazard to *Time*'s journalism was its very structure. Luce and his editors were weekly making decisions for their readers as to what was important and why. Consumers of news who might earlier have sifted through more information now had *Time* editors, writers, and checkers assuming that role: a complex event, episode, or trend, cleverly, knowingly arranged in four hundred words.

Journalism has always involved summary, yet *Time* was redirecting the process of synthesis. "Color," detail, description, often irrelevant, were added to give a *Time* entry authority. "Personality" dominated serious discussions of policy. The world was becoming more complicated, *Time* was making it seem too comprehensible. And because its circulation only rose, few dared question let alone challenge what Luce and Hadden had created: a journalism of reassurance, not information. Lippmann's dream of journalists as philosopher kings was being profitably realized at Time Incorporated's headquarters atop the Chrysler Building. Ever larger numbers of readers, well-to-do and educated, were surrendering their sovereignty over information to *Time* and its imitators.

Victory

Luce's journalism nevertheless not only impressed the middle class but came to destroy *Time*'s first great rival. Beginning in the late 1920s, some advertisers entertained doubts about the *Literary Digest*. Circulation began to fall in the early 1930s from a high of 1.6 million in 1931 to 464,030 in 1938. The magazine that Luce and Hadden had been warned they could not contest was dying. Its reputation plummeted after predicting a Republican victory in 1936. Two years later the *Digest* ceased publication. Time Incorporated purchased the subscription list for twenty-five thousand dollars. The boys had won out, although Luce was too busy with other enterprises to savor either the *Digest's* destruction or his own mastery of informing the middle class.

5

FORTUNE AND "THE MARCH OF TIME"
1930–1936

By the late 1920s, *Time* was proving profitable enough for Luce to begin contemplating fresh ventures. In 1930 came a new magazine, *Fortune*, and several years later, "The March of Time" radio program and newsreel. Of the three, only *Fortune* did not greatly expand Luce's audience. Yet even that magazine succeeded financially and artistically. All constituted departures in established norms of news delivery. *Fortune* offered new and expansive definitions of business journalism. On the radio, "The March of Time" presented a far more structured and dramatic summary of the news than the newly formed radio network news services attempted. "The March of Time" on the screen similarly rewrote the rules of newsreel production.

There were minor properties as well. Even before *Time*'s success was assured, Luce and Hadden briefly owned the *Saturday Review of Literature*. For three years they published an advertising trade journal. In 1932, Time Inc. bought *Architectural Digest*; its modest circulation and perennial operating losses through the decade disappointed Luce. He derived little satisfaction from publishing professional or literary journals. His ambitions remained too great, his fascination with journalistic innovation too overriding.

Fortune

Fortune was the first substantial addition to Time Inc. and the one for which Luce himself deserves the most credit. Hadden had been the senior partner in designing *Time*. Others labored more than Luce in creating "The March of Time." Luce, however, had conceived of *Fortune* and he spent more time and energy directly overseeing its publication than on any other project. Although *Fortune*'s second editor, Ralph Ingersoll, worked harder on the magazine, he was most often carrying out Luce's commands. *Fortune* was Luce's passion, his other publications mere acquaintances. "*Fortune*," wrote one contemporary, "was Luce's real love among his magazines."[1]

Luce weighed creating a business periodical in 1928. He had never shared the antagonism toward free enterprise that he contemptuously identified in 1931 with the "professional culturist." "Your culturist has no difficulty," Luce wrote, "identifying big business with stupidity, crassness, insensitive efficiency, and to put not too fine a point upon it, prostitution."[2] Such a stereotype contradicted Luce's own self-image. In the 1920s he considered himself almost as much a businessman as a journalist. While Hadden handled most editorial tasks, Luce took on the managerial ones associated with publishing: negotiating with printers, brokers of office supplies, and landlords. Unlike Hadden, who exchanged these duties with Luce for a year, Luce enjoyed playing the business executive, especially when *Time* was headquartered in Cleveland and he could mix easily with virtually all the city's chief enterprisers.

The economic boom of the twenties reinforced Luce's predilection toward modern capitalism. At no time in his life did the economy grow with so little inflation as in the 1920s. Luce thought the new era would never end. "I instinctively share, with most Americans," he remarked in March 1928, "an almost fantastic faith in the industrial and commercial future of this country."[3]

Journalism to Luce had been unequal to the task of explaining capitalism's great success. Although he regarded free enterprise as the story of the era, the fourth estate continued to give far more space to sports and politics. Increases in *Time*'s coverage of commerce and industry in the late twenties did not satisfy him. The business world "is in fact the largest of the planets," he told the directors of Time Inc. "The growth of the chain store system is no less significant in the century's development than the decline of the theory of state's rights."[4]

Luce blamed both correspondents and their subjects for this under-coverage. Reporters were by and large ignorant of economics. "The average reporter knows more about astronomy than he does about industry," Luce complained in June 1929. This gap, in turn, left many business correspondents at the mercy of the new public relations specialists explaining a complex financial maneuver in deceptively simple and self-serving terms. Business leaders, too, were at fault. Too many, he argued, abhorred publicity in any form. "An honest analysis of business was regarded as vulgar or Communistic or both," Luce remarked later. "The attitude then, under King Calvin Coolidge, was that something called private business as then organized was the God-given order of the universe."[5]

No newspaper or magazine could be said to have overcome the obstacles to a searching journalism of capitalism. Newspapers serving the commercial classes, notably the *Wall Street Journal*, then had modest followings (before the 1929 stock market crash, the *Journal's* circulation reached a high of fifty-six thousand) and were, as newspapers, by definition limited in the length they could devote to studying individual companies and economic trends. Existing business magazines like *Nation's Business* suffered from an excess of conciseness if not supplication. Business magazines "were simply pap," recalled one Luce aide. "If they weren't written from handouts, they might just as well have been."[6]

Moreover, the fourth estate in the 1920s had failed to come to terms with fundamental changes in large-scale capitalism. The sheer volume of economic activity confused the monitors of the business world. Nostalgia became a substitute for good reportage. Many journalists and their readers could not turn away from the surviving patriarchs of American industrialization, Henry Ford and John D. Rockefeller, even as a second generation of leaders took hold of big business.

Luce's new magazine, in contrast, would describe and promote a new enterpriser. Taking up a phrase *Time* had popularized, Luce spoke of "the coming tycoon." He was neither the founder nor the inheritor of a business, but its manager; not the crude inventor in the Ford pattern, but a well-educated chief executive officer resembling Owen Young of General Electric, who had been trained in a law school, not a laboratory. "Business demands for its direction at the top greater and greater intellectual powers," Luce declared. "Shrewdness is necessary, but it is less and less the shrewdness of the horse trader. Technology is necessary, but it is less and less the technology of the tinker." Companies were becoming corporations, too vast to be entrusted to those who had started—or owned—them. The coming tycoon, Luce declared, "became less and less the owner and more and more the semi-detached or, at any rate, detachable manager."[7]

Luce's appreciation of the new industrial leadership could be seen elsewhere. In *The Modern Corporation and Private Property* (1932), A. A. Berle, Jr., and Gardiner C. Means described managers, increasingly college graduates, a few the products of the new and prestigious graduate schools of business administration, running large-scale enterprises. Normally they held little of the company's stock. Often, they came without the firsthand experience of production, like the president of U.S. Steel who, the joke went, first saw a blast furnace shortly after dying. "The primary responsibility for business leadership in the large corporation," an economist found, "has devolved upon a group of men who are professional managers. Their position is not achieved through ownership. They are salaried experts, trained by education and experience in the field of management."[8]

The leaders of the "organizational revolution" that accompanied a more interdependent economy required a superior business journalism. Lippmann, indeed, viewed the new manager as little more than the coordinator of facts about markets and resources. "The more clearly he realizes the nature of his position in industry," he wrote, "the more he tends to submit his desires to the discipline of objective information." "In no other profession," Owen Young told *Time* in 1929, "is the need for wide information, broad sympathies and directed imagination so great."[9]

Unlike the harried "gentleman from Indiana," whom Luce described as the typical *Time* subscriber, the *Fortune* reader had the hours and curiosity to absorb a far more substantial journalism. He was the thoughtful burgher. He and his counterparts had gone to similar schools; they had developed tastes unknown to the first Ford, who in the late 1920s was underwriting a hillbilly music program on a Detroit radio station. The new enterpriser, Luce concluded, was "a cultivated citizen of the world," quite probably devoted to classical music and high art, overall actively interested in many things.[10]

Luce intended *Fortune* to be structurally *Time*'s opposite. The magazine would carry fewer and longer stories, not crisp summaries but thoughtful explorations. A four-hundred-word entry in *Time* was considered prolix; the standard *Fortune* story might come to ten thousand words. Finally, corporations, not personalities, would be the major focus.

After two years of planning, *Fortune*'s first number appeared in February 1930. The dollar-per-copy charge was enormous; a year's subscription at ten dollars came to twice that of *Time*. But Luce had not intended *Fortune* to be cheap. "It will be as beautiful a magazine as exists in the United States," Luce told his board of directors. "If possible, the most beautiful." A costly heavy paper (one issue weighed two pounds) was used to avoid the shiny glare of *Time*'s and others' stock, and it had to be hand-sewn. The magazine was generously illustrated with photographs, drawings, and paintings. Asked to assess volume one, number one, Owen Young said he was "overwhelmed."[11]

Such extravagance seemed poorly timed as *Fortune*'s debut coincided with the beginnings of the Great Depression. Between 1929 and 1933, national income dropped 50 percent; fifty-one hundred banks failed. The number of full-time employees at U.S. Steel, the nation's largest steelmaker, fell from 224,800 in 1929 to zero on 1 April 1933. Capitalism's greatest crisis should have doomed Luce's enterprise, yet like *Time*, *Fortune* only proved how well insulated some were from the widespread decline. Like Time Inc., many enterprises and industries, including Douglas Aircraft, IBM, zipper manufacturers, and network radio, thrived even amid hard times. Their managers and others benefited from deflation. Circulation rose steadily, from thirty-four thousand in 1930 to ninety-six thousand in 1934. Advertising revenues did drop in 1932 but rose thereafter. By 1934, *Fortune* earned money for Time Inc., between 1930 and 1937 accounting for about 15 percent of the corporation's profits.[12]

Next to Luce himself, much of the responsibility for *Fortune*'s success belonged to Ralph Ingersoll. Despite his skills as a writer, *Fortune*'s young first editor, Parker Lloyd-Smith, proved an ineffective manager. Luce, who normally sought such amateurs (Lloyd-Smith was another class poet from Yale), took the unprecedented step of hiring Ingersoll away from the *New Yorker*. Originally Ingersoll split editorial responsibilities with Lloyd-Smith, who remained in charge in name only. Then either a personal or financial reversal drove him to suicide in 1931 and Ingersoll became editor. Like his former chief at the *New Yorker*, Harold Ross, and *Time* managing editor John S. Martin, Ingersoll was a strong-willed chief. Few on the staff liked him. But he improved the efficiency and profitability of *Fortune*'s operations while ever loyal to

Luce's expectations for the magazine. For several years, Ingersoll ranked as Harry's only friend at Time Inc.[13]

Others at *Fortune*, like their counterparts at *Time*, found Harry an unpredictable, at times distant boss. Unaffected by success or position, he worked closely with writers. Yet he had no time for idle chat or a drink after work. Ingersoll thought Harry feared intimacy with men, no matter how attracted to them. Some simply found him peculiar, especially in his lack of social graces. Upon meeting Luce for the first time in 1934, one writer thought Harry looked "as if he had just swallowed tobacco juice."[14]

Still, the state of the economy, not Harry's eccentricities, provided the greatest challenge to Luce's new venture. Planned to explain prosperity, *Fortune* had to reckon with economic collapse. At least one long story per number covered the dislocation or accompanying governmental initiatives, and in a tone that made the periodical, wrote one historian, "read almost like a reform journal."[15] In 1932, *Fortune* examined unemployment in the largest cities and the housing crisis for the poor. A year earlier, four New York City hospitals had treated ninety-five cases of starvation; twenty of the patients had died. One out of every eight Saint Louis residents in 1932 faced eviction. A year later *Fortune*, dramatically establishing the intimate, intrinsic link between private enterprise and public policy, began to run pieces on the Roosevelt administration's recovery agencies. Suddenly Washington and not New York loomed as the nation's most important source of news. With the New Deal, *Fortune* observed in December 1934, Washington "has paradoxically at last become the capital of the U.S."[16]

Most *Fortune* stories, however, concerned enterprise. At least two per issue were usually uncritical profiles of corporations. Luce and Ingersoll tried to strike a balance by carrying a feature on an older established company like U.S. Steel and one on the rise like Douglas Aircraft. Each number as well included a discussion of an entire industry such as steel rails or whiskey.

Businessmen divided over the prospect of a *Fortune* profile. Most were conditioned to privacy or having their public relations specialists control the flow of all information about their operations. Suddenly they faced the magazine's staff writer and photographer. The chairman of the board of one of America's largest manufacturing concerns, Ingersoll recalled, literally began to weep upon learning that *Fortune* intended to report on his company. Although company representatives were permitted to review the story in advance of publication to check for factual inaccuracies, the editors as at *Time* withstood pressures to alter a story's interpretive slant. Because most profiles proved flattering, such demands came less frequently. And some publicity hungry corporations actually welcomed *Fortune*'s attentions. In New York's publishing and advertising circles, rumors spread that Luce actually obtained compensation from companies in exchange for a *Fortune* story. The missionary's son took offense; aides resented the low charge, one hundred dollars per page, one source indicated Time Inc. received.[17]

Although *Fortune*'s army of editors, writers, and researchers carefully fashioned their new business journalism, there were missteps, most often born of an overenthusiasm for the subjects. An admiring profile of the railroad tycoon Van Sweringen brothers (March 1934) gave no hint of their imminent entry into bankruptcy court. "All four" of their railroads, the magazine found, "are first-class properties, very smartly operated, and financially promising." Similarly, a 1937 treatment of the American Viscose Company (AVC) played to Anglophobes by grossly overstating the profitability of the British-owned operation; AVC was, in fact, in difficult financial straits, losing bitter confrontations with competitors and the Internal Revenue Service.[18]

Fortune conceded space to less economic curiosities. An issue might include extended digressions on baldness, Bryn Mawr College, gardening, Duke Ellington, and guide dogs. Some aimed to enlighten: an introduction to anthropology and reproductions of great artworks. Many of the business stories, in turn, concerned merely colorful as opposed to significant enterprises: the huge King Ranch in Texas, the lobster and bicycle industries. Nearly once a quarter came a film company profile.

Whether describing modern art or the Swift Company, each *Fortune* story included illustrations. Although most American newspapers and magazines had long carried photographs, only the tabloids had begun to try to connect pictures to reportage; others used the photograph haphazardly. At *Fortune*, one photographer recalled Luce saying, "Pictures and words should be conscious partners." With *Fortune* still in the planning stages early in 1929, Luce asked a young photographer based in Cleveland, Margaret Bourke-White, to work for the magazine. Bourke-White had begun to demonstrate that industrial photography, long neglected by skilled photographers, could be high art. "The whole dynamic world of industry lay before me," she recalled. "All over America were railroads, docks, mines, factories waiting to be photographed—waiting, I felt, for *me!*" Luce shared her mission, she recalled: "The camera should explore every corner of industry, showing everything, Mr. Luce explained, from the steam shovel to the board of directors. The camera would act as interpreter, recording what modern civilization is, how it looks."[19]

True to Luce's conception, the camera helped to carry a story. Photographs added force to *Fortune*'s moving February 1932 discussion of the housing crisis. In the new style of 1930s photography captions were all-important: underneath a shot of a Richmond slum—"Back of the fashionable streets." The camera eye added to the impact of other essays, usually about business as well. In a feature on the Swift Company, *Fortune* ran a series of Bourke-White shots of pigs unknowingly and unwisely following a trail to their slaughter.[20]

In a similar attempt to integrate photography and journalism, *Fortune* took up new "candid camera" techniques. For European magazines in the late 1920s and early 1930s, Erich Salomon of Germany had used a smaller, often hidden camera to capture events others missed and newsmakers unposed. Learning of Salomon's work, Ingersoll persuaded him in 1932 to work for *Fortune*. Readers discovered striking and realistic images: the habitually dour President Hoover beginning to grin, diplomats' hats atop a table next to the conference room entrance, powerful investment bankers whispering to each other at a half-closed door. Salomon's work, a Time Inc. history noted several years later, marked a fusion of photography and journalism "getting the camera where you want it and making it record not only a picture but also a fact."[21]

In assembling writers for *Fortune*, Luce proved similarly unorthodox. Unlike rival periodicals, *Fortune* did not invite many notables to contribute stories. Instead, Luce sought a permanent staff. After being rejected by some younger business correspondents for New York newspapers, Luce elected to follow the *Time* practice of employing young men, fresh from Harvard, Yale, and Princeton. It was a risky decision. Virtually none had experience in or reporting on business; unaware of managerial dress codes, some had to be ordered to wear suits rather than sportscoats and dress trousers while on assignment. Many had to be shown how to read a balance sheet. By then, however, Luce had persuaded himself that talented amateurs made better business journalists than glorified bookkeepers.

This in-house training worked with one notable exception. Temperamentally incapable of handling any story dealing with economics, James Agee had been doing features on orchids, jewels, and the American roadside. Luce, sensitive to any challenge to his system and conviction that a good journalist could explain anything, ordered Agee to write a story on the pricing of steel rails, which Harry himself would edit. Despite long conferences with Luce patiently explaining the economics of the matter, "Now, Jim, don't you see . . . ?" Agee could not complete the feature, which Harry in frustration turned over to another writer.[22]

Normally, Harry's reliance on amateurs appeared justified. Most shared his certainty that they could, indeed, describe any firm, industry, or government agency. As amateurs, "Boy and Girl Scouts going places and doing things," one commented at the time, they associated themselves with those readers not thoroughly familiar with a topic. A gently pedagogical clarity absent in the accounts of older business journalism characterized the typical *Fortune* story. Readers completed a *Fortune* story on public utilities able to define a kilowatt, or finishing one on Goodrich, aware of the technology of the zipper. That completeness distinguished *Fortune* from *Time*. *Fortune*, as a monthly carrying fewer and longer pieces, could not affect *Time*'s range. But Luce's business journal did aim for a comprehensiveness the firstborn could not achieve. If anything, a historian observed later, *Fortune* resembled the Progressive era model of informational journalism that Luce and Hadden had eschewed in producing *Time*. "The articles in *Fortune*," Lloyd Morris wrote, "were often as long, and as thoroughly researched, as any McClure dissertation."[23]

Fortune could also startle readers. Two long pieces on controversial European regimes, the USSR (March 1932) and Italy (July 1934), were later criticized for their opinions. The Soviet Union profile was considered too hostile, the Italian feature too kind. Yet each essentially described their subjects. *Fortune* did have its passions. President Roosevelt subsequently asked Archibald MacLeish to become Librarian of Congress in part because of the proadministration tone of his New Deal pieces. In March 1934, Eric Hodgins with Luce's help wrote an unmistakably negative analysis of the European armament industries. "According to the best accountancy figures, it cost about $25,000 to kill a soldier in the World War. There is one class of Big Business Men in Europe that never rose up to denounce the extravagance of its governments in this regard," Hodgins began. "The reason for the silence of these Big Business Men is quite simple: the killing is their business." The *New Yorker* recommended Hodgins's piece for a Pulitzer Prize.[24]

Most of the time, however, passions were controlled. *Fortune* aspired to the new disinterestedness that Lippmann and others had been advocating for the fourth estate. After congratulating Hodgins for his "Arms and the Men" story, Luce added, "Don't get me wrong about any of this. It doesn't mean that *Fortune* might not want to turn around the next month and publish one hell of a fine story whooping it up for the biggest navy in the world."[25] Luce himself, devoted to capitalism, on coming to South Bend in 1929 to write a *Fortune* feature, discovered and reported the dull and dark routine of the assembly line and its "Army." "The South Bend privates are well paid," he wrote. "They labor without complaint and without hope. Were it necessary to recruit the army of South Bend from such as you and I there simply would be no Industrial Age."[26] The *Fortune* writer, MacLeish wrote, "is quite as willing to publish the answers that upset his apple cart of preconceptions as to publish the answers that bear him out."[27]

That skepticism was easily achieved considering the staffing of the magazine. Most, including Agee, MacLeish, and Dwight Macdonald, were would-be poets and essayists and shared the "professional culturist's" adversarial attitude toward business. Working for Harry paid the rent. Politically, most stood well to the left of Luce and the *Time* staff. Macdonald, indeed, embraced Trotskyism. There was no little irony in Luce publishing the most lavish business journal in America and then filling its editorial positions with writers decidedly out of sympathy with their subject. It is perhaps no coincidence that *Fortune*'s most memorable stories to the late 1930s either avoided capitalism or exposed its darker sides.

The presence of MacLeish and others also gave *Fortune* a decidedly literary character. Although *Fortune* contributors did not abandon *Time*'s love of visually evocative adjectives, they were free of having to condense the complex into four hundred words and torment the language in the process. They had the room to write expansively. For staff members like Agee and MacLeish, this license encouraged prose absent in *Time* and, indeed, most periodicals. Describing Swedish securities manipulator Ivar Kreuger on the eve of his suicide, MacLeish wrote, "Saturday, March 12, 1932, was a sunless-white-skied, pale spring-like morning. From Numero Cinq Avenue Victor-Emmanuel you could see the raw light on the roof of the Grand Palais and the open ground with its gravel and its plane trees and the new buds swelling on the trees. . . . Mr. Kreuger drew the bedroom blinds, smoothed the unmade bedclothes and lay down. Looking up he saw the fat, gold stucco cherubs in the ceiling corners of the room. Odd witnesses! He snapped a cartridge in the army type, the 9 mm, and placed his feet together neatly."[28]

MacLeish's Kreuger story exemplified the 1930s "documentary expression," a new, self-consciously "realistic" movement in the arts. The richly textured description in the work of MacLeish and others—the "fat, gold stucco cherubs in the ceiling corners" of Kreuger's room; the rumpled suits and chronic dandruff of New Dealer Harry Hopkins; in the Tennessee Valley, "flat land planted to cotton, worn and warped like a wrecked heel"—gave features an intimate tone. "An imagination that seeks the texture of reality must fix upon particulars," historian William Stott wrote, "and the imagination characteristic of the thirties did."[29]

Although not as heavily edited as *Time*, *Fortune* for all its literary talent was not a writer's magazine. Ingersoll had to strike Agee's critical remark that the restoration of colonial Williamsburg constituted "nationalistic propaganda." Agee's subsequent effort with *Fortune* photographer Walker Evans to profile four Alabama sharecropper families was rejected altogether. Macdonald left after his editors softened his unflattering portrait of U.S. Steel chairman Myron Taylor. "Committed as he is to the *status quo*," Macdonald wrote, "Myron Taylor is also committed to all the absurdities, stupidities, and contradictions that we have discovered in our study of the Steel Corporation."[30]

Such editorial interference, however, remained the exception during *Fortune*'s first seven years. Luce recognized that overediting might rattle (and cost him) his talented pool of authors. Wrote one who joined the magazine in the 1940s, "It had been Henry Luce's reluctant discovery that, with rare exceptions, good writers on business were either liberals or socialists."[31] As a result, few taking the magazine then would have regarded it as merely a more handsome organ of business. Features on subjects about which great capitalists held strong views were not written to reinforce prejudices. Stories of deprivation and government activism were too sensitively drawn to comfort the tired if still thoughtful burgher. "Was there ever a journal," asked a British reviewer of *Fortune* in the 1930s, "that allowed its staff such freedom to bite the editor's hand and mock its readers' ethos?"[32]

The political leanings of *Fortune* writers helped to distinguish the magazine from more conventional and reactionary business periodicals. After *Fortune*'s "Arms and the Men," *Nation's Business* asked, "Do Business Men Want War?" and answered no. That issue also included "Relief Is Ruining My Town" by Ray Bert Westerfield, professor of political economy at Luce's alma mater; the New Deal, Westerfield concluded, had destroyed the work ethic. *Fortune* two months later chose not to indict the federal dole but describe the different forms of relief available as well as the plight of those out of work. *Nation's Business* attacked the Tennessee Valley Authority in December; *Fortune* opted twice to explain it. Philosophical objections to public power were noted only in passing.[33]

There was perhaps no greater sign of *Fortune's* more objective standard than the *Fortune* Survey. Although *Time* for more than a decade had presumed to say what Americans thought, in the early 1930s advances in survey research led by George Gallup made such guesswork less excusable. Using techniques developed in advertising, Gallup and others began to conduct polls on political issues. In early 1935, Ingersoll hired a firm to begin the *Fortune* Survey, to appear in every third issue. Since the publication of Lippmann's *Public Opinion* (1922), MacLeish wrote, introducing the first survey, "there had developed a technique for sampling the opinions of the world which should have interested any journalist who thought about it." If the president of "General Motors can discover by a survey what trend in automobile design is most welcome to General Motors customers, why cannot the editor of a magazine ascertain by the same method the real state of public opinion on matters that vitally concern his readers?"[34]

The great confirmation of the survey's value came in 1936, when of all the primitive and scientific projections of the presidential vote, *Fortune* most closely called the Roosevelt landslide. Even *Fortune's* editors doubted the final tabulations (other nationwide surveys were indicating a closer race) and waited until after the election to reveal how accurate their service had been. Ironically, the most embarrassed forecast—one predicting a Republican victory—had been sponsored by *Time's* once insurmountable rival, the *Literary Digest*.[35]

The survey added to the magazine's ranks among the opinion leadership. President Roosevelt expressed a keen interest and soon regularly consulted with the new measurers of public sentiments. *Fortune's* poll, the president of Harvard declared, "will revolutionize democracy." Each month in 1939, the editors boasted, some five hundred newspaper columnists and radio commentators referred to *Fortune* articles and the survey.[36]

However influential, only a few, just over one hundred thirty thousand in 1939, subscribed to *Fortune*. Put differently, *Fortune's* circulation was one-sixth *Time's*. Although those who took *Fortune*, like their counterparts subscribing to *Time*, did tend to read most if not all the articles, they remained few in number and very well-to-do. In 1932, the typical *Fortune* subscriber earned $21,382; the combined income of all subscribers surpassed the total for all the income taxpayers earned in thirty-three states. Just over 60 percent of all subscribers were "*officers, partners*, or major *executives*"; 46 percent of the men and 30 percent of the women were on the social register. A 1933 study of readers in a suburban New York county found that a small minority took *Fortune* and they resided in the five wealthiest towns; the magazine was virtually unread elsewhere. Even in the most prestigious suburbs, it ranked, at thirty-five readers per thousand adults, behind such periodicals as the *New Yorker* and *National Geographic*.[37] If *Fortune* in the 1930s proved to be Henry Luce's greatest achievement, it remained his least read. MacLeish wrote Harry, "If there were some possible means to get rid of that vast and ritzy bulk and to put the price within possible reach of the educated American public, *Fortune* would become an even greater influence than it now is."[38]

"The March of Time"

To Luce's dismay, two other Time Inc. enterprises of the 1930s, "The March of Time" radio program and newsreel, drew vast audiences. Theirs was a popularity Luce not only had little hand in earning but appeared at times to resent. Lost in London in the late 1930s, he identified himself to a stranger as the editor-in-chief of *Time*. The passer-by had never heard of the publication. He did, however, recall seeing a "March of Time" newsreel. Luce was hurt: "I'm just old-fashioned and pigheaded enough to admit that I don't like everything that's happening."[39] Although long fascinated by the possibilities of photography in reportage, Luce had little interest in such newer forms of mass information as radio. Harry considered himself a man of the printed page. In the early 1930s, he even considered buying a newspaper.

Luce allowed his circulation manager, Roy Larsen, to talk him into "The March of Time" series ventures. Ever concerned with readership, Larsen conceived of "The March of Time" radio series for its publicity value. The marriage of the new magazine and the new medium seemed fitting. Just as Hadden and Luce began *Time*, sales of radio sets took off; the number of homes with radios rose from 400,000 in 1922 to 16.7 million in 1931. Like *Time*'s readership, radio ownership was heaviest outside the South and still slightly disproportionately urban and middle-class. Reaching far more Americans than anything Luce published, radio offered the most efficient means of publicizing his magazine. Despite a growing awareness of Luce's work in certain quarters, many people remained ignorant of *Time* and its founder. While in South Bend in 1929 on assignment for *Fortune*, Luce found to his dismay that few members of the city's business class had ever heard of *Time*. If *Time* were to be written for the gentleman from Indiana, more Hoosier burghers would have to be made aware of the periodical. After experimenting with several different types of radio programs, Larsen and a Cincinnati broadcaster developed the format for a thirty-minute program dubbed "The March of Time," with the magazine to be heavily promoted during the show and the script itself based on entries in the newsweekly.

"The Voice of Time" narrated the program. After a fanfare the Voice declared, "The March of Time!" Then another announced,

There are thousands of Periodicals.
There are hundreds of Magazines.
There are dozens of Journals of Opinion.
There are several Weekly Reviews.
But there is just ONE NEWSMAGAZINE.

VOICE OF TIME

————It is TIME.
On a thousand fronts the history of the world moves swiftly forward—a thousand new facts, new details in the world's history come into being every hour.

TIME, the Weekly Newsmagazine, is the one and only complete record of this swift-changing civilization.

Although Time Inc. retained full editorial control, an advertising agency, Batten, Barton, Durstine, and Osborn, handled the details of putting out "The March of Time" week to week. The Columbia Broadcasting System, the weaker of the two new radio networks, agreed to carry the program, at first for a fee, then free. Because much network air time remained unsold in the early 1930s, CBS was only too happy to pick up Larsen's publicity machine.

Larsen's program consisted of a series of reenacted news events, all introduced by the deep-voiced Voice of Time and accompanied by a twenty-three piece orchestra. Actors played presidents and kings, Italy's Mussolini and Adolf Hitler. (Foreign parts were always done in accented English.) "In one startling exception," broadcast historian Erik Barnouw wrote of "The March of Time," radio "drama and news met."[40] Not always to the delight of the newsmaker. President Roosevelt became annoyed over hearing himself imitated and eventually persuaded the producers to cease doing so.[41] Others, like Britain's Ramsay MacDonald and India's Mahatma Gandhi, had no comparable leverage over a federally regulated medium.

"Playing out" the news could confuse listeners, though the producers took some pains to be accurate. Certain national events, a speech by the president or a vote for Speaker of the House of Representatives, did approach authenticity. Yet even these could be faulted. Many Americans did not yet immediately recognize the president's or the Speaker's voice over the radio. "Reality" for them became problematical. Then, too, many of the dialogues, such as those of El Salvadorean rebel militiamen, were plainly creative exercises, often, in the case of such overseas news, condescendingly so.

Nevertheless, the achievement of "The March of Time" radio program is better understood considering the state of radio news in the early 1930s. The two major networks, CBS and the National Broadcasting Company, had no news gathering divisions. A few prominent "commentators" like H. V. Kaltenborn read headlines from the wire services and offered analysis. Moreover, the difficulty of live or taped transmission often made it impossible to record the voices of the newsmakers themselves. As broadcasting developed portable and remote capacities, "The March of Time" fell into disrepute. Until then, however, it seemed a more than satisfactory approach to radio news.

Although Luce had little to do with "The March of Time" 's production, it possessed many of the features of his journalism. An orchestra and narrator led the listener, much as *Time*'s storybook structure and omniscient "voice" guided the magazine's reader. "The March of Time" script included touches of *Time*style, unusually descriptive and all-knowing. "In the conference room of the rambling, droughty Saint James Palace, warmed by dismal little grate-fires," the Voice began an 11 December 1931 segment. The Voice drew a conclusion in the *Time* manner, and unlike the conventional newspaper or *Literary Digest* account: "Thus ends the Second India Round Table Conference, costing over a million dollars, using 500,000 sonorous words to re-state the opinions already voiced in the first conference and postponing definite agreements to a third conference." Britain's terms "if accepted will condemn India to a self-chosen slavery, will perpetuate Imperial domination and exploitation."

Despite "The March of Time" 's resemblance to his firstborn, Luce tried to kill the series. He objected to the costs (two hundred eleven thousand dollars in 1931) and in February 1932 ordered that it cease production. Later in the year, after a flood of letters, 22,231 in all, some reprinted in *Time*, he relented. Larsen argued that the program had helped to boost *Time*'s circulation during a period when most magazines, because of the depression, were losing subscribers. Indeed, some claimed that only the popular radio comedy program, "Amos 'n' Andy," had a larger audience. "The March of Time" returned late in 1932, remaining on CBS, then NBC, until 1945.[42]

In 1934, Larsen talked Luce into underwriting another project: a newsreel version of "The March of Time." This time, however, journalistic rather than promotional possibilities motivated Larsen. An experienced newsreel camera operator, Louis de Rochemont, had persuaded Larsen that Time Inc. could revolutionize the nonfiction film. The two men, together with former *Time* managing editor John S. Martin, began to plan a *Time* newsreel.

Long shown in theaters before or between feature films, newsreels had been produced almost as afterthoughts by motion picture companies and the Hearst organization. None possessed a journalistic sensibility. Around nine to ten minutes long, each consisted of short footage spliced together. Their agenda was most often light, with sporting events and beauty contests consuming most of a reel. All told, newsreels gave audiences pictures, not stories. The availability of film alone established story selection. Consumers were given virtually no background information.

De Rochemont, Larsen, and Martin concluded that *Time* could offer more. A *Time*-produced newsreel, by interpreting fewer items at greater length, could supply context. "They started with the basic idea," wrote one journalist, "that moving picture audiences, given a chance, would like a change and see, not the bare bones 'This happened here' kind of thing but motion picture stories of *why* and *how* things of importance in the world happen."[43] "The newsreels are stuck in the mud," de Rochemont had complained. "They never get behind the news. What has led up to a given event? What does it portend?"[44]

Although Luce did not involve himself directly in the creation of

"The March of Time" on film, the prospect of a *Time* newsreel did engage him more than the radio program. Filmed news appealed to his visual sense, already evident in *Time*'s language and *Fortune*'s layout. "The radio is important," Luce wrote in 1934. "But actually the greatest supplement to the invention of language itself for the purpose of communication of news-fact is the photograph. And the most potent development of the photograph is the so-called moving picture." Film, however, had not yet been "widely used as a prime instrument of journalism." This was Time Incorporated's opportunity: "to pioneer in the possibilities of the moving picture as an instrument of significant journalism."[45]

At Time Inc., a pattern reemerged. Just as *Time* successfully found a format distinct from the *Literary Digest*, and *Fortune* from other business journals, "The March of Time" separated itself from the established newsreel groups. "The March of Time" came out once a month (most newsreels, weekly) and included as many or fewer segments but at twice the length, around twenty minutes. Its agenda was by comparison serious. Indeed, the newsworthiness of the subject, not the footage at hand, defined a run. And more than film was used to tell a "March of Time" story. The staff produced maps and graphics and provided historical background all to make an occurrence more discernible. "The March of Time" thus separated itself from the field. Unlike its competitors, wrote British filmmaker John Grierson in 1937, "The March of Time" "gets behind the news, observes the factors of influence, and gives perspective to events. Not the parade of armies as much as the race in armaments; not the ceremonial opening of a dam but the full story of Roosevelt's experiment in the Tennessee Valley; not the launching of the *Queen Mary* but the post-1918 record of British shipping. All penetrating, dramatic."[46]

Indeed, "The March of Time" resembled *Time* in its sense of drama and structure. To make its relatively more serious topics palatable, features often stressed conflict; segments took the form of stories, with a beginning, middle, and end. The greater time given each item, observed one historian of the nonfiction film, A. William Bluem, "permitted a journalistic style in which emphasis was divided between the inherent drama of an event and a dramatic technique of presentation. 'The March of Time' sought to establish an ordering, or plotting, of elements within its news presentations, moving toward a dramatic climax."[47] Luce himself had wanted a newsreel with impact. In April 1933, Harry had rejected a newsreel proposal by two outside the company because their prototype, an aide recorded, "gave him no emotional kick, no catch at the throat."[48]

As with "The March of Time" radio program, the Time Inc. newsreel invited some staging of news events, or what Luce dubbed "fakery in allegiance to the truth."[49] Again technical barriers and the greater time and effort then required to transport crews to the news largely accounted for the practice. Film cameras were even more cumbersome than radio equipment and regardless, faking shots had long been a tradition in news photography. De Rochemont himself, as a young man, had persuaded a German saboteur and his jailer to reenact their entry into a Maine jail. Nor was it unusual when de Rochemont cast a Time Inc. office boy as the emperor of Ethiopia, or had a Nazi attack on Jewish stores in Germany redone in the New London, Connecticut, retail district. Some principals—utility president Wendell Willkie and radio commentator Father Coughlin—played their own parts. In a few cases reality was "preenacted," as when a "March of Time" crew filmed the inauguration of Pan American Airways' flying boat service to China prior to the first scheduled departure. Although later condemned, preenactments or reenactments brought few criticisms at the time. Most students of the nonfiction film in the 1930s recognized that technological lags forced compromises. "There was little public discussion," Barnouw wrote, "about the validity of such techniques."[50]

Most followers of the nonfiction film actually hailed "The March of Time." "Here would seem to be recognition of the possibilities of screen journalism," wrote one British critic. "At last here would appear to be a definite attempt to put decent reporting on the screen." Journalist Alistair Cooke called its London debut "far and away the most important thing that has happened for several years."[51] In March 1937, the Academy of Motion Picture Arts and Sciences honored "The March of Time" with a special Oscar.

Such distinctions were, as Cooke for one noted, praise for *Time* itself. A "March of Time" segment structurally resembled a *Time* story. Because *Time* writers helped initially with the scripts, they possessed some of the magazine's style, with phrases like "Gay was Vienna into which Otto of Hapsburg was born twenty-four years ago" and references to "Crafty little Benes of Czechoslovakia."[52] Like *Time*, "The March of Time" often gave great weight in assessing events to individuals. Staged shots of newsmakers were often photographed from a sitting position, thus making each seem larger than life.

"The March of Time" newsreel had a narrator directing information. Westbrook Von Voorhis's "voice of doom" served much the same purpose as his counterparts on the radio "March of Time" and the omniscient point-of-view of the "man in the moon at the end of the century" aimed at in *Time*. Through the maze of modernity, he guided the consumer of information. "We were emotional, we hissed and cheered," George Dangerfield wrote of viewing "The March of Time." "And all the time the narrator's voice rose serenely above our distressing clamor, talking behind the screen like a Greek actor behind his mask. Just such a voice, I feel sure, would have been hired to speak the lines of one of Euripides' suave male gods—those gods who appeared so opportunely at the end of a tragedy, when everything was going up in flames and agnosticism, and explained matters away."[53]

Some critics charged that "The March of Time" 's narrator-as-decisionmaker and clearly defined structure led the newsreel in 1935 and 1936 to propagandizing. Conventional newsreels had lacked the resources or intelligence Time Inc. poured into "The March of Time"; their accounts were too fleeting to be considered dangerous. Bathers along the boardwalk hardly made for agitprop. In contrast, "The March of Time," because it resembled *Time* by presenting the news with skill and with a conclusion, invited criticism. Many movie house operators, loathe to offend any patron, preferred the formless, uncontroversial alternatives.[54] On the left, some attacked a "March of Time" segment on fascism in France as too polite; they did not note "The March of Time" 's unflattering portrait of Father Coughlin or Senator Huey Long, both unpopular with progressives. The reactionary Hearst papers condemned the newsreel's feature on the Soviet Union, which had ended with the line "That the young Soviet is doing a better job of nation-wielding than the last of the imperial rulers none can deny."[55]

Dangerfield thought "The March of Time" suffered from an excess of detachment. Luce's newsreel, he wrote, "is neither candid nor passionate nor partisan, merely excitable. It is neither for the Morgans nor is it against the Masses. It is almost completely irresponsible; it picks out those bits of contemporary history which seem to pack the most punch, and reenacts them with what it likes to think is fairness."[56]

Such sniping continued, especially as a new form of nonfiction film committed to the Left, emerged in the late 1930s. Unlike "The March of Time," the thirties documentary film was an individual rather than a corporate enterprise. It conveyed the artistry and political values of the director-photographer. As self-consciously artistic and political expressions, the documentary film often succeeded, though "reality" was often sacrificed to political ends.[57] Moreover, the progressive critics of Luce's newsreel, echoing the detractors of *Time*, wanted a middle-class or mass medium to serve an ideological mission that their audiences were by no means prepared to absorb. Despite its merits, the documentary film drew small crowds. The *Nation*'s circulation paled against that of *Time*.

And Luce, not the editor of the *Nation*, was becoming a mass communicator. "The March of Time" 's political disengagement hardly affected its popularity. By 1936, some 12 million Americans saw his newsreel each month. Between 1936 and 1942, that figure rose to just under 20 million.[58] One moviegoer, a farmer, wrote to thank Larsen and company. "My womenfolk are always pestering they don't get no amusement" and though tired from a day's work, one night he drove them twenty miles to a theater. Starting to doze off, "I got a poke in my ribs like to have put me off onto the floor; and my wife says, 'Look at this quick,' and I looked and it was this thing called 'March of Time.' And say, let me tell you, if I never get any sleep, I'll drive 20, don't make any difference, if it's 100 miles, to see another."[59] " 'The March of Time' is getting to be habit, like breakfast, the Marx brothers and Charlie Chaplin," wrote a *Washington Star* critic. "Its influence on public thinking should not be minimized."[60]

If Luce cared little for Larsen's filmmaking, his circulation manager had given him an audience—around 14 percent of the population, higher than that for any of his magazines. From England, H. G. Wells wrote Time Inc., "I don't know *Time*. I ought to do so. *Fortune* I know and the March of Time films and I have an unstinted admiration for your group."[61] In March 1936, a prominent midwestern newspaper publisher urged former president Hoover to meet Henry Luce. He was becoming important, John Cowles told Hoover. "The combined total of Time Magazine, plus 'The March of Time' radio programs, plus 'The March of Time' movies, has in my opinion an enormous amount of influence."[62]

6

THE "MIND-GUIDED
CAMERA" MAGAZINE
1933–1940

Several times at casual social encounters beginning in 1934 Clare Boothe Brokaw, a handsome blond divorcée, suggested that Luce start a new magazine. Buy the moribund humor magazine *Life*, she urged him, and turn it into a picture weekly. No general interest American magazine at that time relied extensively on photographs, despite their apparent popularity. Such a periodical might prove immensely popular.

At the time of Brokaw's suggestion, Luce was already pondering the idea of a picture magazine. The success of *Time* and *Fortune* in the early 1930s did not satisfy him. He was not yet ready to live off his dividends, as he had thought he might a decade earlier, and run for public office. His ambitions remained journalistic, and unfulfilled. What should Time Inc. do next? In the fall of 1933, Luce weighed several possibilities: buying a newspaper, starting a ladies' magazine or a picture weekly. The last prospect attracted him most. "We have practically decided to go into the 'experimental stage' on a new magazine," Luce wrote one of his editors in November. "A weekly or fortnightly [review of] current events for large circulation, heavily illustrated."[1]

Thinking about Pictures

Luce's decision seemed a logical step for him and Time Inc. As a prep school editor, he had insisted on running more illustrations in his literary magazine. The uniqueness of *Time*'s style owed much to its layered visual imagery. Moreover, the magazine's editors had demonstrated much ingenuity in arranging pictures. Although at first compelled to use the dull and posed photographs of prominent figures, editors tried to caption each in ways that drew readers to an entry. Under some they placed newsmakers' remarks ("There are not many crooks in Congress") or an arresting snippet from the story itself ("He balanced his budget on a cottage"). In 1932, photographer Edward Steichen called *Time*'s layout of pictures, "one of the most dynamic features of the magazine."[2]

Always eager to go beyond the deadening conventions of newspaper display, *Time* in the early 1930s ran photographs that the dailies had refused to include, with perhaps the most vivid example being that of the naked corpse of a lynched man. The magazine gradually increased its run of photographs. Luce himself ordered a six-page spread on the 1933 London Economic Conference. A year later, *Time* ran a page of photographs of the assassination of King Alexander of Yugoslavia, a layout with a then unique newsreel quality. Readers were left with the sensation of being there.[3]

Fortune was far more generously illustrated. Margaret Bourke-White's work demonstrated the calculatingly artistic possibilities of industrial photography, offering, wrote one, "unique angles upon the world of action—of blast furnaces erupting, of soup being cooked in kettles a thousand gallons at a time, of locomotives being hammered together red hot, of orchids growing under glass." Walker Evans's photography could draw the eye to the commonplace. Photographing the rich and powerful for *Fortune*, Erich Salomon "was the first cameraman to bring to perfection the fine art of clicking the shutter at the exactly wrong moment," wrote one historian of Luce's publications.[4] Together, they and others shooting for the magazine were leaders in the emerging documentary movement of the 1930s, a photography of compelling "realism."

Beyond the offices of Time Inc. were strong indications of popular enthusiasm for the iconographic. Some historians have traced this fervor to the late nineteenth century, when advertisers, magazines, and newspapers discovered the illustration to be a highly effective means of increasing their audiences. The popularity of the motion picture in the new century created even more demand for story telling that went beyond words.[5]

With exceptions, newspapers only halfheartedly tried to satisfy this new visual expectation. In the 1920s, the new tabloids succeeded largely because of their even greater use of the camera. Indeed, newspapers like the *New York Daily News* and *New York Graphic* broke new ground by allowing the camera to tell part of the story. Other dailies, in turn, boosted their pictorial displays in the 1920s and early 1930s. Many followed the *New York Times* in offering a weekly supplement that relied on a German process of reproducing photographs in brownish tones, rotogravure; the Associated Press inaugurated a photo wire service in 1935. Most editors, however, would only travel so far; nearly all had been reporters, not photographers. They had spent their careers agonizing over paragraph construction, not camera angles. Then, too, pictures were thought to be the journalism of the less educated. The tabloids, they reasoned, were lower-class organs, dailies like the "*Porno-Graphic*" a new form of "yellow" or sensational journalism. Following their lead by running numerous photographs, recalled one editor, "might pull down the integrity of the American press."[6]

Still, the preference for photographs as news was not limited to the "gum-chewers" living in the large markets where the tabloids flourished. In 1925, the Cowles family, owners of the *Des Moines Register* and *Tribune*, hired a young journalism instructor at Drake University, George Gallup, to conduct newspaper readership surveys. These in turn revealed an overwhelming and unmet demand for photographs, not only alone, but as part of a news item. When the *Register and Tribune* tested Gallup's findings by adding a Sunday pictorial supplement, circulation rose by 50 percent. Subsequent studies of small and large papers across the country confirmed his results. Readers were three to four times as likely to look at a picture as a news story. Moreover, they welcomed efforts to use the camera as a story-telling device; photographs should relate to type.[7]

Without engaging a survey team, Luce recognized this demand. Photo selection should not be arbitrary but suggest a "mind-guided camera," Luce wrote, which "can do a far better job of reporting current events than has been done." Such "photojournalism," connecting news to images, had an audience, he declared. Indeed, "To see, and to be shown," he wrote in 1936, "is now the will and new expectancy of half mankind."[8]

There was a new technological element as well. Developments in photography made a more vivid, realistic, and inviting image possible. In the 1920s, German manufacturers had perfected a camera far more mobile than the heavy-duty models then in use. The Leica could take up to thirty-six shots before reloading, had a greater depth of field, and in many indoor settings did not require a flash. Thus the intrepid photographer could take more shots more rapidly, giving an editor more pictures from which to choose or, using a group, to compose a series of related photos. Furthermore, these "mini-cameras" encouraged still more candid shooting. For practitioners like Salomon, who began using a Leica in 1932, the mini-cameras saved time lost loading the unit and setting the lens. More newsmakers, less likely to notice the small and flashless camera, might be captured unposed.[9]

In 1935, *Time* cameraman Thomas McAvoy used a mini-camera and specially treated film to photograph President Roosevelt at his desk in the then dark Oval Office. McAvoy's brethren told him he did not have enough light; President Roosevelt agreed. He ignored the photographer, signed a law, drank water, smoked a Camel. McAvoy clicked, and of thirteen of the twenty shots that did come out, *Time* on 25 February 1935 ran six. McAvoy had captured another Roosevelt. The president had heretofore allowed photographers to shoot him eating or swimming. Compared to those of his predecessors "at ease"—Coolidge on the farm or Hoover fishing—Roosevelt struck the pose of the patrician relaxing. But it was a pose. "Although informal photographs of Franklin D. Roosevelt are common," the magazine noted, "Unposed shots showing the natural play of his expressions are rare."[10]

Most newspapers were, in comparison, slow to adapt themselves to the mini-camera revolution. Although tabloids had been experimenting with the photo essay and unposed shots, few had taken up the smaller camera. Dailies normally issued large Speed Graphics or Graflexes to their staff photographers. None offered the photographer the flexibility first of the Rolleiflex, then of the Leica. The Leica had a synchronized flash—the photographer saw his or her subject and shot—whereas the standard camera shutter had to be opened, the bulb fired, the shutter then closed. The operator had to insert manually one sheet of film for each shot. If a photographer used his or her own mini-cam, newspaper developers and engravers complained, because its smaller (1 by 1½ inches) negative required more time and care to develop than the most common Speed Graphic negative (4 by 5 inches) and was more difficult to engrave onto plates for publication. Some dailies simply refused to buy the enlargers necessary to reproduce the new and smaller negatives. Only a few dailies—the *Milwaukee Journal* and the Cowleses' *Des Moines Register* and *Tribune*—even allowed their photographers to use Leicas.[11]

One episode of candid camera work revealed this resistance. At a

University of California function in 1935, Peter Stackpole, a young free-lance photographer from Oakland, used his Leica to capture the image of former president Hoover asleep as the secretary of labor spoke. Returning home, Stackpole could not find a buyer for his snapshot. The *Oakland Tribune*, a staunchly Republican sheet, refused to carry such an unflattering image of Hoover, the party's titular leader. For technical as opposed to partisan reasons, engravers at the rival *Post-Inquirer* would not run it either. Their equipment was not designed for the smaller-sized print. *Time*, however, eagerly carried Stackpole's picture. The magazine, which applied unflattering adjectives to both parties, could not resist the embarrassing if "realistic" photograph of the head of one.[12]

A magazine of photographs taking up this new picture journalism might find an eager audience. The nation's most popular periodicals, the *Saturday Evening Post* and *Collier's*, were well illustrated, but relied more on sketches than photographs. Those pictures they did run had a soft focus or were formal as opposed to harsh, "realistic" portraits. Then, too, in Europe, the commercial success of magazines like *Berliner Illustrierte Zeitung*, for which Salomon had worked, invited American imitators. Several publishers considered starting a picture magazine. Even before Luce's November 1933 memo, the Cowleses had been working on a prototype, as was William Randolph Hearst until financial setbacks forced him to drop the venture. "One of the extraordinary things about the 'picture magazine' in America," Luce wrote later, "was that everybody talked about it, but nobody did anything about it."[13]

The Cowleses' intentions did concern him. Like Luce, young, confident, and unafraid of violating journalistic convention, the Des Moines publishers were certain they could best him. *Time*'s founder, they reasoned, suffered from an eastern education and cultural orientation. They, not Luce, knew the Middle Border. By bringing their magazine out first, the Cowleses could deny Luce the edge he had enjoyed earlier with *Time*.[14] Luce's first two publishing successes, *Time* and *Fortune*, had worked in part because of their novelty; each had conveyed information in new ways. Luce could not afford to have the Cowleses' magazine resemble his own. Imitation had not made him a tycoon.

Luce directed Daniel Longwell in 1934 to plan a picture periodical. In great secrecy, the two men spent Saturdays poring over possible layouts. Together with Laura Z. Hobson, another *Time* staff member, they put together a picture-book history of Time Inc., *Four Hours a Year*; in truth, it was a dry run in pictorial journalism. Photos, not words, told stories. Longwell went to Europe to study the flourishing illustrated magazines. Recognizing the German advantage in photography, Longwell back home met often with a former editor of the *Berliner Illustrierte Zeitung*, Kurt Korff. Expert in photographic display, Korff tried to teach Longwell how to choose the "right" photograph for inclusion. Korff also labored to explain how to lay out a "photo-essay," a succession of shots of a given news event. Finally, Korff urged Longwell and Luce to hire other refugees from Hitler's Reich, including Alfred Eisenstaedt, as photographers.[15]

Despite Longwell's labors, Luce had not yet totally committed himself to the picture magazine. Some lieutenants spoke against it, suggesting that *Time* simply carry more photographs. But as the magazine's picture editor, Longwell had found that *Time* could carry only so many. Then, too, Luce's own specifications for the periodical frustrated planners. Luce wanted the magazine to be relatively inexpensive, though at ten cents it would still be twice the newsstand price of the *Saturday Evening Post* or *Collier's*. He also insisted that it be published on shiny white paper, ideal for photographic reproduction. Pictures in newspapers would look shabby in comparison. Nor did he want his illustrations to have the sepia tone of the rotogravure process or the *Illustrated London News*. Yet no paper producer could offer a reasonably priced stock fitting Luce's design. In other words, Time Inc. could not put out at a dime the kind of magazine he wanted. The pleas of Longwell and the prospect of the Cowleses' entry notwithstanding, Luce hesitated.

The Divorcée

A change in Luce's personal life caused him to abandon that caution. To the amazement of coworkers and friends, and to the dismay of his missionary parents, Luce left his wife for another women. She in turn rededicated Harry to the idea of a picture magazine.

Although one of her grandfathers had also been a preacher, Clare Boothe Brokaw's parents had worked in show business. That calling— like the elder Luces'—left them without a hometown and Clare with Harry's physical restlessness. Otherwise, their backgrounds offered nothing but contrasts. Clare's father abandoned the family when she was still a youngster. Her mother responded by inculcating into her only daughter a will to succeed, all the while scheming to marry her off to someone who could provide the security Clare's father had not. Formal education for Clare was less important (she never finished high school) than a successful catch. Mother Boothe's designs, however, only brought her daughter an unhappy marriage at age twenty. George Brokaw was wealthy but also drank too much and beat his young bride. A divorce left Clare with a nice stipend but no friends. Moving to a fancy apartment in Manhattan, Clare talked her way on to the staff of *Vanity Fair* in 1929. An amply illustrated periodical of wit and style for the well-to-do, *Vanity Fair* was for several years the perfect outlet for Clare; she enjoyed playing the arbiter of correct tastes, of nominating "comers" for the magazine's "Hall of Fame." (She selected Luce for a 1930 issue.) After several years, however, she grew bored and tried her hand at writing plays. Her targets were personal: her ex-husband, other women.

Meeting Luce several times in the early 1930s, she recalled being put off by his manner. On one memorable occasion, he played the White Rabbit, ending a conversation (about a picture magazine) with her by glancing at his watch and declaring abruptly, "Time to go. Good night."

Yet they came to be attracted to each other. It seemed an unlikely pairing. She was elegantly beautiful and blond; Harry still trim but losing his hair. She could never compete with Harry in the realm of knowledge; hers had been a training in charm and calculation, of being clever as opposed to intelligent. Still, they shared certain qualities. His lack of tact resembled her own occasional acidity. Moreover, Clare, unlike his wife Lila, was actively interested in Harry's first love: the fourth estate. Lila could only affect to follow closely his ideas for journalism. Although altogether devoted to Harry, Lila increasingly appeared too removed from his lifework. After one more chance encounter, Henry Luce confessed to the divorcée that he wanted to leave Lila and marry her. An astonished Clare pleaded for time and fled to Florida to be with her mother.

Luce's decision to wed Clare was the most agonizing of his life. Deserting Lila, for whom he still had much affection, pained him. Lila resisted at first, then relented. Luce's parents caused him the most anguish. Like most middle-class Americans at the time, Henry and Elizabeth Luce deeply disapproved of divorce. "Harry's pious family was taking it very hard and thought he was a dirty dog to ditch Lila," Billings wrote in June 1935. His parents' unhappiness left him in torment, distracted from his duties at Time Inc. "Harry said he'd been through hell for weeks," Billings recalled. "Couldn't work, had to walk around the block."[16]

More than his parents' disapproval explained his behavior. Beneath a thickly difficult exterior, Luce could be a man of intense passions, ones he labored mightily and constantly to contain. His love for Clare had stripped him of his self-control. Luce let his emotions—not the church's teachings—reign over him. He married Clare late in 1935. For about five years he remained madly in love.

Back from the Honeymoon

During his two-month honeymoon in Cuba, Harry agreed to publish the picture magazine. Clare, exercising her newly won influence, had the most to do with his decision. But her position enjoyed the vigorous advocacy of Ingersoll as well. Named Time Inc. general manager, Luce's second in command, in November 1935, Ingersoll visited the newlyweds to review year-end budgetary matters with Harry and plead for the picture magazine. Ingersoll had demonstrated as *Fortune* editor an enthusiasm for pictorial display; as general manager he had become involved in planning the picture weekly. At a Havana poolside, Ingersoll excised Harry's lingering doubts; he came back to New York rededicated to the project. "Luce was all for a picture magazine," Billings wrote of his boss's return. A day later Billings described Luce as "completedly absorbed in [the] new magazine. He came prancing happily into my office and cried, 'I'm pregnant'—i.e. with ideas on picture magazines."[17]

Luce's new marital state could still be a distraction. Enamored of Clare, Luce began uncharacteristically taking an early train home, often leaving Ingersoll in charge. And Luce's "perpetual honeymoon," as his aide-de-camp sarcastically dubbed his superior's new life-style, temporarily left to Ingersoll the burden of overseeing preparations for the new periodical and holding Harry to his commitment to the picture magazine. In long memoranda—Ingersoll's forte—he restated earlier justifications. Pictures appealed to everyone, he wrote, the bank president, the truck driver. Advances in photography, moreover, offered journalism a new instrument—for telling stories or capturing events and newsmakers more realistically—that newspapers were not adopting. Time Inc. had to act, he wrote, because "through the next decade the movement of pictures into journalism will be so rapid as possibly to revolutionize the journalistic machinery of the world."[18]

Luce, Ingersoll, and others confronted a host of obstacles to production. The magazine lacked a name. After considering *Showbook* and *Dime*, Luce belatedly recognized his new wife's wisdom and bought the dying *Life* for the rights to its name for ninety-two thousand dollars. For a four-letter word, staffers joked, Luce had already spent more than he and Hadden had needed in 1922 to begin *Time*. Achieving the production values Luce wanted for the new *Life* proved even more time-consuming. Harry insisted that the weekly be published on a coated paper—of a higher grade than *Time* but not so costly as *Vanity Fair*—to give photographs a high reproduction quality. Much of the effect of including vivid newsphotos in newspapers was lost because of dailies' inferior pulp and coarse-screen halftone engraving process. Yet among magazine publishers there had been little demand for the quality and quantity of stock Luce sought. As a result, an aide found most printers he approached unable to meet the publisher's specifications. One Luce operative recalled printers' "general lifting of the hands in holy horror."[19] Finally, the Mead Corporation offered Time Inc. an experimental paper that appeared appropriate.

Luce, Ingersoll, and Longwell still had to determine a formula for the magazine itself. From the outset everyone agreed that through agreements with major syndicated photonews services, *Life* would run photographs of the major news stories of the week. Yet they wondered whether they alone would suffice to fill the projected forty to forty-eight pages of *Life*. Then, too, carrying nothing but the best of the week's syndicated shots might cause *Life* to seem only a variation on the weekly rotogravure sections. And in plotting a magazine Luce always insisted that it appear unique at the crowded newsstand.

For Luce, *Time* offered the key to *Life*'s identity. Like his news-weekly, *Life* would be departmentalized. The magazine would carry a President's Scrapbook similar to *Time*'s Presidency section as well as ones on science and the popular arts. The latter were deemed justified because of their pictorial possibilities. "A painting, a sculpture, or a building is better seen than written about," Luce wrote in a prospectus. "A movie is a story told in pictures."[20]

Luce confessed that the availability of photographs would determine a department's weekly fate. "Not all the types of features will appear in every weekly issue and they may appear in slightly varying order," he wrote. The magazine "is not obligated to report on all the significant news: its obligation is to report in pictures all the significant news which the camera has succeeded in making a pictorial record of." Japan's prime minister might be assassinated, but the editors "may record nothing about it for three or four weeks: [they] will wait until all the good pictures pertaining to that event have arrived."[21]

Putting together a prototype or "dummy" posed an enormous challenge. Their past enthusiasm for photographs notwithstanding, Luce and his editors had previously regarded pictures as supplements to words. Now they had to reverse that order, and their lack of familiarity with photographic layout, despite past meetings with Korff and others, showed. An early attempt dissatisfied everyone, especially experts. One recalled, "the editors hadn't the vaguest notion of picture values and I was thoroughly convinced that they had a definite contempt for photography altogether."[22] Nor could planners decide which types of stories belonged in Life. One prototype seemed middlebrow, another, replete with nudes, too sensational (it also offended President Roosevelt's mother, who had chanced upon a copy). More consultants pored over more dummies, cut and pasted new ones; Ingersoll wrote more memoranda. Indecision over the publication's proper style made everyone jittery.

A related uncertainty involved Life's potential audience. Should the magazine play only to the well-to-do burghers who took Time? Or did Luce seek a larger readership? He denied wishing to compete with the Saturday Evening Post or Collier's, even resorting to obscenity (for him, rare language) when a coworker accused him of such intentions.[23] Yet Luce's prospectuses for Life did not suggest he would limit the periodical's readership to those "busy men" on eastern commuter trains he and Hadden had described in 1922 as potential readers of Time. Instead, Luce spoke of "half of mankind."

One encouraging sign was the sale of some $1.7 million in advertising contracts prior to publication. Time Inc. sales representatives based Life's rates on a circulation of two hundred fifty thousand. Advertisers could extend on a "blanket" basis their contracts set according to this figure for a full year after Life's first number.

With advertising agreements being signed and Life itself nearing production in the fall of 1936, Luce faced yet another crisis. Although Harry in effect served as managing editor, John Martin was his chief lieutenant and expected to be in charge of Life's day-to-day operations. His erratic and irascible behavior, however, caused Luce late in October to turn to Billings, Time's managing editor, who agreed to replace Martin. Billings, too, struggled to achieve the "right" layout for Life, but he eventually proved an ideal choice. Life's weekly publication schedule and multiple deadlines due to its heavy use of illustrations all but required a supremely well-organized manager like Billings. More-over, though a "print man," Billings had what Ingersoll had said *Life's* chief had to possess, "a reverence for pictures."[24] Billings immedi-ately brought order to *Life's* operations and commanded the new staff's respect.

Luce remained in charge as he, Billings, and Longwell oversaw the production of the magazine's first issue, scheduled for the newsstands for 19 November 1936. Ingersoll, left out of the final stages of the mag-azine's creation, continued to compose long memoranda, now largely ignored. "What is most on my mind," Luce wrote his lieutenant, "is *getting things done.*"[25]

Life's first number made deadline. Billings, scrambling for an im-pressive first cover, had found one by Bourke-White "an answer to our prayer."[26] Characteristically, the photographer had managed to make the new Fort Peck Dam seem exotic, its monumental turrets caused some to mistake it for a castle. Inside, she contributed a photo-essay on the workers of New Deal, Montana, who were constructing the dam. *Life* also ran the first aerial shot of the king of England's country resi-dence and one of the recently opened San Francisco Bay Bridge. The theater department featured the newest middlebrow triumph, *Victoria Regina*; the film of the week was Greta Garbo's *Camille*. In addition, *Life* carried a three-page spread of the paintings of contemporary artist John Steuart Curry. And the magazine "went to a party," as the section came to be known, for the British ambassador to France.

"Having Quintuplets"

Within hours of *Life's* arrival at newsstands, the first, seemingly fantas-tic stories began reaching the offices of Time Inc. Vendors across the country reported selling all two hundred thousand issues available to them; some dealers began taking lists of those willing to pay in advance to reserve copies of the next issue. There were stories of people who, after managing to secure a first issue, proudly hosted cocktail parties to show off their prize. Together with subscription sales, *Life* had a first-issue circulation of four hundred thirty-five thousand.

After four weeks that figure rose to five hundred thirty-three thou-sand. No magazine in American history had passed the half-million mark so soon after its initial release. It had taken *Time* ten years to do so. By January 1937, *Life* had a circulation of seven hundred sixty thou-

sand. Newsstands still ran out of copies as the Chicago plant struggled to find enough coated paper to increase *Life*'s run. An aide to
Luce cried, "Having *Life* isn't like having a baby. It's like having
quintuplets."[27]

In 1937, *Life*'s circulation continued to climb. It passed the million mark four months after the first issue. On a West Coast trip in
August, Longwell described *Life*'s arrival at the motion picture studios
at noon on Fridays. "Hollywood is really excited about *Life*," he wrote.
"Copies [are] perused all over the place."[28] By the end of 1937, *Life*
commanded a 1.7 million circulation, still below that for *Collier's* or
the *Saturday Evening Post* but more than twice that of *Time*. And a market test in Worcester, Massachusetts, suggested that *Life* could achieve
a circulation of five million.

Life's publishers could not, however, at first meet this unantici-
pated demand. Production, including the supply of paper stock and
contracting of printing facilities, had been planned for a weekly run of
three hundred fifty thousand. Now faced with caring for quintuplets
rather than one newborn, the company had to pay exorbitant rates for
the treated paper and invest in printing operations, the latter step one
that Luce had hoped to avoid. Vendors continued to complain of running out of *Life*. Recalled one observer, "Newsstand operators assumed
hard-boiled attitudes, hardly deigning to honor requests for copies with
a reply—one ought to know better than to ask for cherries in March."[29]

The far greater crisis involved advertising. *Life*'s prepublication circulation guarantee of two hundred fifty thousand had obviously proven
too modest and Luce's sales representatives had unknowingly worsened
matters prior to *Life*'s first issue by offering advertisers the option after
the first weeks of renewing their contracts at the low rate for a full year.
For advertisers, these contracts made a *Life* ad a bargain. They also
denied the company the revenues needed to cover the higher-than-
expected production costs. For ten cents, Roy Larsen estimated, an
American at the newsstand at the right time on Fridays could buy one
copy of *Life*. Yet it cost Time Inc. fifteen cents to produce that copy;
from advertisers, subscribers, and street sales, the company recovered
six cents.

Time Inc. was losing $3 million a year on *Life*. Advertising cut-
backs due to the 1937–38 recession added to the company's woes. In
1937, Time Inc. showed its lowest profit ($168,430) since 1928. (In
1936, Time Inc. had made $2.7 million.) Its stock fell from a high of
$260 to $138 per share; dividends were eliminated. In December, Luce

announced that there would be no Christmas bonuses. The tycoon confessed, "We are poor again."[30]

For the first half of 1937, Luce and his aides had debated what to do. Advertising rates could be and were raised to reflect the greater circulation, but until November these higher charges did not affect those who had signed prepublication agreements. Curtailing circulation by raising *Life*'s newsstand price to fifteen cents had been considered and then dropped. Reluctantly in June, Luce had gone along with Larsen's recommendation that *Life* seek the largest possible circulation—even though this move meant more short-term losses—and continue to raise advertising prices.

Although some balked at the climbing rates, advertisers eventually fell into line because of indications of the magazine's effectiveness as a promotional vehicle. When Baker's Chocolate, which already held a 65 percent share of the premium cooking chocolate market, increased its *Life* advertising, the company's sales actually rose. Within days of a *Life* advertisement for the Chrysler Highlander automobile, dealers reported being out of the model. Consumers clutching copies of *Life* had literally rushed into showrooms. By 1940, advertisers accepted *Life*; the magazine took in 11 percent of all monies spent on advertising in all magazines.[31]

Madison Avenue had, after all, intersected with Main Street. In 1938, 80 percent of *Life*'s subscribers renewed, "a phenomenal figure," Billings wrote excitedly. Early in 1939, *Life*'s circulation neared 2.4 million. *Life* was beginning to make money.[32]

Billings and Luce had additional cause for celebration. In December 1938, Time Inc. published an exhaustive measure of *Life*'s readership. *Life's Continuing Study of Magazine Audiences* not only analyzed circulation but estimated total audiences by trying to calculate *Life*'s pass-along factor. That is, how many more people read (as opposed to purchased) a copy of *Life*? Criticized at first as in-house propaganda, the *Continuing Study* soon enjoyed wide credibility. Although *Life*'s circulation still fell behind that of the *Saturday Evening Post* or *Collier's*, the *Continuing Study* found that more adults—taking the pass-along factor into account—actually read *Life*. Another survey listed *Life*'s pass-along number at 14, a figure so incredible that the survey team lowered it before calculating *Life*'s total audience, which it figured at just over 17 million, compared to 16 million for *Collier's*. Just over 15 percent of all adults in America read *Life*.[33]

Nevertheless, *Life* was not a people's magazine. Like most periodicals, *Life* had a largely middle-class constituency. Indeed, the magazine's following in that regard much resembled *Time's*. Of the four leading magazines—the *Saturday Evening Post*, *Collier's*, *Life*, and *Liberty* —*Life* was the most popular among younger and well-to-do consumers. *Life* led in every age category except that including those forty-five years and older. In the three wealthiest groups, *Life* led the field. Of the *Continuing Study's* "A" category, those in the "top income group"—executives, "well-to-do merchants, professional men, prosperous farmers," those likely to own a car and a home—37 percent read *Life* to 25.2 percent the *Saturday Evening Post*. Among the upper middle-class "B" group, 31 percent looked at *Life* compared to 26.8 percent the *Saturday Evening Post*. The gap narrowed between *Life* and its rivals only as one descended this income ladder.[34] Class, then, predicted whether one might find *Life* in someone's parlor.

The System

Life's instant success had little to do with editorial consistency. Later, in and outside *Life's* offices came the admission that only after two to three years did the magazine's staff establish a *Life* "look" in story selection and photographic display. The editors did not, Luce's hopes notwithstanding, show a great mastery at judging the week's best pictures. Photographs in early numbers were usually crowded together, not generously surrounded with the white space that in the 1940s and later added to the effect of a *Life* feature. Longwell recalled, "*Life* was not a magazine until two years after its publication, when we learned, by publishing it, how to publish a [picture] magazine." *Life* in 1937 and 1938, Luce wrote, "still wasn't really good but only getting good."[35]

Life's slow evolution was not peculiar. Most new magazines and newspapers—especially ones seeking to break new ground—went through a period of rough experimentation. "The magazine defines itself as it grows," Billings observed in 1937.[36] It had, after all, taken more than five years for *Time* to begin to achieve the tone that Hadden and Luce had intended for their periodical. Yet so great was the audience awaiting a journalism of photographs, that even as *Life* groped to find the right formula and format, Luce did not have to wait as he had with *Time* for the fame that came with widespread consumer acceptance. Looking at the early *Life* issues, a magazine industry analyst concluded in 1944, "By the standards of today's *Life*, they are amateurish indeed—but for eight years ago they must have been good; their acceptance, unlike the acceptance of *Time* some years before, was hearty and immediate."[37]

However awkwardly assembled in its early years, *Life* benefited from being America's first mass-circulation picture magazine. The Cowleses had waited too long: their entry, the biweekly *Look*, did not appear until 5 January 1937, five weeks after *Life*. Luce had beaten them to the newsstand. *Look*, too, won a substantial if less loyal following while avoiding *Life*'s heavy initial operating losses. But by printing *Look* on cheaper stock and giving it a less serious agenda, the Cowles brothers unknowingly made their picture magazine appear a lower-class attraction, one less appealing to some readers and many advertisers.[38] Over the next two decades, *Look* never threatened *Life*'s dominance of the picture magazine field.

In time a debate ensued over who deserved credit for *Life*'s success. Many chose to downgrade Luce's own contribution and emphasize the prepublication counsel of Kurt Korff or Ralph Ingersoll. Korff tutored Longwell in photograph selection and arrangement, and Ingersoll, along with Clare, kept Luce committed to the project. But as *Life* first neared deadline, neither man was actively participating in the preparations, and the staff refused to allow Luce's bride to join their ranks. Given *Life*'s initial shortcomings, all three might have been better utilized. Instead, Luce, Billings, and Longwell had to learn on their own, like the new generation of amateur photographers with Leicas hung around their necks.

Although after the first three weeks Luce left to Billings most of the responsibilities of putting *Life* out, the founder refused to give his editor a free rein. Much to Billings's annoyance, Luce occasionally stepped into his office to criticize the mock-ups of the next issue. Billings, who prized a smooth-running operation, detested his superior's interference. Although "swell on general balance," Billings wrote early in 1937, Luce "botches up details." A photograph lacked "significance," Luce would complain, an issue "pep." In August, Billings wrote, "Luce still fussing with news pictures. He tosses everything up in the air like a juggler—and then ducks out and leaves it to us to catch the pieces as they come down."[39]

Luce was participating in his own brand of collective editing. Since first planning his picture magazine, he insisted that *Life*, like *Time*, be an exercise in group journalism. By definition, *Life* required the active involvement of photographers and the art department in planning stories. Everyone had to collaborate. The vexing problems of choosing a subject that lent itself to visual story telling, and then planning the photo-essay, called for a collective spirit. "*Life* is the true product of group journalism," an office directive noted. "In so far as possible, everyone from researcher, office boy, photographer, out-of-town correspondent, to writer and layout man is supposed to play whatever part he or she can in the stories that go into each issue of *Life*."[40]

Life's group journalism awarded photographers unprecedented prestige. Even before *Life*'s first number Luce recognized that his new periodical could not rely on the photonews services alone for all the "right" pictures. "They might come in," *Life* staffers were warned. "Only a small portion do."[41] Indeed, most pictures reaching Billings's and Longwell's desks were almost predictably dull, shot in the old tradition by photographers unaffected by the miniature-camera revolution. *Life* quickly depended, then, and as no magazine before, on its staff of photographers. Wilson Hicks, who became *Life*'s photo editor in March 1937, recalled, "*Life* has a saying, which is only partly true, that 'There isn't anything wrong with the magazine that a few pictures won't fix.' "[42] In such a situation, photographers could not be treated as hired help, like their counterparts at dailies, but as equals. They were, in fact, billed on the masthead with the writers. This granting of status was eased by the intelligence and skills that Bourke-White and Eisenstaedt had already demonstrated. Nonetheless, it was an unprecedented tribute to a new generation of photographers, coming at a time when few journalism schools taught photography and, recalled one contemporary, the most unflattering stereotype burdened the photographer: "Hollywood cast the press photographer as a helpless chowderhead, slightly stooped in posture, following his glamorous, masterminding reporter and waiting in bewilderment for his command: 'Shoot that.' "[43]

At *Life*, the photographers decided what to shoot. Taking advantage of newer equipment, *Life* photographers aimed for a greater realism. Eisenstaedt specialized in the candid shots, what one admirer later called the " 'no, don't smile' school of portraiture." Eisenstaedt's "portraits are completely honest."[44] Like Eisenstaedt, Peter Stackpole and Thomas McAvoy used Leicas to achieve naturalistic, unposed shots. Others like Carl Mydans had worked for the Historical Section of the Farm Security Administration, which under Roy Stryker had fostered a whole documentary tradition of capturing the commonplace.

"Overshooting" eased their search for the realistic image. *Life* photographers, unlike their colleagues on tightfisted newspapers, were encouraged to take a lot of pictures, in the hope that the right image would be captured or that enough good shots could form a photo-essay. Indeed, at a given news event, *Life* photographers could always be identified: they had four cameras around their necks, all loaded and ready.

The miniature-camera revolution deeply influenced *Life*'s photography. Although there was no "official" camera at *Life*, and staff photographers proved eclectic in their choice of equipment, the Leica's influence was unmistakable. In May 1937, Arthur Cofod, Jr., went to Lakehurst, New Jersey, to pick up a packet of photographs for *Life*'s editors, who had arranged the shipment of film from Germany on the airship *Hindenburg*. Cofod was not a staff photographer, only an amateur. By chance, he had his camera, a ten-year-old Leica, with him. As he and twenty photographers stood on the field to watch the *Hindenburg* approach, the zeppelin suddenly exploded. Cofod had chanced upon one of the great news stories of the year. And as the only photographer on the scene with a Leica, Cofod was able to get the most shots. Running his pictures, *Life* boasted that Cofod had captured "the most complete record of all." "Swell pictures of the *Hindenburg* disaster," an excited Billings wrote, "puts zip into my issue."[45]

Cofod's *Hindenburg* shots were a variation on the photo-essay, first tried in Germany a decade earlier, which wove a narrative with pictures. In a February 1937 issue, *Life* ran two dozen photos by Eisenstaedt of Vassar College. To describe the exclusive women's college, he shot not just Gothic structures but scenes capturing the students' everyday lives, making the experience of attending such an educational enclave real to readers far removed. To *Life*'s publicists, the photographer like Eisenstaedt had become the twentieth-century equivalent of the eighteenth-century essayist. Citing the Vassar photo-essay, an advertisement for *Life* declared, "Together these twenty-four pictures give an impression of college as personal and as homogeneous as any thousand words of Joseph Addison."[46]

Bourke-White, too, offered photo-essays. In a May 1937 number, Bourke-White did a photo-essay on the Lynds' "Middletown," Muncie, Indiana. Her effort better exemplified the essay's—and *Life*'s—possibilities. The Lynds' encyclopedic study had suffered from a clinical tone coveted by sociologists then and later; Bourke-White, in contrast, allowed Muncie to breathe, to appear a real city. Her shots of Muncie's rich and poor conveyed the class divisions that the Lynds, for all their commitment to social equality, could not match with nearly the same force.[47]

Life's "realism" could stand out. Cofod's *Hindenburg* shots spared readers little of the misery of the burned survivors. A 10 January 1938 story on the Sino-Japanese war included two horrifying half-page pictures from the seige of Nanking: one of the bodies of civilians and soldiers executed by the victorious Japanese, another of the head of a man who had resisted their advance. To Luce and Billings, such photographic realism constituted good journalism, and readers should not be spared.[48]

Life's search for the real did not require expertise. Like colleagues at *Time* and *Fortune*, *Life* photographers and writers were talented amateurs, endowed with Luce's assurance that the intelligent lay person could cover any topic. Photographer Carl Mydans recalled an editor one day asking the staff, "Anyone here an expert on brain surgery?" After a pause came a young staff member's reply, "Not yet, but give me ten minutes and I will be."[49]

Life itself was better suited to handle another mission: elucidate high culture to readers. The art of photography itself might be described, as in a January 1938 feature on Berenice Abbott. Pictures were used to explain Wagner's *Ring of the Nibelungs*. Most often, *Life*'s pedagogical mission invited reproductions of great art: four pages in a March 1938 issue on Italian Renaissance painting in American museums. In its first two decades, a *Life* publisher claimed, the magazine spent more than $25 million on color reproductions of masterpieces. *Life*, a journalism school professor concluded, had become "the greatest disseminator of art that mankind has ever known."[50]

Yet *Life* editors shamelessly "packaged" such stories together with ones featuring attractive young women. Hollywood starlets and New York fashion models—not newsmakers—most often adorned a cover. While introducing Picasso's work to millions conditioned only to the mindless Americana of the *Saturday Evening Post* and *Collier's*, *Life* cushioned the shock of the new by having two pages of models along Miami Beach follow the feature. Inside the 15 February 1937 issue, *Life* ran shots of a young woman showing "How to Undress for Your Husband." It may have been an in-house joke, but the editors had concluded that cheesecake helped circulation and kept serving. "I am determined to get charm, sex and glamor into this issue," Billings wrote in October 1937. "Hence, a racy spread on zippers." Luce, too, did not want *Life* to get excessively serious. At a March 1939 conference with Billings, Luce argued that *Life* "needs more charming pictures, more boy-and-girl, more fun." On the eve of World War II, Billings wrote, "We need some sex. Yesterday Sermalino brought two semi-naked models into my office. . . . I decided to use them both for exercise photos showing how to reduce waist [and] to wear wasp-waist corsets. . . . In the excitement over the approaching war, I must not forget other stuff to give the magazine balance and variety."[51]

Such an editorial attitude caused *Life* to be charged with loose morals. Teetotalers objected to Fort Peck Dam workers pictured drinking. In Auburn, Maine, the local YMCA director removed the "Undress for Your Husband" issue from the reading room. A March 1938 photo-essay on "The Birth of a Baby" was banned in Boston and the Bronx.

The prudishness of some *Life* critics obscured the extent to which the magazine upheld traditional values. *Life* was most often only teasing male readers with leggy models. Luce's editors, like their counterparts in film and radio, respected conventional life-styles, noticeably in their handling of the private lives of mass cultural "celebrities," and even at the expense of "reality." When photographer Robert Capa returned from Sun Valley, Idaho, with pictures for one of *Life*'s many stories on Ernest Hemingway, editors referred in the cutlines to the novelist's live-in lover as his wife. They had yet to wed.[52]

Others found the whole enterprise a sham. The *New Republic* disparagingly likened *Life* to the big-city tabloids. Discussing *Life* and *Look* in March 1937, the liberal journal complained, "hardly any mental effort is required to look at a picture and to spell out a few lines of accompanying caption, written in primer English. The attractiveness of such periodicals is enhanced if the pictures are themselves sensational, faintly salacious, or gruesome." At her Virginia finishing school in November 1937, Clare's daughter Ann had to sit impassively as her English instructor observed, "*Life* is a magazine for morons." The *New Yorker* three years later ridiculed *Life* for running a picture of a nude model at a Yale art class. For Luce and *Life*, of course, the photo worked: "This had Yale, it had Art, it had Class, it had America; it had everything, including no clothes on. It was *Life*'s dream come true."[53]

Life's calculating search for "zip" could be dismissed as a concession to circulation. If the editors ran too many starlet covers, inside they discussed art and politics all the while struggling to perfect the newest mass medium, photojournalism. If these treatments fell short of certain standards, seeming middlebrow or even patronizing, the critics of *Life* like those of *Time* forgot that Luce was not publishing a magazine for them or the subscribers to the *New Republic*. Luce had far more to please.

Nevertheless, *Life* could, like *Time*, betray a less than inclusive view of the audience. *Life*'s America was white, often northern European. In May 1939, Noel Busch wrote an especially condescending profile of New York Yankee outfielder Joe DiMaggio. The Yankee Clipper fared better against Pitcher Feller. "Italians, bad at war, are well-suited for milder competition," Busch observed. "Although he learned Italian first, Joe, now 24, speaks English without an accent, and is otherwise well-adopted to most U.S. mores. Instead of olive oil or smelly bear grease, he kept his hair slick with water. He never reeks of garlic."[54]

The camera itself could play favorites. In a December 1937 issue, *Life* ran a double spread on the large and attractive family of Joseph P. Kennedy, a Boston millionaire with political ambitions for himself and his sons and whom Luce had come to know and admire. The Kennedys, like the Roosevelts, photographed well; the spread, Billings wrote, "zips up the issue."[55] Thus could be seen the beginnings of a mutually beneficial relationship between a visually demanding medium and a certain type of political family. *Life* annointed those with good looks.

Other less photogenic leaders suffered at the hands of this new journalism of images. Senator Robert A. Taft of Ohio could not develop the contrived naturalness before the camera that the Roosevelts and Kennedys had turned into an art. Taft was not a political model or starlet. And yet the new camera age all but insisted on those features, however irrelevant to political leadership. In a 19 February 1940 story, *Life* ridiculed Taft, seeking the Republican presidential nomination, for his inept photographic showmanship. Taft had tried while fishing to create a photo opportunity; he was too obvious, *Life* instructed readers. Someone else had caught the fish.[56]

Like *Time*, *Life* purported to summarize, only with pictures rather than words as its instrument of synthesis. In one prospectus, Luce wrote that his new periodical "will be the complete and reliable *record* of all the significant events which are recorded in pictures." When *Life* "tells the story of [an] event it will do so with pictorial finality."[57]

This "finality" could be questioned. Luce himself had acknowledged that not all stories lent themselves to visual display. *Life*, he wrote in a prospectus, "takes for its field not all the news but all the news which now and hereafter can be seen; and of these seen events it proposes to be the complete and reliable record."[58] But was Eisenstaedt's Vassar a true portrait? Or did it disguise the snobbery of such institutions in the 1930s, making the school seem like a cheery state university for the children of those with a bit too much money? Did

Bourke-White really convey or exaggerate Middletown's class biases? Her professionalism, like that of *Time*'s writers, cloaked the extent to which choices were being made for readers about the "real" Muncie. "*Life*'s greatest admirers," wrote two students of the photo magazines in 1942, "are occasionally troubled by a quality of its pictorial journalism which is hard to pin down, but which might be called a subtle distortion of reality. To some extent this seems to result from an overtone which *Life* shares with the other Luce publications, an overtone which conveys a highly conscious, humorless certitude about them, as if they were saying, 'Here are the facts, and here is the truth they add up to, and that's that.' There never seems to be any real doubt that the Luce papers know all the answers."[59]

True to the documentary movement of the 1930s, Luce's picture weekly prized impact over representativeness. Wilson Hicks wrote, "People are sometimes heard to remark that looking at the photograph of an event is 'like being there.' The fact is that, when expertly made, a photograph is better than being there, in a sense it is more real than reality."[60]

Achievement as Temptation

Luce himself savored his greatest journalistic triumph. With the help of others, including a new wife, he had not only provided an outlet for a budding form of expression, photojournalism, but had vastly increased his own audience. With this new following came the temptation to do something more than create still more magazines, perhaps to do what work had kept him from for almost two decades, enter the political arena.

7

FROM PUBLISHER TO
PUBLIC MAN
1933–1940

Life's triumph marked the end of Luce's career as a journalistic innovator. The missionary's son had spent his first seventeen years out of college creating new ways of informing the middle classes. The remainder
of his life went to converting some members of his audience while
keeping others in line. For the American middle, Henry Luce assumed
the post of propaganda minister.

Until the late 1930s, Luce's infrequent public utterances constituted defenses of his labors. He struggled with his stammer most often
to defend the moneychangers and to challenge those on the left critical
of business. Luce's allegiance to capitalism, even in its darkest hours,
had a personal function. Defending free enterprise justified his own
path, as opposed to the rejected ones of politics and religion. Luce defined free enterprise as an alternative statesmanship and in so doing ra-
tionalized the forsaking of his father's call. Like his son, Henry Winters
Luce had been a hard worker and ambitious. But he aspired for God's
kingdom on earth; personal well-being did not follow. With no little
guilt, the son sought to explain why he traveled the profitable, secular
path.

To do so Luce ennobled journalism. Unlike the other captains of
commerce, Luce maintained, publishers could be idealists as well as
businessmen. The mass communicator could both prosper and enjoy a

freedom of action the envy of those they lunched with. Unlike the factory manager, an editor could consider the problems of the world and pose solutions. He was a free agent. Luce dismissed altogether the charge of advertiser interference; "We editors won the war," Luce said of the long struggle with space buyers. Publishers, he wrote, "are quite as free as college professors and quite as brave as statesmen."[1]

Precisely because of Luce's sense of journalism as a calling, he disparaged what he deemed the "please-the-people" or "department-store" theory of some newspaper publishers, who to Luce, had gone too far trying to please all possible readers. Still, Luce himself could be accused of pandering. His magazines were full of what could most generously be dubbed compromises: weekly shots of half-clad nymphs in *Life*, too many film industry profiles in *Fortune*, an excessive weight to personality in *Time*. But they were compromises Luce made without qualms, necessary to lure potential believers into his sanctuary. Others surrendered too much, Luce thought. Sensationalism substituted for seriousness in some publications. In others, the "common-carrier" editor fed his sheet with "twaddle-yards and yards of mediocrity, acres of bad fiction and triviality, square miles of journalistic tripe." In a more spirited vein, Luce declared, "I'll be damned if I'll be a public utility."[2]

Cultivating a Consensus

Luce correctly recognized the new professionalism of the fourth estate—a "revolution" according to Lippmann that freed editors of having to pay excessive heed to the whims of parties or readers.[3] Consumer tastes should not dictate content. The new publishers, respectful of what came to be known as the "social responsibility theory" of the press, disguised their party memberships. Editors tried to serve a wide political spectrum; causes and crusades should be chosen and waged carefully, if at all. Mainly for fear of federal regulators, the emerging national radio news services similarly stood the middle ground.

To Luce, such a journalism of consensus fit his organic view of society. Luce wanted journalism to hold the republic together; national unity was paramount. As an adolescent, he had spoken of the Swiss as "my ideal." A people divided by language and culture nevertheless maintained their nationhood through voluntary association and broadly shared values. The eastern upper classes' preparedness campaign of 1916, he wrote discerningly, might be of dubious military value, but "it emphasizes that first and last, and never-learned lesson of freedom, *obedience*; that if all would be equally privileged, all must equally obey."[4]

Luce's enthusiasm for mass identity with the state caused him to be among the early admirers of Italian dictator Benito Mussolini. As the Great Depression worsened, Luce studied the theories of economist Vilfredo Pareto, commonly considered the intellectual architect of Italian fascism. Pareto had offered the West a model economy, "the corporate state," with stable labor-management relations. In July 1934, *Fortune* in turn presented a generally positive portrait of Pareto's supposed test case, Italy under Il Duce. Italian fascism was made to appear American; Mussolini's system was likened to Secretary of Commerce Herbert Hoover's earlier efforts to create an "associative state" of unions and trade associations. Luce himself wrote an unsigned introduction, which praised without endorsing Mussolini's rule. "No 100 percent journalist can be more than a few percent Fascist, which is to say, he is by definition non-Fascist," he wrote. "But the good journalist must recognize in Fascism certain ancient virtues of the race, whether or not they happen to be momentarily fashionable in his own country. Among them are Discipline, Duty, Courage, Glory, Sacrifice."[5]

Il Duce enjoyed many good press notices in the 1920s and early 1930s. Before his March on Rome, Italy had seemed not only incapable of modernizing its economy but at the brink of chaos, if not communism. Mussolini had, it appeared, brought stability to Italy. In America and Britain a myth was reported as a fact, namely, that, as *Fortune* declared, "Mussolini *did* make the trains run on time." Il Duce himself went to great lengths wooing and fooling the foreign press into believing him a great man. The month after *Fortune*'s Italy feature, one victim of his public relations campaign, the publisher of the Toledo (Ohio) *Blade*, described Mussolini as "the greatest personality of the present century."[6]

Regardless of class, Americans had long been infatuated with strong leadership. Napoleon had been among the most popular heroes in nineteenth-century public school readers and popular periodicals. In the Progressive era, muckraking journalists often framed their stories around powerful individuals. *Time* had gone a step further, by offering the cover story and Man of the Year. In the late 1920s and 1930s, *Time* praised Turkey's Atatürk and Iran's Reza Pahlavi, both brutal dictators, yet like Mussolini, "strong."[7] Even the Studebaker automobile company conveyed this sentiment in the twenties by offering three models: the President, the Commander, and the Dictator.

Nothing attracted Luce to Mussolini more than the dictator's reputed success at singlehandedly bringing together a once divided, downcast people. More than anything, Luce's magazines strove to be instruments of national bonding. From *Time*'s first number, the periodical offered readers an omniscient view of politics and culture, a centrism at times genuine, at other moments, affected or guessed at. *Time* and *Life* steered readers toward a national middle. *Time* similarly championed strong leadership by focusing attention on the presidency, even when, in the 1920s, chief executives were neither strong nor great. Leaders of regions, notably the rural Midwest and South, were not taken seriously, but ridiculed unless, like small-town Kansas editor William Allen White, they displayed a national outlook.

Handling Roosevelt

Given their bias, Luce and his editors should have embraced the Roosevelt presidency. Roosevelt quickly asserted a presidential role in economic recovery and to most appeared the first truly effective and powerful chief executive since Wilson. Moreover, like Luce's boyhood hero, Theodore Roosevelt, Franklin enjoyed exercising his power and offering his vision of his distant cousin's "new nationalism" over regional and economic interests. "Mr. Roosevelt showed a splendid eagerness," Luce remarked in 1937, "not only to relieve distress but also to practice once again the art of government."[8]

Luce could not, however, cheer on the New Deal for long. Initially, some *Time* and *Fortune* entries applauded Roosevelt's initiatives, and Luce himself was enamored of the new president. "What a man! What a man!" he declared after an early meeting.[9] Yet after a year of mostly good words for his active presidency, Luce, if not his writers, began to treat the administration more critically. Although Roosevelt's cheery informality still provided good copy for *Time*'s President's Week section, other aspects of his leadership disquieted the top men of Time Inc. Luce and *Time* editor John Shaw Billings both found Roosevelt arrogant, even condescending. He seemed to experiment too much. Then, too, well-publicized squabbling over policies among cabinet members left Luce with the sense that Roosevelt could not lead his own troops, let alone the nation. Ironically, the president's overreliance on improvisation and his pitting factions against each other, reminded some Luce lieutenants of their editor-in-chief.[10]

New Deal taxes took their toll on Luce. In the 1920s, Secretary of the Treasury Andrew Mellon had repeatedly cut already low income tax rates. His Democratic successors raised them to Luce's fury. Unlike so many Yale classmates, Harry had earned his million. Now the sons of the well-to-do, Franklin Roosevelt and his finance minister, Henry Morgenthau, Jr., insisted on a share of Luce's wealth. He never reconciled himself to progressive taxation.

Roosevelt's more class-based politics clashed with the publisher's organic view of community, a vision much in keeping with his journalism of consensus. A profile of Pittsburgh Luce wrote for *Fortune* praised the Steel City for what he saw as the absence of class antagonisms;[11] for similar reasons, he hailed Mussolini's corporate state. Luce dreaded a nation of self-interested factions.

Roosevelt's unexpectedly overwhelming reelection in 1936 and events in the first half of 1937 only added to Luce's unease. Never in his lifetime had a presidential candidate so clearly rejected middle- and upper-class support and still won handily. Had Time Inc. been too neutral in 1936? Although not prepared to move his publications in the direction of the vehemently anti-New Deal dailies, he did begin to believe that his periodicals should take on the administration more forcefully. Early in 1937 Roosevelt appeared drunk with power. His attempt to pack the Supreme Court with pro-New Deal justices fed middle-class fantasies of an American dictatorship. That spring, the new labor movement's aggressive organizing campaign, which included sitdown strikes, posed a seemingly grave challenge, almost European in its radicalism, to traditional notions about property rights. All the while, some New Dealers persisted in offering a rhetoric ostensibly hostile to free enterprise.

Before a Cleveland audience in November 1937, Luce delivered a strong attack on the New Deal's antibusiness tilt. By then, mistaken fiscal policies had plunged the economy, commonly thought on the road to recovery, into a "Roosevelt recession." Luce believed the tag appropriate. The private sector should be flourishing, he maintained: "Whatever way you look at it, the smallness of our national production is a disgrace, a wicked disobedience of the ancient injunction to increase and multiply." To Luce, the New Deal had placed no faith in business, and "capitalism functions only under conditions of confidence," he declared. Roosevelt "has based his political popularity on the implication that Business is antisocial, unpatriotic, vulgar, and corruptive." Finally, the true "Liberal State" would award more respect to property rights than was an administration idly observing sit-down strikes.[12]

Luce's new defensiveness about capitalism caused a political reorientation at *Fortune*. In mid-1937, he composed several memoranda to the magazine's new publisher and editor. Members of the business community had been complaining to Harry about the seemingly antibusiness tone of some *Fortune* stories. Luce agreed; the periodical had been too objective, especially regarding business and labor. *Fortune*, he wrote, should "acknowledge a bias in favor of private enterprise."[13] Although "suggestions," Luce's observations appeared to have had an impact. The magazine lost some of its bite; the flattering profiles of New Dealers ended. *Fortune* also suffered the departure of two of its more prominent, left-leaning writers, Dwight Macdonald and Archibald MacLeish.

Although Macdonald and others began to associate Luce with the decade's right-wing publishers, Luce and his editors did not romp with the decade's political dinosaurs. He could not take seriously the passively procapitalist politicians like Coolidge a decade earlier or the reactionary Liberty League of the 1930s. In his Cleveland and subsequent addresses, Luce criticized business for its past abuses of power; his political favorites shared and defended his vision of a dynamic, expanding, and socially responsible capitalism. More and more explicitly, Luce and *Fortune* associated themselves with those within a predominantly Republican and eastern business elite seeking a middle ground between the New Deal and reaction. A lead *Fortune* editorial in March 1940 praised the Roosevelt administration for "an impressive array of social enactments." The New Deal accomplished social and regulatory reforms long overdue. The magazine, unlike virtually every other business periodical, hailed the administration's creation of Social Security and public power agencies: "These and dozens of other achievements constitute a magnificent social record, of which the American people and the New Dealers themselves can be justly proud."

The New Deal's shortcomings remained economic. "The New Deal has never succeeded in reducing unemployment substantially below 6,000,000 or about 12 percent of the employable population," *Fortune* observed. Even when recovery seemed assured, early in 1937, the percentage of those out of work was larger than for any other downturn in the previous forty years. Echoing the founder, *Fortune* blamed the administration. "The advocates of government-first" had failed to show faith in the private sector, even as entrepreneurs learned from their errors. "An entirely new spirit is in the air," *Fortune* announced. Enterprisers had become responsible players, some even "business statesmen." And this "new business leadership" deserved better from its government.[14]

Handling the Dictators

Perhaps because free enterprise ranked first among Luce's causes in the mid-1930s, he neglected others. Foreign affairs, a vital matter to him on leaving college, had not engaged him in the 1920s and early 1930s. Until about 1938, he seemed oblivious to the dangerous militarism in Germany and Italy. In his November 1937 talk, Luce referred to Mussolini—whose invasion of a hapless Ethiopia in 1935 had been widely criticized—as "the ablest manager a poor nation ever had."[15]

More insensitive was Laird Goldsborough, *Time*'s Foreign News editor. From the magazine's earliest days, Goldsborough had written virtually all of *Time*'s overseas entries. As one of *Time*'s first writers, Goldie enjoyed a unique autonomy; disgruntled coworkers referred to a standing memo from the editor-in-chief, "Don't touch a word of Goldie's copy."[16] That freedom created problems for *Time* in the 1930s. Goldsborough could not bring himself to abandon a post-Versailles reductionism toward European leaders. He continued to blur fundamental and increasingly obvious differences between the German and British political leadership. Mussolini's invasion of Ethiopia drew no condemnation; the magazine early that year, an office history later found, "showed no particular alarm over 'this thing called Nazi.' "[17]

Most journalists at first underestimated Hitler and strove to rationalize his behavior. In 1933 and 1934, Lippmann deplored the Nazis' persecution of the Jews yet maintained that even under Hitler, Germany could be regarded as civilized. The peace settlement of 1919 had been too harsh, the victors incapable of statesmanship. Like *Time*'s Goldsborough, the *Herald Tribune*'s sage found himself out of sympathy with any European power. "As long as Europe prepares for war," he wrote in May 1934, "America must prepare for neutrality." Popular periodicals like *Collier's* and the *Saturday Evening Post* shared Lippmann's calm. Repeatedly, excuses were offered for Hitler's conduct. Moral condemnation of National Socialism smacked of Wilsonian self-righteousness.[18]

Still, the isolationism of the fourth estate can be overstated. Even in the twenties, many small-town newspapers in the supposedly deeply isolationist Middle West had favored a more active foreign policy. This sentiment grew as the aggressors' territorial violations in Europe, Africa, and Asia continued unchecked. When in October 1937, following Japan's attack on China, Roosevelt vaguely suggested that America join in some sort of international "quarantine," the McCormick and Hearst papers assailed the president. Yet as *Time* noted, most dailies showered him with "more words of approval, some enthusiastic and some tempered, than have greeted any Roosevelt step in many a month."[19]

At *Time*, the handling of the European crisis formed part of a larger crisis over the editorial direction of the newsweekly in the late 1930s. Younger staff writers, many supporting the Left's Popular Front against fascism, detested Goldsborough. None found him more frustrating than Ralph Ingersoll. *Fortune* editor between 1931 and 1935 and Luce's chief aide between 1935 and 1936, Ingersoll had been named publisher of *Time* in 1937. Unlike Harry, Ingersoll embraced the decade's radical spirit. Although he refused to join the Communist party, he participated in party study groups and in characteristically long memoranda, he pleaded with Harry to turn the Luce press leftward. Quietly, Ingersoll tried to instill his own values into *Time*; having like-minded writers helped. Under Ingersoll, *Time* avoided condemning the controversial sitdown strikes while antiunion activities received harsh words. *Time* nevertheless at times remained within a Republican center: FDR's court-packing scheme was introduced in the most unflattering way; a May 1938 cover story on American Communist party head Earl Browder proved no tribute. But privately, party members on the staff bragged of their ability to lace entries with subtle propaganda (dubbed "agitprop"). Billings, until late 1936 *Time* editor, deeply resented the propagandizing. "The old *Time* is now gone forever," he wrote. "Ingersoll has revolutionized and sovietized things."[20]

For two years, Luce lacked the will, the time, and the interest to do anything about Ingersoll's managing of *Time*. *Fortune*'s point-of-view, already being redirected, mattered far more. Although *Time* may have been the firstborn, *Fortune* was the favorite child. His third sibling, *Life*, with a financially costly infancy, proved an enormous distraction. And like Roosevelt, Luce refrained from confrontations whenever possible.

A showdown did come early in 1939, when *Time* designated Hitler Man of the Year. The decision had not been meant as a tribute—Germany had just swallowed much of Czechoslovakia—only as a recognition of his newsworthiness. To Ingersoll's dismay, however, the cover an underling chose flattered the German dictator. At great cost, he ordered at the last minute a new, less appealing portrait. Harry resented both the expense and his aide's passion. Gangster Al Capone, Luce noted, had once graced a *Time* cover. Why the fuss over Berlin's equivalent? "Harry had a different idea of a journalist's functions," Ingersoll recalled. "He believed that a journalist should be amoral—with no responsibility except to be accurate and able to hold the attention of his audience. We drifted apart."[21]

Ingersoll left *Time* in April, taking some staff with him to start a liberal tabloid in New York, *PM*. Luce, who never had been able to bring himself to dismiss Ingersoll, wished him well. Others not sharing Ingersoll's politics and self-estimation celebrated his departure. "What a conceited egotist," Billings wrote in a rare use of an unnecessary word. "Ingersoll always wanted bias in all reporting." A year later, Billings noted, "Luce admitted that Mac Ingersoll was his one great mistake" in Time Inc. personnel. He said Ingersoll was "a good man 'to carry the message to Garcia' but nothing more."[22]

The Crisis of the West

One irony to Ingersoll's departure was that Harry was beginning to abandon his affected journalistic detachment. The editor-in-chief had already begun to hold his own study groups, inviting underlings to long lunches, asking Great Questions. What did Time Inc. stand for? Should his magazines explicitly take positions on the Great Issues of the Day? What were the Great Issues of the Day?

Two books Luce read in the late 1930s, José Ortega y Gasset's *Revolt of the Masses* (1930) and Peter Drucker's *End of Economic Man* (1939), much affected his thinking. Both authors were European liberals deeply disturbed by trends in Continental politics. Americans, ever optimistic, smiling like extras in one of the decade's movie musicals, only dimly realized the extent to which political and economic upheavals since 1914 had shaken the Old World. These crises fostered a mass enthusiasm for extremes that menaced the Lucean ideal of a democratic, capitalistic centrism.

Both Drucker and Ortega attributed the rise of fascism to larger,

111

extraterritorial historical forces. Ortega saw the modern economy's insistence on specialization of education and work fostering a dangerous political and historical illiteracy. The people had become Plato's dreaded mob, foregoing law and custom. This "hyperdemocracy," Ortega wrote, "crushes beneath it everything that is excellent, individual, qualified and select."[23]

Drucker's similarly gloomy assessment of Old World politics impressed Luce as well. Drucker attributed fascism's rise to a loss of faith in a rationally based political and economic order. The masses were less to blame than events. To Drucker, the Great War "showed the individual suddenly as an isolated, powerless atom in a world of irrational monsters" and the Great Depression "proved that irrational and incalculable forces also rule peacetime society." The mediocrity of Europe's postwar political leadership further undermined heretofore accepted norms of governing. Europeans began rejecting modernity itself, bringing about a "return of the demons." "The old orders have broken down, and no new order can be contrived from the old foundations," Drucker wrote. "In despair the masses turn to the magician who promises to make the impossible possible." The magician was the fascist leader, his victims the capitalist and the democrat.[24]

Modern society's potential rejection of tradition and susceptibility to anticapitalist, antidemocratic systems—themes in the works of both Drucker and Ortega—inspired Luce the publisher and participant. Ortega was too pessimistic, Luce told a 1937 audience. A socially responsible mass media could help to counteract the forces Ortega saw undermining liberal thought and institutions. His magazines must continue to remind Americans not only of their history but of the heritage of Western civilization. Thus *Life* and *Fortune* periodically offered generously illustrated history lessons. Luce himself in 1940 helped to found the Council for Democracy, a committee of liberal and moderate journalists and academicians, to promote democracy in American society. "Democracy in Europe was in the most dire peril," wrote one council member, "which meant that in time it might well be in dire peril in the United States."[25]

Drucker's American symbolism encouraged Luce the nationalist. However troubled Europe, Drucker contended, in America hope remained. Although capitalism appeared "doomed . . . certainly as far as Europe is concerned," free enterprise was worth saving. Capitalism "has succeeded beyond its wildest dreams," Drucker wrote. The deadening hand of statism simply had to be held in check, but only for a socially responsible system of free enterprise, one that promoted economic equality, rather than class conflict. "The only justification, the only basis for Economic Man," Drucker argued, "is the promise of the realization of freedom and equality." That promise might be fulfilled in the New World. America had been a model to Europe of capitalism's possibilities. The collapse of the American economy in the early 1930s shocked the Continent, and for many turned fascism into an irresistible temptation. Nevertheless, Drucker found, "the magic power of America as the land of equality still lingers."[26]

Luce's concern over the European crisis might have come regardless of the writings of Drucker and Ortega: the success of *Life*, some coworkers thought, drove him over the top. That is, before the unexpected success of his picture magazine, he had relatively few readers. *Life* forever changed him. By the late 1930s, only chewing gum manufacturer William Wrigley had his name printed on more pieces of paper. "Harry's third baby," wrote a friend, "was too much for him, the demon in the litter." Now, "with those thousands of trucks rolling every week just for him, he became a Big Fellow, virtually a principality." Luce, Thomas Matthews of *Time* recalled, "began to entertain the delusion common among press lords: that he could control and direct the enormous influence his magazines exerted on public taste."[27]

This theme of a publisher suddenly infatuated with power could be seen in a Lucean roman à clef, *The Death of Kings*, by Charles Wertenbaker of *Time*. The Luce character, Louis Baron, declares, "the news magazines, not the newspapers, were the future molders of the country's thought" and "the man who controls public opinion is the man of power in this country." Gathering his chief editors for dinner on the eve of World War II, Louis Baron promotes a new activism. They are the true leaders of America. "We're the kings of the present time," he concludes. "It was the early kings who led the people against the nobles. We're the kings because we wear the crown and wield the scepter of truth."[28]

Whether because of ego or intellect, Luce's mission by 1939 had taken on an international dimension. He had already started to find the once precious time to criticize the New Deal publicly as a threat to free enterprise. Drucker's work suggested that in Europe capitalism and freedom were even more imperiled. Roosevelt must be defeated at home, the dictators abroad, and overcome not by reaction, but by an enlightened enterprise supportive of democratic traditions.

Even before he read *End of Economic Man*, Luce began moving *Fortune* toward this vision. Beginning in December 1938, the magazine sponsored the *Fortune* Round Table. Leaders in business along with several economists, an engineer, a farmer, and a union representative, began meeting to fashion statements on the economy. The first, published in March 1939, noted the disappearance of free enterprise in Russia, Italy, and Germany and warned that it could happen here. In America, federal spending outpaced economic growth and had to be restrained. Subsequent reports echoed Luce's call for a restoration of confidence in business, and a more dynamic, growth-oriented yet socially responsible capitalism.[29]

Other Time Inc. divisions were a step ahead of the editor-in-chief concerning global matters, perhaps none more than "The March of Time" newsreel service. In January 1938, "The March of Time" released the sixteen-minute *Inside Nazi Germany*. To the dismay of theater owners, who loathed upsetting moviegoers, *Inside* invited controversy. Various Nazi horrors were reenacted, with anti-Hitler German-Americans playing those they had left behind. The newsreel described Hitler's advocacy of racial purification and its terrifying consequences for German Jews. Nor were Catholics spared; East Side New York City charwomen played persecuted nuns. Other victims, too, were the political foes of fascism. "Every known liberal today," the Voice intoned, "is either in hiding, in prison, or dead." Nor could Americans, however far from such excesses, rest easy. Producers cast an elderly Hoboken couple as Germans absorbing anti-American propaganda over state radio. Germany was rearming: indeed, Hitler now commanded "one of the great war machines in history," the Voice warned. "And the inevitable destiny of the great war machines of the past has been to destroy the peace of the world, its people, and the governments of their time." After previewing the film, a German diplomat screamed at producer Louis de Rochemont, "God-damn it. Germany's no longer a small country and you'll suffer for this!"[30]

Life, too, disturbed the peace. Germany's March 1938 annexation of Austria inspired a sixteen-page layout that disapprovingly described Hitler's rise to power. The magazine condemned the Nazis' persecution of Jews in Germany and Austria and forecast Hitler's plans for expansion on the Continent.[31] More forcefully, *Life* promoted defense expenditures. Hitler's insatiable appetite, intensified by France and Britain's gift of Czechoslovakia in September 1938, necessitated a build-up. Britain's appeasement suggested new demands on America: "Britain may no longer be able, if willing to try, to stop the march of the fascists." In a theme to be replayed over the next three years, *Life* questioned the British navy's capacity to protect the Americas. For over a hundred years, the British fleet, not the Monroe Doctrine, had frustrated European designs on the Western Hemisphere. The American navy had to be expanded. Airpower similarly rendered obsolete the natural defense of the Atlantic. New long-range bombers, *Life* (with others) forecast, could attack the easternmost United States. America must immediately develop an effective air raid defense network along the coast. The pathetic state of the peacetime army had to be corrected. Finally, American industry, beleaguered by nearly ten years of depression and government harassment, must be put on a war footing. Fear not, *Life* declared in 1939, for "there is still time to prepare."[32]

By late 1938, too, *Time*'s Foreign News section began to cast the dictators darkly. Guest editing *Time* in late November, Luce saw for himself Goldsborough's excessive detachment regarding fascism and removed him from the department. With Goldie gone, *Time* recognized that British prime minister Neville Chamberlain's September 1938 Munich pact with Hitler had only raised false hopes. Critics of Chamberlain's appeasement came in for praise. Hitler's escalating ill-treatment of Jews at home, and expansionist intentions abroad were condemned with an ever-growing consistency. When in March 1939 Germany seized the portion of Czechoslovakia that Chamberlain had not awarded Hitler earlier, *Time* remarked, "the treaty-breaking, lie-telling German dictator . . . threw away all pretence of being anything but a Conqueror."[33]

Such advocacy journalism did not in most instances originate directly with Luce. With the expansion of his empire, Luce monitored rather than managed his periodicals. He wrote memos and hosted luncheons. To keep himself abreast of staff and editorial changes at each magazine, he personally edited each publication for several weeks a year. Although he helped to assemble some antifascist layouts, most propagandizing appears to have been the work of individual editors and writers, few of whom needed prodding. Until the Nazi-Soviet pact of August 1939, Communists and fellow travelers at *Time* followed the party line in opposition to fascism; they prided themselves on their skill at infusing anti-Hitler commentary into the magazine. Others, outside the party circle, independently determined that they could no longer be disinterested journalists in the matter of the European crisis.

The Great Debate, 1940–1941

Should America actively oppose Germany or remain neutral? By early 1939, most American newspapers and periodicals appear to have abandoned the moral reductionism that had equated Germany, France, and England; Hitler's intentions and cruelties had become too apparent. Despite efforts of German government agents, virtually no one in the United States could be found prepared to support the Reich if another European war came. Most publications—even Robert R. McCormick's isolationist *Chicago Tribune*—believed with Time Inc. that America must rearm. Yet a "Great Debate" did emerge over the size of America's military build-up and whether Roosevelt was merely using the crisis as an excuse to extend his powers. Moreover, in the event of a German-British conflict, to what extent should America help Britain? Did a German victory pose a threat to America's security?[34]

At first, most could defer thinking about U.S. participation in another European war. Hostilities began with Germany's attack on Poland in September 1939, but before the Reich's spring 1940 western offensive, there was every reason to believe that the French army—western Europe's largest—and the British fleet—the greatest in the world—could check Hitler. Poland had fallen with shuddering completeness. Yet until April and May 1940, what *Time* dubbed "World War II," was more aptly called the "phony war."

Even during the "phony war" period, colleagues found Luce anxious to engage America in the conflict. After one meeting of senior staff members, one asked Billings, "When is Harry going to declare war on Germany?"[35] When in February the *New Republic*, championing pacifism, denied that war could eradicate European fascism, Luce accused the liberal journal of moral confusion. In memos to his editors, he insisted that they not mislead readers regarding the evils of Nazi Germany. "The responsibility of news-editors," he wrote in February, "is not to becloud the issues."[36]

A visit to the western front stirred Luce all the more. Harry had gone to join Clare, who had persuaded him to ignore his promise to the staff and allow her to do a story for *Life* on the war. Early in May, asleep at the American embassy in Brussels, the Luces were awakened by a maid: *"Les Allemands reviennent."* Germany was invading Belgium. This time, to much surprise, there was no stalemate along the western front. The Low Countries fell as the Germans rushed to the Channel, separating the British and French forces. The British Expeditionary Force found itself surrounded at the port of Dunkirk. In the event of the British army's capture, the Chancellor of the Exchequer secretly arranged to ship British gold and securities to North America. Shorn of its equipment, Britain's army escaped to England. France faced the German army alone.[37]

Luce returned to America more resolved than ever to engage America in the conflict. This might not involve direct military intervention, only aid to the Allies. But the nation had to reckon, finally, with the reality of Hitler. "The American way of life," he told a national radio audience in late May, "is bitterly opposed by mighty and ruthless nations." And "nothing will stop these mighty and ruthless nations—not money or cajolery or friendship—nothing but superior force." Of Luce's address, Billings observed, "Pretty good stuff—but [it] was war mongering."[38]

As earlier, however, others at Time Inc. shared Luce's new commitment. Since late 1938, de Rochemont and Roy Larsen of "The March of Time" had been planning another feature on the German menace. Two years in the making, *The Ramparts We Watched* (1940) offered a history of America's entry into World War I, while clearly warning audiences that they again faced conflict abroad. Producers intermixed historical footage with new sequences dramatizing the Great War's coming to a "typical" American town, New London, Connecticut. True to *Time*'s coloration, nearly all the Americans portrayed in *Ramparts* had a middle-class hue.

The director's point-of-view was unmistakable. This time the innocents faced a much more dangerous German leader. This time America had to rearm before the crisis hour. Otherwise, the fate of Poland, quickly conquered by German aggressors in September 1939, awaited the New World. *Ramparts* ended with footage de Rochemont had taken from a Nazi newsreel on Poland's fall. The film, in possession of British authorities, had been released to "The March of Time" only after assurances that de Rochemont intended to show the German invasion as unjustified and brutal. So terrifying was it that Pennsylvania's state film board banned *Ramparts*. Moviegoers, the board had determined, might be upset.[39]

Ramparts unsettled some critics for other reasons. Documentary filmmaker Pare Lorentz complained that the film, akin to "The March of Time" 's formula, offered only one, tightly organized interpretation of the Great War. Producers deliberately left out information that cast the correctness of America's participation in World War I into doubt. "The March of Time" 's directed synthesis, another complained, "is more dangerous than the regular newsreels, which so far have been for the most part straightforward presentations of events." *Ramparts* and other "March of Time" releases "are crying in almost evangelical tones: 'Turn Back! Forget what we have learned since the First World War. Feel, believe as we did then. America must be first!' "[40]

Luce's periodicals displayed a similarly unmistakable warmindedness. *Fortune* characteristically took the greatest pains and offered the most detail, describing America's military preparedness and economic stake in Asia and Europe.[41] By comparison, *Time* shared less information than opinion, criticizing Roosevelt's caution while hailing the British. Perhaps because of the dark moods of Foreign News writer Whittaker Chambers, *Time* exaggerated the damage German bombers did to English cities during the Battle of Britain.[42]

Life proved the most ardent organ of war. Although editors still favored placing leggy young actresses in shorts on the cover, inside the magazine acquired a new seriousness. One photographer recalled, "My stories were concerned less with skunk fur and more with America's potential to defend itself."[43] Issues reminded readers, many heretofore certain that Americans had always been a peaceful people, of the nation's long military heritage. Others described the fall of France, as news and as a warning. A caption to one photograph of American-built planes being sent to France read, "Like a great cross of hope a boxed American plane is loaded on a French ship. But the year is 1938 and France did not ask for enough."[44] In a special issue, "The Defense of America," *Life* again offered opinion as information. Modern warfare warranted abandoning national traditions. Tanks required trained soldiers, not militiamen, *Life* argued, and a peacetime draft.[45]

Like so much of Luce's journalism, *Life* presented a "knowing" vision of events and issues, as news, not opinion. There were no doubts, no arguments. The dangers were real and could not be discounted. Hitler, *Life* reported in July 1940, "must indubitably anticipate that when America has spent billions on armaments it will some day choose to use its arms, probably against him, rather than suffer economic collapse.

For him, it is obviously the part of wisdom to strike at America before it has organized its terrible potential full strength."[46]

To Luce, more than arms were necessary to defend America: the country had to be united. The ethnic divisions that had followed the Great War, the class antagonisms of the 1930s, had to end. Both he and Clare had concluded that France had fallen and England lay in peril in part because of their failure to overcome their prewar factionalism. America, in contrast, still had time to come together, collectively practicing a voluntary totalitarianism needed to match the Nazis' efficiency and zeal.

By the same token, Luce had come to believe that President Roosevelt could be doing much more to prepare the people for another world war. In a foreword to a book by John F. Kennedy, the young son of U.S. Ambassador to Great Britain Joseph Kennedy, Luce wrote, "America will never be ready for any war, not in one year, nor in two nor in twenty—never until she makes up her mind there is going to be a war." Roosevelt, unlike Luce, appeared less willing to conclude for the public. The president, Luce wrote, "can't really believe we are ever going to fight."[47] At a time when he should have been leading public opinion, Luce believed, the president followed it. (Roosevelt did, in fact, study the new Gallup and *Fortune* polls.) Years later, Luce remained critical of Roosevelt's public caution about American intervention. Roosevelt, Luce remembered, "was overcautious, political."[48]

Finally, Luce criticized Roosevelt's defense plans as not only inadequate, but one more indication of the administration's poor ties to the world of enterprise. Requests for tanks and planes remained too modest, Luce wrote, and given the urgency of rearmament, government-business relations too cool. With other prowar Republican voices, notably the *New York Herald Tribune*, Luce called for a partnership between government and industry, telling one radio audience, "Today we need the services of the ablest industrialists in America for the most efficient arming of America."[49]

Thus Luce expressed his position in the Great Debate. The people, led by Roosevelt or a new president (1940 was an election year), had to find their purpose. Harry, in a sense, had already decided for them. America must face the dictators. He knew what America must do (rearm) and how to achieve that goal (improve government-business ties). And Luce was not to play the passive observer. Rearming America and the Allies had become vital, life-and-death causes to him.

Most Time Inc. writers and editors had little difficulty infusing his views into their work. Most shared his opinion on the conflict; few isolationists worked at Time Inc. Luce's advocacy did upset the professionalism of Billings, *Life*'s editor and one of the few former newspapermen at Time Inc. Luce's "mission," however well considered, did not seem true to the norms of objectivity to which newspapers adhered. Most of the time, however, Billings kept quiet. He was outflanked. "The March of Time," in a sense, had already broken diplomatic relations with Germany. Others followed. *Time* dropped any lingering jadedness toward European politics and was banned in Italy.[50] *Life* labored to shake its vast readership out of complacency. *Fortune* endeavored to prepare the new managers for their greatest challenge.

Luce did not personally order or kill stories. He could not have had he tried. By 1940, he published too many periodicals of too many pages for one man, however dedicated, to oversee; things slipped by. Then, too, he was still willing to be talked out of positions. Although *Life* began running his opinion pieces, on at least one occasion Larsen and Billings dissuaded him from publishing an especially prowar essay he had written upon his return from Europe. " 'Ok,' said Luce," Billings wrote, "sweet and humble. What a man! Most publishers would hand their editors a piece and order it printed. But not Luce, thank God."[51]

Luce could become involved outside of journalism. Soon after his return from the Continent, Luce joined an informal prowar caucus, the Century Group. Anglophilia, an often inherited malady of the East's upper strata, inspired some to participate. Many simply had the same nightmares. With the defeat of France imminent, Hitler was expected to take possession of French colonies in Africa and the Western Hemisphere. Meanwhile, German agents were trying to arrange pro-Nazi coup d'états in Latin America. Finally, lacking sufficient American aid, Britain was thought likely to surrender; with her collapse, the British navy would fall into German hands, either directly or because a pro-German government assumed power. Not only would America lose her valuable trade with Latin America and Europe, a point Lippmann stressed, but the nation's very security would be in jeopardy.[52] *Life*, among other publications, encouraged a panic by publishing various "plans" for the invasion of America. That Hitler had none was not noted. "Our people are justly alarmed for our own safety," Herbert Hoover observed. "And some of them are more panicky than the people in Paris and London."[53]

Luce's participation in the Century Group suggested his admission into the Eastern Establishment. The group consisted of old money, a predominantly Anglo-Saxon, Protestant, Ivy-League college-educated faction of northeasterners, and took its very name from an exclusive New York City club. That they welcomed the son of a lower middle-class China missionary was a signal honor. That he was arguably the nation's most powerful mass communicator helped.

Luce represented the Century Group in meetings with the secretaries of war and state and the president. The publisher urged Roosevelt to give Britain old destroyers, a donation many had been pressing on the administration. As earlier, the president could have been more respectful. "Luce came in and told us about his visit with Roosevelt," Billings wrote. "Roosevelt talked to Luce as if he were a sub-freshman. Also—Roosevelt did all the talking—and Luce couldn't get a word in edgewise."[54]

Within the group, Luce found himself a Roosevelt-like moderating influence. The publisher dissuaded members from urging an American declaration of war on Germany. It would be folly to lead a divided America into conflict, Luce cautioned. In a like spirit, he tempered the group's Anglophilic tendencies by insisting that aid to Britain have strings attached. Ever the realist, Luce noted that Britain might well lose and be governed by a collaborationist or pro-Nazi government. That new regime need not have American weaponry.[55]

The spectre of Hitler drove many within the fourth estate to join the Century Group and other prowar lobbies. In addition to Luce, eight editors, columnists, and a radio commentator belonged to the group. Others, though not members, eagerly used materials supplied by its busy press liaison office. In late May 1940, William Allen White founded another pro-British association, the Committee to Defend America by Aiding the Allies. White, at seventy-two, symbolized all that could be admired about small-town, middle-class America. He was, in other words, perfectly cast for the prowar, eastern elite. And *Time*, among other group publications, rewarded White for his statesmanship, later characteristically confusing its sentiments with the nation's: "Americans wished the U.S. had more editors like him."[56] Lippmann, too, joined the war hawks of the fourth estate. White's opposite in many ways, the New York City–born and bred Lippmann had tried to lead journalism into the new century. To Lippmann, White's small-town style could not keep pace with the complexities of modern America. Yet Germany's victories caused Lippmann, like White, to drop any pretensions to objectivity. He secretly helped to write a radio speech General John J. Pershing, commander of American forces in World War I, delivered on behalf of the destroyer deal.[57]

Although the antiwar or isolationist elements included many prominent newspaper publishers, none commanded the new and popular mass media of the interwar years. Radio increasingly presented war news and opinion favorable to the Allies and the national defense. Radio news "experts" were especially interventionist. CBS's commentators in particular, wrote one historian, "came to believe in one course of action so fervently that they lost the capacity for objectivity." Roosevelt's increasing tilt toward the Allies went unscrutinized. The commentators "ceased offering even constructive criticism of administration foreign policy. . . . Stopping Hitler had become, they felt, a sacred obligation of the American people."[58]

The Second Hero

Amid the debate over intervention, Luce in June combined with other prominent pro-British, Republican publishers in seeking to nominate a GOP presidential candidate sympathetic to their view of the war. Joining him were the Cowles brothers, rival photojournalists and publishers of the largest newspapers in Iowa and Minnesota, and the Reids of the *New York Herald Tribune*, the nation's most prestigious GOP daily.

They had a prospective nominee. Wendell L. Willkie as president of a southern utility had fought the Tennessee Valley Authority without resorting to the reactionary rhetoric of some New Deal critics; Willkie had, in fact, as late as 1939 been a Democrat. An Indiana native, Willkie overflowed with a folksiness that not only disarmed publishers and their minions but made him appear, compared to other possible Republican nominees, dynamic and personable. He even reminded Luce of his boyhood hero. *Time* declared, "For the first time since Teddy Roosevelt, the Republicans had a man they could yell for and mean it."[59] Willkie possessed another advantage. Of any Republican contender, he was the most pro-British. The two front-runners, New York county district attorney Thomas E. Dewey and U.S. senator Robert A. Taft of Ohio, had each been screened by prowar groups; neither would begin to match Willkie's support for aid to Britain. And being pro-British took on added importance in late June, when France surrendered to Germany.

Yet Willkie had no substantial constituency early in 1940. He had never held elective office. Only those few following the TVA's legal battles would have recognized his name. When in late April the Gallup survey first listed Willkie among prospective nominees, 3 percent favored him.[60]

Out of thin air, a Willkie movement grew. *Fortune* editor Russell Davenport, having met Willkie at a *Fortune* Round Table gathering earlier, introduced him to Luce and the Cowles brothers and then helped the attorney draft a declaration of principles, which *Fortune* ran in April. Davenport then quit *Fortune* to assist in managing a Willkie-for-president campaign. Together with others skilled in mass publicity, Davenport cultivated an image for Willkie. The Willkie public relations machinery, wrote one political scientist, "placed before the public not a utilities-identified tycoon or the Akron corporation counsel, but instead a fascinating picture of a homespun, hard-working Indiana smalltown boy; a carelessly dressed, friendly, Horatio Alger type, opposed in a mighty crusade to the Country Squire in the White House."[61]

The Willkie forces were helped as well by Luce, the Cowleses, and the Reids. The *Herald Tribune* ran a three-column, front-page editorial hailing Willkie for president. *Time* and *Life* found Willkie's political forays charming. *Life* on 13 May, a Willkie biographer noted, "published eleven pages of Willkie puffery" as news, complete with the observation "In the opinion of most of the nation's political pundits, Wendell Lewis Willkie is by far the ablest man the Republicans could nominate for President at Philadelphia next month."[62]

Reporters participated in the Willkie phenomenon. Whereas Taft and Dewey kept their distances, Willkie made himself available at virtually any hour of the day or night. He was the only GOP contender who consented to be interviewed while taking a bath. Colorful and frank, he made good copy. As a consequence, in the two months before the national convention Willkie snared more stories in more publications than the two front-runners.[63] By late June, *Time* reported, seven of the country's most prominent columnists, including Lippmann and Dorothy Thompson, had come out for Willkie. The delegates, *Time* observed, "could no longer read the newspapers with any enjoyment for all the important columnists were daily comparing the nomination of anyone but Willkie to the Fall of France."[64]

The columnists and new magazines either mistakenly or deliberately assumed that once they had decided an issue or on a candidate, the country agreed with their opinion. Most Americans, however, did not read or surrender their citizenship to *Time* and Walter Lippmann. Their readers were few, relatively well-to-do and educated. When one columnist suggested to Alice Roosevelt Longworth, a Taft delegate, that Willkie's support came from the "grass roots," she replied with a greater accuracy, "from the grass roots of ten thousand country clubs."[65] But *Time* led in proclaiming the Indiana attorney the people's candidate. Indeed, in late June, Gallup found, Willkie led Dewey and Taft among Republican voters. Not reported was the extent to which these voters were more representative of *Time*'s subscription list than of the nation—younger, wealthier, better educated—or that some Willkie operatives rivaled Tammany Hall in their rascality. Convention delegates received fake telegrams of support for Willkie; a few with mortgages discovered that their bankers favored Willkie and expected an added interest payment during the balloting. The galleries filled with loud young people, some bearing forged passes, all screaming, "We Want Willkie!" Yet Luce's magazines along with the rest of the prowar Republican press failed to reveal such contrivances. Europe must be saved. "A vote for Taft was a vote for the Republican Party," *Time* reported. "A vote for Willkie was a vote for the best man the party had to lead the country in a crisis."[66] Aided by such thinly disguised advocacy, the Hoosier won the nomination on the sixth ballot. Editing *Time* that week, Luce called in Billings to give his interpretation of the conclave; "His theme: the people won over the professional politicians," Billings wrote. That thesis could be seen without qualification in Luce's periodicals. "The people had won," *Time* declared. Privately, Taft complained of losing to a propaganda campaign, "engineered from Wall Street."[67]

The coverage of the Democrats' national meeting in July further conveyed the new, purposeful prejudices of Time Inc. Having ignored the Willkie managers' machinations, *Time* and *Life* exaggerated those of the president's supporters. Roosevelt insisted that he be "drafted" to run for a third term. Party officials went along, engineering a "draft," which *Life* judged to be "one of the shoddiest and most hypocritical spectacles in history."[68] Nevertheless, Roosevelt, unlike Willkie, could rightly claim the support of most members of his party, not just those who drove wood-paneled station wagons and took the *Herald Tribune*.

In the fall, Luce and his peers demonstrated that they had an influence, but over the middle class who took their publications, not the nation. Paul Lazarsfeld's study of public opinion formation in an Ohio county during the 1940 campaign found few voters affected by periodicals. Most voters relied on radio and newspapers. Between 15 and 25 percent of the voters in Lazarsfeld's Erie County, Ohio, survey read magazine articles relating to the election, and *Life* and *Time* were found no more significant than *Farmer's Journal*. Moreover, consumers of magazines tended to use them as elaborations of positions already taken. The readers of periodicals did serve as opinion leaders, likely to be among the more respected, educated, and well-to-do figures in a community.[69] Yet their influence appeared largely limited to their socio-economic class, those predisposed to the GOP. The New Deal's large working-class base effectively robbed town elites of what political leverage they might have commanded a decade earlier, when a laborer might at least hear out his or her employer. In cities like Toledo, a few years earlier the scene of bitter labor-management strife, Willkie met with outright hostility from working people. Elsewhere, laborers tossed telephone books, ashtrays, potatoes, cantaloupes, eggs, oranges, and tomatoes at the GOP nominee. *Time* acknowledged, "He had more assorted sizes and kinds of vegetables thrown at him than anyone since the old Mississippi showboat days."[70]

Willkie also saw his honeymoon with the fourth estate end. Few journalists could ignore his bungling in the fall campaign. Davenport, who had not been well organized as *Fortune* editor, proved an inept campaign director. He was unequal to the task of coordinating the simplest tasks associated with a presidential bid or of holding together the fragile alliance of Willkie volunteers and party professionals. "Seldom has there been more chaos in a presidential campaign," Raymond Clapper wrote, speculating that a Willkie administration "would be almost paralyzed." Lippmann declared himself neutral; Thompson switched to Roosevelt. Even *Time*, to Luce's dismay, reported the foibles of "Amateur Willkie."[71]

Willkie's mistake-ridden "crusade," as he grandiloquently dubbed his effort, revealed the hazards of the new media's role in the political culture. They alone could not make colorful novices political leaders. A candidate's capacity to provide good copy should not have so affected the judgments of reporters and publishers alike. *Time* itself wondered if Willkie were not, after all, a "super-hawker who had sold the Republican convention a bill of goods."[72]

Luce would not give up. Late in September Luce joined the campaign train and wrote a major Willkie address. In the Luce-drafted speech delivered in San Francisco, Willkie dedicated himself and his party "to fight the Battle of America." While granting that "the New

Deal has achieved a number of reforms that were badly needed," Willkie attacked the president for failing to bring about a full recovery. Furthermore, Willkie charged that Roosevelt's initially cautious foreign
policy had contributed to the European crisis. "The administration
must bear a direct share of the responsibility for the present war," Willkie declared. Nor had Roosevelt been able to arouse the people from a
"national insomnia" of isolationism that "has for the most part been
close to the level of 1920." The nation had to be awakened, its domestic production and aid to Britain increased.[73]

However genuine their plea for rearming America and Britain, the
Luce-Willkie assessment of Roosevelt could only be viewed as disingen-
uous. Although he had probably, as Luce surmised, been too respecting
of isolationist opinion, it is by no means clear that any American
leader, however possessed of Luce's self-assurance, could have talked his
people out of their deep disillusionment with the active foreign policy
that accompanied American participation in World War I. Then, too,
the Willkie-Luce speech ignored the role of the candidate's newly
adopted party in the widespread xenophobia. The major opponents of
Roosevelt's halting efforts at national rearmament had included prominent congressional Republicans.

More fundamentally, Luce, like many business managers, never
accepted the restraints on American political leadership. As a publisher, he had to deal with a limited number of groups—advertisers, reporters, editors. Most of the time, he could convert them to his causes.
He could return from Europe in May 1940 shaken by the might of the
German military and find attentive listeners. Underlings might agree,
say nothing, or debate—as long as after a decent interval, they too,
lapsed into silence or took up his position.

Roosevelt, however, had to reckon with far more constituents. He
had to respond to the call of the new British prime minister, Winston
Churchill, that after France fell in June, America declare war on Germany. The president had to cajole the Joint Chiefs of Staff, concerned
over America's rearmament, into agreeing to his requests for sending
military supplies to England. Congressional leaders, whose support was
vital for the revision of neutrality laws, the creation of a peacetime
draft, and augmented defense appropriations, remained fixed on the
path of isolation. Finally, unlike Luce, Roosevelt had to lead all Americans, not the younger middle-class subscribers to Time Inc. publications. Polls repeatedly showed little support for a declaration of war;
most Americans wanted Britain to win, but not if such a victory cost

American lives. The president sought no repetition of the disunity that accompanied America's first European crusade. The people had to be led with caution and guile.

Luce could not see Roosevelt's predicament. The publisher never realized—his unhappiness with presidents, Republican and Democratic, was to continue—that successful chief executives could only lead their people so far. Stepping too much ahead risked a Wilsonian self-destruction.

In October and November, Roosevelt further frustrated Luce. Willkie momentarily gained ground after accusing the president of directing America toward war. But Roosevelt arrested Willkie's belated advance by assuring voters in a Boston speech that American troops would not see action while he remained in office. That pledge infuriated Luce. Ever the "realist," he regarded American participation as probable: Roosevelt was deluding the people, if not himself. Yet it worked. With 55 percent of the vote, Roosevelt easily defeated Willkie and won a third term.

Minister of Information

For Luce, a precedent had been set in 1940. For the first time, he had involved himself and to a lesser degree his publications directly in politics. The success of his periodicals, especially *Life*, may have fostered an exaggerated sense of self-importance. More likely, the stability of Time Inc. gave Luce the time to consider the secular world again. And worry about the West. The failure of the domestic economy to recover fully from the depression and the plight of the Allied cause in Europe had driven Luce into party politics. Although his periodicals had usually conveyed a rightist centrism, only in 1940 had they settled on a leader for that great middle. Until then, the heads of both parties had been alternately praised and lampooned, so as to preserve Time Inc.'s claims to omniscience, to "facts" rather than causes.

Luce denied that his magazines had abandoned their affected objectivity. None of his magazines formally endorsed the Republican standard bearer. "*Time* never was and is not now a Willkie 'backer,' " he told the *New York Times*.[74] In his own election-eve editorial, Luce said only that, given the importance of the contest, he would not "knowingly sit down to a meal" with someone who refused to cast a ballot for one of the candidates.[75]

Still, it was less a matter of Luce becoming a partisan than finding a purpose, one that he possessed to the end of his life. He had determined to assume a public role. America had a new and vital part to play in the world. If Roosevelt refused to articulate that American mission, Luce and his magazines were prepared to do so. At a cost. "He's too deeply involved in national policy to be a good journalist," Billings complained of Harry in June 1940.[76] That was not a criticism Billings had made four or eight years earlier. Yet it was to be raised of Luce for the rest of his life.

HRL in 1937; about to go public.
Courtesy of Cleveland Press *Collection,* Cleveland State University Library.

Holding copies of *Life*, Harry smiles, late 1930s.
Courtesy of Cleveland Press Collection, Cleveland State University Library.

Running for the House, Clare Boothe Luce with her husband, November 1942.
Courtesy of Cleveland Press *Collection, Cleveland State University Library.*

General Dwight D. Eisenhower and Representative Luce, December 1944.
Courtesy of the U.S. Army Signal Corps.

Harry in December 1946. New writers were finding Harry intimidating. Among the staff, there was less of the give and take of the 1930s. *Courtesy of* Cleveland Press *Collection,* Cleveland State University Library.

HRL, January 1947.
Courtesy of Cleveland Press Collection, Cleveland State University Library.

The Ambassadors. At a performance of the Cleveland Orchestra in the mid-1950s, Italian Ambassador to the United States Manlio Brosio, Clare Luce, HRL, and philanthropist Kenyon C. Bolton.
Courtesy of Cleveland Press Collection, Cleveland State University Library.

Harry with President Johnson, September 1965.
Courtesy of the White House.

Harry in January 1964.
Courtesy of Cleveland Press Collection, Cleveland State University Library.

8

THE AMERICAN CENTURY
1941–1950

Luce in 1940 had been committed to intervention. With others in the business and journalistic elite, Harry had concluded that the United States must aid Britain in the world war. Early in 1941, he began to separate himself from some war hawks by advocating an expansive, nationalistic foreign policy. America had become the great power, Luce contended, and must assert the decisive role in the postwar world. Many accused Luce of jingoism, and an initial imprecision, combined with some rhetorical flourishes, invited such attacks. Yet as America entered the war in December 1941, Luce persisted. He devoted most of his energies to the plotting of an American-led postwar economic and diplomatic order. In the postwar years, Luce labored to define his American globalism. He resisted any return to isolationism while warning of a new threat to an American world system, the Soviet Union.

Although by the late 1940s America's political and economic leadership, at times modestly, at times with zest, moved closer to his conception, Luce in most instances served as a publicist rather than an initiator. Those in government, though usually respectful of Luce's readership, normally set the national foreign policy agendas. Luce's magazines were left to report them. In his own formulations, he tended as before to borrow from others.

"The American Century"

In 1941, Roosevelt's still-halting leadership animated Luce. Roosevelt, Luce opined, possessed an excess of caution. An overattention to isolationism kept the administration from stating clearly America's position in the war or goals once the nation found itself, after all, in battle with dictators. Instead, the president's approach early in 1941 consisted of little more than broad references to America as "the arsenal of democracy" and a specific pledge that he would not seek a declaration of war on Germany. "Our national policy is not directed toward war," Roosevelt told a national radio audience in December 1940. "Its sole purpose is to keep war away from our country and our people."[1]

To Luce, however much as Americans might want to defer participation in another world war, they could not base their foreign policy on the avoidance of pain. In several addresses and a February 1941 editorial in *Life*, Luce argued that Americans had to reconcile themselves to the burdens that went with being the most powerful country in the world. "The fundamental trouble with America," he wrote, "has been, and is, that whereas their nation became in the twentieth century the most powerful and most vital nation in the world, nevertheless Americans were unable to accommodate themselves spiritually and practically to that fact." That self-delusion had to cease. Americans could no longer ignore the "one fundamental issue which faces America as it faces no other nation," an issue "peculiar to America and peculiar to America in the twentieth century—now." The twentieth century had become the American Century. Americans had to "accept wholeheartedly our duty and our opportunity as the most powerful and vital nation in the world and in consequence to exert upon the world the full import of our influence, for such purposes as we see fit and by such means as we see fit."

"The American Century" was, in part, a product of the moment. Luce argued with both sides debating America's foreign policy early in 1941. He took issue with those fellow interventionists who emphasized an Anglo-American postwar order, even a political union of the United States and the British Commonwealth. In any arrangement with Great Britain after the war, Luce insisted, America would be the senior partner. America's eclipse of Britain a generation earlier as the world's foremost economic power made a formal political association rank sentimentalism. That same theme of America's moment informed his argument against the isolationists. The United States was no longer a small state, for whom neutrality was not only possible but at times de-sirable. The success of the American economic and political experi-ment left the nation with responsibilities it could no longer shirk.

Much of the essay reflected traditional justifications for American expansionism. At times, Luce appeared to be reviving the nineteenth-century argument of a "Manifest Destiny," that America was duty-bound to share with the world her exceptional political institutions and liberties. There were references to the "open door" of trade, of the need for a developed American economy to secure new markets. Asia, he wrote, could "be worth to us four, five, ten billions of dollars a year."

The bulk of the editorial constituted an admonition. Only near the end did Luce begin to suggest what America's postwar duties might be, and even there he was, like Roosevelt, vague. Luce did not call for a large peacetime army and navy—or even a declaration of war against the Axis powers. Instead, he advocated a secularization of the mission-ary experience, the export of American expertise to the less developed world, and alluded broadly to "America as the principal guarantor of the freedom of the seas, the vision of America as the dynamic leader of world trade."

The nation's role would not be boundless, Luce admitted. "Em-phatically our only alternative to isolationism is not to undertake to po-lice the whole world nor to impose democratic institutions on all mankind including the Dalai Lama and the good shepherds of Tibet. America cannot be responsible for the good behavior of the entire world." The world after the war would still include tyrannies; warfare itself would not be eliminated by America or a "parliament of men." More often, however, Luce offered an expansive assessment of Amer-ica's postwar role. Although freedom would not reign everywhere, Luce expected it to flourish throughout most of the world. "Tyrannies may require a large amount of living space," he wrote. "But freedom requires and will require far greater living space than Tyranny."

On one level, "The American Century" was a deeply personal ex-pression. Its nationalism could be traced to Luce's father and the pride his son took in the American missionary experience; Americans could be the "Good Samaritans of the World." Luce's own nationalism, nur-tured by his parents, had found expression in his senior class oration at Yale in 1920, when Luce had proclaimed America's premiere standing in the world. Then like a wayward Christian, Luce had turned away from world affairs to assemble his communication empire. In the late 1930s, the nationalism of his boyhood returned, and the sense of a calling awakened. Thus in "The American Century" Luce and America are one, each with the "blood of purpose and enterprise and high resolve."[2]

"The American Century" had another source of inspiration. A year and a half earlier, *Life* had carried an essay by Walter Lippmann, "The American Destiny," that included arguments Luce subsequently offered. Indeed, Luce appears to have borrowed from the first two paragraphs of Lippmann's essay. "The American people are profoundly troubled," Lippmann wrote. "They are oppressed by doubt." Yet "the American spirit is troubled not by the dangers, and not by the difficulties of the age, but by indecision." Luce began his editorial, "We Americans are unhappy. We are not happy about ourselves in relation to America. We are nervous—or gloomy—or apathetic." To Lippmann, this mood stemmed from the nation's "refusal to accept the large responsibilities" that accompanied "the American Destiny." "In the lifetime of the generation to which we belong," he wrote, "there has occurred one of the greatest events in the history of mankind. The controlling power in western civilization has crossed the Atlantic," he argued. "What Rome was to the ancient world, what Great Britain has been to the modern world, America is to the world of tomorrow." Americans "have the opportunity, the power, and the responsibilities of a very great nation at the center of a civilized world."[3]

The Luce-Lippmann thesis of historical inevitability had its defenders. Syndicated columnist Dorothy Thompson, the *New York Herald Tribune*'s other oracle, quoted liberally and approvingly from "The American Century." "To Americanize enough of the *world* so that we shall have a climate favorable to our growth is indeed a call to destiny," she wrote, one that Americans should heed. "If we had been doing our part in the world this war would not have happened. Now we must do it or take a back seat in history. This will either be an American century or it will be the beginning of the decline and fall of the American Dream."[4]

Others were less enthusiastic. Radio commentator Quincy Howe praised Luce as "a great editor" and agreed with his assertion that America had in fact become the world's greatest power. Nonetheless, the prospect of something as encompassing as an American Century unsettled Howe. "I do not know that I welcome all the implications of our national future as enthusiastically as Mr. Luce." Perhaps he possessed too great an ambition for his country, akin to Britain's imperialists at the end of the nineteenth century. "Mr. Luce is a prose Kipling," Howe wrote, "a Cecil Rhodes of journalism." Former president Hoover warned, "The stern voice of experience says that America cannot impose its freedoms and ideals upon the twenty-six races of Europe or the world."[5]

Covering War

Although the debate over the American Century continued, the most pressing task for Luce's periodicals remained covering the war itself. The onset of hostilities in September 1939 had helped to push his magazines into more reporting. Long composed from a pile of clippings, *Time* with *Life* now had correspondents actually witnessing rather than summarizing history.

With the war *Life* reporters and photographers embarked on worldwide odysseys. No Luce employees took more risks. In April 1941, two *Life* staff members survived a German U-boat sinking. Margaret Bourke-White found herself the only American photographer in the Soviet Union as Hitler launched his invasion of Russia in June. Ignoring a state ban on photographing and a German air raid on Moscow, Bourke-White filled her hotel bathtub with developing trays and with the help of the American embassy staff smuggled to New York the first visual evidence of Russia at war.[6]

Life proved especially effective describing a global conflagration. The generous displays of photographs, some searing in their capture of death and destruction, made World War II for the *Life* reader the first "living room war." Yet the camera eye alone did not adequately indicate the periodical's informational advantages. *Life* also ran analyses of the conflict, maps, and illustrations. *Life*, Lippmann wrote to a member of the magazine's staff, has "given the most useful and original treatment to the war news of any periodical. Your strategical maps and your articles about tactics have been immensely clarifying to me and, I imagine, to many others who had found these things difficult to visualize through their own imaginations."[7]

Modern war, both *Life* and *Time* insisted, all but required their all-knowing journalism. If the Great Depression and the federal government's response had made keeping abreast of the world a challenge, the Second World War added to the news consumer's burdens. Daily newspapers gave ample coverage to the nation's rush to rearm. "Day after day, our newspapers are bringing us news of plans completed at Washington in weeks, whose details in normal times would have consumed years," *Time* noted. "They are covering stories so big, developments so rapid, that even the early days of the New Deal seem quiet in retrospect." So much going on necessitated the new synthesis. "Here, in one place, the anxious citizen will find reports from every field."[8] *Life* promoted itself no less immodestly: "For *Life*'s new-age journalism makes information about *all* the forces that move and shape our lives easy to understand and absorb—and infinitely exciting. In doing this, *Life* helps great masses of people come to grips with the world as it really is—helps them make more intelligent decisions."[9]

Debating the Future

In February 1942, two months after America entered the war, Luce used *Life* to elaborate his vision of America as the world's salvation. It owed much to his organic view of the Great Society. Europe had fallen prey to Hitler because corrupt and ineffective regimes had sanctioned class and interest-based politics. America "alone among the nations of the earth was founded on ideas and ideals which transcend class and caste and racial and occupational differences," he wrote. And the "American experience is the key to the future." With others, Luce foresaw a new universalism after the war, "a family of nations." But to him, "that family will require an elder brother, strong, brave and, above all, generous. America must be the elder brother of the nations in the brotherhood of man."[10]

Again, a debate ensued. Both the left and right expressed reservations over Luce's conception of America as "the eldest sibling." To Hoover and other old isolationists, it would be inappropriate if not impossible for America to play this role. To Vice-President Henry A. Wallace and other liberal Democrats, the new universalism required no leader.

"Some have spoken of the 'American Century,'" Wallace declared in May. "I say that the century on which we are entering—the century which will come out of this war—can and must be the century of the common man." America might "suggest the freedoms and duties by which the common man must live" and should help to raise the living standards of the world. But "no nation will have the God-given right to exploit other nations." There "must be neither military nor economic imperialism."[11]

Wallace privately sought to downplay his differences with Luce, whom, with Clare, he had become friendly, talking theology and economics. "I do not happen to remember anything that you have written descriptive of 'The American Century' of which I disapprove," he wrote Luce a week after his "Common Man" speech. The vice-president's alternative had been meant for overseas consumption. The phrase, "American Century," he opined, "did rub citizens of a number of our sister United Nations the wrong way."[12]

Isolationists, however, echoed Wallace's public objections. Luce and his allies, Hoover asserted, "want a Pax Americana," though he told a friend he regarded the American Century concept as too confused "to worry about." A more irate Senator Robert A. Taft of Ohio devoted an entire speech to a critique of Luce's proposal. America could not, Taft contended, impose her political values on the world; even an attempt would require a peacetime military establishment that he and other economy-minded Republicans of the old guard could not tolerate. Then, too, Taft noted that America's political and economic values had not helped those parts of the world like Puerto Rico where the United States had been sovereign. The egoism of an American Century upset the Ohioan. "It is based on the theory that we know better what is good for the world than the world itself. It assumes that we are always right and anyone who disagrees with us is wrong," Taft said. "Certainly however benevolent we might be, other people simply do not like to be dominated."[13]

To the criticisms of Taft and others, Luce responded defensively. Detractors had not read his editorials with sufficient care, he insisted. "You can't extract imperialism from the American Century," he told a reporter later.[14] Furthermore, Luce charged his critics with failing to reckon with America's economic and military advantages after victory over the Axis. Soon after Taft's attack Luce remarked, "While Americans realize that they have never entered into any compact with each other or with their forebears to provide well-being for all mankind, they may nevertheless contribute to the welfare of mankind in greater measure than any other nation in history." Luce also rejected as too ambitious Wallace's postwar vision, agreeing with Taft that America could not be everything to every country. "Not every mission is appropriate to the political state," Luce said. "To claim for it an unlimited mission to do good is to invite infinite confusion, ugly strife and ultimately, disaster."[15] Clare simply dismissed one of Wallace's "common man" proposals—that all nations share air routes—as "globaloney."

His critics notwithstanding, Luce resolved to plan for the postwar world, a task he and others believed Roosevelt was neglecting. In assuming this public role, Luce appeared more dedicated than ever to being more than a mass communicator. Unlike some of his peers he had the time to do so: he had delegated most editorial authority to individual editors and virtually all managerial responsibility to Roy Larsen. Perhaps a personal crisis spurred him on. Friends like Wallace described him as troubled following his father's death in December 1941. The missionary's son still could not live easily with his material success.[16]

During Roosevelt's presidency, Luce had little choice but to plot America's future. The administration refused Luce's request for war correspondent credentials. Although the president denied any part in the matter, he was capable of such vindictiveness toward his critics in the news media. And he numbered Harry among them. He had worked hard for Roosevelt's defeat in 1940 and Luce's magazines afterwards enraged the president on more than one occasion. One July 1941 *Time* entry, reflecting Luce's impatience with Roosevelt's leadership, had compared a presidential vacation in Georgia to one of Hitler's periodic retreats to Bavaria. Roosevelt associated Luce and his publications with the most reactionary elements of the fourth estate.[17]

The administration even limited Luce's self-casting as a planner. Before American entry into the war, Luce joined the board of the American Policy Commission, a business leaders' association intending to underwrite research on the postwar economy. Early in 1942, Secretary of Commerce Jesse H. Jones agreed to cosponsor the group, renamed the Committee for Economic Development. Jones insisted, however, on reconstituting the advisory board; he dropped Luce from the list of trustees.[18]

Undeterred by Jones's snub, Luce set out to offer the formulations of his own staff and outside experts on the postwar order. In *Life* editorials Luce and his chief writers tried to add details to the vague and controversial conception of an American Century. *Fortune* proved the most suitable vehicle for such a journalism of contemplation. "The contents of any issue of *Time* was 80 percent dictated by what had happened," a *Fortune* editor recalled. "The contents of any issue of *Fortune* was 80 per cent dictated by what might or might not happen."[19] In that spirit, the magazine introduced an America and the Future section of three to four articles per issue while running a series of editorials and special reports on the domestic economy and foreign relations.

Calling for "a new democratic capitalism," *Fortune* sought to balance the postwar needs of the corporation with political pressures for a greatly expanded federal role in the economy. In the process, the magazine challenged the conventional wisdom of the business community and recognized the Great Depression's impact on American politics. No longer, *Fortune* editorialized in October 1942, did the typical voter "believe as he once believed: that depressions are made in heaven. . . . Henceforth, when occasion demands, he will vote himself more social security, free food, or a job." In the postwar era, *Fortune* warned, both government and business had to accept this new political reality. If only to forestall the "revolutionary militance" that hostile managerial attitudes toward unionization had fostered, business had to acknowledge the right of labor to organize. Government should consider the economic theories of John Maynard Keynes. The British economist had in the interwar years challenged several generations of economic orthodoxy by maintaining that government could play a positive role in free market economies. Through correctly timed deficit spending and tax cuts, Keynes argued, government could prevent severe economic downturns. Although the "new" economics had proven difficult for the Roosevelt administration to accept, *Fortune* urged business leaders to consider elements of Keynes's approach. Prosperity would likely follow the war's end. But if another major depression loomed, the federal government would have to respond through public works expenditures. Vice-President Wallace, whose own postwar intentions cost many a chief executive officer sleep, praised a December 1942 *Fortune* supplement on the domestic economy.[20]

Like earlier proponents of the "open door," *Fortune* saw a vital link between economic growth and overseas markets. Here the magazine even went beyond the free trade proposals of Secretary of State Cordell Hull. The United States, Latin America, Great Britain, and her dominions should agree to end all tariffs on imports. Gradually other nations would be invited to participate in this free market area. "We must," *Fortune* contended, "attack the restrictions and other maladjustments that have stifled economic expansion and the production of wealth in the past." To one historian, *Fortune* more than echoed the views of some eastern business leaders. A "new American frontier" of unimpeded trade would assure economic stability. With Luce's business journal the organ of this internationalism, William Appleman Williams wrote, the "convergence of a sense of economic necessity and a moral calling transformed the traditional concept of open door expansion into a vision of an American Century."[21]

Three Allies, 1941–1943

Luce's postwar order allowed for other great powers, though none, early in the war, the publisher deemed a potential rival. Harry's short list resembled those of others calculating the peacetime strategic balance. He expected both the Soviet Union and China to be active, if only as regional powers. Britain would emerge from the conflict a weakened if still forceful factor in world affairs.

Luce's "American Century" editorial, like Lippmann's "America's Destiny," had been based on the assumption that Britain's days as the world's policeman were over. A visit by Luce to England early in 1942 hardened this view. The British, he wrote, appeared "uncertain and unclear" about the future of their empire and their economy. To his dismay, socialism tempted many. All told, Luce came away convinced that America could not entrust postwar global leadership to the British.[22]

Luce's magazines and newsreels handled the Soviet Union generously. In 1942 and 1943, when Russia alone of the major powers bore the brunt of Axis forces, Time Inc. publications described a valiant, suffering people. The political and economic characteristics of the Soviet Union were ignored. So was the ruthlessness of her leader, Joseph Stalin, whom *Life*'s Bourke-White alone of America's photojournalists had captured smiling. *Time* named Stalin Man of the Year in 1942. The famines and purges of the 1930s, even the Nazi-Russian pact were explained away. Signs that the Russians were abandoning their support for revolution abroad while encouraging political liberties at home were emphasized. "The rights as individuals that U.S. citizens have," *Time* informed readers, "the Russians want and believe they eventually will receive." Again, the Luce press conveyed its enthusiasm—seen in its treatment of Mussolini and others earlier—for a strong leader arbitrarily imposing a modern economic system on a backward people. *Life* observed in March 1943, "It is safe to say that no nation in history has ever done so much so fast."[23]

Life's special issue on Russia (29 March 1943) at the time netted the periodical only praise. There were reports that Stalin himself appreciated the effort. Lippmann judged it "the most advanced development of the photographic journalism which *Life* has invented." Only later, when it was no longer necessary for the American news media to serve the alliance, did the magazine's exaggerations become transparent, and embarrassing. *Life*'s special issue had been a Potemkin village of American journalism, full of what one historian later called "pro-Soviet gush."[24]

Again, however, Luce's journalism was in step. Most newspapers and magazines had begun siding with the Soviet Union after Germany's invasion and Churchill's immediate declaration of an Anglo-Russian alliance. Goodwill for Russia increased with America's entry into the war. In 1942, a prominent New York book publisher urged a ban on all works critical of Russia. Two of *Life's* competitors, *Collier's* and the *Saturday Evening Post*, rivaled one another, wrote one observer later, "in pro-Soviet effusions."[25]

Luce himself took a more restrained view of the Soviet-American alliance. A 1932 visit to the Soviet Union had confirmed his anti-Marxism; *Fortune's* feature on the USSR that year, he complained, "omitted the stink and sourness of Russia." Yet in 1942 and 1943 Luce disliked rather than feared the Soviet Union; he doubted that Stalin would seek to impose his system on the West after the war. The publisher expected Russia to return to its relatively passive foreign policy of the 1930s. "Luce said we must learn to live with Russia as a completely isolated power," Wallace recorded in his diary in February 1943. In a September *Life* essay on American foreign policy, one of Luce's trusted young editorial writers, John K. Jessup, echoed his superior and others. "Ideological differences, though not to be ignored, should not frighten us into thinking we cannot get along with Russia before we have tried," Jessup wrote. Americans should be encouraged by the apparent increasing moderation of the Soviet regime at home. "Nations and even ideas live and change and grow. Russian society is already different from what it was in 1935."[26]

Emotionally, Luce's preliminary postwar order invested the most in China. "You cannot be long with Luce without sensing his kinship with and concern for China," observed Kenneth Stewart in a *PM* profile of the editor-in-chief.[27] Japan's brutal 1937 invasion had turned Luce's affection for his boyhood home into a rage over its fate. He threw himself into fund-raising for China war relief. He urged *Life's* editors to give ample space to China's struggle, "I know there is no more important or interesting occasion in human affairs right now than Embattled China." To Luce, the Japanese occupation of much of China had frustrated the emergence of a "New China," led by Generalissimo Chiang Kai-shek and his Kuomintang Party (KMT). Chiang Luce regarded as the one leader capable of uniting China. Having checked the power of the warlords and almost annihilated the Chinese Communist party, Chiang appeared a strong leader able to modernize a struggling nation. Moreover, Chiang's attempts to revive Confucian thought fascinated the publisher. After the war, Luce believed, Chiang would introduce capitalism to China without disrupting the best of traditional Chinese culture. China, Luce told one audience in April 1942, fights "to reestablish in that nation the best of the past and to go on to greet a new sun shining upon a universal humanity from a universal heaven." This new China, as an ally and regional power, would together with America bring stability to East Asia. Undergoing industrialization, China would also be a market for American imports and American democracy. "Among all the peoples of the earth," Luce remarked, "China most admires and trusts the people of America, believing that the American people have come closest to achieving the conditions of progressive freedom which they now desire to achieve for themselves."[28] Luce's faith in Chiang was reaffirmed during a 1941 visit. With Clare, he visited the wartime capital of Chungking. Chiang and his wife spared no expense as hosts. And Luce returned to New York with an article for *Life* and memos to his editors urging still more coverage of the Asian war.[29]

Others had great expectations for Chiang's regime. Taking no cues from his editor-in-chief, *Life* correspondent Theodore H. White described Chiang in March 1942 as "a first-class fighting man" and "the shrewdest politician in China." Roosevelt himself publicly insisted that China be regarded as the fourth great power, the policeman of postwar Asia. White agreed. "An Allied victory would make China one of the four great powers of the world," he wrote, and "Chiang Kai-shek may have greater influence than any other single human being of our age." In *Life*, Pearl Buck complained in May 1943, "The Chinese are being exalted into persons such as cannot exist in our fallible human race. A dose of common sense is needed."[30]

Two Friends, Two Campaigns

As Time Inc. tried to outline the postwar diplomatic and economic order, Clare Luce entered politics. In October 1940, the publisher's wife had campaigned for Willkie and gained much attention debating Dorothy Thompson over the radio. Two years later, Clare was speaking on her own behalf. Her mother's second husband, Albert Austin, had served a term in the House of Representatives from a suburban Connecticut district only to be defeated with Willkie in 1940. After Austin's death in January 1942, an aide persuaded Clare to run for her stepfather's seat. Supporting her decision, Harry contributed three thousand dollars and the services of an assistant to her campaign; he also wrote some speeches. Clare won narrowly.

In the House, Clare offered many of Harry's views on Roosevelt's foreign affairs as her own. She also resorted to a form of discourse ("globaloney") more appropriate to the theater or *Vanity Fair* than to the House chamber. Her style turned bitter after her only child, from her first marriage, was killed in an automobile accident in January 1944. In the terrible months afterwards Clare recalled prewar promises of peace that had so rankled her husband and accused Roosevelt of being "the only American President who ever lied us into a war because he did not have the political courage to lead us into it."[31] In her most controversial speech, Clare told the 1944 Republican National Convention that the president's isolationist foreign policy had helped to plunge the world into war. Roosevelt's indecision and inadequate military preparedness cost thousand of American lives. (Harry had said as much a year earlier, "Tens of millions of men and women all over the world lie dead or wounded—and a more forthright American foreign policy might have spared them.")[32] Clare spoke of the dead buddy of the army's G.I. Joe, "G.I. Jim," "the heroic heir to the unheroic Roosevelt decade: a decade of confusion and conflict that ended in war." He is the soldier never to return. "Dare we ask if his death was inevitable? Might not skillful statesmanship have helped to unmake war through the '30s?"[33] Clare, like her husband, knew the answer.

Others never forgave her for asking such questions in the first place. Like Harry, she had ignored in her attacks the prewar isolationism rampant in her own party. She now heard the party's isolationists applaud her and progressives hiss. Journalist Quentin Reynolds wrote, "Representative Clare Boothe Luce's charge that President Roosevelt 'lied' us into the war is not the first time a person named Booth treacherously assaulted the President of the United States."[34]

Another friend, Wendell Willkie, seeking the party's 1944 presidential nomination, could not match Clare's partisanship. Willkie's support for many of Roosevelt's foreign and defense policies had infuriated party regulars. By late 1943, Willkie's standing within the party had plummeted. Even rank-and-file voters began deserting him in favor of New York's new governor, Thomas E. Dewey. Efforts by Luce and the Cowles brothers, key editorial supporters in 1940, to boost Willkie came to nothing. They could not, this time, manufacture an image; for Republicans, Willkie had become a too well known quantity. When, in a desperate attempt to salvage matters, Willkie entered the primary in isolationist Wisconsin, voters there rejected him overwhelmingly. Willkie quit the race.

The Wisconsin results did not, as some Willkie enthusiasts feared, portend a reaffirmation of isolationism within the Republican party. The Gallup poll had found 70 percent of Republican voters sampled in the summer of 1942 favoring U.S. membership in a postwar peacekeeping international organization. A year later, a conference of Republican leaders meeting on Mackinaw Island in Lake Michigan had committed themselves to such a body. Although Willkie and his supporters wanted more specifics, the 1944 Republican platform and party nominees promised an active foreign policy. Like Luce, nominee Dewey acknowledged America's arrival; "The building of peace is more than a matter of international cooperation," Dewey told party delegates in June. "God has endowed America with such blessings as to fit her for a great role in the world." Commenting on the Roosevelt-Dewey contest, *Life* exclaimed, "Isolationism is no longer a possible foreign policy for any responsible government. We no longer have a choice between the ostrich and the eagle."[35]

A Tentative New Partisanship

The Republicans' acceptance of globalism fired Luce's partisanship. Indeed, during the last two years of the war, the editor-in-chief moved to the right. He did not join hands with the nation's most conservative publishers as much as he simply parted company with some of his fellow interventionists. His tolerance of the Roosevelt administration, never high, and of one ally, the Soviet Union, declined. He stood by Chiang Kai-shek as correspondents in Chungking, including his own, began to portray the generalissimo's regime as reactionary and corrupt.

This partisanship could be seen first in the 1944 campaign. Although never close to Dewey, Luce did agree to *Life*'s endorsement of the Republican candidate in the fall. For the first time a Luce publication had formally recommended a presidential candidate. While *Time* issued no endorsement, some Roosevelt supporters thought the newsweekly's political reporting pro-Dewey. With only *Time* available in Chungking, an American correspondent and his colleagues "began to think that maybe, after all, Dewey was going to be elected President."[36]

Although most staff members objected to what they perceived as a rightward shift in Luce publications in 1943 and 1944, few could bring themselves to quit the organization. Some, unable to give up the good pay, took up alcoholism or underwent psychoanalysis. They and others, engaging in a newsroom self-censorship, began to write more often in anticipation of what the editors and Harry wanted. "Self-censorship at *Fortune*," recalled one writer, "involved a constant calculation as to whether a particular statement—sometime a sentence or a paragraph—was worth the predictable argument, perhaps with Luce, possibly with some frightened or zealous surrogate. Often one decided that it was not the day for a fight."[37]

As before, however, the Luce press did not lapse into the mindless partisanship of some dailies. Because Luce did not personally oversee the production of each issue of each magazine, anti-Dewey stories did appear on occasion. Luce could only complain. In other instances, his editors simply refused to substitute their assumptions with reporters' findings. With rumors spreading that the president was a dying man, Republicans tried to make Roosevelt's health an issue in the campaign. *Life* editor John Shaw Billings was inclined to believe the worst, until a reporter failed to confirm that Roosevelt's days were numbered. Billings ran her account.[38] Although Luce had concluded that a fourth term "would be the unhappiest thing that could happen to America politically," he personally ordered that his editors not follow the example of the more partisan Republican newspapers of running the least flattering (most sickly) photographs of the chief executive. *Time*, in fact, exposed the practice, showing how pro- and anti-Roosevelt papers ran contrasting shots of the president.[39]

Even Luce's China was not immune to this objectivity. In May 1943, novelist Pearl Buck contributed a critical review of China under Chiang. In the eyes of Theodore White and his fellow reporters in Chungking, monstrous inflation, heavy taxes, corruption, and famine combined to discredit Chiang's ruling faction (though not necessarily Chiang himself). In May 1944, *Life* ran White's harsh assessment of the KMT. The Kuomintang, White wrote, "is dominated by a corrupt political clique that combines some of the worst features of Tammany Hall and the Spanish Inquisition." Although upset over White's findings, Luce agreed to the piece's inclusion and recommended the article to a select list of opinion leaders: "It suppresses none of the 'bad news'—some of which may come as a shock to the friends of China."[40]

A more fundamental change involved Russia. Sometime in late

1943 and early 1944 Luce began to view the Soviet Union as the likely obstacle to an American Century. A new and Russophobic adviser on foreign affairs, William Schlamm, may have contributed to Luce's thinking. More likely, Luce was merely trying to anticipate the postwar order. Roosevelt's cheery forecasts of great power cooperation struck Luce as characteristically evasive and unrealistic. At conferences of the Allies, Russian diplomats had begun to display some stubborness, especially regarding the fate of Eastern Europe. They would not surrender their national interest, Luce averred; America should not.[41]

At the same time, Luce's relations to his writers in New York and correspondents abroad, most of whom did not share his views on Russia, worsened. More complained that Harry was inaccessible. As his organization grew, his contact with his staff became less frequent. Luce had come to rely almost exclusively on a "senior group" of editors and advisers like Schlamm, most close to him in age and ideology. Among the rest there was less of the give-and-take of the 1930s. In chance encounters, he now appeared less attentive. Younger writers found Harry intimidating. His very success created a distance. So did his appearance and manner: the beetle brows, the staccato delivery.[42]

Although an ideological barrier had always existed between some editors and writers at Time Inc., there was a hardening of political differences. Some progressives on the staff had made no secret of their ability on occasion to interject their own views into copy, even though as Luce noted, "editorializing in *Time* is primarily the function of the Senior Editors under the baton of the Managing Editor." With the war ending, though, what one Billings assistant termed *Time*'s resulting "ideological confusion"[43] had to end. Many of his writers, Luce had concluded, were too innocent or too ideologically committed, particularly regarding the Soviet Union, to be entrusted with too much autonomy. A decade earlier, Luce might tolerate Russophiles as defenders of an offensive but as yet harmless experiment. With the likelihood of Soviet-American tensions after the war, however, Russia's champions had to be watched closely. He was more likely to reject certain arguments out of hand or to seek a means of overcoming what he regarded as "the domination of left-wing thought and left-wing terminology" among his writers.[44]

Seeking to bypass his staff's indifference to the Russian challenge, Luce ran in *Life*, 4 September 1944, a guest article by former U.S. ambassador to the Soviet Union William C. Bullitt. Writing from Italy, Bullitt predicted that Stalin—though still America's ally—would soon replace Hitler—still to be vanquished—as the great threat to Europe. It was in America's interest, Bullitt observed, to see postwar Europe democratic. Nevertheless, there was every probability that the "present Soviet imperialists" had designs on Europe. In the next fifteen years, Bullitt believed, Europe would either collapse under the weight of the Red Army or, by establishing a military alliance led by America and Britain, fight World War III to defeat the "new conquerors."[45]

Time, too, began to view Russia negatively after managing editor T. S. Matthews named Whittaker Chambers as Foreign News editor in August 1944. Turbulent political conversions had transformed Chambers into a dedicated Russophobe. In the 1930s, he had not only been a loyal Communist party member but had helped to transmit secret information to Soviet agents operating in America. On leaving the party, Chambers like Schlamm and others became a zealous foe of communism and the Soviet Union. Not without justification, he assumed that those few still in the CP adhered to his former blind faith in a party hierarchy that obeyed every Moscow directive. Some *Time* and *Life* writers, Chambers recognized, were not Party members, only sympathizers or "fellow travelers." Many more were just naive. "They seemed to know little about the forces that were shaping the history of our time," he wrote. "They seemed like little children, knowing and clever little children, but knowing and clever chiefly about trifling things." Chambers was determined to correct them. Autocratically he began to ignore the dispatches of *Time*'s correspondents and instead ran his own syntheses, infused with the view that the Soviet Union's "primary purpose at that moment in history was [the] conquest of the world."[46]

Chambers's most controversial editing performance appeared in the 17 November 1944 cover story. The last third of the entry constituted a harsh attack on American correspondents in China. Having finally been permitted by Chiang to visit Yenan, the section of China controlled by the Chinese Communists, American journalists had discovered much to admire in the leadership of Mao Tse-tung. Mao and his lieutenants had overseen local elections. Their socialism seemed democratic, their hold on the people strong. Most impressively, they had created an effective fighting force. The contrast to Chiang's China could not have been more compelling. Yet Chambers chose to condemn such accounts as wrongheaded, if not "agitprop." Mao's followers were not agrarian liberals but Marxists in close alliance with the Soviets. Chiang's regime, *Time* reported, might be "a dictatorship ruling high-handedly," but it sought "to safeguard the last vestiges of democratic principles in China" and "was fighting an undeclared civil war with Yenan, a dictatorship whose purpose was the spread of totalitarian Communism in China."[47]

Just when it appeared that Luce's magazines were about to declare war on communism in Asia and Europe, an in-house revolt forced Luce to check Chambers's powers. Late in 1944, *Time* foreign correspondents John Osborne, John Hersey, Walter Graebner, and Theodore White, already upset about the Bullitt essay, complained bitterly to their editor-in-chief about Chambers. Their memorial left Luce in a quandary. Of all his writers, he most respected his overseas correspondents; toward both White and Hersey, he felt an almost fatherly attachment, despite growing and deep disagreements over Russia and China. Luce did, however, grant that Chambers might be going too far, seeing Red everywhere. Chambers, Luce wrote in January 1945, "has to some degree failed to distinguish between, on the one hand, the general revolutionary, leftist or simply chaotic trends and, on the other hand, the specifically Communist politics in various countries." While refusing to remove Chambers as Foreign News editor, Luce did dilute his control over overseas dispatches by creating a separate International section with Osborne in charge.[48]

There was perhaps another reason for Luce's compromise. Earlier in the decade, his magazines had disguised advocacy of Willkie and interventionism as news. But other periodicals and newspapers had done that too. In late 1944, however, Bullitt's essay and Chambers's editing stood out. Only the *Reader's Digest*, published by the conservative DeWitt Wallace family, and the more reactionary dailies had taken on Russia. Most of the prestige press with which Luce identified remained pro-Russian, as did those surveyed on the alliance. The war in Europe and Asia still raged; to finish off Hitler and then invade Japan, America still needed the Red Army.

Luce rarely sought to be too far ahead of national opinion. "An editor's job," he told Schlamm, "is to stay ahead of his readers by three weeks, not ten years."[49] His magazines had to wait for political leaders or world crises to make the editor-in-chief's point. Although Luce himself by late 1944 anticipated tensions between America and the Soviet Union, his magazines would only travel so far in setting a foreign policy agenda for readers. To a certain extent, only events themselves—a presidential speech critical of Russia, a Communist coup in Eastern Europe—could justify Chambers's editing.

Until then, *Time* offered two interpretations of Soviet-American relations in 1945. In a March entry (which Luce had originally not wanted to run) Chambers likened Stalin to the tsars in his lust for territories.[50] Echoing Bullitt, a July entry told readers, "Hitler and Mussolini's Fascism is destroyed but in its ruins there is rapidly rising a dictatorship of the left." Other *Time* accounts, however, calmed readers. Russia's need for secure boundaries all but justified its imposition of puppet regimes in Eastern Europe. Moreover, the magazine on several occasions likened Russia's concern over its eastern boundaries with America's hegemony over Latin America. "From the standpoint of lesser nations," *Time* assured readers 5 November, "the Big Two were dangerous not because their foreign policies were so different, but because they were so much alike."[51]

Luce continued to regard Russia with the gravest suspicions. He rejected the argument of some within the administration that America had to view Eastern Europe as part of Russia's "sphere of influence." The Soviet Union, he suspected, had grander designs. When the United States and Great Britain agreed to Russia's demands on the borders and composition of the government of Poland, Luce ridiculed the "realism" of those defending the concessions.[52] In a July memo to his senior editors, Luce wrote, "we accept the premise that Russia is until further notice the No. 1 problem for America," much as "we would all be happy if it didn't exist." The excuse making of American progressives notwithstanding, Russia remained "a totalitarian country" with designs on the world: "she is ready and willing to pursue a dynamic foreign policy in every quarter of the globe."[53]

Clare at first absorbed and then went beyond Harry's assessment of the Soviet Union. Like many Republicans campaigning in 1944, Clare had questioned Russia's moves in Eastern Europe. While praising Russia's war effort, Clare regarded communism, "next to fascism, as the most deadly blight that has ever hit the spirit of man."[54] Politics became religion as she prepared late in 1945 to convert to Catholicism under the instruction of Bishop Fulton J. Sheen, a popular radio commentator, and, like most of his superiors in the Church, a fervent anticommunist. In the *Herald Tribune* in November 1946, Clare argued that Russian Marxism's emphasis on materialism, that the human being "is an animal without a soul," made peaceful coexistence impossible.[55]

The Luces' ranks soon expanded. The war's end had not diminished the press's tendency to define news as conflict. Front pages increasingly became filled with stories playing up Soviet-American disagreements over Eastern Europe and Iran. Some within the fourth estate blamed Russia for the deterioration of the alliance. Indeed, by late 1945, radio commentators like H. V. Kaltenborn of NBC and many dailies were more hostile to the Soviet Union than most *Time* or *Life* entries. And a majority of those Gallup surveyed early in 1946 no longer believed Russia would cooperate with America in world affairs.[56]

Habit and expectation partly explained these shifts. In one sense, the hostility could be regarded as a return to the prewar equilibrium, when the Soviet Union had relatively little support and, in fact, had at times been coupled with fascist states. Then, too, as Luce had feared, Roosevelt, having done little during the war to prepare Americans for a Soviet foreign policy motivated by self-interest, thus invited a large-scale disillusionment with a Russia intent on a substantial sphere of influence. Finally, the Russian leadership itself apparently little understood or cared about the impact its actions had on Western opinion. A *Life* editor observed in May 1945, "Part of the Russian difficulty lies in the fact that they have been so busy ironing out a revolution and winning a war that they have paid no attention to the mores of other nations."[57]

"Living with This Conflict"

Early in 1946 Luce found himself increasingly frustrated by the reluctance of the Truman administration as well as some of the larger and more prestigious newspapers to recognize the new rivalry. Some dailies and periodicals still called for negotiation, still defended or excused Soviet conduct. Truman himself had not quite made up his mind.

Luce had. Angry over what he regarded as an excessively even-handed coverage of a foreign ministers' conference in April 1946, Harry ordered that *Life* carry an editorial that finally revealed his views. "It is time to face the truth," *Life* declared. America and Russia were now rivals for power and influence around the world. Wishful thinking concerning Soviet-American relations fostered during the war had to end. "If we Americans want real peace, we will have to get used to the idea of living with this conflict," *Life* declared. "We shall have to work hard and sleeplessly at the tough game of power politics and diplomacy."[58]

Life continued to run signed articles warning readers about Russia. In June 1946, Wall Street attorney and Republican foreign policy adviser John Foster Dulles wrote a two-part series urging the West to awaken to the prospect of a *Pax Sovietica*. Returning from war-ravaged

Germany, liberal theologian Reinhold Niebuhr concluded in October that "Russia hopes to conquer the whole of Europe strategically and ideologically." Americans had to recognize "the new tyranny" and avoid the errors of the 1930s by actively contributing to the economic stabilization of Western Europe. "It is a very tragic thing to wade through blood and spend the treasures of a generation in order to overcome one tyranny and then be faced with another," he wrote. But "it is better to face the facts and to avoid the mistakes made in confronting the last tyranny."[59]

By 1946, *Time* contradicted itself less often. Individual news entries, combining summary and opinion, appeared more supportive of the Cold War. Of the Soviet Union's claims in Iran, *Time* employed a wartime imagery, observing in February, "Russia donned Mussolini's old mantle as Protector of Islam." Administration "toughness" earned high marks. As Secretary of State James F. Byrnes voiced his unhappiness with the Soviet Union, *Time*'s estimation of him rose. Indeed, the magazine named Byrnes Man of the Year for 1946, as Byrnes came to embody "a nation that had learned that the price of peace could be too high."[60]

Time and *Life* were both anticipating administration policy. Late in 1946, Truman adopted a strategy of "containment" first offered by State Department Russian expert George Kennan. America could not expect to achieve through negotiations normal relations with the Soviet Union. Rather, the United States had to act to "contain" further Russian gains by stabilizing Western Europe through economic aid and military pacts.

To sell Kennan's doctrine, first in Greece and Turkey in February and March 1947, Truman and his advisers engaged in opinion management. Although most Americans regarded Russia as a rival bent on expansion, relatively few wished to commit America militarily or financially in opposition to the Soviet Union. *Time* itself frequently noted a national indifference to growing East-West tensions.[61] In a calculated effort to end this apathy, the administration culled and reversed recent stereotypes: the heroic ally became the menacing aggressor, Stalin became the new Hitler, communism "Red Fascism."[62]

Time, which already had been using the "Red Fascist" imagery, became the willing instrument of the administration's promotional effort. Even before the president announced his doctrine of aid to pro-Western regimes, *Time* had stressed that Greece, which though "tiny and poor and quarrelsome, was worth the world's worry." Greece "was a strategic spot in democracy's worldwide, defensive struggle." A month later, the magazine cheered the announcement of the Truman Doctrine, which called for $400 million in American aid to both Greece and Turkey in their battles against Communists. With a haunting perspicacity, *Time* recognized that "U.S. financial intervention might earn America the resentment, even the hate of beneficiaries. The program opened up a road with no visible end. Along that road were other nations in almost as desperate straits as Greece. Who would be next to need U.S. help?" But "Communist imperialism must be contained. U.S. influence must expand to contain it; otherwise the U.S. might be engulfed."[63]

By early 1947, more and more mass-circulation magazines had adopted the new orthodoxy of the Cold War. America was the dominant world power, her foreign policy altruistic. Russia's hegemony over Eastern Europe was only the beginning of a plan for world conquest. The USSR, *Collier's* insisted in October 1946, "had a gangster government" that understood "nothing but force." The *Saturday Evening Post* described a "world-wide contest between the Soviet Union and the West."[64]

This is not to deny that there were dissenters, only that their ranks thinned. Within Luce's own organization writers gradually converted to the editor-in-chief's views or, in the case of Hersey, White, and others, departed. They and other Cold War critics could still find forums in 1947 in *Look*, the *Atlantic Monthly*, the *New York Times Magazine*, and the smaller-circulating progressive periodicals, the *New Republic* and the *Nation*. But by 1948 even the liberal press no longer carried the once common rationalizations of Soviet diplomacy or condemnations of an expansive American foreign policy. Russia's "truculence," to borrow from *Time*, evoked too many memories. Liberals who had decried Hitler's aggressions in the late 1930s could not help but see parallels in Stalin's ten years later. Many, still adhering to a Wilsonian gospel of self-determination, could not relegate Poland or Czechoslovakia to Russia's sphere of influence.[65]

Solutions

How should the United States respond to this "new tyranny"? At first the Luce press sought largely to remind readers of America's dominance in world affairs and discourage any thoughts of retreat from globalism. The prospect of a *Pax Sovietica* made that untenable. Yet how was Luce's America to deal with the circumstances that, as Niebuhr and others constantly informed *Life* readers, made much of the world vulnerable to the totalitarian temptation? As *Time* and *Life* noted frequently, Soviet gains were not necessarily the result of military aggression. War had left Europe devastated; peace presented the prospect of her colonies free but economically forlorn.

The United States, Luce argued, could save the noncommunist world partly through the creation of an interdependent economic system. "As Americans seek to lead the non-Communist world," he wrote in February 1950, "their chief instrument of *constructive* activity is—Business." A combination of American economic assistance and corporate investment would revive the economies of Western Europe and create new export markets for domestic goods and services. Finally, trade barriers and currency controls, part of what Luce later dubbed "the world's economic irrationality," that inhibited this economic expansion, should be eliminated.[66]

Private investment abroad served several purposes. Corporations themselves would in the long run gain; their export of capital would create demand for American imports. "Direct investments increased the productivity of the nation where they are made," he explained in 1946, "and it is only by increasing other people's productivity that we can balance our trade and permanently enrich the world." Such global economic expansion would also make socialism, appealing in Europe and elsewhere, "seem increasingly sophomoric," he declared. "If American businessmen go abroad, as wealth-makers, as creators of productivity—in short as good capitalists—they will be good salesmen for their system as well as for the country."[67]

Luce's supreme confidence in large-scale capitalism inspired his pleas for greater private economic expansion abroad. Some shared his economic globalism, though mainly out of fear that unless America found new markets the nation would suffer another depression. Luce himself rarely resorted to such gloomy reasoning. He regarded as unlimited the future under the leadership of the typical second-generation corporation "manager" profiled in *Fortune*. American business leaders had abandoned their once exclusive concern with profits and had become socially responsible, Luce reasoned. The new "American Business Economy," he wrote in 1950, "is answerable, and insists on being answerable, to the moral consensus of the community it works in. And that is why, as it undertakes this world task of economic reformation, it deserves the enthusiastic welcome and support of all men of good will."[68]

True to his journalism's emphasis on personality, Luce made his case by stressing an individual's career. The editor-in-chief delighted in Truman's naming of Paul Hoffman in 1948 to coordinate the Marshall Plan of economic assistance to Europe. Since 1930, Luce had been an admirer of Hoffman, head of the Studebaker automobile manufacturing company. He had saved his corporation during the depression while maintaining relatively harmonious labor relations. He also had engaged in what *Life* called "many extracurricular chores," promoting highway safety, participating in the original *Fortune* Round Table, and chairing the Committee for Economic Development; he had even helped to raise money for China relief. The "new Hoffman-type businessmen gravitate naturally toward public service," *Life* observed. Two years later, Luce himself lavished praise on Hoffman as "perhaps the greatest living reformer," one "preaching a change the like of which Europe has not known since its famous Enlightenment."[69] Though not a Diderot, Hoffman did serve Luce's purposes.

Audiences

Did Luce's enthusiasms have an influence? His hold on Republicans was not to be assumed. Luce had become friends with the Senate Republican leader in foreign policy in the late 1940s, Senator Arthur H. Vandenberg of Michigan. Letter-writing constituents inspired by a *Life* or *Fortune* editorial may have indirectly influenced others. But Senator Taft and other old isolationists viewed the Marshall Plan and other Cold War initiatives with suspicion. Luce could not move them.

Most though not all of Truman's circle acted without concern for Luce's views. Although the publisher did have good ties to James V. Forrestal, secretary of the navy, 1944–47, and secretary of defense, 1947–49, Luce was little heeded at the State Department and the White House. The formulation of the Marshall Plan and North Atlantic Treaty Organization cannot be traced to Luce's musings in *Fortune* or elsewhere. Indeed, Truman dismissed him as another Republican party publicist and charted policies with surprisingly little concern for the opinions of the fourth estate. Truman wrote a friend, "Don't worry about what Life, Time or any other Luce (loose) publications may say about you."[70]

This is not to say Truman ignored altogether what Luce and his peers wrote about his administration. The president and others in the administration took *Time* and other Luce publications; yet they did so not for direction but out of self-absorption. Officials wanted to know what Luce's magazines were saying about them, much as actors stayed up after a first night to buy the first newspaper reviews of their opening. If the critics' comments came too late to affect their performance the interest remained. Some, especially at the State Department, read Luce's magazines along with other periodicals and newspapers because of their audiences. Reading *Time*, for example, gave them some clue as to what subscribers across the country were being told (and told to think) about foreign and domestic policies.[71]

As to the business community, did *Fortune*'s call for a foreign policy of corporations affect the new manager? Investments by U.S. corporations in foreign subsidiaries did increase from $12 billion in 1945 to $55 billion in 1967, or twice the rate of growth for domestic assets.[72] However tempting to attribute such activity at least in part to Luce, he was in fact merely publicizing the thinking of the administration and planners for some of the largest corporations.[73] Luce, in that sense, was merely encouraging others to follow. Yet how many others? The majority of the nation's leading executives did not even take *Fortune*. Those who did read an average of seven newspapers and magazines, one or two of them *Time* and *Life*.[74] Luce, then, was not the only publisher with access to the board room.

What power Luce enjoyed among the business leaders involved the distributing as opposed to devising of economic foreign policies. His arguments likely had the greatest impact on some of those subscribers heading companies in smaller cities and towns, far from the great metropolitan areas with their many informal networks of associations. There and not on the pages of *Fortune* business strategies were most often discussed. Although the manager of a corporation in Iowa or Kentucky did not frequent New York's private clubs or travel to Pittsburgh regularly to lunch with the president of Westinghouse, he could through *Fortune* be exposed to the emerging ideology of overseas investment.[75]

"Counterpressure"

To Luce, economic globalism alone would not win the Cold War. A coup in February 1948 left Czechoslovakia with a Communist government. The fall of Czechoslovakia, one of Hitler's prizes during the decade of appeasement, gave a new credence to the "Red Fascism" imagery of the Cold Warriors, including Luce. Moreover, Communists now appeared likely to win in elections in Italy and on the field of battle in China. In ten years "a divided, stunned and defeated U.S. may be trying to adjust itself to a Communist-ruled world," *Time* warned readers. History must not be allowed to repeat itself. "To the leaders and nations who want to commit suicide by yielding to Communist pressure," *Time* declared, "the U.S. needs to bring not only life and help but counterpressure."[76] In 1950, Luce ended an otherwise extended promotion of overseas business activity with the observation, "We must give up the illusion—both comforting and inane—that Soviet Communism is something to be contended with by Food Baskets from Lady Bountiful. Far though we are from its brutality, we must learn to see Soviet Communism as the modern barbarian."[77]

Although by 1948 Truman and his advisers fully shared Luce's concerns over the Soviet Union—one historian has found that as early as 1947 Truman's foreign policy "came increasingly to resemble Henry Luce's American Century"[78]—the publisher regarded the president as too cautious. *Time* judged lame the American response to the Czech coup. *Fortune* attacked as inadequate Truman's defense budgets. *Life* began to liken Secretary of State Dean Acheson to the appeasers of the 1930s.[79]

By early 1950, neither Acheson nor his chief needed Luce's advice on the Cold War. The State Department had drawn up a more expansive policy, National Security Council paper number 68 (NSC 68), that extended America's containment doctrine beyond Europe and called for dramatic increases in defense expenditures. *Fortune* in December 1948 had urged a $18 billion defense budget; the authors of NSC 68 spoke of one of $40 billion. And the new approach rivaled Luce's own American Century in scope. "We are children of freedom," Acheson declared. "We cannot be safe except in an environment of freedom. . . . We believe that all people in the world are entitled to as much freedom, to develop in their own way, as we want ourselves."[80]

What kept Luce from seeing the essential similarities between his views and the administration's? An impression of Truman as inadequate to the task of leadership and, worse, inclined to wait too long to react to the Red menace, partly explained Luce's hostility toward the president. So did partisanship. Luce could not forgive Truman for being a Democrat. Truman's reelection in 1948 had caught Time Inc. pollsters (including *Fortune*'s), and much of the rest of the fourth estate, by surprise. Luce wondered if Time Inc. had indirectly contributed to the president's reelection by being too objective. In the future, Time Inc. handled Truman with even less deference. The president's tumbling popularity in his second term made this change in tone less noticeable at the time.[81]

Still, nothing more enraged Luce than the administration's China policies. Reports of corruption and military blunders had failed to shake Luce's steadfastness toward Chiang. To Luce, Chiang remained China's hope. Trips to China in 1945 and 1946—during the first he met with Communist leaders Mao and Chou En-lai—only reenforced his loyalties to the Nationalist cause. After a November 1945 dinner with Harry, Henry Wallace wrote, "Luce is a very strong admirer of the Generalissimo." He seemed to be "continually modifying his sentences to make sure that all of them contributed to the utmost to make the Generalissimo a hero."[82] To Luce's dismay, however, the Truman administration had at first been unable and then unwilling to save the Nationalists. Western Europe's security preoccupied most American policymakers. As Luce suspected, within the State Department an almost racist contempt for Asia afflicted many. Yet they and others in the administration also had little choice but to be Eurocentric. The slowness with which Congress and even the president agreed to larger military expenditures forestalled direct American intervention in China. Chiang's own political and military blunders, his failure to use effectively what aid America had provided, discouraged Truman from heeding the Nationalists' plea for still more materiel. Then, too, key advisers to Truman, led by Secretary of State George C. Marshall, who in 1946 had tried to mediate the civil war, believed that because the Soviet Union had given little direct support to the Chinese Communists, the United States should concentrate its limited resources where Marshall and others believed the Soviet Union did appear intent on expanding its sphere of influence, Western Europe. Moreover, Marshall and others assumed that the Chinese civil war would continue indefinitely; there was no sense of urgency about China, which for nearly four decades had been in various states of turmoil. When Chiang's military position deteriorated sharply after another of his unsuccessful offensives between December 1947 and March 1948, the administration realized that it was simply too late, not too expensive, to save the generalissimo. Mao's forces marched south; the prospect of a "Red" China loomed. *Life* observed bitterly, "American behavior in and toward China has been the most completely disastrous failure of U.S. foreign policy since the war."[83]

Luce had done all he could to assure a different outcome. Frederick Gruin, White's postwar replacement in China, proved more reliable in his handling of the Kuomintang. Like Luce, Gruin acknowledged but regularly offered excuses for the Nationalists' shortcomings while playing up their aspirations to social reform and democracy. External forces—Soviet support of Mao, and the administration's indifference if not hostility to the Kuomintang—accounted for Chiang's plight. Luce's periodicals by late 1947 and 1948 were demanding that the administration offer substantially more military aid to Chiang.

Time and *Life*'s handling of the Chinese civil war marked one of the few times Luce stood apart from most of the prestige press. His allies on China included the Hearst and Scripps-Howard newspaper chains along with Colonel McCormick's *Chicago Tribune*. Most columnists and radio commentators as well as the *New York Herald Tribune*, however, came to accept the administration's assessments of Chiang and his military position as hopeless. By 1948, virtually none regarded Mao and his followers as agrarian democrats, merely superior soldiers. A massive infusion of American military aid would not stop them.[84]

Although outnumbered, Luce and other pro-Chiang publishers did affect congressional deliberations over Chiang's fate. Their cries for help kept China on the public agenda at a time when the administration preferred to emphasize the need for increased economic aid to Europe. And Luce and others found a receptive audience among Republicans on Capitol Hill. Understaffed, lacking the administration's overseas intelligence-gathering apparatus, members of Congress tended to rely more on the news media—including *Time*—for information on international developments. Luce and others, in that sense, could affect congressional—if not administration—thinking.

Still, there was also an element of opportunism in the Luce-Congress connection. Those in Congress favoring the Nationalists used Luce's coverage of China, especially an October 1947 *Life* report by Bullitt, to promote China aid. Bullitt himself subsequently testified on behalf of greater American support for the Nationalists. But many of those nodding approvingly at the former ambassador acted out of past loyalties or present partisanship. Pro-Chiang leaders, notably Representative Walter Judd of Minnesota, had long been committed to the Nationalist cause. Others in 1947, 1948, and 1949 "discovered" China through *Life* and other periodicals as they frantically searched for a foreign policy issue to hammer away at the Truman administration, which had already taken up the cause of arresting communism's advance in

Western Europe. Luce's magazines, then, did not necessarily convert legislators so much as they served their political needs.[85]

Although Congress forced Truman to increase aid to China in 1948, the president rejected more drastic schemes for some form of direct American military intervention in 1948 and 1949. Soon after Chiang quit the mainland for the island of Taiwan, Truman announced that America would not act to prevent Mao's forces from invading the Nationalists' last outpost. Meanwhile, Marshall's successor at State, Dean Acheson, weighed recommending recognition of the new Chinese Communist government. He ignored the protestations of Luce and a nascent "China lobby" of pro-Chiang American business leaders.[86]

The Cynosure

Furious over China, Luce lost sight of the extent to which his vision of an American Century had been realized. The war's end had left America the great power. "Almost everywhere on the planet," wrote one historian, "the United States became a cynosure with no parallel except perhaps for that of the papacy in Medieval Europe."[87] Although many lacked Luce's enthusiasm, Americans nevertheless seemed reconciled to their new standing. Gone was the perplexity of 1941. Treaties had been signed, armies raised, aid administered, all demonstrating a national will to power. Bickering remained, but not over fundamentals.

9

THE LUCEAN DECADE AND ITS DETRACTORS
1950–1959

The fifties proved to be Luce's decade. His company, with the economy, prospered and expanded. After suffering eight years of Truman, Luce finally had a Republican in the White House, and his wife had an ambassadorship. Large corporations led by the new managers dominated the economy and began to invest substantially overseas. The country seemed to have absorbed much of Luce's ideology. Few doubted the Cold War orthodoxy Luce had been among the first to preach. Most defenders of negotiations with Russia kept silent, and advocates of recognition of Communist China all but disappeared.

Luce's political influence, however, remained indirect. He had wanted to run for the Republican nomination for the U.S. Senate from Connecticut in 1950. Reluctantly letting friends talk him out of making the race, he had surrendered his last chance for elective office.[1] Clare failed in her effort to win the GOP nomination for the Senate two years later. Despite Luce's close involvement in Dwight Eisenhower's election in 1952 and personal ties to his secretary of state, John Foster Dulles, Luce himself had little if any role in the casting of American diplomacy. As before, his magazines promoted rather than initiated policies.

And the Lucean decade ended badly for Harry. Luce found himself, his wife, and his magazines under attack. Some questioned the very fundamentals of his journalism, the ways his periodicals covered culture and news. More often, the critics assailed an institutionalized partisanship, especially at *Time*.

Alternatives to Truman

The decade began with the last and greatest foreign policy crisis of the Truman presidency. Late in June 1950, Communist North Korea invaded South Korea. American troops on Truman's orders moved to stave off the North Koreans; with Russia boycotting the Security Council, U.S. representatives won United Nations endorsement of America's intervention. A largely American UN force then pushed the North Koreans back to the Chinese border. For the first time since the advent of the Cold War, territory under Communist rule had fallen to the West. But in late November, three hundred thousand Chinese soldiers attacked the U.N. army, then under the command of General Douglas MacArthur. After a retreat to the south and then another offensive, the U.N. forces found themselves in a bitter stalemate. For two and a half years, the Korean conflict wore on, as did a fierce debate over both the war in Asia and American foreign policy throughout the world.

The Korean conflict itself brought new converts to Luce's camp. The seeming nakedness of North Korea's aggression and the assumption that the Soviet Union had encouraged the invasion reminded virtually all opinion leaders of Hitler's behavior in the late 1930s. The mistake of appeasing the dictators must not be repeated. That American soldiers were actually under fire aroused the patriotism of others. Former vice-president Henry A. Wallace, the last important critic of the Cold War, endorsed Truman's call to arms. Many recently in the Communist party began to "name names" of others still denying their once fashionable and passionate radicalism.

The Korean War similarly affected attitudes toward Communist China. Between January 1949 and June 1950, some in the press, business, and even missionary work had supported American recognition of Mao's mainland regime. America should follow Britain and other Western nations in accepting the outcome of the Chinese civil war. The Truman administration had weighed such a move, despite conflicting signals from Mao's government, the intense opposition of Republicans in Congress, the "China lobby," and the more conservative voices within the fourth estate.[2] North Korea's march south, however, ended any talk of diplomatic relations. Advocates turned bitter, seeing Mao's hand in North Korea's action, even before Chinese forces actually entered the war. Within days of the invasion, Truman ordered the U.S. navy to the Formosa Straits to protect Taiwan, the last outpost of the anticommunist forces led by Chiang Kai-shek, from an attack from the mainland.

Truman's belated support for Chiang and more timely intervention in Korea did not satisfy Luce. Even before the Korean invasion, Luce had been moving toward a more moralistic definition of the American Century. To Luce, communism assumed the form of civil religion. Anticommunism had to possess an equivalent righteousness. An excessively "realistic" foreign policy, one he associated with Secretary of State Dean Acheson, was an unappealing alternative to those peoples and nations torn between the competing systems of the Cold War. Relatedly, Luce had concluded that the president and Acheson offered an essentially defensive strategy to "contain" communism in Asia and Europe. More had to be done, specifically in Asia, and in the spirit of Luce's American Century. Without directly engaging the Soviet Union and bringing on World War III, America must attempt to win back territories under Communist rule.

Within the Republican party, Luce found a like-minded voice. Since the 1944 presidential campaign, John Foster Dulles had been positioning himself (stories in *Life* had helped) as the GOP's chief foreign policy spokesperson. Luce deeply admired the Wall Street lawyer. Like Luce, Dulles was not only an early critic of Russia but a devout Presbyterian. A religious moralism increasingly crept into Dulles's attacks on communism in the late 1940s. Luce, who along with Clare had been moving in the same direction, approved. Truman's Cold Warriors, especially Acheson, Luce believed, lacked the fervor a global crusade against communism required. And Dulles proposed a crusade. In *War and Peace* (1950) and a May 1952 *Life* article, he offered a doctrine of "liberation." The United States should actively encourage, short of war, disengaging nations from the Soviet sphere. America should channel aid to anticommunist guerillas in Eastern Europe and Asia ("We need not assume fatalistically that China's future is now immutably foreordained, beyond our power to influence") as well as promote an ambitious propaganda campaign of psychological warfare. "We should be *dynamic*," Dulles wrote. "We should use *ideas* as weapons; and these ideas should conform to *moral* principles."[3] With a foreign "Policy of

Boldness," wrote one historian, America would "take the moral and spiritual offensive in the Cold War."[4]

Anticommunism at Home, in the Office

Domestic anticommunism presented a different, more personal problem for Luce and Time Inc. As Cold War anxieties increased in the late 1940s, so did fears of Communist infiltration in the federal government. A *Time* senior editor, Whittaker Chambers, had fueled the anticommunist hysteria in 1948 when he told a House committee that as a courier for Russian spies in the 1930s, he had received secret documents from former State Department official Alger Hiss. As the committee and federal prosecutors pursued the widely covered allegations, Luce forced Chambers's resignation and ended the company's support of his legal fees. He had become a public relations problem. Although Chambers had quit the Party in 1939 and became a fanatical critic of the Soviet Union, readers wrote in protest of having even a former Russian operative on the masthead. (Luce himself, although long aware of Chambers's former Party membership, had not known about his espionage activities and was angered by his editor's failure to tell him about them earlier.) Among much of the staff, Chambers, never popular, had become a pariah; Hiss a martyr. "It's all very exciting," a Luce aide wrote, "but it does us no real good."[5] Even after Hiss's indictment for perjury—in an earlier libel suit he had denied the espionage charges— some liberals never forgave Chambers. Harry inexplicably would not allow Chambers to return to *Time*. A few of his supporters never forgave Luce.[6]

More vexing was the handling of Senator Joseph R. McCarthy, Jr., of Wisconsin. After four unnewsworthy years in the Senate, McCarthy early in 1950 seized the Communists-in-government issue and the attentions of the fourth estate. The Hiss case and others, together with Communist gains in Europe and China, had created a climate of opinion in which the most fantastic allegations of domestic subversion were taken seriously. No one in the early 1950s benefited more from this mood than McCarthy. Usually without evidence, the senator accused various government agencies of harboring Communists. The press, in turn, adhering to the journalistic ideal of objectivity, dutifully reported McCarthy's charges. The wire services proved especially effective conduits. Dailies relegated analyses or criticisms of the senator to the editorial page, broadcast news services to a few commentaries, not their regular newscasts.

Time, in contrast, suffered from no such confusion. The magazine's traditional if controversial mix of news and analysis freed the periodical from serving as McCarthy's stenographer. The magazine both reported and challenged McCarthy's claims, especially when the senator seemed at times on the wane. In *Time*'s brutal if mostly accurate 22 October 1951 cover story—under the portrait the caption read "Demagogue Mc-Carthy"—editors and writers drew upon a two-decade tradition of applying knowing, unflattering detail to assail the "burly, ham-handed" senator. Although rarely missing Sunday mass, he could not always control a passion for very well done steak on Fridays. Worse, of course, "No regard for fair play, no scruple for exact truth hampers Joe's political course."[7]

The cover story conveyed Luce's views. Like most eastern opinion leaders, the publisher could not abide McCarthy's crude style; *Time* had rarely treated provincials kindly. Moreover, McCarthy's emphasis on conspiracies, Luce believed, distracted too many from a critical analysis of Truman's foreign policies. Unlike McCarthy, Luce blamed the loss of China and other Cold War reversals on bad diplomacy, not perfidy. Yet with McCarthy's rise, Luce complained in June 1953, anticommunism had "become for millions of Americans a substitute for thinking."[8]

Still, the editor-in-chief warned *Time*'s editor and others not to allow their loathing of the senator to blind them to his popular appeal or newsworthiness. If the rest of the fourth estate covered McCarthy extensively, so must *Time*. And as the rest of the press highlighted the senator's crusade, *Time* followed. By 1954, McCarthy's activities filled the National Affairs section of *Time*.[9]

Finally Electing a President

McCarthy might be news, but Luce continued to regard Truman as the problem. To Luce, McCarthyism merely reflected a deep frustration over America's vacillating foreign policy. The Republicans must regain the White House in 1952.

To that end, Luce and his magazines promoted Dwight D. Eisenhower for the GOP presidential nomination. Luce's task was simpler than in 1940, when he had last devoted himself so totally to one man's

162

election. Eisenhower, unlike Wendell Willkie, was not a relatively obscure Wall Street attorney but the nation's greatest living war hero.
Eisenhower was not, then, nearly as dependent as Willkie had been on
the thinly disguised advocacy journalism of *Time*, *Life*, and other publications. Eisenhower did draw from Willkie's support within the eastern
Republican financial and business community. The general's few comments on national affairs in the late 1940s suggested that he shared the
corporatist ideology *Fortune* had been espousing for the preceding decade. Backing Eisenhower, however, meant once again rejecting the
candidacy of Senator Robert A. Taft of Ohio, leader of the party's conservative old guard. Although a Taft admirer despite past disagreements
over foreign policy, the publisher accepted the conventional wisdom
that the senator could not win in November. That conviction and a
Luce pilgrimage to Paris, where Eisenhower commanded the new North
Atlantic Treaty Organization forces, settled the matter for the editor-
in-chief. His magazines, boosting the grinning, would-be Cincinnatus,
became as in 1940 willing instruments of one candidate's cause. On the
eve of the Republican convention, with the delegate count close,
Eisenhower managers distributed issues of *Time*, out a day early on
Luce's orders, with a highly prejudiced account of the Taft managers'
"stealing" of delegates. Eisenhower won on the first ballot.[10] Although
probable even without Luce's help, the general's victory appeared to
confirm the view of Harry as a modern kingmaker.

Despite polls showing Eisenhower leading his Democratic opponent, Adlai E. Stevenson, Luce and his periodicals took no chances in
the fall. The press's excessive reliance on surveys falsely forecasting a
Truman defeat four years earlier caused everyone to be cautious. Luce
contributed thirteen thousand dollars and the services of *Fortune* publisher C. D. Jackson and *Life* editor Emmet John Hughes to the Eisenhower campaign. Clare, who had spoken on Eisenhower's behalf before
the convention, continued her efforts in the fall. *Life* formally endorsed
the Republican candidate while *Time*, still without an editorial page,
made little effort to disguise its enthusiasms. Most *Time* writers as well
as editor T. S. Matthews supported Stevenson. Matthews had gone to
Princeton with the Democratic nominee; younger staff members associated with Stevenson's genteel liberalism. But Luce positioned loyalists
to do *Time*'s political coverage and editing.

Eisenhower's easy win left Luce exultant. After twenty years
America had a Republican president. At the office Luce could not
cloak his mood. "Look at him," remarked a *Time* researcher, "only

gravity is holding him down." A despondent Matthews asked, "Harry, now that you've got America how do you like it?"[11] When Eisenhower named corporation presidents to two key cabinet posts, *Fortune* hailed the president-elect's "political audacity." This constituted large-scale capitalism's moment—it must not fail. The new managers of enterprise *Fortune* had so long honored could now help to govern at home and combat communism abroad.[12]

Assuming Luce sought no appointment, the president-elect did not ask Luce to join his team. In the 1940s, Luce would have welcomed being asked to be secretary of state; friends and coworkers had surmised that had two Luce allies, Willkie or Arthur Vandenberg, been elected president, Luce might have been given serious consideration. By 1952, however, the emergence of Dulles as the GOP's Metternich made him the all but inevitable choice.

Eisenhower did offer Clare the ambassadorship to Italy. Excited for her, Harry persuaded his wife to accept. Clare served for four years. Harry went along, careful to distance himself from her so as not to appear a coemissary. He traveled around Europe, commuted frequently to New York, and read. And from his own Rome office he wrote many memos for his editors back home.

Home Office, 1946–1954

Changes at Time Inc. made Luce's move to Rome less of a sacrifice than it might have been earlier. Shifts in the political composition of the periodicals' staffs reduced the tensions that in the mid-1940s had made managing each an occasional struggle for Harry. Then, too, in the late 1940s, Luce and others had spent many hours "rethinking" the magazines as well as such enterprises as "The March of Time."

Part of this stability was born of caution. Luce dreaded diversification. For years and despite ample profits, his company continued to rent its New York City office space rather than build or buy a headquarters facility; accountants bemoaned the arrangement. But Time Inc., Luce argued, had no expertise in real estate. It could put out a magazine. In that spirit, Time Inc. planners chose to deemphasize the company's involvement in such fields as broadcasting. "The March of Time" radio program ceased production in 1945, the motion picture version six years later. After moving toward acquiring the newly formed American Broadcasting Company in 1945, Time Inc. backed out. A venture in television documentary production in the late 1940s proved short-lived. Luce did agree to the purchase of some TV stations in the early 1950s, but only in the 1960s did these properties' substantial profits begin to command top management's attention.[13]

Luce's own energies went into a rethinking of two of his magazines, *Fortune* and *Life*. *Fortune*, at his command, began dealing more exclusively with business and the related topics of labor and government. That reorientation of the magazine and the good economic times accompanying the Korean conflict chipped away at *Fortune*'s disinterestedness. "*Fortune*'s articles mostly read like publicity brochures," novelist Mary McCarthy complained in 1953. So good was the economic news, editor Hedley Donovan recalled, that he introduced a new corporation profile, "the failure story," for relief.[14]

Luce's ambitions for *Life* were of a different order. Still his most popular publication, *Life* sold over 5 million copies a week in 1953. Far more, counting the pass-along factor, actually looked at the magazine. Each week about 26 million read the magazine; over six weeks, some 60 million examined, however casually, at least one issue.[15] Luce responded to such an audience as a cultural missionary. Starlets in cashmere sweaters could grace the covers, and treatment of such leisure industries as film and sports could comprise much of what came between, but each issue, Luce ruled in 1946, must include one "serious offering." "The expanding machine," he opined, had "slowly deadened our aristocratic sense."[16] *Life* could fill the breach. Although *Life* in its first ten years had usually included a feature on the arts or ideas, Luce standardized the practice. Beginning in 1947, *Life* ran a generously illustrated History of Western Man series on the development of society since the Middle Ages. Other special features on religion and science followed. In 1948, the magazine began running excerpts from Winston S. Churchill's gargantuan memoirs. In September 1952, Ernest Hemingway's novel *The Old Man and the Sea* first appeared in *Life*. Most often, reproductions of great art—more and more of them in color—constituted *Life*'s "serious offering." In 1949, a *Life* photographer sent to Rome to shoot the Sistine Chapel found himself imitating Michelangelo, on his back atop scaffolding. In the first six months of 1950, the magazine reproduced seventy-two paintings. Only the Works Progress Administration in the 1930s, *Life* editor Daniel Longwell declared a year later, could be compared to *Life* as an educative force for art and "Harry has been the biggest publicizer and publisher of art in his time."[17]

Life's cultural mission rarely encompassed fiction. The magazine's "documentary" tradition had always distinguished *Life* from two older rivals, the *Saturday Evening Post* and *Collier's*, which continued to devote up to a third of each issue to short stories. Between 1936 and 1965, *Life* ran only twelve fictional works. The magazine, like *Look*, covered the "real." To poet Randall Jarrell, that quality had helped to rob audiences of their imaginations. Twentieth-century celebrities *"are our fictional characters,"* he observed. "Shakespeare or Tolstoy can show us all about someone, but so can *Life*; and when *Life* does it, it's someone real."[18]

Luce's rethinking of his magazine did not affect *Time*. In the late 1940s and early 1950s, Luce had few complaints about his firstborn. The departments and style of the magazine remained essentially unchanged. Under Matthews, *Time* in the 1940s had abandoned some of the more excruciating elements of Timese. Reverted fewer sentences were. *Time* still told stories as stories, however, full of "knowing" detail, possessed of an omniscience tinged by or dripping in biases.

Shifts in personnel had transformed *Time* in other ways. Matthews left soon after the 1952 campaign; he was the last Democrat to hold a key editorial position under Luce. And whereas Matthews had edited heavily to obtain a stylistic consistency, his successors sought a greater political conformity. Those joining *Time* as writers in the late 1940s and early 1950s, in turn, accepted the new regimen. Old timers could see it coming. The magazine no longer hired so many class poets, touched by radicalism, accepting Luce's paychecks for a few years before leaving to write the American *Iliad*. Now "careerists," still male, filled the office. Although usually Democrats, they acquiesced to the magazine's editing routine. They were *Time's* "organization men" (a corporation type first described by *Fortune's* William Whyte, Jr.). "They are company men as sure as any ad salesman," wrote one latecomer. "A *Time* reporter might as well be a junior executive at Hunt Foods or Unilever."[19] Recalled another, "It was almost like joining General Motors." Luce himself observed, "The young people today don't seem as individualistic."[20]

A generational change partly explained this new type of writer. Younger staff members at *Time* in the 1950s had gone to college after radicalism's heyday on campus. The infiltration of Stalinists, mindlessly loyal to party imperatives, into progressive causes in the early and mid-1940s and subsequent tensions with Russia had made the postwar young adult suspicious of the left. Anticommunist witch-hunts at home caused others to dread the consequences of not conforming.

Then, too, those seeking a greater degree of political and editorial autonomy had more options than earlier. During an ambitious effort after the war to recruit returning veterans and younger correspondents with other news services, Luce's aides discovered that some talented young reporters, including Joseph Alsop, Harrison Salisbury, and John Mason Brown, would not entertain offers from Time Inc. Newspapers were beginning to give more reporters by-lines; *Time* entries remained unsigned. To some, reports since 1944 of heavy, politically charged editing discredited *Time*.[21] A self-selection process was at work. Those going to *Time* did so with the understanding that they would be passing the plate and not delivering the sermon. But the plate was full and the pay excellent.

From Rome, Luce did encourage one significant change at Time Inc., the creation of a new sports weekly. Since the mid-1940s Luce had been casting about for an excuse to start another periodical. At a New York meeting in June 1953, Luce suggested and his senior executives quickly agreed that Time Incorporated's next venture be a sports periodical. Luce's own sporting interests were decidedly limited; he had played tennis avidly as a child and tried to take up golf, to the horror of several greenskeepers. He had never, however, been a fan of spectator sports like baseball; indeed, he had once started to leave a World Series game during the seventh inning stretch, thinking it marked the game's conclusion. Yet as he met more and more political and business leaders around the world, he realized the common fascination with sports. Many, to Luce's discomfort, preferred to discuss boxing to the Marshall Plan. At the very least, putting out a sports magazine would render for him socially useful what Luce had regarded as journalistically irrelevant.

Then, too, Harry saw an unfulfilled demand for an upper-class sports journalism. Studies suggested that *Time* and *Life's* readership, disproportionately middle class, had become increasingly concerned with leisure-time activities. Moving to the suburbs, many had taken up golf. Yet existing sports magazines emphasized one sport and were written for a lower middle-class male reader; newspaper sports departments did not play to the affluent suburbanities, but to a mass audience. Coverage of a few popular team sports and boxing filled most columns. Majoritarianism often forced this exclusivity. In one midwestern city in the early

1950s, a daily might sell ten thousand more papers if the popular baseball team had won the night before.[22]

For his publication, Luce envisioned a broader agenda. Much as
Time had redefined a "news digest"; *Fortune*, business journalism; and
Life, the mass magazine, *Sports Illustrated* tried to refashion sports journalism. Without ignoring the more-covered activities, *SI* each week
sought to give equal weight to recreational activities like golf, bridge,
fishing, or hunting, not always treated in the dailies. Using a phrase
offered by the editor-in-chief, *SI*'s first dummy announced, "There's no
end to the wonderful world of Sport."[23] Like *Fortune*, *SI* ran longer and
fewer stories—from six to eight—than appeared in dailies or more specialized sports journals. When *SI* did cover a sporting event or team
amply reported in the dailies, the magazine's feature functioned much
like a *Time* cover story. *SI* "guided" readers by discerning a trend newspapers covered only as a string of individual contests. A good sports
columnist served the same role, but not every daily had one.

More than a year went into the planning of the publication. Away
much of the time, Luce cabled instructions or ideas; when in New
York, he studied dummys and attended his first basketball games and
boxing matches. "What's a left hook?" he pressed an *SI* staff member.[24]
He wanted *SI* to be written for himself, someone who was interested
but not expert in all sports. In addition, he and his planners regarded
SI as a "quality" magazine, read by the same well-heeled subscriber of
the *New Yorker*; *SI* from the beginning stressed upper middle-class pursuits like golf and included *New Yorker*-style sophisticated cartoons. A
few readers complained soon after the magazine's first issue in August
1954 that the "martini set" read *SI*.[25]

SI proved a struggle despite an initially enthusiastic response from
readers. In late 1954, the magazine enjoyed a circulation of just over
five hundred thousand; a Time Inc. survey indicated that as intended,
SI had found its way into the younger, prosperous homes. (One editor
later called *SI* the sports magazine for the two-yacht family.) Yet advertisers hesitated. Most classified *SI* not with the *New Yorker* or a newsweekly but with lower middle-class "men's" magazines, which the more
desirable space buyers avoided. Only slowly did *SI* advertising representatives break down this resistance; not until 1964 did *SI* begin to earn
money for Time Inc. and quiet those who thought that Harry had lost
his touch.[26]

The founding of *SI* and reconsideration and restaffing of Luce's
publications coincided with a major shift in the consumption of the

mass media. Between 1948 and 1960, television entered the American home, with virtually every American household equipped with one or more TV sets by the early 1960s. Americans began spending entire evenings in front of nineteen-inch boxes presenting live drama, quiz programs, and variety hours. Even Luce, having long since overcome his stammer, appeared on several programs; he and Clare regularly watched the criminal lawyer series, "Perry Mason."

Although the home screen came to be regarded as a threat to mass magazines like *Life*, the initial reaction of Luce and his lieutenants was hardly one of alarm. Indeed, many were fascinated by TV. *Life* sponsored one network's telecast of the 1948 national party conventions. And the medium itself provided Luce's picture magazine with fresh and popular copy. Just as *Life* had regularly "gone to the movies" to cover the latest films and their performers, the magazine now joined in the rush to award television actors celebrity status.

Television, then, gave no cause at first for panic at Time Inc.; its rise came at the expense of other mass media, film and network radio. Television's advent had caused consumers to allot less time to reading periodicals, but they did not cancel their subscriptions. In the early 1950s, *Life*'s circulation and advertising pages actually rose.[27]

Technology still favored Luce's magazine. Most network telecasts were in black and white; *Life* had begun to carry more color photographs. Nor had TV robbed *Life* of its tone of "finality." Television news programs could not yet easily relay film or tape to their studios; and the early evening newscasts of the 1950s, like the newsreel before "The March of Time," tended to include available as opposed to well-constructed or important footage. In addition, nightly network news programs were fifteen minutes and not available in many markets. Stations and networks scheduled entertainment, not information, programming most evening hours. Thus despite television, the pictorial summary of the world for many came not nightly from the Magnavox but weekly in an eleven-by-fourteen-inch magazine atop the coffee table.

Audiences

Luce's magazines did not, however, populate most homes. Through the 1950s and 1960s, more Americans took a newspaper than any Luce publication. In some communities, the gap between Luce's audience and the local newspaper publisher's could be enormous. In Wichita, Kansas, more families in 1951—17 percent—read *Life* than any rival; yet 88 percent of all households took the Sunday paper.[28] In 1960, *Life* enjoyed a circulation of about 6 million; *Time* just over 2 million; about 50 million households had one or more television sets. Studies of business leaders found a minority reading *Fortune*. Luce himself acknowledged that *Fortune* "seeks a businessman's audience but many able businessmen don't read period and others don't read good."[29]

Although the composition of the audiences for Luce's two most popular periodicals, *Time* and *Life*, had expanded since the 1930s, the majority of his audience remained middle class. The one-fourth of the adult population taking his most popular magazine was on average more comfortable, better educated. A 1955 study indicated that 38.8 percent of *Life*'s and 54.4 percent of *Time*'s heads of households were professionals or proprietors; 7 percent of all household heads held such positions. Most working-class and farm families, in contrast, consumed *Life* irregularly, casually in a barber or beauty shop or more anxiously in a dentist's waiting room.[30]

As before, many of those taking Luce's magazines, especially *Time*, did so out of a continued frustration over the local orientation of most daily newspapers. ("The nation's press," *Time* observed in July 1962, "always provincial in character, has become even more so.")[31] Then, too, daily journalism's excessive play to events left some readers seeking to master an episode's "meaning" by turning to the newspaper's weekly review, a columnist, a *Time* entry, or a *Life* essay. And in some communities, Luce's readers often served as "opinion leaders" of those within their social strata who lacked the time or energy to follow national and world events.[32]

Nationwide, not even all opinion leaders read a Luce periodical. Those living in New York and Washington, served by newspapers that stressed national and international news, were far less inclined to rely on *Time*. A study of opinion leaders not in government in 1958 found that, of those surveyed most interested and involved in foreign affairs, more took the *New York Times*, including many not living in New York, than read *Time* or another newsweekly.[33] Luce's most attentive audience, then, consisted largely of those in the middle class, less provincial than some in their communities, yet less cosmopolitan and influential than some living closer to the seats of power.

Of those who did depend on *Time*, most, given their socioeconomic status, shared many of Luce's tenets. The American middle class had not been at the forefront of reform since the Progressive era. Its members had always been nationalistic and usually hostile to communism and the Soviet Union. For most, Luce's magazines likely confirmed rather than inculcated political and cultural values.

The Middle-Class Universe

And *Time* and *Life* did convey the middle-class certainties of the fifties. *Life*'s American family was white and middle class, gone to the suburbs. All of the magazines, one historian wrote, "drenched in the romance of progress," saw technology only positively.[34] A consensus was prized. In generally favorable treatments of the budding civil rights movement, *Time* stressed its leaders' moderation and religiosity. Nonconformity, especially in the arts, brought only ridicule. The newsmagazine honored novelists Herman Wouk and James Cozzens in part because of their lack of affiliation with the country's avant garde. And no American writer received more attention from *Time* and *Life* than Ernest Hemingway, whose plain prose and ostentatious manliness were easy for the conventional burgher to comprehend and admire.[35]

Did Luce and his editors deliberately play to their audiences? Luce himself still possessed an organic vision of American society and an Aristotelian fervor for the middle class. "We are a middle class, that is to say classless society," he told a 1957 audience.[36] Moreover, despite a deep interest in religion and philosophy, Luce like many of his subscribers had conventional literary tastes. He liked Wouk's *Caine Mutiny* and long resisted modern art. Although others at Time Inc. had more advanced cultural sensibilities, many by the 1950s shared their readers' suspicions of the less approachable novel or painting.

Luce's magazines thus continued to offer a journalism of reassurance. People explained events. Between 20 August 1945 and 28 September 1963, individuals graced 93.8 percent of all *Time* covers. "Names make news," Luce wrote *Fortune*'s Donovan in January 1956. "People are interested in People."[37] And facts, offered not to fashion an argument but to give audiences the sense of being "in the know." Eisenhower, *Time* noted, had a small steak for breakfast, a Scotch highball before dinner.[38] Such reportage, Dwight Macdonald complained, had created in the postwar era an American preoccupation with irrelevant details, for which he blamed Luce and most American newspapers. Indeed, one analyst of writing found that *Time* readers

171

remembered not the essentials of a weekly summary, but the at times visually evocative, often inconsequential "fact," that Stalin drank vodka or a first reference to a British Labour party leader as "pink, grizzled Welshman Aneurin Bevan." *Time*, Macdonald cried, "gives us something to do with our minds when we aren't thinking."[39]

Critics

In the 1950s, attacks on Luce's journalism grew more numerous. Although he had been a target since the mid-1930s, the barrage grew in intensity as older, more hated press lords like Hearst and McCormick passed from the scene; to some Luce became the individual publisher most easily identified with the shortcomings of American journalism in postwar America.

The Luce press's cultural reportage came under fire. However ambitious, *Life*'s "serious offering," David Cort wrote, applied the magazine's tone of "finality" to usually debated academic issues.[40] To Macdonald, the magazine's attempt to include impressionist painting along with features on horses on roller skates only denied readers the power to discriminate between high and mass culture, creating a mindless "midcult."[41] A *Time* entry on Friedrich Nietzsche infuriated historian Jacques Barzun. The complications of the philosopher's writings were waved off in favor of clever yet dismissive summary. "Friedrich Nietzsche was a pale, crabby hermit who sat in a cheap Swiss boarding house peering beyond good and evil and demanding, at the top of his apocalyptic voice, the rearing of a demonically driven breed of superman." To Barzun, "More dull error could not be compressed into so few words."[42]

More frequently, critics of Luce in the 1950s attacked *Time*'s political prejudices. *Time* had never eschewed editorializing. But the magazine's bias toward entry into World War II, the Willkie and Eisenhower candidacies, or the Cold War could be seen in much of the rest of the prestige press. During the Eisenhower presidency, however, *Time* assumed the role of house organ, compared to much of the fourth estate, uncritical of the president and his cabinet. Stories were fashioned as dramas, with the administration's forces the heroes. *Time* used "knowing" details to prick the president's opponents: one sweated profusely, another avoided picking up the tab at dinner. Rarely did the president and his advisers suffer such treatment. Eisenhower was "sensitive to the mood of the nation" and possessed "equanimity and inner ease."[43] Secretary of State Dulles "both drew upon and nourished US confidence." His "emphasis on US interests had a wholesome effect of stimulating the national prides of other Western nations."[44] Although columnists Walter Lippmann and James Reston regarded the Suez crisis of 1956 as a defeat for the Western alliance, *Time* only praised the administration's handling of the episode and disparagingly quoted Reston's views with the line, "reported nonsensically."[45]

Time's distortions were all obvious when several analysts compared the magazine's treatments of Truman and Eisenhower. In 1946, *Time* described George E. Allen, a friend of both presidents, as Truman's "croniest crony" and "a clown." Eight years later, golfing regularly with Eisenhower, Allen was a "Washington lawyer and friend of presidents."[46] *Time* downplayed scandals exposed in the regulatory agencies early in 1958; seven years earlier, the magazine had enthusiastically recounted wrongdoing in the Truman administration.[47]

As Luce himself liked to note in language his father would have shunned, *Time*'s partisanship reflected the values of most readers. "I am a Protestant, a Republican and a free enterpriser," he declared. "I am biased in favor of God, Eisenhower and the stockholders of Time Inc.—and if anybody who objects doesn't know this by now, why the hell are they still spending 35 cents for the magazine?"[48] T. S. Matthews concluded, "*Time* is more biased, but so are its readers. It's nothing but a Republican magazine."[49]

For the more liberal members of the middle class, however, *Time* ranked as the major journalistic frustration of the fifties. College professors and a small but expanding "new class" of well-educated liberals drawn to Adlai Stevenson could take no solace in Luce's rival newsweeklies. *Newsweek* had yet to distance itself from *Time*; *U.S. News & World Report* stood to Luce's right and lacked any cultural reportage. Because Luce dominated the newsmagazine field, his liberal readers could only complain. More and more did. At Princeton cocktail parties, decrying *Time* had become fashionable. Some published critiques of *Time* and Luce's abuse of power. "In my teaching I try scrupulously to differentiate between fact and opinion," wrote an English professor in the *Nation*, "but Luce can order hundreds of persons to write what he wants them to write and he can use only that part of their writing which he likes. I cast my little vote. He helps make Presidents."[50]

Changes in daily journalism since the 1930s appeared to justify such attacks. In *Time*'s first two decades, an occasional editorial tilt could be excused by comparison. Many newspapers in their reportage still resembled party sheets or echoed the passions of an opinionated owner-operator like Hearst or McCormick. In the 1940s and 1950s, however, more and more dailies ceased mixing opinion and information. Luce himself had encouraged the trend by funding a Commission on Freedom of the Press in the mid-1940s. Chaired by Chancellor Robert M. Hutchins of the University of Chicago, the commission had called on newspapers to be "socially responsible" to all elements of a community. Some of the new generation of newspaper owners, in turn, found the Hutchins commission's recommendations an endorsement of their own management styles. Publishers like John S. Knight and S. I. Newhouse had already begun to assemble what came to be the most popular newspaper chains. Knight and others abhorred the prejudiced journalism of Hearst and McCormick; they viewed their properties as profit centers, not extensions of their political egos. Each should be treated as an autonomous unit, functioning best if left alone. Reporters, in turn, under less pressure to handle stories in a certain way, wondered why the same could not be said of their peers at Time Inc.[51]

Attacks on *Time*'s political reporting in the 1950s, it should be noted, centered around its treatment of personalities, not issues; until the 1960s Luce's antagonists rarely mentioned *Time*'s rigidity toward the Soviet Union and the world. Instead, many within the fourth estate went beyond *Time* and *Life* in deeming Eisenhower's Cold War management too tentative. Syndicated columnists Joseph and Stewart Alsop, ridiculing *Time*'s January 1955 cover story on Dulles, accused the secretary of not having done enough to stop communism in Asia; they later likened Eisenhower's major advocate of lower military expenditures, Secretary of the Treasury George M. Humphrey, to a counterpart in the British cabinet in the 1930s who had cut the air force's request as Hitler prepared for war.[52] Other Washington-based correspondents, increasingly annoyed by *Time*'s fidelity to the administration, pressed the president at press conferences about what they assumed was the inadequacy of his defense budget. Essayists in the then liberal *Commentary* warned against perceptions of a thaw in East-West relations. Stalin's eventual successor, Nikita Khrushchev, could not be trusted. To these writers, one historian observed, the Soviet leader's call for peaceful coexistence "was a cunning device to anesthetize the free world before its eventual subjugation."[53]

Regarding China as well, Luce's magazines reflected a conventional wisdom. China's involvement in the Korean War and subsequent behavior cost the mainland regime dearly. A wide spectrum of political and national opinion leaders believed Mao's government to be not only hostile to the United States but anxious to extend a "Bamboo Curtain" across Asia. In 1956, both major parties' platforms opposed diplomatic relations with mainland China; by the late 1950s the pro-Chiang Committee of One Million included such prominent liberal senators as Paul M. Douglas, Hubert H. Humphrey, Eugene J. McCarthy, and Jacob Javits.[54] Although no publisher of his prominence so closely associated himself with Chiang's American sponsors, Luce's actual role in the lobby was limited. Direction came from the Nationalist embassy in Washington and those in Congress devoted to Chiang. Luce lent his name and donated money. As to his publications, their treatment of Mao was unmistakably negative, their appraisals of Chiang almost reverential. Likening a newsmagazine to a smorgasbord waiter-captain, making the selections for a customer, press critic A. J. Liebling complained, "At Time, Inc., you are likely to get a bit of Chiang Kai-Shek straight out of the deep freeze with every meal." Most major news services, however, not just those tied to the China lobby, ran unsubstantiated and highly critical accounts of China under Mao. To illustrate a 1959 story antagonistic toward China, *Time* reproduced a cartoon by the liberal Herblock of the *Washington Post* picturing Mao with designs on Laos and India.[55]

The Publisher and His Administration

Having supported Eisenhower in 1952 hoping that he and Dulles would indeed take the offensive in the Cold War, the editor-in-chief soon became disheartened. The president seemed temperamentally incapable of launching another crusade. He appeared too eager in 1955 to attend a summit conference with the Soviet leaders, the first in ten years. These assessments only occasionally crept into *Time* and *Life*, usually as asides. Finally, Luce agreed with those who thought that Dulles's frequent misstatements created a host of problems for him and the administration.[56]

Life added to the secretary's woes in January 1956. In an interview, Dulles defended the administration's foreign policies and revealed that on three occasions the country had "gone to the brink" of nuclear war with China in order to keep the peace. An uproar over Dulles's "brinksmanship" followed. Democrats accused the secretary of recklessly endangering the world. Luce came to Dulles's defense. Although the secretary had reviewed a copy of the story, Luce in *Life* denied that Dulles had done so. Unlike most periodicals, which attacked the secretary, *Time* defended him: "Communist aggression has been deterred only by the willingness to go to war rather than cringe before the threats."[57]

Luce admired Dulles too much to abandon him. His moralistic approach to foreign policy offered Luce the rhetorical alternative to communism he had found missing in the Truman era. The secretary possessed a missionary's nationalism. "What we need to do," Dulles told *Life*, "is to recapture the kind of crusading spirit of the early days of the Republic when we were certain that we had something better than anyone else and we knew the rest of the world needed it and wanted it and we were going to carry it around the world. The missionaries, the doctors, the educators, and the merchants carried the knowledge of the great American experiment to all four corners of the globe."[58] "Eisenhower as President left his mark," Luce told an interviewer late in 1956. "But I would say that Foster Dulles has been most articulate on the moral and political problems of the era."[59]

Party loyalties and personal access explained Luce's faithfulness to Dulles and Eisenhower. Luce wanted the first Republican administration in a generation to succeed. He was unprepared to leave Eisenhower's public image in the hands of others, especially reporters he considered essentially unsympathetic to a Republican administration. Moreover, Eisenhower made him welcome in official Washington. For the first time in his life, Luce had regular contact with a secretary of state and president. Dulles took his calls. Eisenhower answered every letter and honored every request for a meeting.[60]

Such access to power did not bring influence. Although Luce and Dulles had become friends, Eisenhower set American foreign policy. The president kept himself at a cordial though steady distance from the publisher. Two former Time Inc. aides, C. D. Jackson and Emmet John Hughes, did work in the White House, but left disillusioned after short tours of duty. Luce himself rarely volunteered advice to the president, who in turn contacted Luce only after a decision had been made and in hopes of goodwill from Time Inc. publications. Eisenhower handled Luce as he did others within the business elite who had championed his entry into politics. At numerous White House stag dinners, the president listened attentively to his wealthy patrons and then sought to convert each to positions already taken.[61] Even concerning China, Eisenhower acted on the basis of his own calculations, invariably hostile to the mainland regime. The president in such matters was predisposed to causes Luce championed. In others, like military spending, Eisenhower ignored the publisher. When in 1960 Luce joined those criticizing the administration's civil defense expenditures as inadequate, Eisenhower politely replied that individuals should pay for their own bomb shelters.[62]

Once, the Luce periodicals combined with other publications and some in Congress to force the president's hand. In October 1957, the Soviet Union launched Sputnik, the world's first satellite, into space. Although the administration had been aware of Soviet missile developments and had inaugurated its own military rocketry program, Eisenhower, committed to containing military expenditures, had refused to publicize the Russians' activities or insist upon a full-scale American space program. With the Sputnik launch, however, Eisenhower lost control of the issue. While most Americans followed the president and refused to panic over the launch, powerful voices in the mass media, led by *Life*, demanded an American response. "The *press* assumed Sputnik meant Soviet superiority and the *press* pushed the panic button," wrote one historian. In the ensuing "media riot," editorialists declared Sputnik a blow to American prestige abroad, a sign of the nation's lost technological edge. "Let us not pretend that Sputnik is anything but a defeat for the United States," *Life* declared.[63] Americans had allowed the material gains of the postwar decade to lull them into complacency. The Republican *Herald Tribune* observed, "This nation has been asleep."[64] The symbolism of a little metal ball—and the administration's casual response to the launch—caused *Life* and other voices to ignore the vast sums already appropriated for missile development; Russia remained behind America in technology and weaponry. Over Eisenhower's objections, Congress, encouraged by the news media's crusade, insisted on a space "race" with the Soviet Union.

Although all the news media embraced America's space program, none proved more enthusiastic than Luce's periodicals. Two years before Sputnik, when space travel only engaged futurists, photographer Margaret Bourke-White had demanded that Luce designate her *Life*'s representative on the first manned lunar mission; Harry had agreed. With the space program underway, coverage did not come cheap. *Life* was already lavishly documenting America's reach for the heavens when in 1959 the periodical paid five hundred thousand dollars for exclusive rights to the stories of the seven men chosen for the manned flights. The space agency and *Life* then cooperated in cultivating an image for the seven. They were modern-day explorers yet remarkably like *Life* subscribers; white, small-town Protestants, good family men, middle class. "It was assumed," Tom Wolfe wrote later, that "the seven astronauts were the greatest pilots and bravest men in America *precisely because of* the wholesome circumstances of their backgrounds." Although the seven were not all so stereotypical, *Life* and the rest of the fourth estate behaved, Wolfe wrote, like the "Victorian gent," laboring to set "the proper emotion, the seemly tone."[65] Film critic Pauline Kael later called the Mercury seven, "Henry Luce's walking apple pies."[66] Such an approach, however, allowed *Life* and others to promote a costly and technically complex operation. Such a "framing" of the space program possessed its own logic: a commitment to space, however expensive, had a Lucean flavor. It offered Americans, wrote one historian, "an image of national purpose that equated technological preeminence with military, ideological, and cultural supremacy."[67]

Domestic Affairs

Luce himself was distracted from selling the space race by personal problems. In January 1958, he suffered a severe heart attack, his first serious illness. Doctors urged him to cut down on his work load, travel less, and quit smoking. After a month's recuperation, however, he resumed old patterns. But he looked older now, his sixty years of frenetic activity showing. A year later Billings, retired from Time Inc., wrote, "I have not seen Luce in five years. He looks old and gray and broken."[68]

Eisenhower offered Luce a respite of sorts in February 1959 when he named Clare ambassador to Brazil. Dulles had first broached the nomination with Harry even before contacting Clare.[69] Harry approved. He planned to set up his own offices in Rio and play the loyal spouse.

It was a role to be denied him. In one of his characteristic one-man crusades, Senator Wayne Morse of Oregon furiously attacked Clare's designation. Morse had been among those westerners resentful of Luce, the eastern publisher and kingmaker, and his magazine's unkind treatment of Morse's switch earlier in the decade from the Republican to the Democratic aisle. ("His brillance has not ripened into wisdom," *Time* remarked in January 1955).[70] Clare's partisan excesses in the 1944, 1948, and 1952 campaigns provided Morse and Foreign

Relations Committee chairman J. William Fulbright with ample ammu-
nition. They asked her to explain her 1944 charge that Roosevelt "had
lied us into war." Had she been, in a 1952 address, recommending capital punishment for Dean Acheson? "If a general loses a division, he is
shot," she had told a Chicago audience. "When Acheson as Under
Secretary of State lost 100 million people a year to communism, including the friendly 500 million Chinese, he was promoted to Secretary of
State."[71] Discussed as well was *Time*'s usually sneering treatment of
South America. In a March story on Bolivia, the magazine's Latin
American edition had quoted an "unnamed U.S. Embassy official" saying "the only solution to Bolivia's problems is to abolish Bolivia." In
La Paz, demonstrators stoned the American embassy; two protesters
died. Even after the Bolivia episode, however, the Brazilian government did not object to Clare's appointment. The Senate overwhelmingly approved her nomination. But Clare, ever confusing politics with
theater, had to have the last word. Within hours of the Senate's vote
she told a reporter, "My difficulties, of course, go some years back when
Senator Wayne Morse was kicked in the head by a horse." When she
refused to retract her statement, Senate Democrats reluctantly (few
liked Morse) came to the Oregon maverick's defense. Luce, furious at
his wife's invective, dictated her letter of resignation. Billings observed,
"As usual, the Luces get their full measure of bad publicity. I am almost
sorry for them—but not quite."[72]

Several months after Clare's withdrawal, Harry considered leaving
his wife. Clare had always been his friend and the two had been very
much in love in the first years of their marriage. Yet they had often
been separated and Luce himself frequently lonely. There had been liai-
sons. Now the sixty-one-year-old editor-in-chief, recently recovered
from a coronary, wanted to marry the twenty-four-year-old granddaugh-
ter of his friend Lord Beaverbrook, the British newspaper publisher.
Clare, still beautiful, but humiliated, managed to dissuade him. He remained faithful thereafter. Having endured this last personal crisis, he
could devote the remainder of his life entirely to public ones.

10

FINAL PURPOSES
1959–1967

Luce's last years were his happiest. Friends found him less restless. Harry himself took no little pride in his magazines' continued success. *Time*'s prejudices might unsettle some journalists and readers, but together with the rest of his publications, the magazine made money for Time Inc. Moreover, in the early 1960s a broad segment of the political spectrum, including most Democrats, adhered to the basic outlines of Luce's American Century. "Above all," wrote one historian, "liberals remained dedicated to that Pax Americana whose benefits to mankind would seem less evident later than at the time."[1] "Let every nation know," John F. Kennedy declared in his 1961 inaugural address, "that we shall pay any price, bear any burden, meet any hardship, support any friend, oppose any foe to assure the survival and success of liberty."

As before, much of Harry's own energies went into contemplating American foreign policy. Stung by criticisms from liberal theologian Reinhold Niebuhr and others, Luce tried to modify the American Century by promoting the "peace through law" movement. International law, not the national interest, should be the basis for keeping the peace. In the world arena, nations might resent an American-imposed order, but not a legal one.

Luce's advocacy retained nationalistic overtones. Criticizing the pragmatist movement in American legal studies, Luce insisted that international law retain a moral foundation. "The truth is that we live in a moral universe," he declared, "and the laws of this country and of any country are invalid and will be in fact inoperative except as they conform to a moral order which is universal in time and space." In this moral order, democratic rights that had developed in Western societies since the 1700s were universals.[2]

Luce's peace-through-law movement never took hold. The editor-in-chief did win converts, including the American Bar Association and, shortly before his death, John Foster Dulles.[3] But the Senate, despite Eisenhower's recommendation in 1959, refused to repeal the Connally amendment, which empowered the United States to reject a decision of the World Court. American diplomatists in the late 1950s and 1960s, though respectful of Luce, failed to share his enthusiasm for a foreign policy of moral legalism.

The National Purpose and Its Champions

In late 1959 and 1960, Luce garnered more support for a reappraisal of America's national mission. Harry had long believed in the importance of maintaining a national consensus in foreign policy. There were always temptations, especially for the prospering middle class of the 1950s, to turn inward. These had to be resisted. Opinion leaders had to formulate or refine goals for the nation. In this assessment Luce found himself joining forces with Lippmann and others, who were disquieted by what they construed to be the lethargic leadership of Eisenhower in his second term. An American aimlessness might, in fact, be costing the West its advantage in the Cold War. In the late 1950s, economic growth in the Soviet Union outpaced that in the United States, and Russia appeared to be similarly overcoming America's long-touted technological edge. Marxism, to these critics, provided the Communist bloc with a purposefulness absent in the West.[4]

Declaring itself the major forum for a "search for national purpose," *Life* carried essays by eight prominent Americans, including Lippmann, in May and June 1960. Although contributors presented many goals, even the more liberal ones included tributes to American globalism. All portrayed the United States as the world's best hope and shared a faith in the nation's capacity for leadership. America's purpose, former Democratic presidential candidate Adlai Stevenson wrote, was "to give our goals universal application." The national mission, former *Fortune* writer and poet Archibald MacLeish declared, was nothing less than "the liberation of humanity."[5]

Luce could not control the debate, however. Many of those joining in his search had been publicly critical of Eisenhower's leadership and unwillingness to spend more money on defense. While quietly sharing some of their sentiments, the publisher had more difficulty with their overall dissatisfaction with American society in the late 1950s. They viewed America in decline, in part because the economic abundance of the decade had fostered a self-centered consumer culture. *The Affluent Society* (1958), a popular indictment of the American economy by former *Fortune* staff member John Kenneth Galbraith, codified these opinions. Instead of being invested in social services, economic resources went to frivolous commodities. Luce, ever defensive about American capitalism, remarked, "I taught Kenneth Galbraith to write. And I tell you I've certainly regretted it."[6]

Ignoring Galbraith, Luce drew two conclusions from the dialogues. The nation must resist the tendency to mediocrity and pursue excellence in the arts and sciences. Through its "serious offerings," *Life* could help. *Life*, he wrote in 1960, should be "dedicated to helping bring about a great humane civilization." And the country had to renew its commitment to winning the Cold War. The publisher told a Senate committee in June 1960, "It is in relation to the cold war that our sense of national purpose can be most sharply defined and will be most profoundly tested. What should be our purpose in the cold war? Very simple: we must win it, and the sooner the better."[7]

This militant sense of the national purpose was not in 1960 peculiar to Luce; it could be seen in the campaign of Democratic presidential candidate John F. Kennedy. Like most prominent Democrats, Kennedy accused the Eisenhower administration of spending too little on defense, of overseeing an America "drifting" and "aimless." In what one *New Republic* contributor a year later called "one of the most nationalistic campaigns in our history," Kennedy championed a renewed, more vigorous prosecution of the Cold War.[8] "The American people were summoned," British journalist Henry Fairlie wrote, "even while they were at peace, to a sense of their mission, to meet a global challenge as he called it."[9]

Kennedy's Cold War rhetoric only partly explained his appeal to Luce. Although Kennedy did seem to possess the dynamism world leadership required, there were also personal ties. Luce had been friends with the candidate's father since the 1930s, when Joseph Kennedy began a family tradition of winning allies in the fourth estate. Luce's publications, in turn, had usually treated Joseph Kennedy and his family admiringly; Luce himself had written the introduction to young Kennedy's first book, *Why England Slept*. The night John Kennedy delivered his acceptance speech before the Democratic convention, his father watched the event on Luce's television set in New York.

Less interested in issues and less reliant on traditional party machinery than previous national candidates, Kennedy stressed an "image" upon which publications like *Life* might focus. The press, not just precinct workers, could bring him victory. Kennedy, with *Life*'s assent, ushered in a new era of politicians as celebrities. *Life* and other magazines could not resist running generous photo-essays on the handsome Kennedy and his beautiful wife. More and more, Americans " 'consume' political figures in much the same sense we consume entertainment personalities in the movies," wrote one columnist in 1957. "Month after month, from the glossy pages of *Life* to the multicolored cover of *Redbook*, Jack and Jackie smile out at millions of readers; he with his tousled hair and winning smile, she with her dark eyes and beautiful face. We hear of her pregnancy, of his wartime heroism, of their fondness for sailing. But what has all this to do with statesmanship?"[10]

In the fall 1960 campaign, Luce's magazines continued to treat Kennedy with an evenhandedness long absent in their political reportage. "Too *damn* evenhandedly," one aide to Republican candidate Richard Nixon complained. When William Benton, one of Luce's few close friends, suggested to Kennedy after the campaign that *Time*'s failure to maul him as it had Stevenson in 1952 and 1956 provided him with his narrow margin of victory, Kennedy agreed. Indeed, the handling of his candidacy by *Time* and *Life* so impressed Kennedy that he asked Benton whether Harry might not be prepared, after so many years, to change parties. Benton assured him that Harry was not about to leave the GOP.[11]

Kennedy's election did not disturb Luce. Some aides suspected that Luce had toyed with having *Life* endorse Kennedy until most of his senior editors recommended the Republican nominee. Although Luce had voted for Nixon, he attended Kennedy's inaugural. At the ball, he and Clare sat in Joseph Kennedy's box.

Office Managers and Managing

Time's campaign coverage of Kennedy did not denote a new objectivity. In March 1960, Luce had named Otto Fuerbringer as *Time*'s managing editor. Fuerbringer, dubbed "the Iron Chancellor," proved even more determined than previous editors to impose conventional Republican, Cold War values on *Time*'s domestic and overseas news. Fuerbringer, one staff writer complained later, was "a very bright guy with a basic 1948 outlook on life."[12] Only illness during the fall 1960 campaign kept Fuerbringer from partisan revisions of election entries. On his return, *Time* stories, including many on Kennedy, were closely rewritten to mirror Fuerbringer's views.[13]

Under Fuerbringer, *Time* continued to be charged with distorting the news. A 1961 survey of Washington correspondents found *Time* to be the most read newsmagazine. Yet of those asked to list the most fair and reliable newsweekly, *Newsweek* received seventy-five votes, *U.S. News & World Report* sixty-six, *Time* nine. Facts littered entries, a *Harper*'s contributor wrote in October 1964, "to provide the appearance of documentation for what are essentially essays."[14] Two years later, New York columnist Murray Kempton told readers, "Young men from *Time* are the only ones I meet on a story whom I automatically identify as enemies rather than colleagues. As a slaughterhouse of moral integrity, *Time* is the Verdun of the young."[15]

Although Luce paid little attention to *Time*'s detractors, he could not ignore a growing crisis at *Life*. For years, expanding circulation and advertising sales had allowed Luce to overlook the magazine's high production costs. From the outset, *Life* had spared no expense getting photographers to a story. Such extravagance, later seen in television news organizations, became less forgivable at *Life* in the late 1950s. Television's continued popularity had finally begun to affect the magazine. More homes had TV sets; more advertisers shifted more of their budgets to the most popular medium. And TV's continued ascendancy denied *Life* and rival mass-circulation magazines *Look* and the *Saturday Evening Post* the flexibility to boost advertising rates as their own costs rose. No longer would some advertisers accept increases. Then, too, the magazines fought among themselves for those readers and advertisers available, bringing down or containing subscription charges and space rates. Luce at first favored fighting for the largest circulation, even though *Life* had to keep per issue charges well below costs. In 1962, he went along with those recommending that *Life* in effect surrender the circulation leadership to *Look* and argue to advertisers that Luce's weekly had the more affluent, desirable readership. But as the company had found with *Sports Illustrated*, many advertisers still resisted buying space on the basis of the quality as opposed to the quantity of the audience.

In the early sixties, too, *Life* began to abandon its original formula for success. The magazine deemphasized photographs and illustrations in favor of more text, even though the weekly's popularity had long been associated with the visual. With television's unrelenting popularity, however, *Life*'s editors persuaded themselves that words, not images, could compete with the living room screen. The magazine began to take on a new identity in its use of signed columns and investigative pieces. Less frequently did *Life* arbitrate trends and taste. Television more and more annointed celebrities.[16]

The White House Subscription

Although thoroughly aware of TV's new role in political communication, President Kennedy took special note of *Time*'s treatment of his presidency. No chief executive since Franklin Roosevelt monitored the fourth estate as closely or took greater offense over what he construed to be hostile reportage, especially in the newsmagazines. *Time* and *Newsweek* reached more influential members of the nation living outside of Washington and New York, Kennedy believed, than any other news service. Moreover, Kennedy, on his first presidential trip to Europe, was struck by how many European leaders read *Time*. Convinced, therefore, that every newsmagazine story on his administration had to be scrutinized, the president had editions of *Time* and *Newsweek* delivered by special messenger the night before they reached subscribers and sometimes Luce himself. A story judged unfavorable invited calls to their Washington bureaus. More went to *Time*. Luce's publication, wrote Kennedy's speechwriter, "was a source of special despair."[17]

Time could, in fact, treat Kennedy roughly. A White House staff report and subsequent independent study indicated that the magazine had been more generous to Eisenhower in his first year, giving Kennedy's predecessor the benefit of doubt denied the new chief executive. The magazine on occasion compared Kennedy unfavorably to Eisenhower. In other issues, *Time* cast itself as the president's Cold War conscience. In a rare and unsubtle placing of a historical figure, James Monroe, on the cover, *Time* asked the president to apply the Monroe Doctrine in Cuba: the United States should invade Cuba, a recent addition to the Soviet sphere. The doctrine provided "a solid rock upon which current U.S. action against Cuba might be based."[18]

Kennedy and Luce argued over such editorializing. In one White

House encounter, the president upbraided the publisher. "Does the average man in the street think that *Time* magazine has been fair to me?" he cried. Luce, now living much of the year in a conservative Phoenix neighborhood, replied as he had to others. *Time's* readers were not average Americans. Luce's well-to-do neighbors, he told the president, "think we've been very kind to you."[19]

On other occasions, the president took the publisher into his confidence in hopes of winning him to his side. Before completing a reappraisal of America's long opposition to mainland China's admission to the United Nations, Kennedy asked Luce to prepare his own report. Luce predictably called for no alteration in U.S. policy. America should continue to regard Chiang Kai-shek's exiled regime as the legal representative of China and block the mainland state's entry into the U.N. Although Harry later credited himself in part with the president's subsequent decision not to alter America's China-U.N. position, Kennedy was apparently only playing to the publisher's vanity. The prospect of his magazines' opposition to any shift did not weigh as large as that within the administration, the Congress, or the Republican party. Yet by treating Luce as a member of court, the ever image-conscious Kennedy could hope for kinder copy in *Time* and *Life*.[20]

For the same reason, Kennedy took the time amid the crisis over the construction of Russian missile installations on Cuba in October 1962 for a private session with Luce and Fuerbringer. Aware of *Time's* saber rattling, Kennedy explained the risks, including a nuclear exchange, to an invasion of the island. Luce found himself arguing against his own newsweekly's position. The president had not wasted precious minutes. *Time* and *Life* together with the rest of the American news media hailed Kennedy's decision to institute a naval blockade of Cuba. *Life* praised the president's "splendid speech" announcing the quarantine, which "gave the American people an enormous sense of clarified purpose." The blockade "is a major turning point in the seventeen-year Cold War. The U.S. has dramatically seized the initiative."[21]

Time and Vietnam

With less effort, Kennedy could count on Luce's endorsement of the administration's Vietnam policy. Luce and his publications had long supported the pro-West Southeast Asian country; Luce himself had become something of an admirer of South Vietnamese president Ngo

Dinh Diem, who, like Chiang, showered the publisher with gifts. Luce hardly objected, then, to the administration's efforts in 1962 and 1963 to provide more military aid and send U.S. military advisers to Diem, under seige from insurgents from Communist North Vietnam.

Time managing editor Fuerbringer, largely on his own, framed Vietnam stories in ways pleasing to the administration. While Saigon correspondents for *Time* and other news services warned of Diem's deteriorating military and political position, *Time*'s Vietnam entries usually gave readers the impression of progress. The writing process itself, relatively unchanged since the 1930s, explained the tone of most accounts. As before, a *Time* entry represented a synthesis based on reports from various bureaus and heavily edited by Fuerbringer and his aides.[22] They normally discarded or rewrote a story by correspondent Charles Mohr, critical of developments in Vietnam, after consulting with the Washington bureau, which in turn relied on evasive or optimistic administration sources.

Time's system broke down in public in the fall of 1963. Fuerbringer had, like Whittaker Chambers nineteen years earlier, convinced himself that Mohr and others shared a defeatist mentality, fostered by difficult working conditions and peer judgments. To Fuerbringer, individual episodes, notably the Buddhist protests of Diem's government, caused correspondents to file stories forgetful of fundamentals, that Diem, for all his liabilities, was America's ally in Vietnam. Fuerbringer's assessment could be seen in an entry he wrote for the Press section of the magazine. "The press corps on the scene is helping to compound the very confusion that it should be untangling for its readers at home."[23] When Mohr threatened to resign, Luce stepped in, ordering Fuerbringer to calm his man in Saigon with another, more sensitive Press column. It proved too much of a restatement; Mohr quit. Among reporters, *Time*'s already marginal reputation for accuracy dropped further. Indeed, one of Luce's first *Time* correspondents, Henry Cabot Lodge, the new ambassador to South Vietnam, defended the Saigon press corps.[24]

Time's behavior stood in contrast with that of another journalistic institution. *New York Times* Saigon correspondent David Halberstam's critical dispatches on Diem had upset Kennedy, who in turn asked the *Times*'s publisher to transfer Halberstam to another post. The newspaper not only refused but hired Mohr after his exit from *Time*. Yet the president did not need to suggest personnel changes to *Time*. Its editor and editor-in-chief both supported his policies and ran a magazine that denied Mohr the relative autonomy Halberstam and others enjoyed. All *Time* entries were heavily rewritten; Mohr's were no exception. *Time* was still being edited to convey a consistent "omniscience."

Editors like Fuerbringer, it should be noted, were not being "managed" by Washington. Rather, because they shared administration objectives, they willingly offered official explanations. There were generational factors. Fuerbringer had begun his career as a military writer during a popular war; others his age and with different news organizations—as well as older U.S. Army officers in Vietnam—assumed that military-press relations should again be harmonious, not adversarial. America's cause and that of the press should be one and the same. Some younger correspondents with dim memories of World War II, who saw the conflict differently, struck veteran hands as impertinent.[25]

Skepticism could be mistaken for hostility. American reporters in the early 1960s did not question the correctness of America's budding involvement in Southeast Asia. Their dissatisfaction with the war, as Mohr and others later acknowledged—like that of China reporters a generation earlier—initially involved Diem's ineffectual rule and his ham-handed handling of the press. Subsequent tensions between the American military in Vietnam and the press concerned battle tactics, excessively cheerful war progress reports, and access to information, not the morality of U.S. participation.[26]

Luce himself became less directly engaged in such matters. In April 1964, he stepped down as editor-in-chief. Harry had turned sixty-six. Five years earlier, he had designated his successor, *Fortune* managing editor Hedley Donovan. Among the careerists joining Time Inc. after World War II, Donovan came from the Midwest and more closely resembled the "new manager" of the corporation Time Inc. had become. Although sharing many of Luce's political values, Donovan possessed none of his boss's eccentricities. He fit more easily into the establishment. Although the two shared a concern about the rightness of public policy, Donovan lacked Luce's righteousness.[27] Now "Editorial Chairman," Luce visited New York frequently, offering criticisms and suggestions; Donovan, however, made more and more decisions.

One of the first involved the presidential campaign. Upon becoming president after Kennedy's death in November 1963, Lyndon Johnson, like his predecessor, sought Luce's favor. And Luce found himself liking the new chief executive. Developments in the Republican party only bound Luce closer to Johnson. While *Time* and *Life* promoted more conventional candidates for the party's first prize, the magazines virtually ignored the quiet and skillful efforts of managers of Senator Barry M. Goldwater of Arizona. Goldwater, the leader of a new, more militant breed of conservatives, fared badly in most contested party primaries. Moreover, off-the-cuff remarks and ghost-written treatises left moderate and liberal opinion leaders nervous about his foreign and domestic policies. But the senator's agents had carefully mastered the delegate selection process in nonprimary states, and one contested primary victory in California earned Goldwater the nomination. Although Clare, increasingly to Harry's right, had seconded the senator's nomination at the convention, Luce did not object when Donovan and others recommended that *Life* endorse Johnson in the fall. Virtually all the major Republican dailies did the same. Luce "backed off from Goldwater in 1964," Dwight Macdonald wrote, "but he wasn't, after all, senile."[28]

In the year after his reelection, Johnson reluctantly ordered an escalation of America's participation in Vietnam. South Vietnam's deteriorating military position, the president's counselors had determined, required an "Americanization" of the war. The number of U.S. military personnel rose from twenty-three thousand advisers to one hundred eighty thousand combat troops. The United States, *Time* reported in January 1966, "had irrevocably committed itself to the nation's third major war in a quarter-century."[29]

Time applauded Johnson's move. In a newly introduced editorial page, *Time* declared, "Lyndon Johnson will not allow the U.S. to be pushed out of Vietnam. For if that were to happen, Americans would only have to make another stand against Asian Communism later." *Time* added, "Despite all its excruciating difficulties, the Vietnamese struggle is absolutely inescapable for the U.S. in the mid-60s—and in that sense, it is the right war in the right place at the right time."[30]

Luce himself consistently supported America's involvement. To the end he remained confident that the United States could prevent the fall of the South. Then, too, he viewed Vietnam as a vital testing arena—the first since Korea—of America's leadership. Like many within the administration, Luce had concluded that the nation had to make a stand in Southeast Asia, regardless of the cost. Vietnam had symbolic value. There, Luce wrote, "after twenty years of effort and experience, the United States will be able to make clear to all mankind what rules of international order we intend to uphold and in what ways we will preserve purposes with power."[31]

189

At first, Luce fit comfortably into a consensus on behalf of American intervention in Vietnam. Even David Halberstam wrote in 1964 that America had no choice. "Just as our commitment in Korea in 1950 has served to discourage overt Communist border crossings ever since, an anti-Communist victory in Vietnam would serve to discourage so-called wars of liberation." Although less certain than Luce of America's capacity to resolve the crisis, Halberstam called Vietnam "a strategic country in a key area, it is perhaps one of only five or six nations in the world that is truly vital to U.S. interests." In an April 1965 editorial, "The Anguish of Power," the *Washington Post* used arguments seen in "The American Century" a quarter-century earlier in support of Americanization. Great Britain's decline left America the responsible power. The United States "cannot admit disinterest [*sic*] in any crisis," the *Post* intoned. "We are influenced by every act of injustice and tyranny that takes place everywhere in the globe."[32]

The *Washington Post*, Halberstam, and others in due course ceased speaking of the inescapability of American involvement in Vietnam; at the outset, however, support for intervention in Southeast Asia, like that for the Cold War and World War II, commanded broad support within the fourth estate. The Vietnam conflict was not initially "*Time Magazine*'s War," as some might later surmise; it was not a peculiarly Lucean "cause," but a crisis most reporters and commentators believed warranted U.S. resolution. The editor of *Newsweek*, whose magazine slowly separated itself from *Time* and other prowar voices, later admitted, "I rarely questioned the basic wisdom of America's commitment to 'holding Southeast Asia.' "[33]

Still, as during earlier Cold War episodes, Luce's publications, notably *Time*, conveyed a striking, if pained, certitude about America's course. The tone was not one of glory but of grim resolution. Vietnam, *Time* reported in individual stories and battle shots, was not a splendid little war. Moreover, the newsweekly recognized that most Americans backed U.S. involvement without enthusiasm. "Most Americans may be unhappy about U.S. involvement in Viet Nam, but few could in honor condone the bloody chaos that would swiftly engulf that land if the world's richest and least hungry nation were to meekly fold its tents and withdraw."[34]

That view transformed *Time* into a virtual extension of the administration. Although wishing Johnson more Periclean, more specific and forthright in his war aims, the magazine still absorbed whole administration justifications for involvement and claims of progress. This attitude shaped reportage. When Saigon correspondent Frank McCulloch learned early in 1965 that marines would be deployed at Da Nang airfield, Time editors, on assurances to the contrary from Johnson himself, spiked the story. The marines landed soon thereafter.[35] Time restated rather than examined the assumption widely held within the administration—based on negligible intelligence—that China bore the major responsibility for North Vietnam's aggression.[36] The absence of antagonism between the president and Luce's newsweekly caused even Donovan to complain in a note to Fuerbringer in June 1966, "Occasionally a kind of cheerleader tone turns up in [Time's] treatment of the war and Washington's decisions."[37]

Relatedly, Time showed no tolerance for critics of the war. Much if not all the mainstream and conservative press had difficulty treating the budding peace movements of 1965 and 1966 seriously; they seemed too detached from the national consensus on behalf of the war. Time tended to dismiss their arguments out of hand while running administration defenses, including, on one occasion, a letter from presidential adviser McGeorge Bundy to 127 Washington University faculty members upset over Americanization.[38] Unlike some national news services, Time even showed disrespect for such congressional (as opposed to academic) dissenters as Senators J. William Fulbright, chairman of the Foreign Relations Committee, and Robert F. Kennedy, brother of the late president. Time's reports of their dissatisfaction with the war and American foreign policy were, in truth, sustained refutations of their positions. In a cover story, Time remarked, "Fulbright's central thought was entirely unthinkable: the U.S. must stop hoping for ultimate global victory."[39] Nor could Time abide the growing skepticism of some within the press, notably columns by Lippmann and Reston questioning Johnson's conduct of the war or his goals. The New York Times came under fire when Time praised columnist Cy Sulzberger for being more loyal to the president than his newspaper.[40]

Luce's other magazines were not always so predictable. In Fortune, one of Luce's more conservative writers frequently boosted intervention, yet rarely did he and others do so on economic grounds, that the stabilization of Vietnam was essential for a Southeast Asian "open door."[41] In editorials, which were placed near the front of the magazine, Life embraced the conflict. Beyond page four, however, readers received mixed messages. Life showed an openness to campus dissent trivialized by other news services. In April 1965, the picture weekly carried articles by four college students and Yale University chaplain

William Sloane Coffin, Jr., explaining their opposition to the war.[42] Then, too, *Life*'s hunger for pictures could subvert the most supportive of editorial positions. While Fuerbringer labored to set the properly pro-Diem tone in *Time* entries in the summer and early fall of 1963, *Life* ran shots of Diem's Buddhist opponents setting themselves on fire in protest of his regime. As both *Life* and *Time* offered words on the war's purposes and objectives, *Life* more graphically than any other medium displayed images of war's horrors. Ever in search of the real, *Life* ran battle shots, notably those by Larry Burrows, of bloodied Americans. One, of a wounded U.S. helicopter crew chief, appeared on the cover.[43]

Life's most fearsome rival eschewed this documentary quality. Nightly television newscasts consisted of reading wire service accounts of U.S. military "body counts" of enemy dead. Network crews did show skirmishes in the field, but rarely blood. Their efforts tended to be episodic, with few exceptions, uncritical. Until early 1968, more sustained explorations of U.S. policy constituted little more than defenses of American participation.[44]

The View from Phoenix

From Phoenix or during periodic visits to New York, Luce was satisfied merely to monitor his magazines' coverage of war. He had no cause for regretting retirement. Donovan and individual editors set "policy" regarding Vietnam during periodic meetings of editors. They remained persuaded that despite the increasing number of American casualties, Time Inc. should continue to favor the Americanization of the war. Trips to Saigon strengthened their resolve. After one, Donovan wrote a February 1966 *Life* editorial defending America's participation and suggesting that militarily, the United States would by year's end have seized the initiative; South Vietnam would, at a price, be saved. A delighted Luce called Donovan's essay "the best thing written on Vietnam, ever."[45]

Time's Vietnam coverage, Luce contended, served readers well. The eventism of daily newspapers and evening newscasts, the emphasis on the particular, only confused the great audience. "The American press had failed," he told an audience in November 1966, "to put a burning Buddhist or a jungle terror into perspective."[46] *Time* entries, in contrast, constantly strove to explain and justify American involvement, no matter how grim the news of the previous seven days.

192

Much of Luce's time now went not to endorsements of war but to retirement, and friends thought he was finally happy. Boundless energies once expended on journalism and the world he poured into bridge and golf. Theology, an interest since the 1950s, became an intellectual obsession, though he still found time in the evenings for mysteries. There remained an unbridled curiosity. Clare introduced him to the hallucinatory drug LSD, which she had been trying after a doctor friend extolled its virtues. Harry enjoyed his trips. During one he directed a symphony; during another he spoke to God.[47]

Even in his late sixties, however, Luce busied himself too much. He continued to travel often; he sought to be admitted to mainland China, closed to American journalists, to interview Chou En-lai. He smoked and argued to excess. Then late in February 1967 Luce suddenly felt tired; he had trouble eating. Clare took him to the hospital. Although doctors found nothing wrong, they had him spend the night. At 3:00 the morning of 28 February, a nurse heard an editor's blasphemy. She found him dead in the bathroom adjoining his room.

Public tributes came easily. Luce made the covers of both *Time* and *Newsweek*. In a statement, Johnson praised the publisher. But of the mourners at the funeral in New York later in the week, the prominent politicians were Republicans; Luce had, in the end, most often been their minister of information.[48]

Time Inc. without Harry

Within a year of Harry's death, Donovan broke ranks with Johnson over the Vietnam war. It was a gradual and group-directed disengagement. Opinion leaders in the press and business, once accepting of America's build-up, had begun to question the administration's conduct of the war. America had nearly five hundred thousand troops in Vietnam by the end of 1967, with no end in sight. Although still dismissive of the organized peace movement, more and more doubted the possibility of a military solution in Southeast Asia. Donovan, with closer ties to the nation's elite than Luce, began to share these misgivings. Beginning in October 1967, *Life* editorials urged the administration to seek a negotiated settlement; *Time* questioned the military capabilities of the South Vietnamese armies. Johnson complained to Donovan, "I don't think this would have happened if Harry were still alive."[49]

The North Vietnamese Tet campaign early in 1968 seemed to justify Donovan's change of heart. Although American and South Vietnamese forces inflicted heavy losses on the North Vietnamese and Viet Cong, their ability to launch the offensive and strike in urban areas secure since 1965 destroyed what lingering credibility the administration and military had with the fourth estate. Johnson rejected another troop increase, agreed to negotiations, and declined to stand for reelection. In Vietnam, America had failed Luce's great test of national will.

Johnson's change of heart had its effects on Time Inc. Because *Time*, unlike some other national news services, had persisted in associating itself with the administration on the war, Donovan acted to bring the magazine back to the center. He replaced Fuerbringer as *Time's* managing editor with Henry Grunwald in May 1968. Although Grunwald, like Donovan, was no liberal, no one ever called him the Iron Chancellor. He showed far greater respect for differing opinions and soon granted a most unLucean concession: the awarding of by-lines. The magazine conveyed a new if still circumscribed tolerance for liberal Democrats and the emerging counterculture. One of many bitter former *Time* employees spoke of the magazine's post-Lucean identity with "the new Establishment, which is more interested in co-optation than repression."[50]

Competitive forces had partly compelled changes. Until the late 1960s, *Time* editors, including Fuerbringer, had rarely taken rival newsweeklies into account. But *Newsweek*, under the ownership of the *Washington Post* beginning in 1961, gained a new respect by trying to acquire a separate editorial identity. Although the two magazines tended to share agendas and assumptions, *Newsweek* lacked *Time's* tone of certainty on some issues, notably the war. *Newsweek* relied less heavily on prointervention, administration sources, instead seeking out congressional and academic voices. Such efforts and the carrying of columnists—some of whom had begun to criticize the war—made *Newsweek* appear more objective than Luce's weekly, especially as support for the war began to wane. Although *Time's* share of the newsmagazine market remained steady, advertisers gave Time Inc. cause for concern by showing more interest in *Newsweek*. As a result, Grunwald and others began to study *Newsweek* with a new respect, adopting some of its approaches in the process of revising Luce's first publication.[51] By the late 1970s, the two magazines seemed more alike than dissimilar. Differences remained; *Newsweek* still appeared the more liberal of the two. Each cultivated the center, however, by framing most stories around what sociologist Herbert Gans called "enduring values."[52]

Life changed as well, though too late to save Luce's picture weekly. Under editor Ralph Graves (1969–72), the magazine tried to return to an emphasis on the visual. Graves also strove to cut production costs through reductions in staff and article length. Yet forces beyond his control, especially sharp increases in postal delivery rates, defeated him. The former practice of cheap subscription deals struck to raise circulation had not only become far more expensive but no longer impressed advertisers. They had started to doubt the value of buying space in a magazine part of whose circulation had been virtually given away. Rivals *Saturday Evening Post* and *Look* could not overcome similar obstacles. With *Look*'s end in 1971, *Life* was the last illustrated mass-circulation magazine. Late the next year, *Life*, too, ceased publication.

Although Donovan and others blamed the Post Office, advertisers bore most of the responsibility. More and more, space buyers, reversing their long standing rule-of-thumb, regarded magazines as best suited to reach specialized audiences, ones denoted by class or interest or sex. When *Ladies' Home Journal* named as editor Shana Alexander of *Life* in 1969, and she began to turn the women's magazine toward *Life*'s emphasis on world events at the expense of traditional women's issues, many advertisers abandoned the publication. For a mass audience, advertisers could turn to network television. An ad in *Life* reached fewer potential consumers than one on a popular television program; when divided by the total audience, a higher or comparable charge for a thirty- or sixty-minute "spot" was more "efficient," that is, less expensive per viewer. A full-page color ad in *Life* in 1970 cost $64,200 and reached 8.5 million homes. Yet CBS charged slightly less, $64,000, for a sixty-second spot during a professional football game that might be viewed by three times as many people.[53]

Television had hurt *Life* in other ways. TV's gradual use of live satellite transmissions made *Life*'s often elaborate, always expensive, efforts to photograph certain events a waste of resources; the network news divisions were able to bring more images of breaking stories home every night. Those hungry for picture-news did not have to wait for the mail carrier. The steady increase in color set sales cost *Life* those advertisers who preferred to promote their products in color rather than in black and white. In 1955, an advertising agency handling a tomato soup account wanted the red to be seen, and had to run copy in *Life*; in 1970, the same agency, selling the same soup, could reach even more potential buyers with color television receivers.

Other Luce publications better adapted themselves to television and related distractions. Studies since the early 1950s had suggested that mainly because of TV, readers on average allotted less time to reading magazines. Yet like daily newspapers, Luce's publications had responded to such findings slowly. Only in the late 1960s and 1970s did *Time* and *Fortune* begin to redesign their layouts and reduce article length in concessions to consumers of information.

Although Time Inc. launched several new magazines and eventually revived *Life* as a monthly in 1979, its most successful new periodical in the 1970s was perhaps the least Lucean. Popular from the first number in March 1974, *People* focused exclusively on individuals at work and play. The magazine covered politicians and even an occasional intellectual and included a section on odd or admirable unknowns, but the greatest space went to the celebrities of television, film, and popular music. Text was minimal, so as not to test the capacities of a television generation. Although resembling *Life* in many ways, *People* pandered to popular taste more and lacked the original picture magazine's aspirations (or pretensions) to enlighten as well as to amuse.[54]

Legacy (1): Luce the Imperialist

Luce's own reputation suffered enormously following his death. By the late 1960s, the consensus over the Cold War, firm a decade earlier, had come apart. To liberals and moderates alike, Vietnam had painfully revealed that there were, after all, limits to America's power. The more righteous critics of American interventionism not surprisingly began looking for villains and their publicists. Luce's name could be seen on most lists. His authorship of "The American Century" cast him as the first press lord of American globalism. No publisher of Luce's prominence had so identified himself and his publications with the warrior state. Luce "did not hitch his wagon to a star—he put its weight behind the juggernaut of American power," the *Nation* observed in March 1967. "In this sense he picked the right time to die, when it seemed as though his ideas had triumphed and before the consequences of this triumph could return to haunt him."[55]

In "The American Century," Luce had, if nothing else, correctly anticipated the course of American foreign policy. The nation did abandon a long tradition of diplomatic and military isolation. By 1970, the United States had military commitments to forty-seven nations and

375 major bases and 300 minor facilities overseas. A country whose peacetime army in 1935 had numbered one hundred eighteen thousand thirty-five years later had a million troops stationed abroad.[56]

Luce could only have hoped for such an outcome when he wrote "The American Century" early in 1941. Despite America's growing economic and cultural interests abroad, Luce had determined that isolationists and the Roosevelt administration were unwilling to accept what Lippmann had earlier called the "American Destiny." Luce, more bluntly than the columnist, stated the obvious. America, not Britain, ranked as the world's greatest power. Properly exercised, that advantage could be a force for both global stability and democratic capitalism.

Nor did Luce have qualms about America's ability to lead the world. The missionary's son had never questioned America's capacity for good works. In north China during his boyhood, Luce recalled, the British and Germans were cruel to the Chinese, the Americans generous. That almost innocent view, shaped when the nation had largely avoided the world, gave him and others no cause to expect any but great things during an American Century. The missionary impulse drove him to demand nothing less: America had a duty or calling. "I was never disillusioned with or by America," he once told his senior editors and writers, "but I was, from my earliest manhood, dissatisfied with America. America was not being as great and good as I knew she could be, as I believed with every nerve and fiber God Himself had intended her to be."[57]

There were related certainties. Luce had been among the first to recognize the emergence of the modern corporation. To Harry, this transformation in capitalistic organization was to be celebrated. He could not help but see hope in the "new managers" of the giant enterprises. He saw too much of himself in their education and—by ostensibly being "socially responsible" to the community and nation—their purposefulness. Furthermore, Luce regarded the export of capitalism by large-scale industries to be vital to the stabilization of the world economy and the maintenance of an American Century.

Luce could not, however, impose his globalism on business or lay readers or policymakers, much as journalists and others who overstate their importance might wish to believe. The American mind was not a "blank screen," as one historian wrote, commenting on Luce's support for Nationalist China.[58] In a given week, perhaps a fifth of the adult population read or skimmed a Luce periodical. But that did not in and of itself denote political power. True, Luce's magazines were assembled

197

to have an impact no newspaper and few rival periodicals could match; subscribers often spoke of his magazine as vital in helping themselves render information coherent. Yet they had other sources of news: newspapers, radio, television, friends, and neighbors. And more often than some of Luce's detractors admitted, such "rival" services shared all or key elements of his globalism. Then, too, although successive administrations beginning with Eisenhower's courted Harry, they did so out of respect for his readership, not because they needed his guidance. They based their policies on many considerations: congressional opinion, perceptions of the Russian and Chinese leadership, a revulsion over the appeasement of the 1930s. These factors, not a *Life* editorial, dominated meetings of the National Security Council or cabinet.

Nevertheless, Luce willingly served—along with much of the fourth estate—as a publicist for what came to be known as the national security state. Making most if not all of the same assumptions of those establishing policy, Luce and others reported American Cold War initiatives uncritically. A younger generation, with different memories, came to assume an "adversary" stance, and wondered why Luce and his peers had lacked the resolve to do the same.

Luce's magazines in that regard affected opinion by not upsetting it. His periodicals reached a largely comfortable, disproportionately Republican constituency. In the early 1940s, Luce had challenged some of that readership by championing internationalism. He never again took such risks. His magazines were more moderate than some, *Time* was to the left of *U.S. News*, *Fortune* more progressive than *Business Week*. Nevertheless, all his magazines might have shown more tolerance for the critics of the national security state, however few in number initially. All might have been less nationalistic in their view of the world and America's role.

Legacy (2): Luce the Mass Communicator

Luce's missionary impulses also had pedagogical overtones. Harry had always defined journalism's agenda broadly. From the first number, *Time* had included "back of the book" departments on education, the arts, and sciences, which tried to define news as more than politics and diplomacy. *Fortune* had originally tried to teach business leaders about art and anthropology. *Life* labored to educate perhaps most of any Luce publication. Journalism, to Luce, had "the inner duty to see, to know, to tell, to teach."[59] The fourth estate should regard itself, he remarked late in his life, as an instrument of education. It should, he quoted his father, "make a man feel at home in the universe."[60] In his magazines, the results, detractors noted, often resembled his political reportage in their tone of "finality" on normally debated intellectual and artistic subjects. Most often, critics decried the "middlebrow" definition of culture in Luce's magazines, or *Life*'s potential for confusing tastes by carrying in the same issue features on Toulouse-Lautrec and women's underwear. But perhaps Luce deserved credit for the effort; no other publisher with his readership aspired to such a function. Soon after Harry's death, a critic of the mass media acknowledged, "One thing you could say for Henry Luce: when you picked up one of his magazines, especially *Time*, you really felt his presence. Think of it—all those pages, pictures, words, long series on snakes and Art and whatever happened to the Holy Roman Empire."[61]

A generation later, his magazines commanded no such comments. They had become "properties" run by a new generation of publishers unlike Harry in their ease with their tasks. They had not been raised by missionaries. They did not suffer Harry's unstated anxieties about good works. Occasionally they tried, even in *People*, to educate. Yet the most effective instrument of a cultural mission had been *Life*, and after its resurrection the magazine could not win back its once substantial classroom roster. It had fallen to other mass media, specialized publications, network and public broadcasting, and new newspaper health and science sections, to play the pedagogues. They, in turn, lacked *Life*'s great audience.

Still, Luce's longer news agenda offered only one sign of his impact on American journalism in the second half of the twentieth century. His magazines and "The March of Time" radio program and newsreel came to affect both the style and structure of news delivery in rival periodicals, newspapers, and broadcast services. And although Harry's detractors still wish to blame him for the excesses of the Cold War, he had the greatest influence, not on American foreign policy or public opinion, but on the practices of journalism itself.

The most important practice involved new forms of summary. Every successful twentieth-century innovation in mass communication—the newsmagazine and picture magazine, radio and television news, the newspaper analysis and column—conveyed the news in fewer words or with pictures and images. With more leisure-time distractions, the new consumer of information wanted synthesis, news guided by an expert or "omniscient" group of talented writers, a skilled photographer, or a camera operator. Luce and Hadden had recognized this need for mediated transmission in creating *Time*'s stylized summary of a week's news in four hundred words or less. They were just ahead of others in developing radio newscasts, which had been little more than headlines read with affected authority. Newspapers followed, first in the 1930s with the analytical column and weekly reviews, then in the 1960s and 1970s with still more analysis, changes that had the effect of providing less information, more guidance. "The March of Time" crafted aural and visual images into an understandable whole; TV news services, acknowledging their debt to the Luce newsreel, followed in the 1950s and 1960s. *Life*'s at times too deliberate, often admirable, effort to substitute the camera for words—to offer "finality" through pictures—could be viewed in television news as well. TV news features, too, in the manner of a longer *Time* entry, often "told stories," with a beginning, middle, and end.[62]

Time's emphasis on individual newsmakers, especially presidents, helped to set a pattern for the entire fourth estate. Earlier generations of journalists had often framed stories around individuals, but *Time* gave this approach a new emphasis with the cover story, replete with colorful and irrelevant attention to single news figures in many entries. Although Luce himself was certain—and millions of paid subscriptions proved—that many middle-class readers preferred this kind of reportage, it hardly constituted an advance for mass communication. Many if not most events and trends could not be explained in terms of individuals, however often *Time* remembered to include their middle names or eating habits. Luce protégé Theodore H. White, Wilfrid Sheed wrote, "wrote for the Personality Press, and the *modus operandi* seemed to be to catch top people in expansive moments and deduce history from that."[63]

Close students of the news understood *Time*'s limits. Among journalists, *Time* never won respect as a news-gathering organization. Two decades after Luce's death, reporters and editors most often read *Time* for its packaging of information; scoops were not expected. The magazine continued to confuse "knowing" details with new and important ones. When Dean Fischer of *Time* asked what a presidential candidate had eaten for breakfast on election morning, 1972, a jaded observer wrote, "Not for nothing was Fischer a golden boy at *Time*."[64] One veteran journalist wrote, "anyone who reads the national and international reporting every day of one of the national newspapers rarely, if ever, learns anything additional that is significant when he turns to his weekly copy of *Time*."[65]

Other readers, unable or unwilling to read a prestige newspaper, found *Time*'s formula far more satisfying. Its very palatability reassured the new burghers living in an increasingly complex world. That, after all, had been Luce's first mission: not to make the twentieth century the American Century, but to keep people informed. Luce sought to rescue consumers from newspapers in the 1920s that either buried readers in the sensational or the local, or, in the rare case of the *New York Times*, offered far more information, much of it in deadening prose, than a "busy man" could expect to absorb. Later in the twentieth century, most American dailies and virtually all local television newscasts continued to devote the most space or time to local news. In providing a national perspective, network television and cable news services competed with *Time* and other newsweeklies. Yet like newspapers, TV news suffered from eventism. *Time* still had an outward-looking middle-class audience in search of summary.

Luce in one sense, however, had succeeded too well. Luce, T. S. Matthews wrote in 1967, "set a style in journalism that was mocked, denounced, at last imitated."[66] By the late 1970s all his publications had lost their original distinctiveness. New periodicals competed with *Sports Illustrated*. The daily *Wall Street Journal* gradually won a national readership by offering the comprehensive business reporting that Luce had found so wanting when he had first proposed *Fortune* to his board of directors. Even newspapers, long mired in conventions that had made *Time* and *Life* attractive alternatives, worked to improve the readability of their copy and expand their use of photographs. *Time*'s storybook style and visual imagery had become an ideal type for many journalists, including even the once gray *Wall Street Journal* and *New York Times*. "If *Time* magazine is not as influential among the print media as it once was," wrote *Business Week*'s editor-in-chief in May 1979, "it is because so many publications, both magazines and newspapers, have borrowed, copied, and stolen journalistic techniques that Luce invented."[67]

Luce's journalism of synthesis similarly invested the fourth estate with new powers. Condensing and refashioning news allowed the new communicator not to report some things. Presenting too much or contradictory information might upset the overall tone of a story. Luce's story-telling techniques, complained a British journalist in 1973, tended to make "everything a little too orderly, a little too neat."[68] But

201

Harry expected no less. *Time* entries had to have omniscience, *Life* pictures finality. A Luce writer had to be able to make up his mind. Often the editor made it up for him—adhering to a "policy" of Time Inc. After Luce, the control over the construction of synthesis did change. Writers at *Time* enjoyed more autonomy; *Newsweek* had already been in the process of awarding their staff members greater control over their copy. Newspapers, too, had become more respecting of individual reporters' feelings. Yet this shift by no means brought consumers closer to reality. Reporters, too, could have causes or, more likely, be guided by peer values. They could prize a story's effect over its accuracy. Television news producers, like their predecessors at *Life* and "The March of Time," might similarly favor impact over ambiguity. And millions might delude themselves under the impression that theirs was an "information age" rather than one barely better informed than that described by Lippmann in 1922 in *Public Opinion*.

For his part, Luce never lost that self-confidence, nurtured in north China and unshaken in early manhood, that led him to believe that he and others could summarize and comment on the world. "He thought the world could be understood by most people," one of his former editors recalled, "and once they understood it, they would want to put things straight."[69] Lippmann's jeremiads about the failure of journalism in the early 1920s only encouraged Luce. Formulas could be devised to inform the middle classes. After several martinis late in 1962, he told the publisher of the *Encyclopedia Britannica* that Time Inc. could assemble a rival reference work.[70] Such self-assurance rubbed off on most who worked for him; John Kenneth Galbraith described writing for *Fortune* as the decisive experience of his young adulthood. "Never after did I find anything I couldn't explain."[71] Harry himself searched for explanations more ardently and confidently than any of his employees. To the end, Luce remained positive that explanations could be found, whether in law or theology or political science, to bring order to a complex society. He was still looking when he died.

AFTERWORD, 2001

The century closed American, after all. Just over two decades after Luce's death, the Soviet Union, America's great rival after World War II, began to collapse. Eastern European nations long subject to Soviet control achieved independence. The Berlin Wall fell. It was a moment that Luce would have savored. America no longer had a serious rival for world hegemony.

Yet, the end of the Cold War carried an unexpected price tag for Luce's journalism. With the disappearance of the Russian threat, interest in world affairs dropped sharply. Americans ran away from the commitment to globalism that Luce had urged upon them in his 1941 "American Century" essay. Indeed, the national appetite for serious journalism fell as well. The nation's news agenda began to resemble one that Luce and Hadden had confronted in the 1920s: preoccupied with scandal and stunts.[1] More than world peace accounted for this change in the audience. Since the 1970s Americans had turned inward in other ways. A new identity politics prompted many women and ethnic and racial minorities to eschew an older national identification. Other factors, including increasing levels of education, income, and leisure time, had caused more consumers, especially younger readers, to develop more specialized tastes.[2] The great success stories in periodical publishing were not mass magazines like *Time* or *Life*, but ones that catered to more narrow interests.[3] Luce's heirs had tried to seize upon this trend, but with little enthusiasm and limited success.

One topic still commanded mass attention: the celebrity culture of film and television stars and popular musicians. "No society," cultural critic Neal Gabler wrote, "has ever had as many celebrities as ours or has revered them as intensely."[4] Luce's magazines, especially *Life*, had always understood the celebrity appeal. *People* magazine, founded by Time Inc. in 1974, had gone even further in taking show business celebrities seriously—and prospered greatly. The magazine became a necessity in many a waiting room. *American Scholar* editor Joseph Epstein told of a dentist acquaintance in the early 1990s "who claims to have practically lost his practice when he canceled his office subscription to *People*."[5]

The journalism of celebrity presented a dilemma for the traditional news media. Earlier in the century, editors at Time Inc. could award a cover story to a film star every now and then as a concession to those household members more interested in Rita Hayworth than Harry Truman. By the late twentieth century, editors could no longer be so stingy. The intense marketing of individual celebrities as well as the competition for readers forced their hand.[6] Consumers voted at the newsstand. A March 1987 *Time* cover on South Africa was a flop; *Newsweek's* April 1987 issue on arms control proved the worst selling of the year. As the editor of *People* explained, "Young is better than old, pretty is better than ugly, music is better than movies, movies are better than sports, and anything is better than politics."[7] *People* had been a trendsetter, cultural critic Jonathan Yardley acknowledged on the occasion of the magazine's twentieth anniversary, "But the trend is not one calculated to please anyone who believes that journalism has obligations higher than the vending of trashy celebrity and the accrual of profit."[8]

Time's extravagant 1998 dinner celebrating its 75th anniversary treated celebrities as the co-equals of politicians and world leaders. Former head of the Soviet Union Mikhail Gorbachev sat with actress Sophia Loren, his wife with film star Kevin Costner. The prominence given celebrities like Costner, Tom Hanks, and Tom Cruise, historian Richard Norton Smith complained, "illustrated just how far Hollywood has come, not merely in selling magazines but also in defining mainstream culture and in obliterating traditional barriers between politics and entertainment."[9]

At the same time, staying informed about the rest of the news agenda became easier. In many larger towns and cities, opinion leaders could have the *New York Times* delivered daily. The expansion of television news and the advent of all-news cable television networks made every home a potential information center. Critics might challenge the value of television news programs, especially those produced by individual stations. Nevertheless, the availability of so many new news services in the late twentieth century removed a long-time justification for subscribing to a magazine like *Time*—as did the spread of news sites on the internet and the steady growth of analysis in newspaper reportage.[10]

Time's editors had to decide whether they could continue to honor Luce and Hadden's original specifications and present knowing summaries of the week's news. Indeed, one could argue that the explosion of information sources in the 1980s and 1990s made adherence to *Time*'s original mission all the more important. While other news media might emphasize the attack on an Olympic skater, much as 1920s newspapers had overattended to that decade's sensational crimes, *Time* would tell readers what really mattered.[11] But, the number of Americans who wanted their journalistic vegetables appeared to be declining, and, mindful of this shift, *Time*'s editors retreated to the dessert cart. Rather than fight the prevailing trends of daily journalism, as Luce and Hadden had as young editors, their successors often played to them. An Iowa couple having septuplets, a story that Luce and Hadden would have relegated to the back of the magazine, earned a cover and thirteen pages in a December 1997 issue.[12] Between the two national party conventions in 1968, *Time* had invested nine pages and a cover on the brutal Nigerian civil war. Thirty-two years later, the magazine ran a cover story on professional golfer Tiger Woods.[13]

Time had changed in significant ways. Television, editors averred, had altered preferences in the presentation of news. They accordingly redesigned *Time* to carry more photographs and less text. No longer did the magazine affect to offer a summary of every important event, especially ones overseas.[14] Early in 1998, *Time*'s deputy managing editor admitted, "We're not the magazine of record anymore."[15] Pages given to international stories dropped from 24 percent in 1985 to 14 percent in 1995.[16] Even important domestic news sometimes took a back seat. The issue after Bill Clinton's election as president in 1992, *Time* ran a cover on prehistoric man; the Arkansas Democrat adorned *Newsweek*'s front.[17] "The magazine has evolved," correspondent Lance Morrow wrote in 1998, "into a mix of news and features that play off the news instead of simply recapping it."[18]

"The trademark *Time* cover more than ever before avoided conventional news," a longtime correspondent observed in the early 1990s. "The cover was more often a topic (the environment) or an idea (ethics) than an individual. Rather than being driven by events when there wasn't compelling news, the magazine concentrated on national problems and trends."[19] This departed from Luce's formula of placing individuals on the cover and using them as metaphors for news. The new cover policy had begun under Henry Grunwald, *Time*'s editor from 1968 to 1977. "It was no longer easy," Grunwald wrote, "to find individuals to personify what was significant in American society. Many subjects had grown too large and too complicated, too much the result of group effort and trends."[20] Frequently, critics charged, the trend was short-lived or inadequately reported.[21] Covers in April and May 1998 dealt with the future of money, the potency pill, and careers.[22] Inside came fewer stories, and more autonomy to correspondents as well as signed opinion pieces that made sections resemble opinion-leading periodicals like *The New Republic*. "We no longer feel that *Time* is an institution that must speak with one Olympian voice," the magazine's chief of correspondents remarked in 1990.[23] Some features took on the appearance of old *Life* or *People* pieces. The April 20, 1998, issue devoted four pages to a Catholic lay worker fighting gang warfare on Chicago's near north side, ten to the Shroud of Turin, and five to Disney's Animal Kingdom theme park.[24]

Time often substituted anticipatory coverage for its usual guided, after-the-fact summaries. This shift was first seen in the magazine's treatment of show business. Once, *Time* had been content to wait for a film to be a box office success before awarding it much attention. By the 1980s, it was laboring to stay ahead of the curve by devoting pages to a motion picture or television mini-series *not yet seen by the general public*. Prior to its 1983 telecast, the ABC mini-series, *The Winds of War*, received a cover and six pages.[25] The 1999 feature film, *The Phantom Menace*, netted a cover and an eleven-page spread, as well as the four-page transcript of an interview between the director George Lucas and television journalist Bill Moyers, a month before it opened.[26] The week before the 2000 Republican National Convention, Republican nominee-to-be George W. Bush appeared on the magazine's cover. The week after the convention, when the news magazine would have normally featured the nominee and a long analysis of the conclave itself, the magazine cover featured Tiger Woods, who was about to play in a major tournament.[27]

Despite such constant reinvention, *Time* had plainly passed into a sedentary state. Although not wanting for advertisers coveting the publication's upper-middle-class demographics, its circulation failed to increase between 1970 and 1997.[28] All of the news magazines had similar problems. Between 1993 and 2000 the percentage of adults who reported reading any of the news magazines dropped from 24 to 12 percent.[29] For some time, politicians had realized that they were better served wooing other newspeople, especially those who worked in television or for one of the nation's prestige dailies. "We had become largely irrelevant in journalistic and political communities in this country," a contributing editor confessed in 1992. "We weren't read as we used to be by decision makers, as often and with as much care."[30] "While nothing is what it once was," press critic Eric Alterman wrote in 1998, "this is nowhere truer than at *Time*."[31]

Sports Illustrated, which most resembled *Time* of the company's major publications, underwent similar changes and loss of prestige. In the 1990s, *SI* found itself contending with the all-sports cable network, ESPN, and its popular *SportsCenter* newscast as well as rival cable sports channels and an explosion of radio sports-talk programs. Fans and players began to favor ESPN over *SI*. ESPN started and heavily promoted its own sports magazine. *SI* could still sometimes set the agenda for the sports culture, most remarkably when a reporter recorded the bigoted rantings of Atlanta Braves pitcher John Rocker late in 1999. But *SI* struggled, like *Time*, to remain relevant in a new sports culture of nightly highlights and instant opinions. Increasingly, *SI* staffers realized, too many knew their publication only because of its annual issue devoted to female models in abbreviated swimsuits only a professional model would wear.[32]

"Pointless Men"

In the mid-1980s the leaders of Time Inc. were all too mindful of their company's dilemma. Although virtually all of their holdings made money, the company was not enjoying the kind of spectacular success from new magazines that Luce had experienced. *People* was the one noteworthy—to some, notorious—exception. Attempts to compete with the *Washington Post* and *TV Guide* and to create a new picture weekly had proven costly failures.[33] The great achievement at Time Inc. after Luce had been the cable television unit, which included Home Box Office (HBO), a premium cable channel, as well as individual cable systems. Indeed, Time Inc.'s cable activities had been the most dynamic performer in terms of profits. In 1984, the company's video group accounted for 46 percent of the company's operating profits.[34] Still, Time Inc. appeared committed to periodicals. In 1984, the company turned down an opportunity to purchase the relatively new and then struggling ESPN.[35] A year later, Ted Turner offered to sell Time Inc. a 50 percent ownership of his all-news cable network, CNN. Time Inc. president Richard Munro turned him away after an adviser told him Turner did not fit the company image, saying that Turner "drinks too much, spends money crazily and chases women."[36]

Nevertheless, the magazines' place within Time Inc. began changing for the worse. Luce and his successors had imposed a separation of "church" and "state." That is, business considerations should not affect the production of the magazines. But in 1986, Munro installed Nicholas J. Nicholas as his second in command. Nicholas had relatively little background in publishing; he was a manager, not an editor or writer. And, he acted as a manager, insisting that the magazines increase their revenues, even if doing so required cost-cutting that diminished the editorial product. Layoffs and reductions in expense accounts followed. Editors began basing their decisions in part on market research.[37]

Wall Street partly accounted for the new pressures. The company's overall performance dissatisfied financial analysts, which caused the price of Time Inc. stock to slide. The undervalued shares left the company vulnerable to a hostile takeover. An outside investor could acquire effective control of Time Inc. and draw on the company's substantial annual revenues from the magazines and cable television unit to finance still more acquisitions.[38]

In this environment, Munro realized, Time Inc. could best escape a shotgun marriage by finding a corporate mate of its own choosing. Several factors complicated locating a partner, including the determination of all senior executives that Time Inc. would control any combined entity. There was less consensus as to whether Time Inc. should remain true to its journalistic mission by joining forces with a large newspaper chain. Munro did hold preliminary discussions with the Gannett newspaper group.[39] As Munro weighed the company's options, two senior executives proposed something even more dramatic.

In 1987, Nicholas Nicholas and Gerald Levin, who was with the video group of Time Inc., and, like Nicholas, possessed little background in the company's magazine activities, persuaded Munro to turn away from print. Henry Luce's company should cease considering itself an essentially journalistic institution and merge with an entertainment conglomerate. The future would belong to those companies that extended their activities from journalism to communication generally, and from print to video. "Most of our asset base and expansion possibilities center on entertainment and on our established position in cable and programming," Levin wrote in an August 1987 memo. "Publishing is more limited. The new Time Inc., then, would be an entertainment oriented communications company."[40] That redefinition would include not just the production of messages, but, via cable, their distribution. The ideal partner, like Time Inc., owned cable systems but also produced television programming and feature films. Combined with the right conglomerate, Time Inc. could become a major—if not the major—communication company in the world.

Munro settled on Warner Communications, the successor to the Warner Brothers motion picture company. Headed by Steven Ross, Warner produced feature films and television series as well as sound recordings and operated television cable systems. To the Nicholas-Levin faction, Warner was an excellent fit. At HBO, Levin had regularly dealt with Warner executives and producers and was comfortable with the prospect of a partnership. Unlike some older Time Inc. hands, Levin believed that the future did not allow for the construction of a thick wall separating magazine or print journalism from a broadcasting or cable enterprise. More importantly, it would reward those enterprises that planned for a convergence of print and non-print media. At the same time, it would enrich those who sought the vertical integration that would result from combining production and distribution. In that regard, Warner's cable holdings were as desirable as its entertainment units. Early in 1989, when the merger was announced, Time Inc. had the nation's second largest cable system, Warner's was fifth. Combined, Time Warner controlled 12 percent of the nation's cable market.[41] It would be as if Henry Luce had tried to buy a minority interest in the Post Office.

Similar arguments had been made to Luce several years before his death. Time Inc. President James Linen had recommended in late 1965 that the company purchase United Artists, then a very profitable filmmaking concern. Luce vetoed the plan. Time Inc., he declared, played an essentially educational role. It should not enter the entertainment business.[42] Indeed, it should sell its five television stations, all money-makers, precisely because commercial networks, and not Time Inc., controlled their programming and stressed entertainment.[43] Luce's will specified, "Time Inc. is now, and is expected to continue to be, principally a journalistic enterprise, and, as such, an enterprise operated in the public interest."[44]

The prospect of combining with Warner dismayed the Old Guard of editors who had known and worked for Luce. They evoked the founder's distinction between information and entertainment. Hedley Donovan and others did not think that the journalistic culture of Time Inc. could co-exist with the show business sensibilities that pervaded Warner. In addition, Donovan found nothing inevitable about combining with an entertainment concern. Other publishing companies, notably the owners of the *New York Times, Washington Post,* and *Chicago Tribune,* essentially rejected Levin's model and invested mainly in other newspapers. Munro himself had weighed combining Time Inc. with the Gannett newspaper chain.[45]

Other trends in the mass media, however, blurred the differences between the news and entertainment media that had been clear to Luce and his loyalists. None was more pronounced than the rise of *infotainment,* that is, news that dealt uncritically with the entertainment industry and celebrity culture. Infotainment largely involved promotion rather than reportage. Initially, infotainment was limited to TV programs like the syndicated *Entertainment Tonight* and periodicals like *People.* But infotainment gradually crept into other media. Network morning news and prime time "magazine" programs as well as local TV newscasts willingly hyped forthcoming feature films as, occasionally, did *Time* and *Newsweek.*[46]

Loyalists understood something else as well. Much as some disliked Harry for his beliefs, at least he had them. Creating a magazine empire left him dissatisfied. He wanted to save America, and the world. He was a publisher with convictions, however controversial. Nicholas and Levin, in contrast, were mere builders. They would not have impressed Harry. Poring over a business story set for publication in the 1950s, Luce wrote, "I resent the fact that these men are fighting for a huge chunk of the 'national estate' without there seeming to be any point to the fight. None seems to stand for a damn thing. This is the sort of thing that turns one against capitalism. I resent having these great companies owned by pointless men like these."[47]

An unexpected and costly complication came soon after Munro and Ross announced their merger. Paramount Communications, another entertainment conglomerate, sought to prevent the marriage by launching a hostile takeover of Time Inc. To stave off Paramount, Time Inc. and Warner had to renegotiate their agreement. Time Inc., which had originally planned an exchange of stock, now had to borrow $11.2 billion to purchase the Warner shares. Although approved in July 1989, the merger left the new conglomerate with a huge debt.[48] As a result, Time Warner spent much of the 1990s trying to recover. And Luce's magazines paid a price. Belt-tightening and a soft advertiser demand forced all of the periodicals to cut costs. By 1997, the number of correspondents at *Time* had been reduced from 150 to 100.[49] In this new world, "marketing" periodicals became more important, with editors often determining covers and layouts based on the conclusions of focus groups and surveys.[50]

Although some merger proponents, notably Ross, had foreseen profitable "synergies" created by collaborations between Time Inc. and Warner properties, these failed to happen. In 1994, the British business weekly, *The Economist*, cited Time Warner as one of several prominent examples of a failed corporate fad. "In the media industry," the journal observed, "synergy-driven acquisition strategies have succeeded only in draining away profits and alienating staff who have little incentive to work together."[51] Although Time Warner's overall position improved through the 1990s, a *Time* editor charitably described Time Warner as "an extremely successful dysfunctional family."[52]

The union of Time Inc. and Warner created other problems for Luce's periodicals. Prior to the merger, everyone at Time Inc. understood magazines to be the company's primary business. After 1989, journalism formed only a part of Time Warner's overall activities. Warner was the larger entity. "We're now like the tender to a battleship," one veteran magazine writer cried.[53] One executive dismissed the magazines as "basically software."[54] In 1998, periodicals accounted for 23.2 percent of Time Warner revenues.[55] When Time Warner itself became a *Fortune* story, journalistic autonomy came into question. A *Fortune* consultant resigned in 1991 charging that editors interfered with his calculation of the extravagant annual compensation awarded Time Warner chairman Ross—$78.2 million in 1990.[56] More problematic was the entertainment industry itself. Did Warner films receive more attention and more favorable reviews in Luce's magazines? A 1990 *Time* cover story on Scott Turow's new novel did not note that Warner Books was Turow's publisher and that Warner Brothers was about to release a film adaptation of an earlier novel by the writer. Although no pattern emerged, cross-ownership at the very least created the appearance of a conflict of interest.[57]

Undaunted by such concerns and his company's red ink, Levin, who had succeeded Ross as head of Time Warner, successfully engineered another major merger. After seeking to purchase 49 percent of the NBC network, Time Warner paid $7.5 billion in stock in 1996 for Ted Turner's cable television and entertainment company, which included CNN and a huge library of old Hollywood feature films and cartoons. "There are so many ways this works for all involved," remarked one Warner executive. The nation's largest media company, Time Warner towered over such communication giants as Disney, CBS, and Rupert Murdoch's News Corporation.[58]

Levin's vision became increasingly clear, if not necessarily reassuring. CNN stood as a case study in corporate synergy by self-consciously connecting its programming to Time Inc. "brands." CNN renamed its nightly sportscast CNN/SI.[59] Far more ambitious was a documentary program *NewsStand*, tied to different Time Warner periodicals. "It's a lot easier to get a show's mission conveyed to viewers," a CNN producer explained, "when you're associated with a well-known magazine like *Time*."[60]

The first program proved a journalistic catastrophe. Aired in June 1998, *NewsStand: CNN and Time* claimed that in 1970 the U.S. military had secretly attacked American defectors in Laos with a deadly nerve gas. An independent investigation, prompted by criticisms of the telecast, found that the producers, all from CNN, had insufficient evidence for their grave assertion. CNN issued an apology and fired two producers while another resigned. *Time* was left trying to explain why it had carried a two-thousand-word version of the story, written by a CNN correspondent and producer, despite the misgivings of its own correspondents.[61] "Gerald Levin and Ted Turner melded their legions in 1996 expecting to forge a unique, multimedia newsgathering force with all the potential power and riches of such a union," wrote one press critic. "So far, the results range from mixed to disastrous."[62] Observed two others, "The history of recent mergers suggests that when media companies synergize their brands they do not add to them. They dilute them."[63]

Entering an Infinite Space

Convinced that the future rested with new technologies, Levin sought yet another partner. Early in 2000, he struck a deal with Steven Case of AOL. The leading internet service provider, AOL would pay $165 billion in stock to acquire Time Warner. It represented the largest corporate acquisition in American history. Levin would remain chief executive officer. One observer dubbed the merger "probably the most significant development in the Internet business world to date."[64]

The AOL Time Warner combination was consistent with Levin's plan to transform Time Inc. By coupling Time Warner with AOL, Levin gambled that Case and AOL represented the future. To Levin, the future was no longer in print but in internet providers like AOL; Time Warner under Levin had been unable to fashion its own internet service. Moreover, Wall Street overwhelmingly preferred high technology stocks like

AOL compared to Time Warner. Indeed, AOL's high stock price—what *Time* dubbed its "helium-supported Internet valuation"—made its acquisition of Time Warner possible. For his part, Case regarded Time Warner as part of his strategic plan: AOL would only grow if it could provide subscribers with *content providers*, a turn-of-the-century shorthand for magazines and motion pictures. Even more attractive to Case were Time Warner's substantial cable holdings. More advanced internet services would require the broadband services that cable, as opposed to telephone lines, could provide. That Time Warner's cable systems might be the most desirable part of its dowry undoubtedly would have horrified Luce, to say nothing of the Warner Brothers.[65]

Case was very much a builder, much as Luce had been, several generations earlier, though the connection largely ended there. In his own way, Luce had overseen a journalistic revolution by encouraging much of the news media to move toward guided synthesis. Yet Luce was also very much the child of missionaries. Each of his magazines above all should have a larger purpose, not just expand and prosper. To Luce that meant advancing his vision of mature capitalism and American globalism. Personal wealth was secondary. This is not to say that Luce disliked making money. "I was poor once and I saw no merit in it if you can honestly avoid it," he told a colleague. But he was not a man obsessed with personal wealth.[66] In 1998, Levin earned just over $250 million, about twice Luce's total worth when he died.[67] Case aspired, like Levin, to create a media conglomerate far larger and more encompassing than anything Luce or his contemporaries could have imagined. However, Case and Levin had no apparent ideology, at least not one that they sought to promote. Their ambitions were for their corporate holdings, not their country or the world. Where Luce had declared the twentieth century to be American, Case spoke of the twenty-first as "the internet century," a forecast Levin dutifully echoed.[68] All in all, it would be more about distributing messages than the messages themselves.

The AOL Time Warner combination constituted the most prominent example of the trend to media monopoly. The relaxation of antitrust concerns in the 1980s and 1990s and a mindless preoccupation with American firms competing globally had encouraged a wave of mergers that threatened to reduce the number of independent voices to a precious few. By the century's end, contended the most prominent critic of such concentration, "the country's most widespread news, commentary, and daily entertainment are controlled by six firms," one of them AOL Time Warner.[69] If nothing else, the merger revived questions first raised in the wake of the Time Warner marriage. Would *Time* and other AOL Time Warner periodicals cover their parent company critically, if at all? Or would they become mere appendages that had to attend to the bottom line more than traditional journalistic standards? Their superiors were no longer men like Luce who first and last were journalists. "Essentially and always, Luce was a reporter and writer and editor like ourselves," *Time* observed in its memorial tribute.[70] Steve Case had no background in journalism, unless one counted his high school newspaper work.[71]

Although the trend to bigness was distressing on many levels, other tendencies were consoling. While large mass media corporations joined forces, cable and the internet fractured the national audience itself. AOL might try to encourage but it could not compel subscribers to view *Time*'s web site. Nor could Time Warner's cable systems control viewers' preferences for news channels other than CNN or entertainment programming not manufactured by Warner Television.[72] Facing new rivals on cable, CNN began losing viewers soon after the Time Warner purchase.[73] The internet portended even more audience fragmentation. "The Internet is an infinite space," a *Wall Street Journal* columnist argued. "No matter how big AOL Time Warner becomes, it diminishes the space available to others by exactly zero. We are a far cry from the day when three networks could control everything Americans watched and one telephone company carried all our communications."[74] The AOL Time Warner merger dismayed Michael Lewis, a journalist who studied new technology. AOL had ignored "the first lesson" of the internet boom, "the way new technology and new ideas are likely to be introduced these days. That is, willy-nilly, from the bottom up." Lewis wrote, "Almost certainly the future of this sort of technology will not be imposed from above by some huge company."[75]

Finally, synergies remained elusive or unworkable within a vast organization. Despite increased cross-promotion, even *Sports Illustrated*'s swimsuit issue was losing some of its appeal.[76] *SI*'s biggest scoop of 1999 had nothing to do with thongs, but John Rocker. His interview enormously embarrassed his employer, the Atlanta Braves, which was owned by Time Warner. Earlier that year, Time Warner's extravagant feature film, *Wild Wild West*, could not escape the scorn of those writing reviews for the company's own periodicals and of theater-goer indifference.[77] *Time*'s cover story on the AOL merger included a page-long attack by Victor Navasky.[78] It was a dissenting opinion that upset the magazine's original design. No longer was there one voice, but many, even at *Time*.

CHRONOLOGY

3 April 1898	Born, Tengchow [Penglai], China.
1908–1913	Attends Chefoo School, Chefoo [Yantai], China.
1913–1914	Travels to United States via Europe.
1914–1916	Attends Hotchkiss School, Lakeville, Connecticut.
September 1916	Enters Yale University.
1918–1919	2d Lieutenant, U.S. Army.
June 1920	Receives A.B., Yale University.
1920–1921	Studies at Oxford; tours Europe.
August–September 1921	Reporter, *Chicago Daily News*.
September 1921–February 1922	Joins friend Briton Hadden on staff of *Baltimore News*; the two begin planning weekly newspaper.
1922–1923	Moving to New York, Luce and Hadden prepare "news-weekly," *Time*.
3 March 1923	*Time*, vol. 1, no. 1.
23 December 1923	Marries Lila Hotz of Chicago.
28 April 1925	Son, Henry III, born.

August 1925	*Time*'s operations moved to Cleveland.
August 1927	*Time* returns to New York.
18 May 1928	Son, Peter Paul, born.
28 February 1929	Hadden dies; Luce soon thereafter assumes effective ownership of Time Inc.
February 1930	*Fortune*, vol. 1, no. 1.
6 March 1931	First "March of Time" radio program.
1 February 1935	First "March of Time" newsreel.
5 October 1935	Divorces Lila Luce.
23 November 1935	Marries Clare Boothe Brokaw.
23 November 1936	*Life*, vol. 1, no. 1.
Spring 1940	Joining Clare in Europe, witnesses beginning of German western front offensive, World War II; returns urging American aid to Britain.
Summer–Fall 1940	Becomes heavily involved in Wendell Willkie campaign for president.
17 February 1941	Essay "The American Century" appears in *Life*.
3 November 1942	Clare elected to first of two terms, U.S. House of Representatives, Connecticut.
29 March 1948	*Time* carries essay "Struggle for Survival," urging Americans to take offensive in "Cold War" against the Soviet Union.
19 April 1951	Delivers first of many addresses urging "peace through law."
Summer–Fall 1952	With his wife works for election of Republican Dwight Eisenhower, who wins in landslide in November.
1953–1956	Appointed by Eisenhower, Clare Luce serves as U.S. Ambassador to Italy; Luce sets up offices in Rome.
16 August 1954	*Sports Illustrated*, vol. 1, no. 1.
5 February 1958	Suffers heart attack, reported as severe cold.
30 April 1959	After a bitter encounter with the Senate Foreign Relations Committee and Senate

confirmation of her nomination to be U.S. ambassador to Brazil, Clare Luce resigns before assuming the position.

16 April 1964	Retires as Time Inc. editor-in-chief.
28 February 1967	Dies of heart attack, Phoenix, Arizona.
4 March 1967	Buried, Mepkin Plantation, South Carolina.

NOTES AND REFERENCES

1. INTRODUCTION

1. Robert T. Elson, *The World of Time Inc.*, 2 vols. (New York: Atheneum, 1968–73), 1:447–48.

2. W. Rich to Frank Norris, 5 July 1940, Daniel Longwell Papers, Box 29, Columbia University, New York City.

3. Roosevelt to Luce, 20 November 1940, Roosevelt Papers, President's Personal File, Roosevelt Library, Hyde Park, New York.

4. *Business Week*, 6 March 1948, 6; Pauline Kael, "Raising Kane," *New Yorker*, 27 February 1971, 49–50, 52, 57.

5. Theodore H. White, *In Search of History* (New York: Harper & Row, 1978), 126.

6. U.S., Congress, Senate, Government Operations Committee, Subcommittee on National Policy Machinery, *Organizing for National Security*, Hearings, 86th Cong. 2d sess., 1960, 923.

7. Ralph Ingersoll, quoted in "*Time*: The Weekly Fiction Magazine," *Fact* 1 (Jan.–Feb. 1964):3.

8. Joseph Epstein, *Ambition: The Secret Passion* (New York: E.P. Dutton, 1980), 147. Compare with Epstein, "Henry Luce and His Time," *Commentary*, November 1967, 35–47.

9. W. A. Swanberg, *Luce and His Empire* (New York: Charles Scribner's Sons, 1972), 472.

10. Joan Shelley Rubin, "Swift's Premium Ham: William Lyon Phelps and the Redefinition of Culture," in *Mass Media between the Wars: Perceptions*

of Cultural Tensions, 1918–1940, ed. Catherine L. Covert and John D. Stevens (Syracuse, N.Y.: Syracuse University Press, 1984), 12.

11. David Cort, "Once Upon a Time Inc.," *Nation,* 18 February 1956, 134.

12. Raymond Williams, *The Long Revolution* (London: Chatto and Windus, 1961); James W. Carey, "The Communications Revolution and the Professional Communicator," *Sociological Review Monographs,* no. 13 (January 1969), 23–25.

13. William F. Buckley, Jr., *The Jeweler's Eye* (New York: G. P. Putnam's Sons, 1968), 340–43.

2. THE MISSIONARY'S SON, 1898–1920

1. Sherwood Eddy, *Pathfinders of the World Missionary Crusade* (New York: Abingdon-Cokesbury Press, 1945), 54.

2. Clifton J. Phillips, "The Student Volunteer Movement and Its Role in China Missions, 1886–1920," in *The Missionary Enterprise in China and America,* ed. John K. Fairbank (Cambridge, Mass.: Harvard University Press, 1974), 106–7.

3. B. A. Garside, *One Increasing Purpose: The Life of Henry Winters Luce* (New York: Fleming H. Revell, 1948), 62–63.

4. Eddy, *Pathfinders,* 54.

5. Nettie Fowler McCormick to Elizabeth Root Luce, 12 December 1906, McCormick Papers, Series 1B, Box 24, State Historical Society of Wisconsin, Madison; Kenneth Stewart, "The Education of Henry Luce," *PM Picture News,* 27 August 1944, M7.

6. Stewart, "Education," M8. See also Jane Hunter, *The Gospel of Gentility: American Women Missionaries in Turn-of-the-Century China* (New Haven: Yale University Press, 1984), 104–5.

7. John K. Jessup, ed., *The Ideas of Henry Luce* (New York: Atheneum, 1969), 379–81. For like sentiments, see Pearl S. Buck, *My Several Worlds: A Personal Record* (New York: John Day Co., 1954), 5.

8. Henry R. Luce, "To See Life in Its Full Dimensions," *Fortune,* January 1967, 88.

9. *Yale Courant,* 2 May 1891, 192; 16 May 1891, 207; 18 April 1891, 169; 10 October 1891, 22–23; John Kobler, *Luce: His Time, Life, and Fortune* (Garden City, N.Y.: Doubleday, 1968), 28.

10. John Hersey, "Henry Luce's China Dream," *New Republic,* 2 May 1983, 27–28; Kobler, *Luce,* 33.

11. Gilbert A. Harrison, *The Enthusiast: A Life of Thornton Wilder* (New Haven: Tickner & Fields, 1983), 361.

12. Luce to parents, [?] January 1909, Luce Family Correspondence, Time Inc. Archives, Time-Life Building, New York City.

13. Luce to parents, 21 September 1913, Luce Family Correspondence.

14. Luce to Nettie Fowler McCormick, 30 October 1916, McCormick Papers, Series 2B, Box 152.

15. Draft of sermon, 3 June 1906, Luce Family Correspondence.

16. Nettie Fowler McCormick to Henry Winters Luce, 14 December 1906, McCormick Papers, Series 1B, Box 24.

17. Henry Winters Luce to H. G. Buehler, 19 September 1916, Hotchkiss School, Lakeville, Conn.; Luce to parents, 26 January 1913, Luce Family Correspondence.

18. Luce to Henry Winters Luce, 25 June 1916, Luce Family Correspondence.

19. School theme attached to letter to parents, 4 November 1913, Luce Family Correspondence.

20. Gamaliel Bradford, "Charles Sumner," Yale Review 4 (April 1916): 556; Luce to parents, 29 March 1916, Luce Family Correspondence.

21. Ellsworth Huntington, "The Success of Missionary Children," Missionary Review of the World 58 (February 1935):74–75.

22. Luce to Miss Dolph, 24 March 1912, Luce Family Correspondence.

23. Hotchkiss Record, 22 October 1915, 2; 30 November 1915, 1, 3; Erdman Harris, "Harry Luce at Hotchkiss," Hotchkiss Alumni News, July 1964, 8.

24. Hotchkiss Record, 28 January 1916, 1.

25. Elson, World of Time, 1:30, 31.

26. Luce to parents, 8 August 1916, Luce Family Correspondence.

27. Luce to Nettie F. McCormick, 2 October 1916, McCormick Papers, Series 2B, Box 152.

28. Luce to parents, 8 April 1916, 10 January 1918, Luce Family Correspondence.

29. Henry Seidel Canby, College Sons and College Fathers (New York: Harper & Bros., 1915), 5, 175, 176.

30. William E. Wickenden, "Education and the New Age," in Toward Civilization, ed. Charles A. Beard (New York: Longmans, Green and Co., 1930), 256. A June 1901 survey indicated that at ten schools (Columbia, Cornell, the University of Cincinnati, Harvard, Missouri, Stanford, Virginia, Washington State, West Virginia, and William and Mary) virtually all work was elective; thirty-four reported that 70 percent or more was elective to fifty-one (mostly in the South) reporting that more than half of all courses were required. George Wilson Pierson, Yale: College and University, 1871–1937 (New Haven: Yale University Press, 1952), 264 n.

31. Yale Daily News, 1 April 1919, 2.

32. Luce to James A. Pike, 23 December 1961, Pike Papers, Box 16, Syracuse University, Syracuse, N.Y.; Luce to Nettie F. McCormick, 6 November 1916, McCormick Papers, Series 2B, Box 152.

33. Pierson, Yale, 451.

34. *Hotchkiss Record*, 18 April 1916, 2.

35. Luce to parents, 29 March 1916, 14 May 1917, Luce Family Correspondence.

36. David M. Kennedy, *Over Here: The First World War and American Society* (New York: Oxford University Press, 1980), 188.

37. Elson, *World of Time*, 1:40.

38. Walter Lippmann, *Public Opinion* (New York: Macmillan, 1922), 365. See also Lippmann, *Drift and Mastery* (Englewood Cliffs, N.J.: Prentice-Hall, 1961), 100; Ronald Steel, *Walter Lippmann and the American Century* (New York: Random House, 1980), 44–49; Stephen L. Vaughn, "Prologue to *Public Opinion*: Walter Lippmann's Work in Military Intelligence," *Prologue* 15 (Fall 1983):151–64.

39. Mary Mander, "The Journalist as Cynic," *Antioch Review* 38 (Winter 1980): 91–107.

40. In August 1914, Luce made the distinction of others between a "good" and "bad" trust, and expressed dismay to Mrs. McCormick over a district court's attempt to break up Harvester Company. Luce to McCormick, 11 August 1914, McCormick Papers, Series 2B, Box 136.

41. Epstein, *Ambition*, 130. See also Pierson, *Yale*, 306.

42. Noel F. Busch, *Briton Hadden* (New York: Farrar, Straus & Co., 1949), 41; Elizabeth Root Luce to Nettie F. McCormick, 16 May 1919, McCormick Papers, Series 2B Box 172.

43. Elizabeth Root Luce to Nettie F. McCormick, 27 May 1921, McCormick Papers, Series 2B, Box 177.

44. *Yale Daily News*, 26 April 1920, clipping, Luce file, Alumni Records Office, Yale University.

45. Luce to Nettie F. McCormick, 3 December 1919, McCormick Papers, Series 2B, Box 167.

3. TIME BEGINS, 1921–1923

1. Luce to parents, 28 October 1920, Luce Family Correspondence; Linda Simon, *Thornton Wilder: His World* (Garden City, N.Y. Doubleday: 1979), 30.

2. Jack Alexander, "Up from Akron," *Saturday Evening Post*, 18 August 1945, 44.

3. Story on missing Northwestern student, *Chicago Daily News*, 24 September 1921, 1; Elson, *World of Time*, 1:54–55.

4. Luce to Nettie Fowler McCormick, 6 December 1921, McCormick Papers, Series 2B, Box 177.

5. Edward L. Bernays, *Biography of an Idea: Memoirs of a Public Relations Counsel* (New York: Simon & Schuster, 1965), 363–64; Luce to Nettie F. McCormick, [6 February 1922], [27 April 1922], McCormick Papers, Series 2B, Box 182.

6. Emil J. Emig, *Reading Habits of Newspaper Readers* (Gainesville, Fla.: University of Florida Press, 1928), 13.

7. Bruce Barton, "What Difference Does It Make?" *Collier's*, 3 January 1925, 7. A survey of twenty-three hundred prominent Chicago business and professional men before the war showed 86 percent reading more than one paper; 39 percent read more than two. Walter Dill Scott, *The Psychology of Advertising in Theory and Practice* (Boston: Small, Maynard & Co., 1921), 379.

8. Elson, *World of Time*, 1:5–6.

9. H. L. Mencken, *Newspaper Days 1899–1906* (New York: Knopf, 1968), 14. See also John L. Given, *Making a Newspaper* (New York: H. Holt & Co., 1914), chap. 12.

10. Oliver Gramling, *AP: The Story of News* (New York: Farrar & Rinehart, 1940), 296–97.

11. Andrew Lang, Walter Leaf, and Ernest Myers, trans., *The Complete Works of Homer* (New York: Modern Library, 1935), 148, 258. This portion of the *Iliad* was translated by Lang, whose labors were among the more popular in the early twentieth century. Thomas Stanley Matthews, *Name and Address: An Autobiography* (New York: Simon & Schuster, 1960), 217.

12. Busch, *Hadden*, 53–54.

13. Luce to parents, Easter 1917, Luce Family Correspondence. Luce repressed this style in several signed pieces in the *Saturday Review of Literature*. See, for example, "The Press is Peculiar," 7 March 1931, 646–47.

14. Max Beerbohm, "Enoch Soames: A Memory of the Eighteen Nineties," *Century Magazine*, May 1916, 1–19; Luce to parents, 23 April 1916, Luce Family Correspondence.

15. Review, 29 January 1901, reprinted in Beerbohm, *Around Theatres* (London: Rupert Hart-Davis, 1953), 120; Beerbohm, *The Dreadful Dragon of Hay Hill* (London: William Heinemann, 1928), 40–41. One Time Inc. editor saw a Beerbohm influence on Hadden as well. Daniel Longwell to Alex Groner, 26 June 1957, Longwell Papers, Box 26.

16. Walter Lippmann, *Liberty and the News* (New York: Harcourt, Brace & Howe, 1920), 79, 82; Leo Rosten, *The Washington Correspondents* (New York: Harcourt, Brace, 1937), 7.

17. Daniel Czitrom, *Media and the American Mind* (Chapel Hill: University of North Carolina Press, 1982), 106–7; Norval Neil Luxon, *Niles' Weekly Register* (Baton Rouge: Louisiana State University Press, 1947).

18. Scott, *Psychology of Advertising*, 380–88. See also Glenn Frank, "The Seven Deadly Sins of American Journalism," *Century Magazine*, July 1923, 478.

19. Silas Bent, *Strange Bedfellows* (New York: Horace Liveright, 1928), 245; Walter Lippmann and Charles Merz, "A Test of the News," supplement to *New Republic*, 4 August 1920; Gay Talese, *The Kingdom and the Power* (New York and Cleveland: World Pub., 1969), 162–63.

20. Quoted in *Columbia Journalism Review* 18 (November–December 1980):73.

21. Silas Bent, *Ballyhoo* (New York: Boni & Liveright, 1927), 113. See also Herbert Brucker, "Glut of Occurrences," *Atlantic Monthly*, August 1935, 195–205.

22. Rush Welter, *Popular Education and Democratic Thought* (New York: Columbia University Press, 1967), 256. See also Robert Bremner, *From the Depths: The Discovery of Poverty in the United States* (New York: New York University Press, 1956), chap. 9.

23. Ray Stannard Baker, *American Chronicle: The Autobiography of Ray Stannard Baker* (New York: Charles Scribner's Sons, 1945), 183; Otis L. Graham, Jr., *An Encore for Reform: The Old Progressives and the New Deal* (New York: Oxford University Press, 1967), 12.

24. Harvey N. Davis, "Spirit and Culture under the Machine," in *Toward Civilization*, ed. Beard, 289. Suggestive on the decline of muckraking are Thomas C. Leonard, *The Power of the Press: The Birth of American Political Reporting* (New York: Oxford University Press, 1986), 194; Richard L. McCormick, "The Discovery that Business Corrupts Politics: A Reappraisal of the Origins of Progressivism," *American Historical Review* 86 (April, 1981):272–74.

25. Charles A. and Mary R. Beard, *America at Midpassage* (New York: Macmillan, 1939), 740–41.

26. Preston W. Slosson, *The Great Crusade and After 1914–1928* (New York: Macmillan, 1930), 360–61.

27. *New Haven Journal-Courier*, 12 February 1922, clipping, Hadden file, Alumni Records Office, Yale University.

28. William L. Shirer, *20th Century Journey: A Memoir*, vol. 1: *The Start 1904–1930* (New York: Simon & Schuster, 1976), 44.

29. *New York Times*, 3 March 1923, clipping, Hadden file, Alumni Records Office, Yale University.

30. Frederick J. Hoffman, *The Twenties: American Writing in the Postwar Decade* (New York: Collier Books, 1962), 21, 25; Paul A. Carter, *The Twenties*, 2d ed. (New York: Thomas Y. Crowell, 1975), 12–13.

31. Scott Fitzgerald to Edmund Wilson, [May 1921], in *The Letters of F. Scott Fitzgerald*, ed., Andrew Turnbull (New York: Charles Scribner's Sons, 1963), 326; Paul Johnson, *Modern Times: The World from the Twenties to the Eighties* (New York: Harper & Row, 1983), 215.

32. Ellis W. Hawley, *The Great War and the Search for a Modern Order* (New York: St. Martin's Press, 1979), 52–55. Luce, angry over the Republicans' support for Prohibition, voted against Hoover when he first ran for president in 1928.

33. *Time*, 3 March 1923, 1, 2.

34. Jessup, ed., *Ideas of Luce*, 220.

35. *Time*, 31 October 1927, 36, 38; 25 March 1925, 12; Frank Luther

Mott, *A History of American Magazines*, 5 vols. (Cambridge, Mass.: Harvard University Press, 1930–68), 5:309, 311.

36. Lippmann, *Public Opinion*, 16, 363, 364.

37. Luce to Nettie F. McCormick, [5 August 1922], McCormick Papers, Series 2B, Box 182.

38. See, e.g., *Time*, 24 January 1927, 6; 19 September 1927, 38.

39. Pierson, *Yale*, 364; William Lyon Phelps, "Time," *Yale Alumni Weekly*, 16 February 1922, clipping, Hadden file, Alumni Records Office, Yale University.

40. *Time*, 3 March 1923, 3.

41. Busch, *Hadden*, 87.

4. "TIME WILL TELL," 1923–1938

1. James A. Linen, address, 25 February 1958, Robert W. Desmond Papers, Box 85, State Historical Society of Wisconsin.

2. Transcript of Time Inc. oral history of Daniel Longwell, 18 August 1957, 7–8, Longwell Papers, Box 26.

3. Luce to Nettie Fowler McCormick, [6 February 1922], McCormick Papers, Series 2B, Box 182.

4. Busch, *Hadden*, 181–82.

5. Elson, *World of Time*, 1:121.

6. Diary of John Shaw Billings, 6 March 1931, John Shaw Billings Papers, South Caroliniana Library, University of South Carolina, Columbia.

7. American Society of Newspaper Editors, *Proceedings of Fifteenth Annual Convention April 15–16–17, 1937*, (hereafter, ASNE), 70.

8. Peter F. Drucker, *Adventures of a Bystander* (New York: Harper & Row, 1979), 225.

9. Andrew Kopkind, "Serving *Time*," *New York Review of Books*, 12 September 1968, 24. See also Eric Hodgins, "The Magazines," in *While You Were Gone*, ed. Jack Goodman (New York: Simon & Schuster, 1946), 412–14; Nelson Lichtenstein, "Authorial Professionalism and the Literary Marketplace," *American Studies* 16 (Spring 1978):42–44.

10. Matthews, *Name and Address*, 246–57; Matthews, "Tall, Balding, Dead Henry R. Luce," *Esquire*, September 1967, 131, 183; Billings Diary, 9 July 1933, 24 July 1933, Billings Papers.

11. Billings Diary, 6 June 1935; *Des Moines Register*, 19 April 1933, clipping, Billings Papers, scrapbook vol. 24.

12. Alfred Kazin, *Starting Out in the Thirties* (Boston: Atlantic-Little, Brown, 1962), 103.

13. ASNE, *Proceedings 1937*, 69. Another magazine success story in the interwar years, the *Reader's Digest*, abbreviated articles from other publications

and, like *Time*, relied on neophytes. In 1936, only two of the periodical's thirty-two-member staff had worked for a magazine before joining the *Digest*. "The Reader's Digest," *Fortune*, November 1936, 122.

14. Matthews, *Name and Address*, 221–22.

15. *Des Moines Tribune*, 18 April 1933, clipping, Billings Papers, scrapbook vol. 24.

16. *Time*, 29 August 1927, 6; 31 October 1927, 38; 12 December 1927, 10.

17. ASNE, *Proceedings 1937*, 70.

18. *Brooklyn Eagle*, 4 September 1913. Before the ASNE, Martin said he most admired sportswriting in daily newspapers. See *Proceedings 1937*, 76.

19. Joseph J. Firebaugh, "The Vocabulary of *Time* Magazine," *American Speech* 15 (October 1940):233.

20. ASNE, *Proceedings 1937*, 71; Mott, *History of American Magazines*, 5:316.

21. Quoted in *Time*, 8 March 1948, 63.

22. Ibid., 16 January 1933, 9–10; note on clipping from 10 December 1928 *Time* entry, Billings Papers, scrapbook vol. 24.

23. Donald J. Lehnus, *Who's On Time?* (New York: Oceana, 1980), 9.

24. *Time*, 27 December 1926, 2.

25. Ibid., 9 November 1936, 16–18; David Cort, *The Sin of Henry Luce* (Secaucus, N.J.: Lyle Stuart, 1974), 73.

26. Helen MacGill Hughes, *News and the Human Interest Story* (Chicago: University of Chicago Press, 1940), 284–85.

27. Warren I. Susman, " 'Personality' and the Making of Twentieth Century Culture," in *New Directions in American Intellectual History*, ed. John Higham and Paul K. Conkin (Baltimore: Johns Hopkins University Press, 1979), 212–34; Robert S. Lynd, *Knowledge for What?* (Princeton: Princeton University Press, 1940), 51; Theodore P. Greene, *America's Heroes: The Changing Models of Success in American Magazines* (New York: Oxford University Press, 1970), 71–73, 78–81, 90–92, 98, 106, 109, chaps. 4–5.

28. Otis Chatfield-Taylor, "The Timeditors," *Ringmaster*, November 1936, 7.

29. ASNE, *Proceedings 1937*, 69; Luce to Dwight Macdonald, 31 July 1934, Macdonald Papers, Yale University, New Haven, Conn.

30. Billings Diary, 8 November 1930, Billings Papers.

31. *Time*, 9 January 1928, 11; 30 January 1928, 14; Herbert Brucker, *The Changing American Newspaper* (New York: Columbia University Press, 1937), 78–79.

32. *Time*, 23 May 1932, 10–11; 15 February 1937, 17.

33. Cort, "Once Upon," 134.

34. *Time*, 9 May 1932, 13; 13 June 1932, 17–18.

35. Billings Diary, 24 February 1930, Billings Papers.

36. Ibid., 2 November 1936, 8. See also 3 January 1927, 7.

37. Edmund Wilson, "Thoughts on Being Bibliographed," *Princeton Library Chronicle* 5 (February 1944):53; "The Reminiscences of Thomas S. Matthews" (1958), Oral History Collection of Columbia University, 35; memorandum, Luce to Billings, [20 August 1936], Billings Papers.

38. *Time*, 27 June 1932, 7; *Time* clipping, c. August 1932, Billings Papers, scrapbook vol. 24.

39. Busch, *Hadden*, 194.

40. Harold Ross to Luce, 23 November 1936, copy in James Thurber Papers, Yale University.

41. Bernard De Voto, "Distempers of the Press," *Harper's*, March 1937, 447.

42. Insert, *Standard Rate and Data Publications*, January 1935; Elson, *World of Time*, 1:373–74; Paul F. Lazarsfeld, "How Cities Differ in Their Magazine Reading Habits," *Sales Management*, 15 February 1936, 218–20, 262; 1 March 1936, 296–97, 322, 324.

43. Time Inc., *Time for Concentration* (New York: Time Inc., 1931), 36; Time Inc., "1931 Buying Plans of 350,000 Families," Time Inc. Archives; *Historical Statistics of the United States*, 2 vols. (Washington: U.S. Government Printing Office, 1975), 2:646.

44. Time Inc., "The Income of *Time* Families" (July 1941), Time Inc. Archives.

45. *Time for Concentration*, 41 ff; *Advertising and Selling*, 27 May 1931, 58–59.

46. Time Inc., "*Time* for Business and Industry" (1939), 17, 19, 51, Time Inc. Archives. See also Robert S. and Helen Merrell Lynd, *Middletown in Transition* (New York: Harcourt, Brace, and World, 1937), 260.

47. Time Inc., "More New Car Buyers. . . . " (1939), Time Inc. Archives.

48. David Cort, "Ignorant, Soulless, and Amateur," *Nation*, 16 April 1960, 340.

49. Carl Becker, *Progress and Power* (New York: Knopf, 1949), 71, 72.

50. Samuel P. Hays, "The New Organizational Society," in *American Political History as Social Analysis* (Knoxville: University of Tennessee Press, 1980), 256–63.

51. Luce, speech, 27 May 1939, Billings Papers; Cort, "Ignorant," 340.

52. Joan Shelley Rubin, " 'Information, Please!': Culture and Expertise in the Interwar Period," *American Quarterly* 35 (Winter 1983):505. See also her "Self, Culture, and Self-Culture in Modern America: The Early History of the Book-of-the-Month Club," *Journal of American History* 71 (March 1985):782–806.

53. Emphasis added. *Time*, 21 April 1924, 29.

54. Ibid., 24 December 1923, 33.

55. Richard Norton Smith, *An Uncommon Man: The Triumph of Herbert Hoover* (New York: Simon & Schuster, 1984), 173.

56. Gramling, *AP*, 315.

57. Silas Bent, "The Art of Ballyhoo," *Harper's*, September 1927, 493; John R. Brazil, "Murder Trials, Murder, and Twenties America," *American Quarterly* 33 (Summer 1981):165.

58. Bent, *Ballyhoo*, 36.

59. *Fortune*, December 1934, 55.

60. S. K. Ratcliffe, "America's Columnists," *Fortnightly Review*, August 1939, 167, 169; D. Steven Blum, *Walter Lippmann: Cosmopolitanism in the Century of Total War* (Ithaca: Cornell University Press, 1984), 173.

61. Quoted in Curtis D. MacDougall, *The Press and Its Problems* (Dubuque, Iowa: William C. Brown Co., 1964), 198. See also Alfred McClung Lee, *The Daily Newspaper in America* (New York: Macmillan, 1937), 531; Laura Vitray, John Mills, Jr., and Roscoe Ellard, *Pictorial Journalism* (New York: McGraw-Hill, 1939), 343.

62. Brucker, *Changing American Newspaper*, 56–58, 69–72.

63. Frank Angelo, *On Guard: A History of the Detroit Free Press* (Detroit: Detroit Free Press, 1981), 173.

64. Oswald Garrison Villard, *Some Newspapers and Newspaper-men* (New York: Knopf, 1923), 98; Louis M. Lyons, *Newspaper Story: One Hundred Years of the Boston Globe* (Cambridge, Mass.: Harvard University Press, 1971), 317.

65. Oswald Garrison Villard, *The Disappearing Daily* (New York: Knopf, 1944), 101; Marguerite Young, "Ignoble Journalism in the Nation's Capital," *American Mercury* 34 (February 1934):239–43; George Seldes, *Lords of the Press* (New York: Julian Messner, 1938), 75.

66. Lyons, *Newspaper Story*, 265. See also James B. Beddow, "Midwestern Editorial Response to the New Deal, 1932–1940," *South Dakota History* 4 (Winter 1973):1–17.

67. "The Press and the Public," supplement to *New Republic*, 17 March 1937; *Chicago Tribune*, 4 November 1936, 6; Virginius Dabney, "The Press and the Election," *Public Opinion Quarterly* 1 (April 1937):122–25.

68. Quincy Howe, *The News and How to Understand It* (New York: Simon and Schuster, 1940), 71; Robert Dallek, *Franklin D. Roosevelt and American Foreign Policy, 1932–1945* (New York: Oxford University Press, 1979), 109; Lippmann to Robert A. Taft, 29 April 1939, Lippmann Papers, Yale University. On the columnists' political coloration, see "The Press and the Public."

69. Seldes, *Lords*, 144; George Wolfskill and John A. Hudson, *All but the People: Franklin D. Roosevelt and His Critics, 1933–1939* (New York: Macmillan, 1969), 188, 192.

70. Graham J. White, *FDR and the Press* (Chicago: University of Chicago Press, 1979), chaps. 4–6, esp. p. 71.

71. John Cowles, "American Newspapers," in *America Now*, ed. Harold E. Stearns (New York: Charles Scribner's Sons, 1938), 356, 365, 367; Willard Grosvenor Bleyer, "Freedom of the Press and the New Deal," draft of paper for annual convention of American Association of the Schools and Departments of Journalism, 27 December 1933, 10, 12, Bleyer Papers, Box 3, University of Wisconsin Archives, Madison. See also Harold L. Ickes, *America's House of Lords* (New York: Harcourt Brace, 1939); "The Press and the People—A Survey," *Fortune*, August 1939, 64, 70, 74; Paul F. Lazarsfeld, Bernard Berelson, and Hazel Gaudet, *The People's Choice: How the Voter Makes Up His Mind in a Presidential Campaign* (New York: Columbia University Press, 1948), 126–29. Cf. White, *FDR and the Press*, 97–98.

72. Memorandum, Jack Lait to all editors, 3 April 1936, Billings Papers; *Time*, 12 October 1936, 16–17; 2 November 1936, 12–14.

73. De Voto, "Distempers," 447.

74. *New York Herald Tribune*, 21 February 1941.

75. *Time*, 7 April 1924, 27; 5 December 1927, 2, 4.

76. Leo Rosten, *Washington Correspondents*, 172–73; Elson, *World of Time*, 1:168.

77. Wolcott Gibbs, "*Time . . . Fortune . . . Life . . . Luce*," *New Yorker*, 28 November 1936, 19–25.

78. Dwight Macdonald, "*Time, Fortune, Life*," *Nation*, 22 May 1937, 585.

5. *FORTUNE* AND "THE MARCH OF TIME," 1930–1936

1. Drucker, *Adventures*, 227.

2. Luce, "Press is Peculiar," 646.

3. Jessup, ed., *Ideas of Luce*, 218.

4. Elson, *World of Time*, 1:129.

5. Jessup, ed., *Ideas of Luce*, 223, 385.

6. "The Reminiscences of Eric Hodgins" (1968), Oral History Collection of Columbia University, 49.

7. Jessup, p. 221.

8. Robert Aaron Gordon, *Business Leadership in the Large Corporation* (Berkeley: University of California Press, 1945), 318.

9. *Time*, 6 January 1930, 13; Walter Lippmann, *Preface to Morals* (New York: Macmillan, 1929), 256–57; Jessup, ed., *Ideas of Luce*, 221.

10. Jessup, ed., *Ideas of Luce*, 222.

11. Elson, *World of Time*, 1:130.

12. Not counting investment income. James Howard Lewis, "The Saga of *Time, Life, Fortune*," *Magazine World* 1 (February 1945):12.

13. Another editor later complained of Ingersoll, "He's the only fellow in the company that Luce really seems to want to be 'palsy-walsy' with." Billings Diary, 1 April 1939, Billings Papers. On Ingersoll and Time Inc., see Roy

Hoopes, *Ralph Ingersoll: A Biography* (New York: Atheneum, 1985), 79–91; Ingersoll, answers to Time Inc. company history questionnaire, 28 March 1956, Ingersoll Papers, Box 94, Boston University.

14. Hilton Howell Railey, *Touch'd with Madness* (New York: Carrick and Evans, 1938), 223; Hoopes, *Ingersoll*, 91.

15. R. Alan Lawson, *The Failure of Independent Liberalism 1930–1941* (New York: G. P. Putnam's Sons, 1971), 161.

16. "No One Has Starved," *Fortune*, September 1932, 22, 24; "Washington, D.C.," *Fortune*, December 1934, 55.

17. Hoopes, *Ingersoll*, 89–90; Elson, *World of Time*, 1:209.

18. David Reynolds, *The Creation of the Anglo-American Alliance, 1937–1941* (Chapel Hill: University of North Carolina Press, 1982), 164; "Bachelors of Railroading," *Fortune*, March 1934, 59.

19. Margaret Bourke-White, *Portrait of Myself* (New York: Simon and Schuster, 1963), 62, 64.

20. "Hogs," *Fortune*, February 1930, 56–57; "Housing: The Needs," *Fortune*, February 1932, 63.

21. Time Inc., *Four Hours a Year* (New York: Time Inc., 1936), 21, 37, 44–45; Hoopes, *Ingersoll*, 89; *Fortune*, September 1932, 32–36, 51.

22. Dwight Macdonald, *Against the American Grain* (New York: Random House, 1962), p. 165 n.

23. Lloyd Morris, *Postscript to Yesterday* (New York: Random House, 1947), 315; Railey, *Touch'd*, 222.

24. *Fortune*, March 1934, 52; Eric Hodgins, *Trolley to the Moon* (New York: Simon and Schuster, 1973), 366. On Roosevelt and MacLeish's work, see R. H. Winnick, ed. *Letters of Archibald MacLeish, 1907–1982* (Boston: Houghton Mifflin, 1983), xiv.

25. Hoopes, *Ingersoll*, 98.

26. "The Unseen Half of South Bend," *Fortune*, March 1930, 57.

27. *Fortune*, July 1935, 66.

28. Ibid., May 1933, 52.

29. William Stott, *Documentary Expression and Thirties America* (New York: Oxford University Press, 1973), 132–33; "Harry Hopkins," *Fortune*, July 1935, 58; "TVA," *Fortune*, May 1935, 93–94.

30. Lawrence Bergreen, *James Agee: A Life* (New York: Dutton, 1984), 146; Dwight Macdonald, *Memoirs of a Revolutionist* (New York: Farrar, Straus, & Cudahy, 1957), 9; Macdonald to author, 29 May 1978, with a copy of original draft of the story, also in Macdonald Papers, Yale University.

31. John Kenneth Galbraith, *A Life in Our Times: Memoirs* (Boston: Houghton Mifflin, 1981), 259; Hoopes, *Ingersoll*, 91; "Reminiscences of Hodgins," 48.

32. Philip French, "His Death Gave Life to His Legend," *New York Times Book Review*, 8 July 1984, 31.

33. *Nation's Business* 22 (August 1934):30, 32, 34, et seq.; "On the Dole," *Fortune*, February 1934, 54–60, 146, et seq.; Paul H. Hayward, "The Other Side of TVA," *Nation's Business* 22 (December 1934):23–26, 44, 46–47; "This Project is Important," *Fortune*, October 1933, 84, 86, 97.: "TVA," *Fortune*, May 1935, 93–99, 140, 170.

34. *Fortune*, July 1935, 65–66; Hoopes, *Ingersoll*, 100–102.

35. J. J. O'Malley, "Black Beans and White Beans," *New Yorker*, 2 May 1940, 22; Harold F. Gosnell, "How Accurate Were the Polls?" *Public Opinion Quarterly* 1 (January 1937):100.

36. *Fortune*, February 1940, 185–87; Hoopes, *Ingersoll*, 101. See also Richard W. Steele, "The Pulse of the People: Franklin D. Roosevelt and the Gauging of Public Opinion," *Journal of Contemporary History* 9 (October 1974):195–216.

37. George A. Lundberg, Mirra Konarovsky, and Mary Alice McInerny, *Leisure: A Suburban Study* (New York: Columbia University Press, 1934), 322; *Fortune*, October 1933, 24.

38. MacLeish to Luce, [c. 20 July 1938], in *MacLeish Letters*, ed. Winnick, 292.

39. Raymond Fielding, *The March of Time, 1935–1951* (New York: Oxford University Press, 1978), 135.

40. Erik Barnouw, *A History of Broadcasting in the United States*, 3 vols. (New York: Oxford University Press, 1965–70), 1:277.

41. Telegram, Charles J. Gilchrist to Stephen T. Early, 15 January 1934; letter, Henry A. Bellows to Early, 17 January 1934, Franklin D. Roosevelt Papers, Official File, Roosevelt Library.

42. Warren Susman, ed., *Culture and Commitment, 1929–1945* (New York: George Braziller, 1973), 18; *Time*, 13 June 1932, 48; 27 June 1932, 2.

43. "Pictorial Journalism," *Christian Science Monitor*, Weekly Magazine Section, 30 October 1935, 15.

44. Fielding, *March of Time*, 31.

45. Luce to Billings, 24 August 1934, Billings Papers.

46. John Grierson, "The Course of Realism (1937)," in *Grierson on Documentary*, ed. Forsyth Hardy (London: Faber and Faber, 1966), 201–2.

47. A. William Bluem, *Documentary in American Television* (New York: Hastings House, 1965), 36.

48. Billings Diary, 22 April 1933, Billings Papers.

49. Elson, *World of Time*, 1:237.

50. Erik Barnouw, *Documentary* (New York: Oxford University Press, 1974), 131.

51. Alistair Cooke, "History in the Making," *Listener*, 20 November 1935, 931; Paul Rotha, *Documentary Film* (London: Faber and Faber, 1935), 91.

52. Fielding, *March of Time*, 82, 84.

53. George Dangerfield, "*Time* Muddles On," *New Republic*, 19 August 1936, 43.

54. William P. Montague, "Public Opinion and the Newsreels," in *Public Opinion in a Democracy*, supplement to *Public Opinion Quarterly* 2 (January 1938):51.

55. Fielding, *March of Time*, 56, 64.

56. Dangerfield, "*Time* Muddles On," 44.

57. On this point, see William Alexander, "*The March of Time* and *The World Today*," *American Quarterly* 29 (Summer 1977):182–93.

58. Fielding, *March of Time*, 139; Bluem, *Documentary*, 35.

59. "Pictorial Journalism," 15.

60. Quoted in Time Inc., *Four Hours a Year*, 31.

61. Recorded in Billings Diary, 7 September 1935; note in scrapbook, Billings Papers.

62. Cowles to Hoover, 9 March 1936, Hoover Papers, Post-Presidential Papers-Individuals, Box 307, Hoover Library, West Branch, Iowa.

6. THE "MIND-GUIDED CAMERA" MAGAZINE, 1933–1940

1. Luce to Billings, 1 November 1933, Billings Papers.

2. Edward Steichen, " 'News'-Photography," in *America as Americans See It*, ed. Fred J. Ringel (New York: The Literary Guild, 1932), 290; *Time*, 4 March 1929, 24; 15 February 1933, 12.

3. Rick Friedman, "40 Years of Pictures; Newsmagazine Style," *Editor & Publisher*, 23 March 1963, 47–48; Elson, *World of Time*, 1:270; *Time*, 29 October 1934, 18–19.

4. James Howard Lewis, "The Saga of *Time, Life*, and *Fortune*" *Magazine World* 1 (May 1945):9, 11.

5. Daniel J. Boorstin, *The Image: A Guide to Pseudo-Events in America* (New York: Harper & Row, 1961), 13–14; Neil Harris, Introduction to *Land of Contrasts 1880–1901* (New York: George Braziller, 1970), 8.

6. Basil L. Walters, "Pictures vs. Type Display in Reporting the News," *Journalism Quarterly* 24 (September 1947):193; Simon Michael Bessie, *Jazz Journalism* (New York: E. P. Dutton & Co., 1938), 223, 230–31.

7. John Drewry, "A Picture-Language Magazine," *Magazine World* 1 (November 1945):19. See also Gallup's remarks, ASNE *Proceedings 1937*, 85; Bert W. Woodburn, "Reader Interest in Newspaper Pictures," *Journalism Quarterly* 24 (September 1947):197–201.

8. "A Prospectus for a New Magazine" [1936], 1, second draft, Billings Papers.

9. "The U.S. Minicam Boom," *Fortune*, October 1936, 125–29, et seq; Erich Salomon, *Portrait of an Age* (New York: Macmillan, 1967), 217.

10. *Time*, 25 February 1935, 15–17.

11. "U.S. Minicam Boom," 129; Vitray, Mills, and Ellard, *Pictorial Journalism*, 84–92; Walters, "Pictures," 194.

12. Wilson Hicks, *Words and Pictures* (New York: Harper & Bros., 1952), 82–83.

13. Otha Cleo Spencer, "Twenty Years of *Life*: A Study of Time Inc.'s Picture Magazine and Its Contributions to Photojournalism" (Ph.D. diss., University of Missouri, 1958), 124, 128.

14. Ingersoll, answers to company questionnaire, Ingersoll Papers.

15. Transcripts of Time Inc. oral history of Daniel Longwell, 31 January 1956, 6 March 1956, Longwell Papers, Box 26; memorandum, Longwell to Billings, 7 February 1946, Longwell Papers, Box 27; Spencer, "Twenty Years of *Life*," 128–29, 149; Time Inc., *Four Hours a Year*; Jackson Edwards, "One Every Minute," *Scribner's Magazine*, May 1938, 19.

16. Billings Diary, 6 June 1935, Billings Papers.

17. Ibid., 27 February 1936, 28 February 1936; Martha Weinman Lear, "On Harry, and Henry and Ike and Mr. Shaw," *New York Times Magazine*, 22 April 1973, 48; Hoopes, *Ingersoll*, 140.

18. Hoopes, *Ingersoll*, 141, 144–46.

19. Spencer, "Twenty Years of *Life*," 201.

20. "A Prospectus for a New Magazine" [1936], 5, first draft, Billings Papers.

21. Ibid., 4.

22. Alexander King, *Mine Enemy Grows Older* (New York: Simon & Schuster, 1958), 192.

23. Longwell transcript, 31 January 1956, 12, Longwell Papers.

24. Ibid., 18.

25. Elson, *World of Time*, 1:295.

26. Billings Diary, 5 November 1936, Billings Papers.

27. Elson, *World of Time*, 1:297.

28. Longwell to Billings et al., 18 August 1937, Longwell Papers, Box 27.

29. J. L. Brown, "Picture Magazines and Morons," *American Mercury* 45 (December 1938):406.

30. James Howard Lewis, "The Saga of *Time*, *Life*, and *Fortune*," *Magazine World* 1 (November 1944):13; Elson, *World of Time*, 1:329–31.

31. Spencer, "Twenty Years of *Life*," 265; Paul Deutschman, "The First Ten Years of *Life*," unpublished ms. (1946), 31–32, Time Inc. Archives.

32. Billings Diary, 11 March 1939.

33. Elson, *World of Time*, 1:342–43.

34. Spencer, "Twenty Years of *Life*," 282, 289.

35. Luce to Billings et al., 15 July 1941, Billings Papers; Longwell transcript, 31 January 1956, 1, Longwell Papers.

36. Billings Diary, 2 February 1937.

37. James Howard Lewis, "The Saga of *Time, Life,* and *Fortune*," 11.

38. Gardner Cowles, *Mike Looks Back* (New York: n.p., 1985), 60–63, 110.

39. Billings Diary, 26 January 1937, 16 March 1937, 11 August 1937.

40. Undated memo about proposed editorial organization and second draft, "Editorial Organization and System for *Life*," 19 October 1936, Billings Papers.

41. Undated memo about proposed editorial organization.

42. Hicks, *World and Pictures*, xiv.

43. Carl Mydans, *More Than Meets the Eye* (New York: Harper & Bros., 1959), 8.

44. Stanley Rayfield, "The Wonderful World of Alfred Eisenstaedt," *Popular Photography* 37 (October 1955):139.

45. Billings Diary, 7 May 1937; *Life*, 17 May 1937, 28.

46. *Life*, 26 April 1937, 63; Karin B. Ohrn, "Photographs as Political Statements: A Case Study of Picture Editing in the German Illustrated Press and Its Impact on American Picture Magazines, 1926–38," Paper delivered at the convention of the Association for Education in Journalism, Houston, Texas, 1979.

47. *Life*, 10 May 1937, 15–25.

48. Ibid., 10 January 1938, 50–51.

49. Mydans, *More Than Meets*, 10.

50. Spencer, "Twenty Years of *Life*," 396; *Life*, 3 January 1938, 40–45; 7 March 1938, 50–53; 21 March 1938, 26–31.

51. Billings Diary, 25 October 1937, 29 March 1939, 25 August 1939; *Life*, 15 February 1937, 42–43; 4 March 1940, 56–59, 66–67.

52. Richard Whelan, *Robert Capa: A Biography* (New York: Knopf, 1985), 172. On the national media's respect in the 1930s for traditional morals, see Warren I. Susman, *Culture as History: The Transformation of American Society in the Twentieth Century* (New York: Pantheon, 1984), 159–60.

53. *New Yorker*, 2 March 1940, 9; Stephen Shadegg, *Clare Boothe Luce: A Biography* (New York: Simon & Schuster, 1970), 112; *New Republic*, 24 March 1937, 197. See also *New Republic*, 10 February 1937, 5–6.

54. Quoted in Roy Blount, Jr., "Legend: Joe DiMaggio Made It Look Easy," in *The Ultimate Baseball Book*, ed. Daniel Orkent and Harris Lewin (Boston: Houghton Mifflin, 1981), 209.

55. Billings Diary, 11 December 1937.

56. *Life*, 19 February 1940, 20–21.

57. First prospectus, 3, 4.

58. Second prospectus, 3.

59. John R. Whiting and George R. Clark, "The Picture Magazines,"

Harper's, July 1943, 168. See also James C. Curtis and Sheila Graham, "Let Us Now Appraise Famous Photographs: Walker Evans and Documentary Photography," *Winterthru Portfolio* 15 (Spring 1980):1–23.

60. Hicks, *Words and Pictures*, 11.

7. FROM PUBLISHER TO PUBLIC MAN, 1933–1940

1. Luce, "Giving the People What They Want," supplement to *Public Opinion Quarterly* 2 (January 1938):63; Luce, "Press is Peculiar," 647.

2. Luce, "Giving," 63; Elson, *World of Time*, 1:366.

3. Walter Lippmann, "Two Revolutions in the American Press," *Yale Review* 20 (March 1931):433–41.

4. Luce to parents, 29 March 1916, Luce Family Correspondence.

5. *Fortune*, July 1934, 45; Jessup, ed., *Ideas of Luce*, 94 ff; Hodgins, *Trolley*, 374–75.

6. John M. Harrison, *The Blade of Toledo* (Toledo: Toledo Blade, 1985), 247; *Fortune*, July 1934, 47. See also Bruce Bliven, "Worshiping the American Hero," in *America*, ed. Ringel, 128.

7. *Time*, 21 February 1927, 13; 25 April 1938, 18–19.

8. Luce, address, 10 November 1937, Billings Papers.

9. Elson, *World of Time*, 1:208.

10. Matthews, "Tall, balding," 131; Drucker, *Adventures*, 234.

11. "Pittsburgh," *Fortune*, December 1930, esp. 48, 52; W. A. Swanberg, *Luce and His Empire*, 83–84.

12. Luce, address, 10 November 1937.

13. Elson, *World of Time*, 1:314; Daniel Bell et al., *Writing for Fortune* (New York: Time Inc., 1979), 18.

14. "Business-and-Government," *Fortune*, March 1940, 38–39.

15. Luce, address, 10 November 1937.

16. *High Time*, 1 February 1939, 4, Billings Papers.

17. Mary Fraser, "The Ideology of *Time*," 21 July 1953, memorandum, Billings Papers, scrapbook box 66a.

18. Steel, *Walter Lippmann*, 330–34; Roberta S. Siegal, "Opinions on Nazi Germany: A Study of Three Popular Magazines, 1933–1941" (Ph.D. diss., Clark University, 1950), 24–25, 39.

19. *Time*, 18 October 1937, 19; Travis Beal Jacobs, "Roosevelt's Quarantine Speech," *Historian* 24 (August 1966):483–502; Warren F. Kuehl, "Midwestern Newspapers and Isolationist Sentiment," *Diplomatic History* 3 (Summer 1979):283–306.

20. Billings Diary, 14 February 1938, Billings Papers. The actual number of Party members at Time Inc. appears to have been small. Most, John K.

Jessup recalled, worked at *Architectural Digest*. See Bell et al., *Writing for Fortune*, 20, 42–43.

21. Wolcott Gibbs, "A Very Active Type Man," *New Yorker*, 2 May 1941, 27.

22. Billings Diary, 1 April 1939, 2 April 1939, 20 June 1940, Billings Papers.

23. José Ortega y Gasset, *The Revolt of the Masses* (New York: W. W. Norton, 1932), 18.

24. Peter F. Drucker, *The End of Economic Man* (New York: The John Day Co., 1939), 23 and passim.

25. Raymond Swing, *"Good Evening!": A Professional Memoir* (New York: Harcourt, Brace and World, 1964), 216–18; Richard W. Steele, *Propaganda in an Open Society: The Roosevelt Administration and the Media, 1933–1941* (Westport, Conn.: Greenwood Press, 1985), 79; Jessup, ed., *Ideas of Luce*, 41.

26. Drucker, *End of Economic Man*, 44, 50. At Luce's urging, Drucker went to work for *Fortune*.

27. Matthews, "Tall, Balding," 132; Wilfrid Sheed, *Clare Boothe Luce* (New York: E. P. Dutton, 1982), 79; *Business Week*, 6 March 1948, 101.

28. Charles Wertenbaker, *The Death of Kings* (New York: Random House, 1954), 24, 37.

29. *Fortune*, March 1939, 59.

30. Fielding, *March of Time*, chap. 8, pp. 194, 195, 196. See also Otis Ferguson, *"Time* Steals a March," *New Republic*, 9 February 1938, 19.

31. *Life*, 28 March 1938, 11–27.

32. Ibid., 19 December 1939, 45–46. Earlier, *Fortune* had described the U.S. Army as "a pigmy force," ranked eighteenth in the world. Both Greece and Belgium, the magazine reported, could put more men into the field. "Who's in the Army Now?" *Fortune*, September 1935, 21.

33. Quoted in Fraser, "Ideology," 40–43, 50–51; Swanberg, *Luce*, 159.

34. Siegel, "Opinions," 47, 51, 56; Philip E. Jacob, "Influences of World Events on U.S. 'Neutrality' Opinion," *Public Opinion Quarterly* 4 (March 1940):48–65; Dexter Perkins, "Was Roosevelt Wrong?" *Virginia Quarterly Review* 30 (Summer 1954):360.

35. Hubert Kay, quoted in Billings Diary, 15 September 1939.

36. Memorandum, Luce to editors, 17 February 1940, quoted in Cort, *Sin*, 210; "The Moral Urge Toward War," *New Republic*, 12 February 1940, 198–99.

37. Reynolds, *Creation of Anglo-American Alliance*, 104; Clare Boothe, *Europe in the Spring* (New York: Knopf, 1940), 223–24.

38. Billings Diary, 22 May 1940; Luce, "America and Armageddon," *Life*, June 1940, 40, 100.

39. Fielding, *March of Time*, chap. 11; *Life*, 12 August 1940, 69–75.

40. Margaret Frakes, "Time Marches Back," *Christian Century* 57 (16 October 1940):1277–78. See also review by Pare Lorentz, *McCall's*, October 1940, 4, 96.

41. See *Fortune* advertisement, *Life*, 29 December 1941, 61; William Appleman Williams, *The Tragedy of American Diplomacy* 2d ed. (New York: Dell, 1972), 198.

42. Cort, *Sin*, 252–53.

43. Mydans, *More Than Meets*, 12–13.

44. *Life*, 24 June 1940, 32; 28 October 1940, 23 et seq.

45. Ibid., 22 July 1940, 57 ff.

46. Ibid., 57.

47. Luce, Introduction to *Why England Slept*, by John F. Kennedy (New York: 1940), xv.

48. Kobler, *Luce*, 122.

49. Luce, "America and Armageddon." See also editorial "The Presidency," *New York Herald Tribune*, 10 October 1940.

50. John P. Diggins, *Mussolini and Fascism: The View from America* (Princeton, N.J.: Princeton University Press, 1974), 26, 318.

51. Billings Diary, 25 May 1940, 23 July 1940, Billings Papers.

52. Lippmann, "The Economic Consequences of a German Victory," *Life*, 22 July 1940, 65–71; Julian Bach, Jr., to Lippmann, 20 June 1940, Lippmann to Bach, 25 June 1940, Lippmann Papers; Helen Hill and Herbert Agar, *Beyond German Victory* (New York: Reynal & Hitchcock, 1941), 66–68.

53. Herbert Hoover, *Addresses upon the American Road, 1940–1941* (New York: Charles Scribner's Sons, 1941), 4; *Life*, 24 June 1940, 16–18. See also *New York Herald Tribune*, 12 October 1940; Hendrik Willem Von Loon, "Invasion," *Scholastic*, 4 November 1940, 29–30, 40–41.

54. Billings Diary, 4 June 1940, Billings Papers.

55. Mark Lincoln Chadwin, *The Hawks of World War II* (Chapel Hill: University of North Carolina Press, 1968), 76, 84–85.

56. Quoted in Walter Johnson, *William Allen White's America* (New York: Henry Holt & Co., 1947), 566.

57. Steel, *Lippmann*, 385.

58. David Holbrook Culbert, *News for Everyman: Radio and Foreign Affairs* (Westport, Conn.: Greenwood Press, 1976), 206. See also Richard W. Steele, "The Great Debate: Roosevelt, the Media, and the Coming of the War, 1940–1941," *Journal of American History* 71 (June 1984):83–84.

59. *Time*, 8 July 1940, 14. See also the first Willkie cover story, *Time*, 31 July 1939, 42–45.

60. George H. Gallup, *The Gallup Poll: Public Opinion, 1935–1971*, 3 vols. (New York: Random House, 1971), 1:222.

61. Donald Bruce Johnson, *The Republican Party and Wendell Willkie* (Urbana, Ill.: University of Illinois Press, 1966), 65–66.

62. Steve Neal, *Dark Horse: A Biography of Wendell Willkie* (Garden City, N.Y.: Doubleday, 1984), 76.

63. *Time*, 1 July 1940, 14; *Life*, 24 June 1940, 25–26.

64. *Time*, 8 July 1940, 12.

65. Neal, *Dark Horse*, 99.

66. *Time*, 8 July 1940, 13; Allen Hoover to Thomas T. Thalken, 23 March 1978, Herbert Hoover Papers, Post-Presidential Papers-Subject, Box 77. Gallup, *Gallup Poll*, 1:231.

67. James T. Patterson, *Mr. Republican: A Biography of Robert A. Taft* (Boston: Houghton Mifflin, 1971), 229; H. E. Spangler to Lawrence Richey, 27 May 1940, Hoover Papers, Post-Presidential Papers-Subject, Box 77; *Time*, 8 July 1940, 10, 12, 14; Billings Diary, 28 June 1940.

68. *Life* 29 July 1940, 16.

69. Lazarsfeld, Berelson, and Gaudet, *The People's Choice*, 134–36; Lazarsfeld and Patricia Slater, "Problems and Techniques of Magazine Research: Content Analysis," *Magazine World* 1 (September 1945):36.

70. Quoted in Neal, *Dark Horse*, 164.

71. Ibid., 149; *Time*, 9 September 1940, 15; Matthews, *Name and Address*, 253; Lippmann to Luce, 30 September 1940, Lippmann Papers.

72. *Time*, 9 September 1940, 15.

73. *New York Times*, 22 September 1940; Elson, *World of Time*, 1:442.

74. *New York Times*, 11 September 1940. A month later, he wrote of *Life*'s "strictly non-partisan spirit." Luce, "This Great Moment," *Life*, 21 October 1940, 29.

75. Luce, "This Great Moment," 29–30. This incongruous remark inspired still another *New Yorker* jab at Luce, E. B. White, "Dinner with Henry Luce," *New Yorker* 2 November 1940, 23.

76. Billings Diary, 6 June 1940.

8. THE AMERICAN CENTURY, 1941–1950

1. Dallek, *Roosevelt and American Foreign Policy*, 275.

2. Luce, "The American Century," in Luce, *The American Century* (New York: Farrar and Rinehart, 1941), 7, 23–24, 30, 36–37, 40. The original manuscript is in Yale in World War II Collection, Box 5, Yale University. See also Alexander Hehmeyer to Bernhard Knollenberg, 24 March 1941, in the same collection.

3. Lippmann, "The American Destiny," *Life*, 5 June 1939, 47, 73; Luce, *American Century*, 3. Lippmann's *Life* entry was based on his February 1938 lectures at the University of Chicago. See the first and third lectures, Lippmann Papers, Box 233.

4. Dorothy Thompson, "The American Century," *New York Herald Tribune*, 21 February 1941.

5. Hoover, *Addresses*, 110; Luce, *American Century*, 53, 55.

6. "The Sinking of the 'Zamzam,' " *Life*, 23 June 1941, 21–27; Bourke-White, *Portrait*, chap. 15.

7. Lippmann to Rachel Albertson, 2 November 1939, Lippmann Papers, Box 85. In the first months of America's involvement in the war, the government discouraged the photographing of American dead. Gradually this restraint was relaxed. See, e.g., *Life*, 14 May 1945, 40B–40C.

8. *Time*, 22 July 1940, 55. Just as it had during the first, confusing years of the depression, *Time*'s circulation rose sharply again during the war, from 791,768 in 1940 to 1,560,233 in 1946. *Magazine Circulation and Rate Trends, 1940–1974* (New York: Association of National Advertisers, 1976), 23.

9. *Life*, 15 December 1941, 135; John N. Brooks, *The Big Wheel* (New York: Harper & Bros., 1949), 19–20.

10. Luce, "America's War and America's Peace," *Life*, 16 February 1942, 85, 91.

11. Henry A. Wallace, *PM*, 10 May 1942.

12. Wallace to Luce, 16 May 1942, transcript in Wallace oral history, 1575, Columbia University.

13. Ronald Radosh, *Prophets on the Right* (New York: Simon and Schuster, 1975), 138–39.

14. Kenneth Stewart, "Where Luce Stands on Politics and the Future," *PM Picture News*, 10 September 1944, M15.

15. Jessup, ed., *Ideas of Luce*, 122–23.

16. Carbon of letter, Wallace to James S. Crutchfield, 2 February 1943, and Wallace Diary, 5 March 1943, in Wallace oral history, 2265, 2410.

17. Elson, *World of Time* 2:73; *Time*, 14 July 1941, 12; Richard W. Steele, "News of the 'Good War': World War II News Management," *Journalism Quarterly* 62 (Winter 1985):713; White, *FDR and the Press*, 53, 133–35; Luce to Roosevelt, 23 October 1943, Roosevelt Papers, President's Secretary's File; John J. McCloy to Stephen T. Early, Roosevelt Papers, President's Personal File; file memo, 31 August 1944, and T. D. B. to Early, 31 August 1944, Early Papers, Roosevelt Library.

18. Sidney Hyman, *The Lives of William Benton* (Chicago: University of Chicago Press, 1969), 263–69; Karl Schriftgiesser, *Business Comes of Age: The Story of the Committee for Economic Development* (New York: Harper & Row, 1960); Robert M. Collins, "Positive Business Responses to the New Deal: The Roots of the Committee for Economic Development," *Business History Review* 52 (Autumn 1978):385–91.

19. Hodgins, *Trolley*, 443.

20. Wallace Diary, 1 February 1943, in Wallace oral history, 2259; editorial, "Freedom from Want," *Fortune*, October 1942, 127; "The Domestic Economy," supplement to *Fortune*, December 1942, 4–5, 15; Richard Bissell, Jr., "The Anatomy of Public Spending," *Fortune*, May 1942, 94–95 et seq.,

and *Fortune*, June 1942, 105, 108, et seq. See also John K. Jessup, "America and the Future: I—Our Domestic Economy," *Life*, 13 September 1943, 105–6, 108, et seq.

21. Williams, *Tragedy*, 201; "Pacific Relations," Supplement to *Fortune*, August 1942, 22; "Relations with Britain," Supplement to *Fortune*, May 1942, 14.

22. Luce, "England Revisited," memorandum, 24 March 1942, Longwell Papers, Box 29.

23. Bourke-White, *Portrait*, 183–84; Fraser, "Ideology."

24. William L. O'Neill, *A Better World: The Great Schism. Stalinism and the American Intellectuals* (New York: Simon and Schuster, 1982), 59; Lippmann to John Philip Sousa III, 29 March 1943, Lippmann Papers; Walter Graebner to William H. Standley, 6 May 1943, Longwell Papers, Box 28.

25. O'Neill, *Better World*, 59, 78; John Lewis Gaddis, *The United States and the Origins of the Cold War, 1941–1947* (New York: Columbia University Press, 1972), 32–42; Paul Willen, "Who 'Collaborated' with Russia?" *Antioch Review* 14 (September 1954):259–83; Ralph B. Levering, *American Opinion and the Russian Alliance, 1939–1945* (Chapel Hill: University of North Carolina Press, 1976), chap. 5.

26. John K. Jessup, "American and the Future, II—Our Foreign Policy," *Life*, 20 September 1943, 108; Wallace Diary, 1 February 1943, in Wallace oral history, 2259; Elson, *World of Time*, 1:172.

27. Stewart, "Education of Luce," M7; Luce to Lippmann, 24 September 1940, Lippmann Papers.

28. Luce to John Shaw Billings et al., 29 November 1939, Billings Papers; ad, *New York Herald Tribune*, 17 October 1940, 14; Jessup, ed., *Ideas of Luce*, 199; "Pacific Relations," 19. See also Lloyd E. Eastman, "The Kuomintang in the 1930s," in *The Limits of Change: Essays on Conservative Alternatives in Republican China*, ed. Charlotte Furth (Cambridge, Mass.: Harvard University Press, 1976), 191–210.

29. Luce, address, 24 June 1941, Wendell Willkie Papers, Lilly Library, Indiana University, Bloomington, Ind.; Luce, "China to the Mountain," *Life*, 30 June 1941, 82–86 et seq.

30. Pearl S. Buck, "A Warning about China," *Life*, 10 May 1943, 53; Theodore H. White, "Chiang Kai-Shek," *Life*, 2 March 1942, 71, 80. See also Charles Wertenbaker, "The China Lobby—The Legacy of T. V. Soong," *Reporter*, 15 April 1952, 6–7.

31. *New Haven Journal-Courier*, 20 October 1944, clipping, Luce file, Alumni Records Office, Yale University.

32. Clare Boothe Luce, address, 11 June 1943, Willkie Papers.

33. *PM*, 28 June 1944.

34. Shadegg, *Clare Boothe Luce*, 197.

35. *Life*, 16 October 1944, 34; *New York Times*, 29 June 1944; Robert

A. Divine, *Foreign Policy and U.S. Presidential Elections: 1940–1948* (New York: New Viewpoints, 1974), 91.

36. Richard Watts, Jr., "Reading Luce in China," *New Republic*, 3 December 1945, 740.

37. Galbraith, *Life*, 258, 262. See also Warren Breed, "Social Control in the Newsroom," *Social Forces* 33 (May 1955):326–35.

38. Jeanne Perkins Harman, *Such is Life* (New York: Thomas Y. Crowell, 1956), 95–96.

39. Elson, *World of Time*, 2:92; Luce to Willkie, 8 June 1944, Willkie Papers; *Time*, 30 October 1944, 13, 14.

40. Luce to Hoover, 26 April 1944, Hoover Papers, Post-Presidential Papers-Individuals, Box 441; Theodore H. White, " 'Life' Looks at China," *Life*, 1 May 1944, 103; Buck, "Warning"; John King Fairbank, *Chinabound: A Fifty Year Memoir* (New York: Harper & Row, 1982), 253.

41. "An Isolationist Reaction?" *Fortune*, April 1943, 116, 118.

42. Eric Hodgins to Luce, 22 September 1943, Billings Papers; Wertenbaker, *Death of Kings*, 352–53; Matthews, *Name and Address*, 247; Louis Kronenberger, *No Whippings, No Gold Watches* (Boston: Little, Brown, 1970), 119–20.

43. Fraser, "Ideology," 92; Luce to John Osborne, 11 July 1945, Billings Papers; Merle Miller, *That Winter* (New York: William Sloan Associates, 1948), 67.

44. Luce to David Hulburd, 26 September 1944, Billings Papers.

45. William C. Bullitt, "The World from Rome," *Life*, 4 September 1944, 95, 98, 103.

46. Whittaker Chambers, *Witness* (New York: Random House, 1952), 477–78, 497; Allen Weinstein, *Perjury: The Hiss-Chambers Case* (New York: Knopf, 1978), 626.

47. *Time*, 13 November 1944, 42, 45; White, *In Search*, 209. On the accuracy of the reports of Mao's headquarters, compare Kenneth E. Shewmaker, *Americans and Chinese Communists, 1927–1945: A Persuading Encounter* (Ithaca: Cornell University Press, 1971), 162–73, to Warren W. Tozer, "The Foreign Correspondents' Visit to Yenan in 1944: A Reassessment," *Pacific Historical Review* 41 (May 1972):207–24.

48. Luce to John Shaw Billings, 6 January 1945; Billings to Charles Wertenbaker, 15 January 1945, Billings Papers; Weinstein, *Perjury*, 344; T. S. Matthews, *Angels Unawares* (New York: Ticknor & Fields, 1985), 173.

49. Kobler, *Luce*, 16.

50. Billings Diary, 19 February 1945; Matthews, *Angels*, 172; *Time*, 5 March 1945, 36–37.

51. Quoted in Fraser, "Ideology," 124–26.

52. Quoted in Lloyd Gardner, *Architects of Illusion* (Chicago: Quadrangle Books, 1970), 53; Billings Diary, 26 February 1945.

53. Luce to senior editors, 16 July 1945, Billings Papers; Luce to Roy Alexander et al., 15 March 1946, C. D. Jackson Papers, Box 57, Eisenhower Library, Abilene, Kans.

54. *Greenwich Time*, 10 August 1944, clipping in Longwell Papers, Box 29.

55. *New York Herald Tribune*, 26 November 1946.

56. 52 to 35 percent, according to Gallup, *Gallup Poll*, 1:565. Gallup states that in June 1946, or just as *Time* and other publications were beginning to be consistent in their hostility toward Russia, twice as many of those surveyed (58 to 29 percent) already believed that the USSR was intent on being the ruling power in the world as considered its behavior defensive. This ratio remained constant through the late 1940s. Cf. George Quester, *Political Science Quarterly* 93 (Winter 1978–79):660. On the press and the early Cold War, see Ralph B. Levering, *The Cold War, 1945–1972* (Arlington Heights, Ill.: Harlan Davidson, 1982), 27–28.

57. Fillmore Calhoun, "The Russians," *Life*, 7 May 1945, 40; Levering, *American Opinion*, 202. See also Leo K. Adler and Thomas G. Paterson, "Red Fascism: The Merger of Nazi Germany and Soviet Russia in the American Image of Totalitarianism, 1930's–1940's," *American Historical Review* 75 (April 1970):1048–51.

58. *Life*, 27 May 1946, 36; Elson, *World of Time*, 2:161.

59. Reinhold Niebuhr, "The Fight for Germany," *Life*, 21 October 1946, 65, 72; John Foster Dulles, "Thoughts on Soviet Foreign Policy," *Life*, 3 June 1946, 112–18 et seq.; *Life*, 10 June 1946, 118–20 et seq.

60. *Time*, 24 February 1947, 35; 13 May 1947, 25; 13 May 1946, 22.

61. See, e.g., *Time*, 8 April 1946, 25; 24 March 1947, 17.

62. Thomas Paterson, *On Every Front: The Making of the Cold War* (New York: W. W. Norton, 1979), chap. 6. One tactic was to "leak" the Kennan memo justifying containment. A *Time* reporter was among the receivers. Elson, *World of Time*, 2:161. See also Adler and Paterson, "Red Fascism," 1056–59.

63. *Time*, 24 February 1947, 35; 24 March 1947, 20.

64. Ronald Samuel Reinig, "America Looking Outward: American Cold War Attitudes during the Crucial Years, 1945–1947, as Reflected in the American Magazine Medium" (Ph.D. diss., Syracuse University, 1974), 487 and passim.

65. Richard H. Pells, *The Liberal Mind in a Conservative Age: American Intellectuals in the 1940s and 1950s* (New York: Harper & Row, 1985), 104–5, 107, 127; George E. Simmons, "The 'Cold War' in Large-City Dailies of the United States," *Journalism Quarterly* 25 (December 1948):354–59, 400; Steel, *Walter Lippmann*, 487, 490.

66. Jessup, ed., *Ideas of Luce*, 249; Luce, "The Reformation of the World's Economies," *Fortune*, February 1950, 59.

67. Jessup, ed., *Ideas of Luce*, 244; "Pt. IV," *Fortune*, February 1950, 90–91.

68. Luce, "Reformation," 62–63. See also ad, *Time*, 20 August 1951, 74–75.

69. Luce, "Reformation," 60; *Life*, 19 April 1948, 48.

70. Truman to Ethel Noland, 13 August 1949, in *Off the Record: The Private Papers of Harry S. Truman*, ed. Robert H. Farrell (New York: Penguin, 1980), 161; Walter LaFeber, "American Policy-Makers, Public Opinion and the Outbreak of the Cold War, 1945–1950," in *The Origins of the Cold War*, ed. Yonosuke Nagai and Akira Iriye (Tokyo: University of Tokyo Press, 1977), 43–65. Truman appears to have relied most heavily on State Department advisers long antagonistic toward the Soviet Union. See Ernest R. May, *"Lessons" of the Past: The Use and Misuse of History in American Foreign Policy* (New York: Oxford University Press, 1973), chap. 2, esp. pp. 30, 35; Daniel Yergen, *Shattered Peace: The Origins of the Cold War and the National Security State* (Boston: Houghton Mifflin, 1977).

71. Nancy Bernkopf Tucker, *Patterns in the Dust: Chinese-American Relations and the Recognition Controversy, 1949–1950* (New York: Columbia University Press, 1983), 144–45.

72. Raymond Vernon, "The Role of U.S. Enterprise Abroad," *Daedalus* 98 (Winter 1969):113.

73. David W. Eakins, "Business Planners and America's Postwar Expansion," in *Corporations and the Cold War*, ed. David Horowitz (New York and London: Monthly Review Press, 1969), 155; Robert A. Pollard, *Economic Security and the Origins of the Cold War, 1945–1950* (New York: Columbia University Press, 1985), 7–9. The administration, not the business community, Pollard argues, initiated this economic globalism.

74. Edward C. Bursk, "New Dimensions in Top Executive Reading," *Harvard Business Review* 35 (September–October 1957):93–112.

75. Raymond Bauer, Ithiel de Sola Pool, and Lewis Anthony Dexter, *American Business and Public Policy* (New York: Atherton, 1963), chap. 10.

76. *Time*, 29 March 1948, 29, 32. Eight years later, Luce referred to this long *Time* entry, suggesting its closeness to his own position. Memorandum, Luce to C. D. Jackson, 14 February 1956, Jackson Papers, Box 58.

77. Luce, "Reformation," 63.

78. Norman D. Markowitz, *The Rise and Fall of the People's Century: Henry A. Wallace and American Liberalism 1941–1948* (New York: Free Press, 1973), 180.

79. John P. Mallan, "Luce, Burnham, and the American World Revolution," *Harvard Studies in International Affairs* 3 (June 1953):52.

80. John Lewis Gaddis, *Strategies of Containment* (New York: Oxford University Press, 1982), 108; "The Arms We Need," *Fortune*, December 1948, 77–78. Compare *Fortune*'s enthusiasm for larger defense expenditures with Wil-

liam Bradford Huie, "How Many Armies Do We Need?" *Nation's Business* 52 (February 1949):47–48.

81. Luce to Andre Laguerre, 16 February 1949, Longwell Papers, Box 29; John C. Merrill, "How *Time* Stereotyped Three U.S. Presidents," *Journalism Quarterly* 42 (Autumn 1965):563–70.

82. Wallace Diary, 1 November 1945, in Wallace oral history, 4213.

83. *Life*, 5 April 1948, 28; Warren I. Cohen, "The United States and China since 1945," in *New Frontiers in American-East Asia Relations* (New York: Columbia University Press, 1983), 134–35; Steven I. Levine, "A New Look at American Mediation in the Chinese Civil War: The Marshall Mission and Manchuria," *Diplomatic History* 3 (Fall 1979):349–75; William Whitney Stueck, Jr., *The Road to Confrontation: American Policy toward China and Korea* (Chapel Hill: University of North Carolina Press, 1981), 56–58; Warren I. Cohen, "Acheson, His Advisers, and China, 1949–1950," in *Uncertain Years: Chinese-American Relations, 1947–1950*, ed. Dorothy Borg and Waldo Heinrichs (New York: Columbia University Press, 1980), 15, 16; John Lewis Gaddis, "The Strategic Perspective: The Rise and Fall of the 'Defensive Parameter' Concept, 1947–1951," in *Uncertain Years*, ed. Borg and Heinrichs, 66–69, 72.

84. Tucker, *Patterns*, 145–47, 152. For an example of such coverage, see *New York Herald Tribune*, 24 November 1946.

85. William C. Bullitt, "A Report to the American People," *Life*, 13 October 1947, 35–37; "The China Lobby," *Reporter*, 15 April 1952, 16; Stueck, *Road*, 54; H. Bradford Westerfield, *Foreign Policy and Party Politics: Pearl Harbor to Korea* (New Haven: Yale University Press, 1955), 261–62; Tang Tsou, *America's Failure in China, 1941–50* (Chicago: University of Chicago Press, 1963), 462, 468–74. On Congress-press relations, see James Reston, *The Artillery of the Press: Its Influence on American Foreign Policy* (New York: Harper & Row, 1967), 72–73.

86. Tucker, *Patterns*, 99, 161; Cohen, "Acheson," 34, 42, 49; Cohen, "The United States and China," 136–38.

87. Ernest R. May, "Writing Contemporary International History," *Diplomatic History* 8 (Spring 1984):107.

9. THE LUCEAN DECADE AND ITS DETRACTORS, 1950–1959

1. *New Haven Register*, 1 February 1950, clipping, Luce File, Alumni Records Office, Yale University; Swanberg, *Luce*, 289, 290.

2. Tucker, *Patterns*; Cohen, "Acheson," 34, 42.

3. John Foster Dulles, "A Policy of Boldness," *Life*, 19 May 1952, 154, 158; Swanberg, *Luce*, 356–58; Luce to Dulles, 12 April 1950, Dulles Papers, Box 48, Princeton University, Princeton, N.J. See also Dulles, *War or Peace* (New York: Macmillan, 1950), chaps. 13, 20, 21, p. 175; Ronald W. Prues-

sen, *John Foster Dulles: The Road to Power* (New York: Free Press, 1982), 439–40, 446–47; Mark G. Toulouse, *The Transformation of John Foster Dulles*, (Macon, Ga.: Mercer University Press, 1985), esp. ch. 8.

4. Robert A. Divine, *Foreign Policy and U.S. Presidential Elections: 1952–1960* (New York: New Viewpoints, 1974), pp. 24–25. See also, the Editors of *Fortune, USA: The Permanent Revolution* (New York: Prentice-Hall, 1951), 244, 247; "MacArthur and the National Purpose," *Fortune*, May 1951, 72.

5. Billings Diary, 20 August 1948, Billings Papers; Elson, *World of Time*, 2:240–42.

6. John Chamberlain, *A Life with the Printed Word* (Chicago: Regnery Gateway, 1982), 68–69; Weinstein, *Perjury*, 534–35.

7. *Time*, 22 October 1951, 22. See also Thomas C. Reeves, *The Life and Times of Joe McCarthy* (New York: Stein & Day, 1982), 384; Edwin R. Bayley, *Joe McCarthy and the Press* (Madison: University of Wisconsin Press, 1981), 168–69. After the October 1951 cover story, McCarthy unsuccessfully tried to organize an advertiser boycott of Luce's magazines.

8. Jessup, ed., *Ideas of Luce*, 128.

9. David M. Oshinsky, *A Conspiracy So Immense: The World of Joe McCarthy* (New York: Free Press, 1983), 185, 417; Elson, *World of Time*, 2:271–76, 280.

10. *Time*, 10 March 1967, 32; Robert Griffith, "Dwight D. Eisenhower and the Corporate Commonwealth," *American Historical Review* 87 (February 1982):89–90, 97–100; "The Reminiscences of Clare Boothe Luce" (1968), Oral History Collection of Columbia University, 8, 91, 92.

11. Kobler, *Luce*, 180.

12. Editorials, "Eisenhower Puts Business on the Spot" and "George Humphrey? Of Course!" *Fortune*, January 1953, 76, 79; Schriftgiesser, *Business*, 160–61.

13. *New York Times*, 6 July 1951; *Business Week*, 15 March 1952, 20.

14. Curtis Prendergast, *The World of Time Inc.* (New York: Atheneum, 1986), 474; Mary McCarthy, "The Menace to Free Journalism in America," *Listener*, 14 May 1953, 792; Luce, "Directive for Editorial Development of *Fortune*," attachment to letter, Bradford A. Warner to Ferdinand Eberstadt, 8 July 1948, Eberstadt Papers, Box 103, Princeton University.

15. *Forbes*, 15 August 1953, 15.

16. Quoted in Susman, ed., *Culture and Commitment*, 318. See also Alan C. Carlson, "Luce, *Life* and 'The American Way,' " *This World*, no. 13 (Winter 1986), 56–58, 60–62, 66–70.

17. Daniel Longwell to Andrew Heiskell, 29 November 1951; Longwell to Luce, 22 June 1951, Longwell Papers, Box 28; Dora Jane Hamblin, *That Was the Life* (New York: W. W. Norton, 1977), 296.

18. Norman Jacobs, ed., *Culture for the Millions* (Princeton, N.J.: Van Norstrand, 1961), 173; newsletter, *Inside Look*, February 1953, 4, Longwell Pa-

pers, Box 27; John Raeburn, *Fame Became Him: Hemingway as Public Writer* (Bloomington, Ind.: Indiana University Press, 1984), p. 173.

19. Andrew Kopkind, "Serving *Time*," 23–24; Kronenberger, *No Whippings*, 135, 146–47.

20. *New York Post*, 26 December 1956, 6 January 1957; "The Reminiscences of Robert C. Christopher" (1982), Oral History Collection of Columbia University, 23.

21. Eric Hodgins to Luce et al., 21 September 1945, Billings Papers.

22. *Proceedings 1952* (Washington: American Society of Newspaper Editors, 1952), 85–86; memorandum, Longwell to Luce, 2 August 1949, Longwell Papers, Box 28.

23. Mini-dummy in Robert W. Desmond Papers, Box 84, State Historical Society of Wisconsin.

24. Gerald Holland, "Lunches with Luce," *Atlantic Monthly*, May 1971, 63.

25. Luce to Roy Larsen et al., 17 August 1954, Jackson Papers, Box 57.

26. Elson, *World of Time*, 2:357; Prendergast, *World of Time*, 144, 154.

27. Leo Bogart, "Magazines since the Rise of Television," *Journalism Quarterly* 33 (Spring 1956):154, 156; *Business Week*, 19 January 1957, 97; Hollis Alpert, "What Killed *Collier's*?" *Saturday Review*, 11 May 1957, 42.

28. *Advertising Agency*, 4 May 1951, 122.

29. Luce to Emmet John Hughes, 4 March 1956, Jackson Papers, Box 58; Edward C. Bursk, "New Dimensions in Top Executive Reading," *Harvard Business Review* 35 (September–October 1957):93–112.

30. Daniel Starch and staff, *Fiftieth Consumer Magazine Report* (Mamaroneck, N.Y.: Daniel Starch and staff, 1955), 19. See also Alfred Politz Research, Inc., *The Audiences of Nine Magazines* (New York: Alfred Politz Research, Inc., 1958); *Advertising Age* 31 (15 February 1960):36–63.

31. *Time*, 27 July 1962, 56; Bernard C. Cohen, "Mass Communication and Foreign Policy," in *Domestic Sources of Foreign Policy*, ed. James N. Rosenau (New York: Free Press, 1967), 196–97; Bernard C. Cohen, *The Press and Foreign Policy* (Princeton, N.J.: Princeton University Press, 1963), 116–18.

32. Robert K. Merton, "Patterns of Influence: A Study of Interpersonal Influence and of Communications Behavior in a Local Community," in *Communications Research, 1948–1949*, ed. Paul F. Lazarsfeld and Frank N. Stanton (New York: Harper & Bros., 1949), 204–5.

33. James N. Rosenau, *National Leadership and Foreign Policy* (Princeton, N.J.: Princeton University Press, 1963), 193–203.

34. Christopher P. Wilson, "The Rhetoric of Consumption: Mass Market Magazines and the Demise of the Gentle Reader, 1880–1920," in *The Culture of Consumption*, ed. Richard Wightman Fox and T. J. Jackson Lears (New York: Pantheon, 1983), 50. See also *Life*'s special issue, "The American and His Economy," 5 January 1953.

35. Raeburn, 127–28, 131; Arthur M. Schlesinger, Jr., "*Time* and the Intellectuals," in *The Politics of Hope* (Boston: Houghton Mifflin, 1962), 230–36; Richard Lentz, "Resurrecting the Prophet: Dr. Martin Luther King, Jr., and the News Magazines" (Ph.D. diss., University of Iowa, 1983), 100, 104–5.

36. Henry R. Luce, "The Character of the Businessman," *Fortune*, August 1957, 109.

37. Luce to Hedley Donovan, 2 January 1956, Jackson Papers, Box 58; Time Inc. newsletter, *f.y.i.*, 28 September 1963, 1, Desmond Papers, Box 86.

38. *Time*, 7 September 1959, 9; Richard Wightman Fox, "Breathless: The Cultural Contradictions of Daniel Bell," *American Quarterly* 34 (Spring 1982):71.

39. Macdonald, *Against*, 401; Rudolf Flesch, *How to Write, Speak and Think More Effectively* (New York: New American Library, 1960), 68–69, 131, 148.

40. Cort, "Once Upon," 136–37.

41. Macdonald, *Against*, 12–13.

42. Jacques Barzun, *The House of Intellect* (New York: Harper & Row, 1961), 41.

43. Merrill, "How *Time* Stereotyped," 568. See also Gary Wills, "Timestyle," *National Review*, 3 August 1957, 129; Jigs Gardner, "*Time*: The Weekly Fiction Magazine," *Nation*, 15 August 1959, 65–67.

44. *Time*, 3 January 1955, 9–10, 13–14; Ben H. Bagdikian, "Time Study," *New Republic*, 23 February 1959, 12.

45. *New York Post*, 24 December 1956.

46. Ben H. Bagdikian, *Providence Journal*, 13 October 1958.

47. David A. Frier, *Conflict of Interest in the Eisenhower Administration* (Ames, Iowa: Iowa State University Press, 1969), 14, 151, 173, 183.

48. Quoted in *Newsweek*, 13 March 1967, 68.

49. *New York Post*, 6 January 1957.

50. H. J. Sachs, "Henry Luce and I," *Nation*, 4 July 1953, 13; Karl E. Meyer, "Triumph of the Smooth Deal," *Commentary*, December 1958, 463.

51. Douglass Cater, *The Fourth Branch of Government* (New York: Vintage, 1959), 101–4; William L. Rivers, *The Opinionmakers* (Boston: Beacon Press, 1965), 174–80. On Knight, see Edwin Fahey's fawning profile in *New York Herald Tribune*, 13 November 1960, and *Time*, 13 February 1950, 64–65; on Newhouse, see Robert Shaplen, "The Newhouse Phenomenon," *Saturday Review*, 8 October 1960, 55–57, 63.

52. Joseph and Stewart Alsop, *The Reporter's Trade* (New York: Reynal, 1958), 91, 246.

53. Pells, *Liberal Mind*, 350. Cf. analysis of Cold War developments by James Marlow, *Washington Star*, 10 November 1959.

54. "The China Lobby," *Reporter*, 15 April 1952, 4–24; 27 April 1952,

5–22; Stanley D. Bachrack, *The Committee of One Million* (New York: Columbia University Press, 1976); Ross Y. Koen, *The China Lobby in American Politics* (New York: Macmillan, 1960); Cohen, "United States and China," 147.

55. Felix Greene, *A Curtain of Ignorance: How the American Public Has Been Misinformed about China* (Garden City, N.Y.: Doubleday, 1964), 86–89, 153–57; *Time*, 14 September 1959, 29; 12 October 1959, 28–32; A. J. Liebling, *The Press* (New York: Ballantine, 1961), 166.

56. Telegram, Luce to C. D. Jackson, 14 May 1955, Jackson Papers, Box 58; Jackson Log, 20 July 1956, Jackson Papers, Box 56; Swanberg, *Luce*, 356; Jessup, ed., *Ideas of Luce*, 21.

57. Quoted in Daniel J. Leab, "Dulles at the Brink: Some Diverse Reactions from 10 Years Ago," *Journalism Quarterly* 43 (Autumn 1966):548; James Shepley, "How Dulles Averted War," *Life*, 16 January 1956, 70–72, 77–78. See also Robert J. Donovan, "When Dulles Took the Spirits out of *Life*," *Washington Journalism Review* (November 1985):38–39; *Life*, 20 January 1956, 20; "The Reminiscences of James R. Shepley" (1965), John Foster Dulles Oral History Project, Princeton University, 16–18, 28, 32, 33.

58. Shepley, "How Dulles Averted War," 80, later quoted in *Time*'s entry on the secretary's death, "Freedom's Missionary," 1 June 1959, 12.

59. *New York Post*, 3 January 1957.

60. Luce to Eisenhower, 10 January 1957, Eisenhower Papers, President's Personal File-502, Box 951; Eisenhower to Luce, 24 January 1955, Eisenhower Papers, White House Memorandum Series-24, Box 3.

61. Stephen E. Ambrose, *Eisenhower the President* (New York: Simon and Schuster, 1984), 113–14; "Reminiscences of Clare B. Luce," 91.

62. Luce to Eisenhower, 2 July 1960; Eisenhower to Luce, 8 August 1960; Ann Whitman Papers, Name File, Box 21, Eisenhower Library; "The Reminiscences of Henry R. Luce" (1965), John Foster Dulles Oral History Project, 7, 9, 11. See also Blanche Wiesen Cook, *The Declassified Eisenhower: A Divided Legacy of Peace and Political Warfare* (New York: Penguin, 1984), 40; Cohen, "United States and China," 148.

63. Walter A. McDougall, *The Heavens and the Earth: A Political History of the Space Age* (New York: Basic Books, 1985), 145, 148; *Life*, 14 October 1957, 34–37; *Life*, 21 October 1957, 19–30, 35; Samuel Lubell, "Sputnik and American Public Opinion," *Columbia University Forum* 1 (Winter 1957):15–21.

64. *New York Herald Tribune*, 7 October 1957; *Life*, 14 October 1957, 35.

65. Tom Wolfe, *The Right Stuff* (New York: Farrar, Straus & Giroux, 1979), 140–42, 156–60; Henry R. Luce, "Speculations about A.D. 1980," in *The Fabulous Future: America in 1980*, ed. Editors of *Fortune* (New York: E. P. Dutton, 1956), 181; Robert Sherrod, "The Selling of the Astronauts," *Columbia Journalism Review* 12 (May-June 1973):17–18.

66. Pauline Kael, "The Sevens," *New Yorker*, 17 October 1983, 178.

67. Michael L. Smith, "Selling the Moon: The U.S. Manned Space Program and the Triumph of Scientism," in *Culture of Consumption*, ed. Fox and Lears, 177; editorial, *Life*, 21 October 1957, 35.

68. Notation in Billings scrapbook, 120, Billings Papers, Box 53.

69. "Memorandum of Conversation with Mr. Henry Luce, 19 January 1959," John Foster Dulles Papers, General Correspondence and Memorandum Series, Box 1, Eisenhower Library.

70. *Time*, 17 January 1955, 27.

71. *Chicago Tribune*, 25 October 1952, clipping, J. William Fulbright Papers, BCN 135, File 17, University of Arkansas, Fayetteville, Ark.; U.S., Congress, Senate, Committee on Foreign Relations, *Nomination of Clare Boothe Luce . . .* , Hearing, 86th Cong., 1st sess., 15 April 1959.

72. Billings scrapbook notation, 119, Billings Papers, Box 53; "It's Over," *Reporter*, 14 May 1959, 2.

10. FINAL PURPOSES, 1959–1967

1. Allen J. Matusow, *The Unraveling of America: A History of Liberalism in the 1960s* (New York: Harper & Row, 1984), 11.

2. Luce, "Moral Law in a Reeling World," *Christian Century* 67 (3 May 1950):553–54; Jessup, ed., *Ideas of Luce*, pt. 3; Daniel Bell, "The End of American Exceptionalism," *Public Interest*, no. 41 (Fall 1975), 204.

3. Dulles, address to New York State Bar Association, 31 January 1959, Dulles Papers, Box 143; "The Reminiscences of Henry R. Luce" (1965), John Foster Dulles Oral History Project, 11, 12, 14.

4. Luce, Introduction to *Beyond Survival*, by Max Ways (New York: Harper & Bros., 1959), xi–xii; Luce, "The Promised Land," *New Republic*, 6 December 1954, 20; John W. Jeffries, "The 'Quest for National Purpose' of 1960," *American Quarterly* 30 (Fall 1978):453–55.

5. John K. Jessup et al., *The National Purpose* (New York: Holt, Rinehart, and Winston, 1960), 21, 47.

6. Galbraith, *Life*, 264.

7. U.S., Congress, Senate, Government Operations Committee, National Policy Machinery Subcommittee, *Hearings*, 86th Cong., 2d sess., 1960, 913; Prendergast, *World of Time*, 42–43; "Mr. Luce's Cold War," *Nation*, 9 July 1960, 22.

8. Alexander Walsh, "Kennedy and the Meaning of Sacrifice," *New Republic*, 16 October 1961, 16.

9. Henry Fairlie, *The Kennedy Promise* (Garden City, N.Y.: Doubleday, 1972), 87; Matusow, *Unraveling of America*, 10.

10. William V. Shannon, *New York Post*, 11 November 1957, quoted in

Herbert S. Parmet, *Jack: The Struggles of John F. Kennedy* (New York: Dial Press, 1980), 438. See also David E. Koskoff, *Joseph P. Kennedy: A Life and Times* (Englewood Cliffs, N.J.: Prentice-Hall, 1974), 428.

11. Hyman, *Lives of Benton*, 538; Hedley Donovan, *Roosevelt to Reagan: A Reporter's Encounter with Nine Presidents* (New York: Harper & Row, 1985), 70.

12. David Shaw, *Los Angeles Times*, 3 May 1980.

13. Donovan, *Roosevelt to Reagan*, 73.

14. Otto Friedrich, "There are 00 Trees in Russia," *Harper's*, October 1964, 64; William L. Rivers, "The Correspondents after 35 Years," *Columbia Journalism Review* 1 (Spring 1962):7.

15. *New York World-Telegram and Sun*, 31 March 1966, clipping, Westbrook Pegler Papers, Box 76, Hoover Library. See also "*Time*: The Weekly Fiction Magazine," *Fact* 1 (January–February 1964):3–23.

16. R. Smith Schuneman, ed., *Photographic Communication* (New York: Hastings House, 1972), 237, 357; Prendergast, *World of Time*, 51; James K. Glassman, "One Life to Live," *New Republic*, 9 February 1987, 40.

17. Theodore C. Sorensen, *Kennedy* (New York: Harper & Row, 1965), 316–17; Donovan, *Roosevelt to Reagan*, 70; Merrill, "How *Time* Stereotyped," 566–70; Jessup, ed., *Ideas of Luce*, 368–69; *Time*, 29 November 1963, 19.

18. *Time*, 21 September 1962, 17, 21; *Time*, 12 October 1962, 22.

19. Peter Collier and David Horowitz, *The Kennedys: An American Drama* (New York: Summit Books, 1984), 281 n. See also Kenneth P. O'Donnell and David F. Powers, *"Johnny, We Hardly Knew Ye": Memories of John Fitzgerald Kennedy* (Boston: Little, Brown, 1972), 408.

20. Compare Luce's own memoir of this episode in Jessup, ed., *Ideas of Luce*, 370, to Roger Hilsman, *To Move a Nation: The Politics of Foreign Policy in the Administration of John F. Kennedy* (Garden City, N.Y.: Doubleday, 1967), chap. 22; Warren I. Cohen, *Dean Rusk* (Totowa, N.J.: Cooper Square Publishers, 1980), 166–67, 281.

21. *Life*, 2 November 1962, 4, 36–41; *Time*, 2 November 1962, 15–29; Prendergast, *World of Time*, 35–36; Montague Kern, Patricia W. Levering, and Ralph B. Levering, *The Kennedy Crises* (Chapel Hill: University of North Carolina Press, 1983), 136, 138, 140.

22. John L. Steele, "The News Magazine in Washington," in *The Press in Washington*, ed. Ray Eldon Hiebert (New York: Dodd, Mead, & Co., 1966), 58–60. For an example of *Time*'s early optimism concerning the war, see 12 October 1962, 35.

23. *Time*, 20 September 1963, 62; David Halberstam, *The Powers That Be* (New York: Knopf, 1979), 464.

24. *Time*, 11 October 1963, 55–56; John Horenberg, *Between Two Worlds: Policy, Press, and Public Opinion in Asian-American Relations* (New York: Frederick A. Praeger, 1967), 41–42; Stanley Karnow, "The Newsmen's

War in Vietnam," *Nieman Reports* 16 (December 1963):3–8; David Halberstam, *The Making of a Quagmire* (New York: Random House, 1965), 270–74.

25. Halberstam, *Powers That Be*, 457. A similar generational split, Edward Fouhy argues, affected television. See his "Effect of the Vietnam War on Broadcast Journalism: A Producer's Perspective," in *Vietnam Reconsidered*, ed. Harrison Salisbury (New York: Harper & Row, 1984), 91–92.

26. Charles Mohr, "Once Again—Did the Press Lose Vietnam?" *Columbia Journalism Review* 22 (November–December 1983):55; Henry Fairlie, "We Knew What We Were Doing When We Went into Vietnam," *Washington Monthly* 5 (May 1973):26; Kern et al., *Kennedy Crises*, 191; John Mecklin, *Mission in Torment* (Garden City, N.Y.: Doubleday, 1965), chap. 4; Daniel C. Hallin, *The "Uncensored War": The Media and Vietnam* (New York: Oxford University Press, 1986), 40–42, 48, 58.

27. Joan Simpson Burns, *The Awkward Embrace: The Creative Artist and the Institution in America* (New York: Knopf, 1975), 143–45, 161.

28. Dwight Macdonald, *Discriminations* (New York: Grossman, 1974), 274; *Cleveland Press*, 14 January 1964.

29. *Time*, 7 January 1966, 15.

30. Ibid., 14 May 1965, 30.

31. Prendergast, *World of Time*, 196.

32. *Washington Post*, 26 April 1965; Halberstam, *Quagmire*, 315, 319; Hallin, *"Uncensored War,"* 95.

33. Osborn Elliott, *The World of Oz* (New York: Viking, 1980), 91. See also Reston, *Artillery*, 94.

34. *Time*, 22 April 1966, 19.

35. Halberstam, *Powers That Be*, 477.

36. *Time*, 7 January 1966, 15–16, 21; 11 March 1966, 23; 18 March 1966, 32; Cohen, *Rusk*, 173, 280–89.

37. Prendergast, *World of Time*, 247.

38. *Time*, 7 May 1965, 25. On the press's at times critical handling of the antiwar movement, see Nathan Blumberg, "Misreporting the Peace Movement," *Columbia Journalism Review* 10 (Winter 1970–71):28–32; Todd Gitlin, *The Whole World is Watching: Mass Media in the Making and Unmaking of the New Left* (Berkeley: University of California Press, 1980), chaps. 2–3.

39. *Time*, 22 January 1965, 15–16, 18; 4 March 1966, 26–27; 29 April 1966, 25–26.

40. Ibid., 11 March 1966, 64–65. See also ibid., 22 April 1966, 63–64. On some of the Washington press corps's growing doubts about the war, see Kathleen J. Turner, *Lyndon Johnson's Dual Wars* (Chicago: University of Chicago Press, 1985), chap. 6.

41. Edmund K. Faltermayer, "The Surprising Assets of South Vietnam's Economy," *Fortune*, March 1966, 110–13, is one exception. Other articles stressed the political or military imperatives for intervention. See Charles J. V.

Murphy, "Vietnam Hangs on U.S. Determination," *Fortune*, May 1964, 159–62, 227–30, and "Vanishing Margins in Vietnam," *Fortune*, September 1964, 110. In "The Vietnam War: A Cost Accounting," *Fortune*, April 1966, 119–23, 254, 259, William Bowen warned that the administration was underestimating the financial costs of U.S. involvement.

42. *Life*, 30 April 1965, 31–32.

43. Ibid., 21 June 1963, 24–25; 6 September 1963, 29–30A; cover, 16 April 1965; 11 February 1966, 20–25.

44. George Bailey, "Interpretive Reporting of the Vietnam War by Anchormen," *Journalism Quarterly* 53 (Summer 1976):319–24; Hallin, *"Uncensored War,"* chap. 4; Michael Arlen, *Living-Room War* (New York: Viking, 1969), 45–50, 142–48; Michael Arlen, "The Falklands, Vietnam, and Our Collective Memory," *New Yorker*, 16 August 1983, 70, 72–75; Michael Mendelbaum, "Vietnam: The Television War," *Daedalus* 111 (Fall 1982):157–70. Between August 1965 and August 1970, about 3 percent of all network evening news film from Vietnam showed dead or wounded. Lawrence W. Lichty, "Comments on the Influence of Television on Public Opinion," in *Vietnam as History: Ten Years after the Paris Peace Accords*, ed. Peter Braestrup (Washington: University Press of America, 1984), 158. A sample in Hallin, *"Uncensored War,"* 129–30, suggests a somewhat higher number showed casualties on the screen.

45. Prendergast, *World of Time*, 241–42; editorial, *Life*, 25 February 1966, 27–31. "The Reminiscences of Hedley Donovan" (1968), Oral History Collection of Columbia University, 94–95, 104.

46. Luce, "To See Life in Its Full Dimensions," *Fortune*, January 1967, 88. In the wake of the networks' treatment of the Israeli invasion of Lebanon in 1982, this attack on the episodic aspect to Vietnam reportage was revived. See, e.g., Todd Lindberg, "Of Arms, Men & Monuments," *Commentary*, October 1984, 51–56.

47. Sheed, *Clare Boothe Luce*, 125; Martha Weinman Lear, "On Harry, and Henry and Ike and Mr. Shaw," *New York Times Magazine*, 22 April 1973, 56.

48. The Rockefeller brothers, Richard Nixon, and Barry Goldwater were the more prominent Republicans attending. The only Democrat listed by the *Times* at the services, former postmaster general James A. Farley, had been out of national politics since 1940. *New York Times*, 4 March 1967.

49. Prendergast, *World of Time*, 236, 248 ff; Donovan, *Roosevelt to Reagan*, 103; editorials, *Life*, 20 October 1967, 4; 15 March 1968, 4; Peter Braestrup, *Big Story*, abridged ed. (New Haven: Yale University Press, 1983), 41.

50. Andrew Kopkind, "Serving *Time*," 26; Richard Pollack, *"Time* after Luce," *Harper's*, July 1969, 45, 48; John Tirman, "Doing *Time*," *Progressive*, August 1981, 46–49, 51; David Shaw, *Los Angeles Times*, 1 May 1980, 3 May 1980.

51. *Wall Street Journal,* 12 July 1967; Elliott, *World of Oz,* 50; Pollack, "*Time* after Luce," 44, 48; *New York Times,* 30 November 1968; Shaw, *Los Angeles Times,* 3 March 1980. In *Deciding What's News* (New York: Pantheon, 1979), 319, Herbert J. Gans argues that despite *Newsweek's* efforts to establish a separate identity, in the late 1960s and 1970s the two magazines were essentially addressing the same audiences; virtually no differences by income, age, or education can be discerned from Daniel Starch and staff, *Consumer Magazine Report* (Mamaroneck, N.Y.: Daniel Starch and staff, 1968), 53, 65. *Time's* share of the newsmagazine field did drop slightly from 49 percent in 1961 to 48.7 percent in 1970; *Newsweek's* rose, apparently at the expense of both *Time* and *U.S. News & World Report,* from 27.7 percent in 1961 to 29.7 percent in 1970. Association of National Advertisers, *Magazine Circulation and Rate Trends, 1946–74.*

Nor is it clear, as *Newsweek* veterans delighted to report, that their treatment of the civil rights movement in the 1960s was any more forward thinking than *Time's.* See Lentz, "Resurrecting the Prophet," 694–96, 924.

52. Gans in *Deciding What's News* offers the most devastating case for sameness.

53. Fred Fedler, *An Introduction to Mass Communication* (New York: Harcourt, Brace, and Jovanovich, 1978), 343; Chris Welles, "Can Mass Magazines Survive?" *Columbia Journalism Review* 11 (July 1971):12–13. A. J. van Zuilen, *The Life Cycle of Magazines* (Uithoorn, Holland: Graduate Press, 1977), is the most exhaustive analysis of the death of *Life* and other illustrated mass magazines. The *Wall Street Journal's* account, 11 December 1972, offers the company line.

54. On *People,* see Prendergast, *World of Time,* 431–40; William S. Maddox and Robert Robins, "How *People* Magazine Covers Political Figures," *Journalism Quarterly* 59 (Spring 1981):113–15; Jan Benzel, "*People's* Choice," *Washington Journalism Review* 6 (December 1984):34–37; Nora Ephron, *Esquire,* March 1975, 12, 14, 47.

55. *Nation,* 20 March 1967, 358; Joseph Epstein, "Henry Luce and His Time," *Commentary,* November 1967, 39.

56. Terry H. Anderson, *The United States, Great Britain, and the Cold War 1944–1947* (Columbia, Mo.: University of Missouri Press, 1981), 184.

57. Jessup, ed., *Ideas of Luce,* 379, 381.

58. James Reed, *The Missionary Mind and American East Asian Policy, 1911–1915* (Cambridge, Mass.: Harvard University Press, 1983), 198.

59. Luce, "Giving," 66.

60. Luce, "To See Life."

61. Arlen, *Living-Room War,* 51; *Life,* 16 October 1964, 82–88, 147–48.

62. Edward J. Epstein, *News from Nowhere* (New York: Random House, 1973), 4–5; Doris A. Graber, *Mass Media and American Politics,* 2d ed. (Washington: Congressional Quarterly, 1984), 227. On *The March of Time's* influ-

ences on television news, see Burton Benjamin, "The Documentary Heritage," *Television Quarterly* 2 (February 1962):29–31 and Fred W. Friendly, *Due to Circumstances Beyond Our Control* (New York: Random House, 1967), xv.

63. Wilfrid Sheed, "Brass Bands and Raspberries," *New York Review of Books*, 9 November 1978, 6; W. Lance Bennett, *News: The Politics of Illusion* (New York: Longman, 1983), 7–13; Gans, *Deciding*, 9.

64. Timothy Crouse, *The Boys on the Bus* (New York: Ballantine, 1973), 386–87. Journalists surveyed several years after Luce's death ranked *Time*'s reporting well below that of most other national news services and such "prestige" papers as the *New York Times*. John W. C. Johnstone et al., *The Newspeople: A Sociological Portrait of American Journalists and Their Work* (Urbana: University of Illinois Press, 1976), 88 and Table 5.7. See also David Shaw, *Los Angeles Times*, 1 May 1980.

65. William V. Shannon, review of *Reckless Disregard*, by Renata Adler, *Washington Post National Weekly Edition*, 1 December 1986, 35.

66. Matthews, "Tall, balding," 132.

67. *Business Week*, 21 May 1979, 10; editorial, *New York Times*, 1 March 1967; Galbraith, in *Writing for "Fortune,"* 179; Lloyd Wendt, *The Wall Street Journal* (Chicago: Rand McNally, 1982), chap. 15.

68. Rudolf Klein, "Lords of the Press," *Commentary*, January 1973, 74. See also W. Lance Bennett and Murray Edelman, "Towards a New Political Narrative," *Journal of Communication* 35 (Autumn 1985):156–71.

69. Thomas Griffith, "The No-Fault Society," *Atlantic Monthly*, May 1977, 26; Daniel Bell, "Henry Luce's Half Century," *New Leader*, 11 December 1972, 13.

70. William Benton to Paul Hoffman, 28 December 1962, Benton Papers, Box 177, University of Chicago.

71. Galbraith, in *Writing for "Fortune,"* 119.

AFTERWORD, 2001

The author thanks Robert E. Drechsel for commenting on an earlier draft of the Afterword, as well as Courtney Bond for her careful editing.

1. David Kamp, "The Tabloid Decade," *Vanity Fair* (February 1999):66–70, 75–79; Jim Mann, "Isolationist Trend Imperils Activist Foreign Policy," *Los Angeles Times*, 14 February 1995; Howard Kurtz, "Tuning Out Traditional News," *Washington Post*, 15 May 1995; James L. Baughman, *Republic of Mass Culture: Journalism, Filmmaking, and Broadcasting in America since 1941*, 2d ed. (Baltimore: Johns Hopkins University Press, 1997), 230–31.

2. See, e.g., Robert N. Bellah, et al., *Habits of the Heart: Individualism and Commitment in American Life*, updated ed. (Berkeley: University of California Press, 1996); Robert D. Putnam, *Bowling Alone: The Collapse and Revival of*

American Community (New York: Simon & Schuster, 2000); Jackson Lears, "Mastery and Drift," *Journal of American History* 84 (December 1997):981–84.

3. David Abrahamson, *Magazine-Made America: The Cultural Transformation of the Postwar Periodical* (Cresskill, N.J.: Hampton Press, 1995). *Life*, revived as a monthly in 1978, ceased regular publication in 2000. Its circulation had fallen to 1.5 million and was operating at a loss. Alex Kuczynski, "*Life* Magazine to End Monthly Publication after May Issue," *New York Times*, 18 March 2000.

4. Neal Gabler, *Life the Movie: How Entertainment Conquered Reality* (New York: Knopf, 1998), 7.

5. Aristides, "Nicely Out of It," *American Scholar* 62 (Autumn 1993):494.

6. Joshua Gamson, *Claims to Fame: Celebrity in Contemporary America* (Berkeley: University of California Press, 1994), esp. 40–44, 59–78.

7. Mary W. Quigley, "Magazine Cover Roulette," *Washington Journalism Review* (July–August 1988):19–20.

8. Jonathan Yardley, *Monday Morning Quarterback* (Lanham, Md.: Rowman & Littlefield, 1998), 69.

9. Richard Norton Smith, "Let Us Entertain You," *New York Times*, 12 March 1998; Jim Yardley, "*Time* Goes to a Party (Its Own)," *New York Times*, 4 March 1998. See also Ted Koppel, "Journalism under Fire," *Nation*, 24 November 1997, 23.

10. Bruce Porter, "The Newsweeklies: Is the Species Doomed?" *Columbia Journalism Review* (March–April 1989):23–24; Martin Mayer, *Making News* (Garden City, N.Y.: Doubleday, 1987), 237.

11. This was, in fact, the strategy of *The Economist*, a British business weekly that devoted substantial space to political and governmental news and published an American edition. It much resembled the old *Time*. *The Economist*, however, made little effort to compete directly with *Time* or *Newsweek* for circulation.

12. Lance Morrow, "The *Time* of Our Lives," *Time*, 9 March 1998, 91. See also Walter Isaacson, "Luce's Values—Then and Now," *Time*, 9 March 1998, 195.

13. *Newsweek* also did a cover and ran nine pages on the story. Alicia C. Shepard, "Into the Fray," *American Journalism Review* (January–February 1998):22.

14. *Time*, 23 August 1968, 18–24, 27–28; 14 August 2000.

15. Porter, "The Newsweeklies," 24–25; Alex S. Jones, "For News Magazines, a 'Softening,'" *New York Times*, 29 June 1988.

16. Robin Pogrebin, "At Work and at Play, *Time*'s Editor Seeks to Keep Magazine Vigorous at 75," *New York Times*, 9 March 1998.

17. The figures are for all issues, 1985 and 1995, calculated by Hall's Magazine Editorial Reports, cited in Robin Pogrebin, "Foreign Coverage Less Prominent in News Magazines," *New York Times*, 23 September 1996.

18. Patrick M. Reilly, "The Instant-News Age Leaves *Time* Magazine Searching for a Mission," *Wall Street Journal*, 12 May 1993.

19. Richard M. Clurman, *To the End of Time: The Seduction and Conquest of a Media Empire* (New York: Simon & Schuster, 1992), 296–97. See also Deirdre Carmody, "One More *Time*: Magazine is Reborn," *New York Times*, 13 April 1992.

20. Henry Grunwald, *One Man's America: A Journalist's Search for the Heart of His Country* (New York: Doubleday, 1996), 414, 459–61; Prendergast, *World of Time*, 328.

21. James Fallows, *Breaking the News: How the Media Undermine American Democracy* (New York: Pantheon, 1996), 152–55; James L. Baughman, "The Transformation of *Time* Magazine," *Media Studies Journal* 12 (Fall 1998):124–26; William Triplett, "Alive!" *American Journalism Review* (October 1994):28, 29–30, 31; Judith Adler Hennessee, "*Time's* Man of the Year," *Vanity Fair* (January 1985):83, 98.

22. *Time*, 20 April 1998, 27 April 1998, 4 May 1998, and 18 May 1998.

23. Deirdre Carmody, "*Time* Speaking with a New Voice," *New York Times*, 4 June 1990. See also, Porter "The Newsweeklies," 25–26.

24. *Time*, 20 April 1998, 34–37, 66–70.

25. Ibid., 7 February 1983, 70–75.

26. Ibid., 26 April 1999, 79–89, 90, 92–94.

27. Ibid., 7 August 2000 and 14 August 2000. Changes in the news media fostered this redefinition. New information media had created a 24-hour news cycle; major events were recounted quickly and analyzed at length. A weekly magazine that emphasized such occurrences risked having a very short shelf life. Then, too, other news media began defining news as what was to happen. See Bruce Feiler, "News in Future Tense," *New York Times*, 23 November 1998. As a former *New York Times* editor noted, soothsaying was also cheaper than actual reporting. Max Frankel, "Rushing the Seasons," *New York Times Magazine*, 25 July 1999, 19–20.

28. One advertising trade journal's "Hot List" of 1999 listed two Time Inc. periodicals, *Time* and *Fortune*, see *MediaWeek*, 6 March 2000, M14.

29. "Internet Sapping Broadcast News Audience," Pew Research for People and the Press, 11 June 2000, <www.people-press.org/media00sec1.htm>.

30. Reilly, "The Instant-News Age Leaves *Time* Magazine Searching." See also Randall Rothenberg, "Magazine Industry Had Better Learn Some of the New Tricks," *Advertising Age*, 16 August 1999, 29.

31. Eric Alterman, "Old *Time* Media, New *Slate*," *Nation*, 30 March 1998, 22.

32. Michael MacCambridge, *The Franchise: A History of Sports Illustrated Magazine* (New York: Hyperion, 1997), 335–37, 340, 353–56, 358, 401–2, 403; Brian Stein, "ESPN Gives *Sports Illustrated* a Run for Its Money," *Wall Street Journal*, 8 June 1999; Jeff Pearlman, "At Full Blast," *Sports Illustrated*, 27 December 1999, 60–64.

33. Edwin Diamond, "Trouble in Paradise," *New York Magazine*, 3 March 1986, 50–55; Grunwald, *One Man's America*, 555; Geraldine Fabrikant, "*Time* Pulls Plug on Picture Week," *New York Times*, 7 November 1986.

34. Geraldine Fabrikant, "A Media Giant Loses Its Swagger," *New York Times*, 1 December 1985. See also Les Brown, "*Time* Marching On with Video," *New York Times*, 2 January 1980; Sandra Salmans, "Time Inc. in the Video Age," *New York Times*, 7 March 1983.

35. MacCambridge, *The Franchise*, 253–54.

36. Clurman, *To the End of Time*, 78–79.

37. Geraldine Fabrikant, "*Time's* Cable Head Named President," *New York Times*, 18 July 1986; Lester Bernstein, "Time Inc. Means Business," *New York Times Magazine*, 26 February 1989, 25, 42–44; Connie Bruck, *Master of the Game: Steve Ross and the Creation of Time Warner* (New York: Simon & Schuster, 1994), 256–57; Clurman, *To the End of Time*, 301.

38. Fabrikant, "A Media Giant Loses Its Swagger,"; idem, "Time Plans to Buy Back Up to 16% of Its Shares," *New York Times*, 20 June 1986; Bernstein, "Time Inc. Means Business," 22; Laura Landro, "Time Inc. Has Big Plans after a Difficult Year," *Wall Street Journal*, 17 March 1986.

39. Clurman, *To the End of Time*, 86–92.

40. Ibid., 150–51, 152, 155–56; Bruck, *Master of the Game*, 259.

41. James Bennet, "Time Out," *New Republic*, 24 April 1989, 23; Floyd Norris, "Time Inc. and Warner to Merge, Creating Largest Media Company," *New York Times*, 5 March 1989; Elizabeth Jensen, "'What's Up, Doc?' 'Vertical Integration,'" *Wall Street Journal*, 16 October 1995; Connie Bruck, "Jerry's Deal," *New Yorker*, 19 February 1996, 57.

42. Prendergast, *World of Time*, 214–15. Subsequent loses on a minority investment, made shortly after Luce's death, in another film studio appeared to confirm the Founder's misgivings. According to the company history, Time Inc. wrote off $10.5 million on its 5 percent investment in MGM. Ibid., 381–83.

43. Clurman, *To the End of Time*, 38–39. The stations were sold in 1970, though because Luce's successor had concluded that their value had peaked. See Prendergast, *World of Time*, 273–74.

44. Bruck, *Master of the Game*, 264.

45. Ibid., 266–67; Clurman, *To the End of Time*, 162–63; Hedley Donovan, *Right Places, Right Times: Forty Years in Journalism, Not Counting My Paper Route* (New York: Holt, 1989), 441.

46. Daniel C. Hallin, *We Keep America on Top of the World: Television and the Public Sphere* (London: Routledge, 1994), ch. 5. Coverage anticipating Stanley Kubrick's final film, *Eyes Wide Shut*, provided an extraordinary example of infotainment-as-hype across media. See Katherine Rosman, "Why the Media Kept Their Eyes Wide Shut," *Brill's Content* (October 1999):86–90.

47. Clurman, *To the End of Time*, 30–31. See also ibid., 171; and Byron Dobell, "Clouds in Magazine Heaven," *New York Times Book Review*, 19 January 1986, 23.

48. "Time Warner," *Business Week*, 22 July 1991, 70; Robert J. Cole, "Time, in Rebuff to Paramount, Bids for Warner," *New York Times*, 17 June 1989.

49. Kurt Andersen, "The Outsider," *New Yorker*, 31 March 1997, 47. See also Robert Sam Anson, "Time Warp," *Esquire* (March 1992), 163–64.

50. Anson, "Time Warp," 87–88; Deirdre Carmody, "Beyond the Tinkering at Time Inc.," *New York Times*, 27 September 1993.

51. "Hopelessly Seeking Synergy," *Economist*, 20 August 1994, 53. See also Randall Rothenberg, "Time Warner's Merger Payoff," *New York Times*, 31 December 1990; Richard W. Stevenson, "Moving to End a Battle for Time Warner's Soul," *New York Times*, 22 February 1992; "Time Warner," *Business Week*, 22 July 1991, 72–74; Roger Cohen, "Steve Ross Defends His Paycheck," *New York Times Magazine*, 22 March 1992, 45; Roger Lowenstein, "After Two Years, Time Warner Marriage Still Has to Bloom," *Wall Street Journal*, 18 June 1991; Bruck, "Jerry's Deal," 63, 64. The absence of synergy was partly explained, ironically, given the cries of some critics of media conglomeration, by the autonomy that Levin awarded his many divisions. Brett Pulley, "Morning After," *Forbes*, 4 October 1999, 54–55.

52. Daniel Okrent, "Happily Ever After?" *Time*, 24 January 2000, 42.

53. Clurman, *To the End of Time*, 32.

54. Reg Black, magazine division CEO, quoted in Anson, "Time Warp," 162.

55. *Advertising Age*, 16 August 1999, S2.

56. Laura Landro, "Writer Quits *Fortune* Top-Pay List, Citing Interference," *Wall Street Journal*, 26 June 1991. See also Robin Pogrebin, "*Fortune* Bucks Critics and Covers Its Parent," *New York Times*, 23 March 1998.

57. Deirdre Carmody, "From the Pages of *Time*, a Story for *Newsweek*," *New York Times*, 18 June 1990.

58. Martin Peers and J. Max Robins, "Turner Takes a Time Share," *Variety*, 25 September 1995, 1, 110–11; G. Craig Endicott, "100 Leading Media Companies," *Advertising Age*, 16 August 1999, S2; Anita Sharpe, "Used to Being Boss, Ted Turner Is Mulling His Time Warner Role," *Wall Street Journal*, 27 November 1995; Diane Mermigas, "Done Deal; Time Warner, Turner to Merge," *Electronic Media*, 25 September 1995, 1, 44; Mark Landler, "Time Warner Bids $8.5 Billion for Turner Broadcasting System," *New York Times*, 30 August 1995; Bruck, "Jerry's Deal," 55, 58–59, 61. As in the case of the Time Warner merger, the combination also forestalled a possible hostile takeover. Geraldine Fabrikant, "The Motives for a Mating Dance," *New York Times*, 31 August 1995.

59. MacCambridge, *The Franchise*, 400–1.

60. Lawrie Mifflin, "Not Just 'Larry King Live,'" *New York Times*, 8 June 1998.

61. Robin Pogrebin and Felicity Barringer, "CNN Retracts Report That U.S. Used Nerve Gas," *New York Times*, 3 July 1998; Lawrie Mifflin, "Time Orders Investigation on Accuracy of CNN Report," *New York Times*, 22 June 1998; editorial, "The CNN-Time Retraction," *New York Times*, 3 July 1998.

62. Neil Hickey, "Ten Mistakes That Led to the Great CNN Time Fiasco," *Columbia Journalism Review* (September–October 1998):32.

63. Tom Rosenstiel and Bill Kovach, "The Bad Business of Media Mergers," *New York Times*, 14 January 2000.

64. Scott Rosenberg, "AOL and Time Warner's Marriage of Insecurity," *Salon*, 10 January 2000, <www.salon.com>.

65. Holman W. Jenkins, Jr., "The Last Crazy Internet Valuation?" *Wall Street Journal*, 12 January 2000; Rosenberg, "AOL and Time Warner's Marriage of Insecurity,"; Marc Gunther, "These Guys Want It All," *Fortune*, 7 February 2000, 71–76, 78; Okrent, "Happily Ever After?" 39–40; Martin Peers, Nick Wingfield, and Laura Landro, "Media Blitz," *Wall Street Journal*, 11 January 2000; Mark Leibovich, "A Match for the Media Age," *Washington Post National Weekly Edition*, 17 January 2000, 6–7.

66. Robert T. Elson, "To Make 'Journalist' A Good Word," in *Henry R. Luce, April 3, 1898–February 28, 1967* (New York: n. p., 1967), 16–17.

67. Joshua Cooper Ramo, "A Two-Man Network," *Time*, 24 January 2000, 49.

68. Gunther, "These Guys Want It All," 72.

69. Ben H. Bagdikian, *The Media Monopoly*, 6th ed. (Boston: Beacon Press, 2000), viii, xxi. See also Rifka Rosenwein, "Why Media Mergers Matter," *Brill's Content* (December 1999–January 2000):93–95.

70. "A Letter from the Staff," *Time*, 10 March 1967, 11.

71. Howard Kurtz, "When the News Is All in the Family," *Washington Post National Weekly Edition*, 17 January 2000, 7; Neil Hickey, "Coping with Mega-Mergers," *Columbia·Journalism Review* (March–April 2000):16–17, 19–20; Rosenstiel and Kovach, "The Bad Business of Media Mergers"; William Safire, "Th-Th-That's All, Folks!" *New York Times*, 4 May 2000.

72. See, e.g., Mark Landler, "From Gurus to Sitting Ducks," *New York Times*, 11 January 1998; "Mind Control? (Not Yet)," *Brill's Content* (December 1999–January 2000):105–9.

73. Mark Landler, "CNN Ratings Head South. Calling O.J., Calling O.J.," *New York Times*, 14 July 1997; Lawrie Mifflin, "In This War, CNN Has Real Competition," *New York Times*, 5 April 1999; Jim Rutenberg, "As Ratings Dip, Ted Turner and CNN Uneasily Face Milestone," *New York Times*, 5 June 2000.

74. Jenkins, "The Last Crazy Internet Valuation?"

75. Michael Lewis, "AOL: Almost Obscenely Large," *Wall Street Journal*, 13 January 2000. See also Leibovich, "A Match for the Media Age," 6. For a much more positive view of the merger, see Anthony B. Perkins, "AOL Beats the Odds—Again," *Wall Street Journal*, 12 January 2000.

76. MacCambridge, *The Franchise*, 389–91. On February 26, 2000, Turner's TNT cable channel ran *Sports Illustrated Swimsuit TV Special 2000*. It failed to finish in the top fifteen programs in the basic cable ratings for the week. The only two Turner networks channels to make the list were professional wrestling programs. See *Electronic Media*, 6 March 2000, 46.

77. As *Brill's Content* noted in a "synergy snapshot," Time Warner's *Entertainment Weekly* not only ran a critical review, but carried a cover story on "all the bad buzz about the film. The magazine's assessment was dead-on: *Wild Wild West* ended up as perhaps the summer's biggest belly flop." *Brill's Content* (December 1999–January 2000): 94; Benjamin Svetkey, "Even Cowboys Get the Blues," *Entertainment Weekly*, 9 July 1999, 20–27; Owen Gleiberman, "Men in Bleccch," *Entertainment Weekly*, 9 July 1999, 40–41.

78. Victor Navasky, "Is Big Really Bad? Well, Yes," *Time*, 24 January 2000, 52.

BIBLIOGRAPHIC ESSAY

BIOGRAPHICAL TREATMENTS OF LUCE

Luce has been the subject of two biographies, John Kobler, *Luce: His Time, Life, and Fortune* (Garden City, N.Y.: Doubleday, 1968), and W. A. Swanberg, *Luce and His Empire* (New York: Charles Scribner's Sons, 1972). Swanberg's is far more comprehensive and researched; it is also unrelentingly hostile. More stimulating if far less consistent in their views of Harry are commentaries in Dwight Macdonald, *Discriminations* (New York: Grossman, 1974), and in the Macdonald Papers, Yale University, as well as Joseph Epstein, "Henry Luce and His Time," *Commentary*, November 1967, 35–47, and *Ambition: The Secret Passion* (New York: E. P. Dutton, 1980). John K. Jessup, ed., *The Ideas of Henry Luce* (New York: Atheneum, 1969) contains most of Luce's important writings as well as a perceptive introduction by a former aide. In David Halberstam, *The Powers That Be* (New York: Knopf, 1979), Luce appears frequently. See also Andrew Kopkind's incisive "Serving *Time*," *New York Review of Books*, 12 September 1968, 23–28.

Two newspaper features on Luce proved especially insightful: Kenneth Stewart's three-part profile in New York *PM*, (27 August 1944, 3 September 1944, and 10 September 1944), and the *New York Post*'s ten-part series (24 December 1956–6 January 1957). Wolcott Gibbs's profile of Harry, written entirely in Timese, "Time . . . Fortune . . . Life . . . Luce," appeared in the *New Yorker* and was reprinted in Gibbs's *More in Sorrow* (Boston: Houghton Mifflin, 1958).

THE LUCE FAMILY

Most of Luce's papers are in the Time Inc. Archives, Time-Life Building, New York City; a smaller portion has been donated to the Library of Congress. Access to both collections is restricted. There is also much correspondence between the Luces, including young Harry, and family benefactor Nettie Fowler McCormick, in the McCormick Papers, State Historical Society of Wisconsin, Madison.

On Luce's father, B. A. Garside, *One Increasing Purpose: The Life of Henry Winters Luce* (New York: Fleming H. Revell, 1948), is reverential but all that is available in book-length form. See also Robert E. Speer, *A Memorial of Horace Tracy Pitkin* (New York: Fleming H. Revell, 1903), and Sherwood Eddy, *Pathfinders of the World Missionary Crusade* (New York: Abington-Cokesbury Press, 1945). On the Student Volunteer Movement and China missionaries in the late nineteenth century, I most benefited from Paul A. Varg, *Missionaries, Chinese, and Diplomats: The American Protestant Movement in China, 1890–1952* (Princeton: Princeton University Press, 1958); John K. Fairbank, ed., *The Missionary Enterprise in China and America* (Cambridge, Mass.: Harvard University Press, 1974); and Valentin H. Rabe, *The Home Base of American China Missions, 1880–1920* (Cambridge, Mass.: Harvard University Press, 1978). James Reed, *The Missionary Mind and American East Asian Policy, 1911–1915* (Cambridge, Mass.: Harvard University Press, 1983) is helpful on the shift in attitudes toward the missions. John Hersey, "Henry Luce's China Dream," *New Republic*, 2 May 1983, 27–32, discusses Henry Winters Luce; see also Hersey's novel about a China missionary, *The Call* (New York: Knopf, 1985).

GROWING UP

On missionary children, see Jane Hunter, *The Gospel of Gentility: American Women Missionaries in Turn-of-the-Century China* (New Haven: Yale University Press, 1984); Sarah R. Mason, "Missionary Conscience and the Comprehension of Imperialism: A Study of the Children of American Missionaries to China, 1900–1949" (Ph.D. diss., Northern Illinois University, 1978); Ellsworth Huntington, "The Success of Missionary Children," *Missionary Review of the World* 58 (February 1935):74–75; and Pearl Buck's memoir, *My Several Worlds: A Personal Record* (New York: John Day, 1954), and letters reprinted in Theodore F. Harris, *Pearl S. Buck: A Biography* (New York: John Day, 1971). On the Chefoo School, the biographies of one of Luce's school classmates, Thornton Wilder, were helpful. See Gilbert A. Harrison, *The Enthusiast: The Life of Thornton Wilder* (New Haven: Ticknor & Fields, 1983); Linda Simon, *Thornton Wilder: His World* (Garden City, N.Y.: Doubleday, 1979); and Richard H. Goldstone, *Thornton Wilder* (New York: Saturday Review Press, 1975), which also discusses Wilder's years at Yale with Luce; they were not close. On Hotchkiss, the school's Alumni Office has a Luce file, as well as issues of the *Literary Monthly* and *Record*. See also Harris Erdman, "Henry Luce at Hotchkiss," *Hotchkiss Alumni News*, July 1964, 6–9; Noel F. Busch, *Briton Hadden* (New York: Farrar, Straus, & Co., 1949); and Lael Tucker Wertenbaker and Maude Basserman, *The Hotchkiss School: A Portrait* (Lakeville, Conn.: The Hotchkiss School, 1966). On Yale, George Wilson Pierson, *Yale: College and University 1871–1937* (New Haven: Yale University Press, 1952), the formal history of the college, was most useful. I also checked issues of the *Yale Daily News*; the Alumni Records Office has Hadden and Luce files, both of which have letters and clippings of value.

NEWSPAPERS AND MAGAZINES IN THE 1920s AND 1930s

On journalism in the interwar era, the most valuable scholarly treatments are Alfred M. Lee, *The Daily Newspaper in America* (New York: Macmillan, 1937); Leo C. Rosten, *The Washington Correspondents* (New York: Harcourt, Brace, 1937); and Michael Schudson's provocative *Discovering the News* (New York: Basic Books, 1978) and "The Politics of Narrative Form: The Emergence of News Conventions in Print and Television," *Daedalus* 111 (Fall 1982):97–112.

My characterizations of the press in the 1920s owed the most to two sources, the papers themselves, and a large body of critical literature written by editors and reporters. Newspapers examined include the *Brooklyn Eagle*, the *New York Times*, the *New York World*, the *Chicago Tribune*, the *Chicago Daily News*, and the *Chicago Herald-American*. My sample of newspapers has a "big city" bias. My concern, however, was with those papers Luce and Hadden read. When planning *Time*, they did not scrutinize most big and small papers or the emerging tabloids. One reporter's perspective was gained by examining the diaries of John Shaw Billings, South Caroliniana Library, University of South Carolina, Columbia; Billings was a correspondent for the *Eagle* in the late 1920s.

The most helpful critical works were Silas Bent's two delightful collections, *Ballyhoo* (New York: Boni & Liverwright, 1927) and *Strange Bedfellows* (New York: Horace Liverwright, 1928); Herbert Brucker, *The Changing American Newspaper* (New York: Columbia University Press, 1937); John L. Given, *Making a Newspaper* (New York: H. Holt & Co., 1914) and Oswald Garrison Villard's city-by-city cataloging of horrors, *Some Newspapers and Newspapermen* (New York: Knopf, 1923), and *The Disappearing Daily* (New York: Knopf, 1944). See also Quincy Howe, *The News and How to Understand It* (New York: Simon and Schuster, 1940), which includes a discussion of the newsmagazine as well as newspapers. Linda Weiner Hausman, "Criticism of the Press in U.S. Periodicals, 1900–1939: An Annotated Bibliography," *Journalism Monographs*, no. 4 (August 1967), is an invaluable guide. On press coverage of Roosevelt, George Wolfskill and John A. Hudson, *All But the People: Franklin D.*

Roosevelt and His Critics, 1933–1939 (New York: Macmillan, 1969), and James B. Beddow, "Midwestern Editorial Response to the New Deal, 1932–1940," *South Dakota History* 4 (Winter 1973):1–17, offer the traditional view. Graham White, *FDR and the Press* (Chicago: University of Chicago Press, 1979), sees objectivity reigning; Roosevelt, as White himself admits, identified the press with his political enemies, and that perception shaped his administration's handling of reporters.

Lippmann's *Liberty and the News* (New York: Macmillan, 1920) and *Public Opinion* (New York: Macmillan, 1922) both deal extensively with the complications and shortcomings of the press. His mood improved with "Two Revolutions in the American Press," *Yale Review* 20 (March 1931):433–41. See also Ronald Steel, *Walter Lippmann and the American Century* (New York: Random House, 1980).

One of Lippmann's rivals for attention in the twenties, H. L. Mencken, wrote extensively on journalism. His memoir *Newspaper Days 1899–1906* (New York: Knopf, 1968) and "Journalism in America," in *Prejudices (Sixth Series)* (New York: Knopf, 1927), belie the arguments of Schudson and others that journalism had reached a professional plateau by the 1920s. Mencken's contempt for most of his peers is also clear in his essay in *Civilization in the United States*, ed. Harold Stearns (New York: Harcourt, Brace, 1922); see also John Macy's essay in the Stearns collection. Under Mencken's editorship (1924–33), the *American Mercury* frequently ran reviews of the press's performance. Almost all took a dim view of the fourth estate.

The standard works on the modern American magazine include Frank Luther Mott, *A History of the American Magazine* 5 vols. (Cambridge, Mass.: Harvard University Press, 1930–68); Theodore Peterson, *Magazines in the Twentieth Century*, 2d ed. (Urbana: University of Illinois Press, 1964); John Tebbel, *The American Magazine: A Compact History* (New York: Hawthorn Books, 1969); and James Playsted Wood, *Magazines in the United States*, 2d ed. (New York: Ronald Press, 1956). Eric Hodgins, "The Magazines," in *While You Were Gone*, ed. Jack Goodman (New York: Simon and Schuster, 1946), is a thoughtful, analytical history by a Time Inc. vice-president. Robert Cantwell, "Journalism: The Magazines," in *America Now*, ed. Harold E. Stearns (New York: Charles Scribner's Sons, 1938), is also insightful; Cantwell worked for Time Inc. Paul F. Lazarsfeld and Rowena Wyatt, "Magazines in Twenty Cities: Who Reads What?" *Public Opinion Quarterly* 1 (October 1937):29–41, attempts to determine which sections of the country had the largest magazine circulations.

TIME AND TIME, INC.: OVERVIEWS

Robert T. Elson, *The World of Time Inc.*, 2 vols. (New York: Atheneum, 1968–73), and Curtis Prendergast, *The World of Time Inc.* (New York: Atheneum, 1986), both commissioned by Time Inc., are occasionally critical and unusually well documented. The authors relied extensively on oral histories and documents at the Time Inc. Archives to which scholars unaffiliated with Time Inc. lack unrestricted access. *Business Week*, 6 March 1948, and *Forbes*, 15 August 1953, ran profiles of the company. See also James Howard Lewis, "The Saga of *Time*, *Life*, and *Fortune*," *Magazine World* 1 (November 1944):10–15; (February 1945):10–15; (May 1945):8–11, 30.

On *Time*'s founding and first decade, I depended most on Elson's account and Busch's biography of Hadden. Helpful, too, were materials, mostly clippings, in the Hadden and Luce files, Yale University Alumni Records Office. The Walter Lippmann Papers, Sterling Memorial Library, Yale University, contain Time Inc. materials as well as some Hadden letters and a prototype of *Time*. Luce's letters to Nettie Fowler McCormick were also revealing. See also Otis Chatfield-Taylor, "The Timeditors," *Ringmaster* (November 1936):6–8, 43; John S. Martin's remarks to the 1937 meeting of the American Society of Newspaper Editors, published in *Proceedings*; and David Cort, "Once Upon a Time Inc.," *Nation*, 18 February 1956, 134–37.

FORTUNE

On the history of *Fortune*, I again relied heavily on Elson, though there was much useful material in Roy Hoopes, *Ralph Ingersoll: A Biography* (New York: Atheneum, 1985), and James Howard Lewis, "The Saga of *Time*, *Life*, and *Fortune*," *Magazine World* 1 (February 1945):10–15. Dwight Macdonald's bitter "*Fortune* Magazine," *Nation*, 8 May 1937, 527–30, should be read. Luce's talks on business and business journalism, reprinted in *Ideas of Henry Luce*, ed. Jessup, were invaluable.

On *Fortune*'s early staff, see Laurence Bergreen, *James Agee: A Life* (New York: Dutton, 1984); Margaret Bourke-White, *Portrait of Myself* (New York: Simon and Schuster, 1963); Vicki Goldberg, *Margaret Bourke-White* (New York: Harper & Row, 1986); Jonathan Silverman, *For the World to See: The Life of Margaret Bourke-White* (New York: Viking, 1983); Peter F. Drucker, *Adventures of a Bystander* (New York: Harper & Row, 1979); and John Kenneth Galbraith, *A Life in Our Times: Memoirs* (Boston: Houghton Mifflin, 1981). C. Zoe Smith, "An Alternative View of the 30s: Hine's and Bourke-White's Industrial Photos," *Journalism Quarterly* 60 (Summer 1983):305–10, analyzes Bourke-White's love of machines. Some of James Agee's *Fortune* and *Time* articles have been reprinted in *James Agee: Selected Journalism*, ed. Paul Ashdown (Knoxville: University of Tennessee Press, 1985). See also Daniel Bell et al., *Writing for Fortune* (New York: Time Inc., 1979), for the reminiscences of various staff members and R. H. Winnick, ed., *Letters of Archibald MacLeish, 1907 to 1982* (Boston: Houghton Mifflin, 1983), for some telling correspondence during MacLeish's years with Harry. Eric Hodgins's oral history at Columbia

University proved very helpful; unfinished, his autobiography, *Trolley to the Moon* (New York: Simon and Schuster, 1973), barely covers his *Fortune* career. Hilton Howell Railey's memoir, *Touch'd with Madness* (New York: Carrick & Evans, 1938), is bizarre.

Some *Fortune* articles have been published in book form, including Duncan Norton-Taylor, *For Some the Dream Came True* (Secaucus, N.J.: Lyle Stuart, 1981), Editors of *Fortune, USA: The Permanent Revolution* (New York: Prentice-Hall, 1951); idem., *The Fabulous Future* (New York: E. P. Dutton, 1956); and idem., *America in the Sixties: The Economy and Society* (New York: Harper & Row, 1960).

On *Fortune*'s postwar planning, Robert M. Collins, "Positive Business Responses to the New Deal: The Roots of the Committee for Economic Development," *Business History Review* 52 (Autumn 1978):369–91; David W. Eakins, "Business Planners and America's Postwar Expansion," in *Corporations and the Cold War*, ed. David Horowitz (New York: Monthly Review Press, 1969); Sidney Hyman, *The Lives of William Benton* (Chicago: University of Chicago Press, 1969), and Karl Schriftgiesser, *Business Comes of Age* (New York: Harper and Row, 1960), are especially helpful.

"THE MARCH OF TIME"

Relatively little has been written on "The March of Time" radio news program. Both Elson and Erik Barnouw, *A Tower of Babel* (New York: Oxford University Press, 1966), describe the series. Far more has been done with the newsreel version, with the best treatment Raymond Fielding, *The March of Time, 1935–1951* (New York: Oxford University Press, 1978). See also his *The American Newsreel, 1911–1967* (Norman: University of Oklahoma Press, 1972); Erik Barnouw, *Documentary* (New York: Oxford University Press, 1983); Richard Meran Barsam, *Nonfiction Film: A Critical History* (New York: E. P. Dutton, 1973); A. William Bluem, *Documentary in American Television* (New York: Hastings House, 1965); Lewis Jacobs, ed., *The Documentary Tradition* (New York: Hopkinson and Blake, 1971); and Roger Manvell, *Films and the Second World War* (New York: Delta, 1974). The better contemporary analyses are Alistair Cooke, "History in the Making," *Listener*, 28 November 1935, 931, and George Dangerfield, "*Time* Muddles On," *New Republic*, 19 August 1936, 43–45. William Alexander, "*The March of Time* and *The World Today*," *American Quarterly* 29 (Summer 1977):182–93, provocatively compares the affected realism of Luce's newsreel with a more radical effort.

LIFE

The best studies of Luce's picture magazine are Loudon Wainwright, *The Great American Magazine* (New York: Knopf, 1986) and Otha Cleo Spencer,

"Twenty Years of *Life*," Ph.D. dissertation, University of Missouri, 1958. Both Wainwright and Spencer had full access to the Time Inc. Archives and interviewed many of those involved in the magazine's planning and publication. See also Rick Friedman, "50 Years of Pictures; Newsmagazine Style," *Editor & Publisher* (23 March 1963), 47–48; James K. Grossman, "One *Life* to Live," *New Republic*, 9 February 1987, 36–40; Jackson Edwards, "One Every Minute," *Scribner's Magazine* May 1938, 17–23; John Drewry, "A Picture-Language Magazine," *Magazine World* 1 (November 1945):19, 46; and John R. Whiting and George B. Clark, "The Picture Magazines," *Harper's*, July 1943, 159–69. The Billings Papers at the University of South Carolina and the Daniel Longwell Papers at Columbia University contain insiders' perspectives on *Life's* planning and first years.

My view of photography and the documentary movement was greatly influenced by William Stott, *Documentary Expression and Thirties America* (New York: Oxford University Press, 1973). See also James C. Curtis and Sheila Grannen, "Let Us Now Appraise Famous Photographs: Walker Evans and Documentary Photography," *Winterthru Portfolio* 15 (Spring 1980):1–23. Also helpful were "U.S. Minicam Boom," *Fortune*, October 1936, 125–29; *Journalism Quarterly* 24 (September 1947):193–249; Daniel D. Mich and Edwin Eberman, *The Technique of the Picture Story* (New York: McGraw-Hill, 1945); Stanley E. Kalish and Clifton C. Edom, *Picture Editing* (New York: Rinehart and Co., 1951); Susan Sontag, *On Photography* (New York: Farrar, Straus and Giroux, 1977); and Vicki Goldberg, ed., *Photograph in Print* (New York: Simon and Schuster, 1981). Consult, too, the treatise on photojournalism by *Life's* first photo editor, Wilson Hicks, *Words and Pictures* (New York: Harper and Brothers, 1952), as well as the autobiographies of such *Life* photographers as Bourke-White and Carl Mydans, and Richard Whelan, *Robert Capa: A Biography* (New York: Knopf, 1985). The contributions to *Life* by Bourke-White, Alfred Eisenstaedt, Mydans, W. Eugene Smith, among others, can be seen in book-length reproductions of their photographs. Time Inc. has assembled self-tributes, among them, *Life: The First Decade* (New York: New York Graphic Society, 1980); *Life: The Second Decade* (New York: New York Graphic Society, 1984); and *Life: The First Fifty Years. 1936–1986* (Boston: Little, Brown, 1986).

On *Life* in the postwar era, see Allan C. Carlson, "Luce, *Life* and 'The American Way,'" *This World*, no. 13 (Winter 1986), 56–74; Leo Bogart, "Magazines since the Rise of Television," *Journalism Quarterly* 33 (Spring 1956):153–66; Dora Jane Hamblin, *That Was the Life* (New York: W. W. Norton, 1977); Jeanne Perkins Harman, *Such is Life* (New York: Thomas Y. Crowell, 1956); and Stanley Rayfield, ed., *How Life Gets the Story* (Garden City, N.Y.: Doubleday, 1955). See also William Brinkley's satirical novel, *The Fun House* (New York: Random House, 1961), and John Raeburn, *Fame Became*

Him: Hemingway as Public Writer (Bloomington, Ind.: Indiana University Press, 1984), on *Life* and the novelist's public image.

On *Life*'s woes and eventual demise, Prendergast's account in *World of Time* is more satisfactory on management's initial grappling with the problem than its decision to kill the periodical. See also David Cort, "Face-Lifting the Giants," *Nation*, 25 November 1961, 424–26; A. J. van Zuilen, *The Life Cycle of Magazines* (Uithoorn, Holland: Graduate Press, 1977); and Chris Welles, "Can Mass Magazines Survive?" *Columbia Journalism Review* 11 (July 1971): 7–14.

CLARE BOOTHE LUCE

Sylvia Morris is working on a formal biography of Clare Luce. Until then, the pickings are slim. Stephen Shadegg's biography, *Clare Boothe Luce* (New York: Simon and Schuster, 1970), is too admiring and sometimes simply inaccurate. Insightful if even more cozy is Wilfrid Sheed, *Clare Boothe Luce* (New York: E. P. Dutton, 1982). I found myself relying most on Sheed, a close friend of Mrs. Luce, both for details on her early life and her relations with Harry. Unlike Sheed, I could not dismiss Margaret Chase Harriman, "The Candor Kid," *New Yorker*, 4 January 1941, 21–26, 28–29; 11 January 1941, 22–25, 29–30, which seemed closer to the mark than most, and Martha Weinman Lear, "On Harry, and Henry and Ike and Mr. Shaw," *New York Times Magazine*, 22 April 1973, 10–11, 47, et seq.

Clare Luce's papers are at the Library of Congress and a useful oral history at Columbia University. The Herbert Hoover Papers, Hoover Library, West Branch, Iowa, include many exchanges between Clare and the former president. At the Eisenhower Library, Abilene, Kansas, some correspondence relating to her and her ambassadorial appointments remains closed.

WRITERS AND EDITORS

Many editors and writers have written memoirs of their days with Harry or been the subject of biographies or contemporary profiles. These include, in addition to those listed in the *"Fortune"* and *"Life"* sections above, John Chamberlain, *A Life with the Printed Word* (Chicago: Regnery Gateway, 1982); Whittaker Chambers, *Witness* (New York: Random House, 1952); Allen Weinstein, *Perjury: The Hiss-Chambers Case* (New York: Knopf, 1978); David Cort, *The Sin of Henry R. Luce* (Secaucus, N.J.: Lyle Stuart, 1974); Laura Z. Hobson, *Laura Z: A Life* (New York: Arbor House, 1983); Louis Kronenberger, *No Whippings, No Gold Watches* (Boston: Little, Brown, 1970).

The first volume of Ralph Ingersoll's autobiography, *Point of Departure* (New York: Harcourt, Brace & World, 1961), ends as he joins Time Inc.; the second volume was never published. Roy Hoopes, *Ralph Ingersoll: A Biography* (New York: Atheneum, 1985), often effectively argues for Ingersoll's significance. Ingersoll's relations to Harry are also discussed in Wolcott Gibbs's profile "A Very Active Type Man," *New Yorker*, 2 May 1942, and 9 May 1942; a portion of Ingersoll's papers, with a few Time Inc. materials, are at Boston University.

Thomas S. Matthews, like many, left Luce's fold bitter and this tone affects his autobiography, *Names and Address: An Autobiography* (New York: Simon and Schuster, 1960), and to a lesser extent his funeral oration, "Tall, Balding, Dead Henry Luce," *Esquire*, September 1967, 131–32. Matthews's *Angels Unawares: Twentieth Century Portraits* (New York: Ticknor and Fields, 1985), includes telling tributes to Agee and Chambers.

Some who quit composed novels based on their years with Time Inc., with a character unmistakably Lucean often the villain. See Ralph Ingersoll, *The Great Ones* (New York: Harcourt, Brace, 1948), and Charles Wertenbaker, *The Death of Kings* (New York: Random House, 1954). In Merle Miller, *That Winter* (New York: William Sloan Associates, 1948), and John Brooks, *The Big Wheel* (New York: Harper and Bros., 1949), editors like Matthews contest the heroes. More disturbing than readable is John S. Martin, *General Manpower* (New York: Simon & Schuster, 1938). The author, *Time*'s influential managing editor in the early 1930s, enthusiastically projected a near future smacking of fascism.

LUCE CONTEMPORARIES

Some biographies and memoirs of Luce's contemporaries and friends are helpful, including Sidney Hyman, *The Lives of William Benton* (Chicago: University of Chicago Press, 1969); Steve Neal, *Dark Horse: A Biography of Wendell Willkie* (Garden City, N.Y.: Doubleday, 1984); Ronald W. Pruessen, *John Foster Dulles: The Road to Power* (New York: Free Press, 1982); and Mark G. Toulouse, *The Transformation of John Foster Dulles: From Prophet of Realism to Priest of Nationalism* (Macon, Ga.: Mercer University Press, 1985). Valuable, too, are two essays on Luce's friend, advertising agent Bruce Barton, who, like Harry, was a minister's son uneasy about his secular path. See James A. Neuchterlein, "Bruce Barton and the Business Ethos of the 1920s," *South Atlantic Quarterly* 76 (Summer 1976):293–308; and Leo P. Ribuffo, "Jesus Christ as Business Statesman: Bruce Barton and the Selling of Corporate Capitalism," *American Quarterly* 33 (Summer 1981):206–31.

On Luce and Eisenhower, Stephen E. Ambrose, *Eisenhower the President* (New York: Simon & Schuster, 1984), is the most useful biography. Robert Griffith, "Dwight D. Eisenhower and the Corporate Commonwealth," *American Historical Review* 87 (February 1982):87–122, similarly discusses the role of Luce and other sponsors of Eisenhower's entry into politics. In Blanche Wiesen

Cook, *The Declassified Eisenhower: A Divided Legacy of Peace and Political Warfare* (New York: Penguin, 1984), the author of "The American Century" plays John the Baptist; the half-baked plans of Time Inc. executive C. D. Jackson to "roll back" communism during his brief period in the administration are given great play.

LUCE'S CRITICS

In the 1950s and 1960s, criticisms of Luce and the journalism that he and others practiced were frequent. The more famous include Ben Bagdikian, "Time Study," *New Republic*, 23 February 1959, 9–15, a longer version of which appeared in the *Providence Journal* and *Providence Bulletin* in October 1958; Jacques Barzun, "The Public Mind and Its Caterers," in *The House of Intellect* (New York: Harper and Row, 1961); Otto Friedrich, "There are 00 Trees in Russia," *Harper's*, October 1964, 59–65; Dwight Macdonald, *Against the American Grain* (New York: Random House, 1962); Arthur M. Schlesinger, Jr., "*Time* and the Intellectuals," in *The Politics of Hope* (Boston: Houghton Mifflin, 1962); and Gary Wills, "Timestyle," *National Review*, 3 August 1957, 129–30. "*Time*: The Weekly Fiction Magazine," *Fact* 1 (January–February 1964):3–23, takes testimony from the many worthies abused by Luce's newsweekly.

John C. Merrill, "How *Time* Stereotyped Three U.S. Presidents," *Journalism Quarterly* 42 (Autumn 1965):563–70, attempts to prove systematically *Time*'s partisanship during the Truman, Eisenhower, and Kennedy presidencies. Merrill's effort has been updated by Fred Fedler and others in *Journalism Quarterly* 56 (Summer 1979):353–59, and 60 (Autumn 1983):489–96.

LUCE AND AMERICAN FOREIGN POLICY, 1923–1945

Of the vast literature on U.S. foreign policy since the 1930s, relatively few works deal directly or at length with Luce. Studies of Mussolini, including Denis Mack Smith, *Mussolini* (New York: Knopf, 1982), and John P. Diggins, *Mussolini and Fascism: The View from America* (Princeton: Princeton University Press, 1972), examine the Italian dictator's relations with the American press. Hitler's reputation in three popular magazines, *Liberty, Collier's*, and the *Saturday Evening Post*, is analyzed in Roberta S. Siegel, "Opinions on Nazi Germany: A Study of Three Popular American Magazines, 1933–1941," Ph.D dissertation, Clark University, 1950.

On interwar American diplomacy and the news media, see Travis Beal Jacobs, "Roosevelt's Quarantine Speech," *Historian* 24 (August 1962):483–502; Warren F. Kuehl, "Midwestern Newspapers and Isolationist Sentiment," *Diplomatic History* 3 (Summer 1979):283–306; and Richard W. Steele, *Propaganda in an Open Society: The Roosevelt Administration and the Media* (Westport,

Conn.: Greenwood Press, 1985). Luce and other mass communicators figure prominently in Mark Lincoln Chadwin's study of the interventionists, *The Hawks of World War II* (Chapel Hill: University of North Carolina Press, 1968). Luce's "American Century" editorial and the reactions of others were reprinted in Henry R. Luce, *The American Century* (New York: Farrar and Rinehart, 1941). See also Luce's introduction to *Why England Slept* by John F. Kennedy (New York: Wilfred Funk, 1940), and Clare Boothe, *Europe in the Spring* (New York: Knopf, 1940).

The press's handling of the Soviet alliance is discussed in William L. O'Neill, *A Better World: The Great Schism: Stalinism and the American Intellectual* (New York: Simon & Schuster, 1982); Ralph B. Levering, *American Opinion and the Russian Alliance, 1939–1945* (Chapel Hill: University of North Carolina Press, 1976), and Paul Willen, "Who 'Collaborated' with Russia?" *Antioch Review* 14 (September 1954):259–83. See also John Lewis Gaddis, *The United States and the Origins of the Cold War, 1941–1947* (New York: Columbia University Press, 1972).

THE PRESS AND THE EARLY COLD WAR

The news media in the early Cold War have inspired little detailed investigation, especially the extent to which publications like *Time* and *Life* bore responsibility for the hardening of attitudes toward the Soviet Union. Of the "New Left" and "Post-Revisionist" histories of the Cold War's beginnings, virtually no scholar assigns the press a role in policy formulation. Figures like Luce are ignored or regarded as spear carriers.

The Truman administration turned to the news media, several argue, to promote new directions already set. On this and related points, see Thomas Paterson, *On Every Front: The Making of the Cold War* (New York: W. W. Norton, 1979); Walter LaFeber, "American Policy-Makers: Public Opinion and the Outbreak of the Cold War," in *The Origins of the Cold War in Asia,* ed. Yonosuke Nagai and Akira Iriye (Tokyo: University of Tokyo Press, 1977), 43–65. See also Leo K. Adler and Thomas G. Paterson, "Red Fascism: The Merger of Nazi Germany and Soviet Russia in the American Image of Totalitarianism," *American Historical Review* 75 (April 1970):1046–64. The rapidity with which mainstream periodicals accepted the government's images can be seen in Ronald Samuel Reinig, "America Looking Outward: American Cold War Attitudes during the Crucial Years, 1945–1947, as Reflected in the American Magazine Medium," Ph.D dissertation, Syracuse University, 1974. *Life* fares even worse in John P. Mallan, "Luce, Burnham, and the American World Revolution," *Harvard Studies in International Affairs* 3 (June 1953):46–65, and "Luce's Hot-and-Cold War," *New Republic,* 28 September 1953, 12–15.

On the relations between the press and the federal government as the

Cold War continued, several works are helpful, especially concerning Luce's periodicals, including Douglass Cater, *The Fourth Branch of Government* (New York: Random House, 1959); Michael Baruch Grossman and Martha Joynt Kumar, *Portraying the President: The White House and the News Media* (Baltimore: Johns Hopkins University Press, 1981); James Reston, *The Artillery of the Press: Its Influence on American Foreign Policy* (New York: Harper and Row, 1967); William L. Rivers, *The Opinionmakers* (Boston: Beacon Press, 1965). On *Time* in Washington, see John L. Steele, "The Newsmagazines in Washington," in *The Press in Washington*, ed. Ray Eldon Hiebert (New York: Dodd, Mead, 1966), 50–62. See also Montague Kern et al., *The Kennedy Crises* (Chapel Hill: University of North Carolina Press, 1983). Unlike some popular writers on the fourth estate, James Aronson, *The Press and the Cold War* (Boston: Beacon Press, 1970), argues that reporters essentially accepted the Cold War mentality of the government; they were not "deceived" or misled. On the intellectual community's anti-Communist fervor, see Richard H. Pells, *The Liberal Mind in a Conservative Age: American Intellectuals in the 1940s and 1950s* (New York: Harper and Row, 1985).

On Luce and China, some of the essays in *The Limits of Change: Essays on Conservative Alternatives in Republican China*, ed. Charlotte Furth (Cambridge, Mass.: Harvard University Press, 1976), along with some of Luce's own writings in Jessup ed., *Ideas of Luce*, and elsewhere, help to explain Luce's tolerance of the Kuomintang. *Time-Life* correspondent Theodore H. White's analysis of the Chinese civil war was written with Annalee Jacoby, *Thunder Out of China* (New York: William Sloane Associates, 1946); Luce vigorously objected to some sections of the book. Some of White's dispatches are in the Billings Papers. Although White's memoir *In Search of History* (New York: Harper and Row, 1978), is forgiving of Harry, those participating in the round-table "China Reporting Revisited," *Nieman Reports* 37 (Spring 1983):30–34, are not. See also John King Fairbank, *Chinabound: A Fifty Year Memoir* (New York: Harper and Row, 1982); Felix Greene, *A Curtain of Ignorance: How the American Public Has Been Misinformed about China* (Garden City, N.Y.: Doubleday, 1964); and Richard Watts, Jr., "Reading Luce in China," *New Republic*, 3 December 1945, 740–42. Luce and his publications loom in Sterling Seagrave's hysterical *The Soong Dynasty* (New York: Harper and Row, 1985). On the other side, Kenneth E. Shewmaker, *Americans and Chinese Communists, 1927–1945: A Persuading Encounter* (Ithaca: Cornell University Press, 1971), revives Whittaker Chambers's charge that American journalists—though not White—were naive about the Chinese Communist party; Shewmaker, in turn, is attacked in Warren W. Tozer, "The Foreign Correspondents' Visit to Yenan in 1944: A Reassessment," *Pacific Historical Review* 41 (May 1972):207–24.

Of those reviewing the history of Sino-American relations in the 1940s, Nancy Bernkopf Tucker, *Patterns in the Dust: Chinese-American Relations and the Recognition Controversy, 1949–1950* (New York: Columbia University Press,

1983), carefully measures the impact of the "China lobby" and press in the administration's deliberations. See also Dorothy Borg and Waldo Heinrichs, eds., *Uncertain Years: Chinese-American Relations, 1947–1950* (New York: Columbia University Press, 1980); William Whiting Stueck, Jr., *The Road to Confrontation: American Policy toward China and Korea* (Chapel Hill: University of North Carolina Press, 1981); and Tang Tsou, *America's Failure in China, 1941–1950* (Chicago: University of Chicago Press, 1963).

On China, the United States, and Luce after 1949, Warren I. Cohen, *Dean Rusk* (Totowa, N.J.: Cooper Square Publishers, 1980), offers the perspective of a policymaker who shared Luce's antipathy for the Communist regime. Warren I. Cohen, "The United States and China since 1945," in *New Frontiers in American-East Asia Relations* (New York: Columbia University Press, 1983), reviews recent scholarship, little of which awards much power to Luce and his fellow China lobbyists. In contrast, the China lobby takes on mythic proportions in Ross Y. Koen, *The China Lobby in American Politics* (New York: Macmillan, 1960). Somewhat more calm treatments include a two-part series in the *Reporter*, 15 April 1952 and 29 April 1952; and Stanley D. Bachrack, *The Committee of One Million* (New York: Columbia University Press, 1976). Felix Greene, *Curtain of Ignorance*, contends that most national news organizations, including ones unassociated with the lobby, were hostile to the mainland regime in the 1940s and 1950s.

LUCE AND OPINION LEADERSHIP

For a discussion of the limited role of mass communicators like Luce and public opinion itself, especially in foreign policy, see Norman A. Graebner, "Public Opinion and Foreign Policy: A Pragmatic View," in *Interaction: Foreign Policy and Public Policy*, ed. Don C. Piper and Ronald J. Terchek (Washington: American Enterprise Institute, 1983), 11–34. Doris A. Graber, *Mass Media and American Politics* 2d ed. (Washington: Congressional Quarterly, 1984), offers a good introduction to recent scholarship on the press and public opinion. Also helpful is James N. Rosenau, *National Leadership and Foreign Policy* (Princeton: Princeton University Press, 1963). Although the influence of Luce's publications on readers can never be determined exactly, Robert K. Merton's study of "opinion leaders," *Time* readers in a small town, "Patterns of Influence: A Study of Interpersonal Influence and of Communications Behavior in a Local Community," in *Communications Research, 1948–1949*, ed. Paul F. Lazarsfeld and Frank N. Stanton (New York: Harper and Bros., 1949), suggests that many took the magazine merely for the sake of "being in the know." The influence of *Time* readers, moreover, was largely confined to those sharing their relatively elevated socioeconomic status.

COVERING THE FIFTIES

Both Edwin R. Bayley, *Joe McCarthy and the Press* (Madison: University of Wisconsin Press, 1981), and Elson, *World of Time*, discuss *Time's* attacks on McCarthy. The uproar over Dulles's 1956 "brinkmanship" *Life* interview is ably recounted in Daniel J. Leab, "Dulles at the Brink: Some Diverse Reactions from 10 Years Ago," *Journalism Quarterly* 43 (Autumn 1966):547–50; in the *Washington Journalism Review* 7 (November 1985), Robert J. Donovan, then a senior correspondent in Washington, shares a revealing recollection of the prepublication release of the interview. The Dulles Papers and Oral History Project at Princeton University contain much material on the episode. On *Life* and the space program, see Tom Wolfe, *The Right Stuff* (New York: Farrar, Straus and Giroux, 1979); Walter A. MacDougall, *The Heavens and the Earth: A Political History of the Space Age* (New York: Basic Books, 1985); and Robert Sherrod, "The Selling of the Astronauts," *Columbia Journalism Review* 12 (May–June 1973):16–25. The National Purpose debate is reviewed in John W. Jeffries, "The 'Quest for the National Purpose' of 1960," *American Quarterly* 30 (Fall 1978):451–70, and Henry Fairlie, *The Kennedy Promise* (Garden City, N.Y.: Doubleday, 1972).

VIETNAM, LUCE AND THE PRESS

Both the Kobler and Swanberg biographies, as well as Prendergast, *World of Time*, and Halberstam, *Powers That Be*, deal at length with Luce and his periodicals' coverage of Vietnam. See also Halberstam's *Making of a Quagmire* (New York: Random House, 1965); two forums on the press and war in the *Columbia Journalism Review* 3 (Fall 1964) and 10 (Winter 1970–71); John Hohenberg, *Between Two Worlds: Policy, Press, and Public Opinion in Asian-American Relations* (New York: Frederick A. Praeger, 1967); Stanley Karnow, "The Newsmen's War in Vietnam," *Nieman Reports* 16 (December 1963):3–8; John Mecklin, *Mission in Torment* (Garden City, N.Y.: Doubleday, 1965); Charles Mohr, "Once Again—Did the Press Lose the War in Vietnam?" *Columbia Journalism Review* 22 (November–December 1983):51–56; and Harrison Salisbury, *Vietnam Reconsidered* (New York: Harper and Row, 1984), pt. 2. Two impressive studies have narrowed the commonly assumed gap between Luce's position on the war and those of the *New York Times* and CBS. See Todd Gitlin, *The Whole World is Watching: Mass Media in the Making and Unmaking of the New Left* (Berkeley: University of California Press, 1980), and Daniel C. Hallin, *The "Uncensored War"* (New York: Oxford University Press, 1986).

TIME AFTER LUCE

Prendergast is the most complete record of Time Inc. after Luce's death. Harry's successor, Hedley Donovan, is one of the subjects of Joan Simpson

Burn's collective biography, *The Awkward Embrace* (New York: Knopf, 1975), and Donovan's memoir of relations with various chief executives, *Roosevelt to Reagan* (New York: Harper and Row, 1985), touches on Time Inc. matters. Donovan's ascension did not end the criticisms of his predecessor's journalism. Richard Pollack, "*Time* after Luce," *Harper's*, July 1969, 42–52, gives the new regime decidedly mixed reviews. Even more harsh toward *Time* itself is John Tirman, "Doing Time," *Progressive*, August 1981, 46–49, 51. See also Judith Adler Hennessee, "*Time*'s Man of the Year," *Vanity Fair*, January 1985. *Newsweek*'s effects on *Time* are discussed in A. Kent MacDougall's *Wall Street Journal* feature, 12 July 1967; the autobiography of *Newsweek* editor Osborn Elliott, *The World of Oz* (New York: Viking, 1980); and David Shaw's excellent three-part series on the newsmagazines, *Los Angeles Times*, 1–3 May 1980, which also has material on *Time* during Luce's last years. Most impressive of these post-Lucean analyses is sociologist Herbert J. Gans's *Deciding What's News* (New York: Pantheon, 1979), which, comparing *Time*, *Newsweek*, NBC, and CBS, stresses the shared values of all four news services.

Serious financial setbacks for Time Inc. in the mid-1980s are described in *New York Magazine*, 3 March 1986; *New York Times*, 1 December 1985, sec. 3, pp., 129; and Christopher Byron, *The Fanciest Dive* (New York: W. W. Norton, 1986).

AFTERWORD, 2001

Much new work on Henry Luce and his publications has appeared since the publication of the first edition of this book in 1987. Robert E. Herzstein, *Henry R. Luce: A Political Portrait of the Man Who Created the American Century* (New York: Charles Scribner's, 1994), is a well-researched treatment, though Alan Brinkley's forthcoming authorized biography should prove definitive and even more insightful. John B. Judis, *Grand Illusion: Critics and Champions of the American Century* (New York: Farrar, Straus & Giroux, 1992), traces the fate of Luce's famous concept into the early 1990s. More intellectually ambitious is Oliver Zunz, *Why the American Century?* (Chicago: University of Chicago, 1999), though Luce himself is barely mentioned. *Diplomatic History* 23 (Spring and Summer 1999) published a two-part roundtable on the legacy of the "American Century" in U.S. foreign relations. Luce's second marriage is examined in Ralph G. Martin, *Henry and Clare: An Intimate Portrait of the Luces* (New York: G. P. Putnam's Sons, 1991), while Sylvia Jukes Morris completed a formal biography of Clare Luce in *Rage for Fame: The Ascent of Clare Boothe Luce* (New York: Random House, 1997).

Valuable memoirs by senior editors include Hedley Donovan, *Right Places, Right Times; Forty Years in Journalism, Not Counting My Paper Route* (New York:

Henry Holt & Co., 1989), and Henry Grunwald, *One Man's America: A Journalist's Search for the Heart of His Country* (New York: Doubleday, 1996). Sam Tanenhaus, *Whittaker Chambers: A Biography* (New York: Random House, 1997), is a masterful treatment of a controversial *Time* writer and editor. The career of Theodore H. White has inspired E. J. Dionne, Jr., "Did Teddy White Ruin Coverage of Presidential Campaigns?" *Media Studies Journal* 11 (Winter 1997); Thomas Griffith, *Harry and Teddy: The Turbulent Friendship of Press Lord Henry R. Luce and His Favorite Reporter, Theodore H. White* (New York: Random House, 1995); Joyce Hoffmann, *Theodore H. White and Journalism as Illusion* (Columbia: University of Missouri Press, 1995); and Robert G. Kaiser, "The First Insider: How Teddy White Revolutionized Political Reporting in America," *Washington Post Magazine*, 17 July 1988. *Life* photographers continue to merit attention. See especially Glenn G. Willumson's excellent *W. Eugene Smith and the Photographic Essay* (New York: Cambridge University Press, 1992), as well as James R. Mellow, *Walker Evans* (New York: Basic Books, 1999), and Belinda Rathbone, *Walker Evans* (Boston: Houghton Mifflin, 1995).

Individual Time Inc. periodicals have been examined in Michael MacCambridge, *The Franchise: A History of* Sports Illustrated *Magazine* (New York: Hyperion, 1997); Kevin S. Reilly, "Dilettantes at the Gate: *Fortune* Magazine and the Cultural Politics of Business Journalism in the 1930s," *Business and Economic History* 28 (Winter 1999):213–22; and Carolyn Kitch, "Twentieth-Century Tales: Newsmagazines and American Memory," *Journalism and Mass Communication Monographs* 1 (Summer 1999):119–55. *Time* (9 March 1998) celebrated its 75th anniversary with some telling essays by Lance Morrow and Walter Isaacson. See also Erika Doss's forthcoming collection on *Life*. David Abrahamson, *Magazine-Made America: The Cultural Transformation of the Postwar Periodical* (Cresskill, N.J.: Hampton Press, 1995), is a very competent overview.

The Time Warner merger has been the subject of two books, Connie Bruck, *Master of the Game: Steve Ross and the Creation of Time Warner* (New York: Simon & Schuster, 1994), and Richard M. Clurman, *To the End of Time: The Seduction and Conquest of a Media Empire* (New York: Simon & Schuster, 1992). Clurman gives more detail on Time Inc. Bruck subsequently wrote a very valuable essay on Time Warner CEO Gerald Levin, "Jerry's Deal," *New Yorker*, 19 February 1996, 55–59.

More specialized studies relating to Luce and his publications included T. Christopher Jespersen, *American Images of China, 1931–1949* (Stanford: Stanford University Press, 1996); Patricia Neils, *China Images in the Life and Times of Henry Luce* (Savage, Md.: Rowman & Littlefield, 1990); and James L. Kauffman, *Selling Outer Space: Kennedy, the Media, and Funding for Project Apollo, 1961–1963* (Tuscaloosa: University of Alabama Press, 1994).

INDEX

ABOUT THE AUTHOR

James L. Baughman is a professor in the School of Journalism and Mass Communication, University of Wisconsin–Madison, where he teaches journalism history. Born and raised in Warren, Ohio, he earned his B.A. from Harvard and his M.A. and Ph.D. in history from Columbia University.

Professor Baughman is the author of *Television's Guardians: The Federal Communications Commission and the Politics of Programming, 1958–1967* and *The Republic of Mass Culture: Journalism, Filmmaking, and Broadcasting in America since 1941.*

DATE DUE
